Puritan Political Ideas

1558–1794

THE AMERICAN HERITAGE SERIES

THE AMERICAN HERITAGE SERIES

Puritan Political Ideas

1558–1794

Edited by

EDMUND S. MORGAN

Yale University

Hackett Publishing Company, Inc.
Indianapolis/Cambridge

This book was originally published as a volume in the American Heritage Series under the general editorship of Leonard W. Levy and Alfred Young.

Printed in the United States of America

09 08 07 06 05 04 03 1 2 3 4 5 6 7

For further information, please address:

Hackett Publishing Company, Inc.
P.O. Box 44937
Indianapolis, IN 46244-0937

www.hackettpublishing.com

Cover design by Rick Todhunter and Abigail Coyle
Printed at Sheridan Books, Inc.

Library of Congress Cataloging-in-Publication Data

Puritan political ideas, 1558–1794 / edited by Edmund S. Morgan.
p. cm.
Originally published: Indianapolis: Bobbs-Merrill, c1965
(The American heritage series; 33).
Includes bibliographical references and index.
ISBN 0-87220-687-4 (pbk.) — ISBN 0-87220-688-2 (cloth)
1. Political science—United States—History. 2. United States—Politics and government—Sources. I. Morgan, Edmund Sears.

JA84.U5P87 2003
320.5'5—dc22

2003056159

The paper used in this publication meets the minimum requirements of American National Standard for InformationSciences—Permanence of Paper for Printed Library Materials, ANSI Z39.48-1984

∞

FOREWORD

The historical reputation of Puritanism in America has vastly and deservedly improved since the time of H. L. Mencken, James Truslow Adams, and Vernon Parrington. They depicted the Puritan fathers as joyless, dark-minded, petty entrepreneurs who believed in human depravity and a predestined elect, erected a theocratic state, and tyrannized their subjects within an inch of their lives. Doctrinal intolerance, an established church, witch hunting, and clerical elitism were synonymous with Puritanism, which was treated mainly as a religious creed that burned out by the eighteenth century. We know now, thanks to Samuel Eliot Morison, Kenneth Murdock, Ralph Barton Perry, Perry Miller, and most recently, Edmund S. Morgan, that Puritanism was a very complex system of beliefs and institutions with as much diversity, creativity, and vitality as the Enlightenment. Although it was nothing if not religious, from its core to its peripheries, it expressed itself in education, literature, morality, philosophy, and in every other phase of culture including political theory.

Puritan political theory, like Puritanism itself, had many facets and left a lasting influence on American development. Notwithstanding elements of autocracy, elitism, and theocracy that dominated early seventeenth-century Puritan political thought, Puritanism was a bridge from medievalism to the Enlightenment across which travelled many of our most cherished concepts of democratic constitutionalism. The social compact theory of government and representative government, government by the voluntary consent of the governed and for the good of the people, natural law and natural rights, written constitutions and constitutional limitations on the power of government, religious liberty and separation of church and state, and the exceptional importance of the individual—all may be found in Puritan political ideas.

Nor were these ideas late developments influenced by Locke and the American frontier. Locke was a mere teenager when Thomas Hooker of Connecticut, who was by no means a democrat or tolerationist, declared that the choice of public officers "belongs unto the people by God's own allowance" and that "it is in their power also, to set the bounds and limitations of the power and place unto which they call them. Reasons. 1. Because the foundation of authority is laid, firstly, in the free consent of the people." As Professor Morgan comments in his introduction to this volume, "the only novelty in Locke's explanation of the formation of government was the apparent absence of God from the proceedings . . ." Anyone studying the origins of American political thought and of American constitutionalism must turn to the Puritan theorists.

Professor Morgan, in this unique collection, focuses upon three ideas that lay at the root of Puritan political theory and have had a continuing significance in our history: calling, covenant, and the separate spheres of church and state. The selections show the origin of these ideas in the writings of the early English Puritans before the colonization of America, in seventeenth century New England, and finally in new contexts in the eighteenth century. One may read these documents as primary sources of Puritan thought per se, as sources of American intellectual history, or as sources of a political theory that flowered in the early years of the new constitutional republic.

This book is one of a series of which the aim is to provide the essential primary sources of the American experience, especially of American thought. The series when completed will constitute a documentary library of American history, filling a need long felt among scholars, students, libraries and general readers for authoritative collections of original materials. Some volumes will illuminate the thought of significant individuals, such as James Madison or Louis D. Brandeis; some will deal with movements, such as those of the Antifederalists or the Populists; others like this volume, will be organized around special themes.

Many volumes will take up the large number of subjects traditionally studied in American history for which, surprisingly, there are no documentary anthologies; others will pioneer in introducing new subjects of increasing importance to scholars and to the contemporary world. The series aspires to maintain the high standards demanded of contemporary editing, providing authentic texts, intelligently and unobtrusively edited. It will also have the distinction of presenting pieces of substantial length that give the full character and flavor of the original rather than the usual butchered snippet. The series will be the most comprehensive and authoritative of its kind.

Leonard W. Levy
Alfred Young

CONTENTS

DOCUMENTS

Part One

THE ENGLISH BACKGROUND

Part Two

THE NEW ENGLAND PURITANS

Part Three

EIGHTEENTH-CENTURY TRANSFORMATIONS

INTRODUCTION

From time to time in human history, the course of events challenges men to think about the way they live with one another. The Protestant Reformation of the sixteenth century, coinciding with the rise of national states, produced such a challenge. By causing men to reconsider their relationship to God, it led them to probe their relationships with their fellow men and particularly with the men whom they acknowledged as their rulers.

The ideas that resulted from this reconsideration, whether about God or man, were not altogether new. The guidebook of the Reformation was not the ninety-five theses of Martin Luther or the Institutes of John Calvin, but the Bible. And though it was a new experience for most men to read the Bible, especially in their own language, and though the numbers who could and did read it increased spectacularly with the Reformation, the Bible had always been the principal sourcebook of Christian thought, and none of the ideas men now discovered in it had been entirely absent in the intellectual equipment of the Middle Ages. Change in Christian thought, even so radical a change as the Reformation, has usually been a matter of emphasis, of giving certain ideas a greater weight than was previously accorded them or of carrying one idea to its logical conclusion at the expense of another. In this way one age slides into the next, and an intellectual revolution may be achieved by the expression of ideas that everyone had always professed to accept. Or a change brought about by other forces—by war or rebellion, growth or decline—may be justified and rationalized simply by a rearrangement of old ideas.

Nevertheless, whether the Reformation merely rationalized change or caused it, it did make men think; and if they thought with ideas already familiar, they managed a rearrangement, a new scale of emphasis, that was to affect profoundly the way men have regarded one another ever since, especially in the English-speaking world.

The Puritans were English Protestants who thought that the Church of England as established under Henry VIII and Elizabeth retained too many vestiges of Rome. In the 1640's and 1650's they reorganized not only the church but also the government of England and for eleven years ran the country without a king. When the monarchy was restored in 1660, Puritans were disgraced, but their work could not be wholly undone. Moreover, in the 1630's they had carried their ideas to the New World, where the king could not undo them.

This book offers first a few sample expressions of Puritan ideas about government and the state before the founding of the American colonies (it does not attempt to present the ramification of Puritan ideas in England after 1640); secondly, it offers a larger number of the major expressions of these ideas in seventeenth-century New England; finally, it offers some expressions of these ideas and of others derived from them, in new contexts in eighteenth-century New England. Although Puritan political ideas met with no serious direct challenge in America, the passage of time and the waning of the religious impulse altered emphases and evoked interpretations that fitted the old ideas to a more secular society.

The selections are in most instances complete and self-explanatory units, in which every reader can discern for himself the kind of ideas that the Puritans and their intellectual descendants emphasized at different times and in different circumstances. But it may be worthwhile to identify here three particular ideas that lay at the root of Puritan political thought; even when they were not mentioned. One we may designate as the idea of calling; the second as the idea of covenant; and the third as the idea of the separate spheres of church and state. All three were closely related and were frequently discussed together in Puritan writings; but if we first grasp them as individual concepts we may form a clearer understanding of their relationship and the implications of one for the others, and of how they evolved together in the eighteenth century.

The Calling

Prior to the Reformation, it was common to speak of the special summons or vocation by which God called certain men to serve Him as priests, monks, or bishops. The notion already existed, of course, that every man was placed by God's command in a particular station in life, but monks and churchmen performing holy services for God were thought to have a special direct calling to their tasks. The Protestant reformers, and especially the Calvinists and Zwinglians from whom the Puritans took their intellectual descent, extended the doctrine of calling to cover all honest human activities. God called men from sin to salvation; called them to be husbands or fathers, masters or servants; called them to the particular trade by which they served society and made a living. Before undertaking any new enterprise, voyage, or job a man must discern his "call" from God to it. The Puritans who founded New England searched their souls for many months to ascertain whether they had a call to the New World. The activity by which a man earned his living came to be known familiarly as his "calling," but the same word applied to his status as a son or a father, a ruler or a subject.

In emphasizing this idea, neither the Puritans nor other

Protestants supposed that God's calling of a man to a particular task or station would be signified by a direct visitation of the Holy Spirit. The Age of Revelation, they believed, had ceased with the writing of the Bible, and man could look for no further messages from God until the millennium. He must study the recorded Word of God, examine his God-given capacities and opportunities, and discern for himself what his calling was. Reason would dictate, for example, that he had no calling to a task for which God had given him no talents. If his fingers were all thumbs, he obviously had no calling to be, say, a silversmith.

Reason also dictated a number of things to the Puritans that had not been so evident in earlier centuries. God never, they decided, called a man to an activity that benefited him without producing some good also to his fellow men. On this ground (and others) they condemned gambling as an occupation—and likewise prayer. Prayer was the duty of every man, but to make a calling of it, as monks did, was to live from the labor of others, just as a gambler did, producing nothing for society. A calling always meant work. Brief periods of recreation were permissible, in order to enable a man to resume work refreshed, but idleness was incompatible with any calling.

Underlying the doctrine was an assumption that every calling involved certain known functions and duties and that a man fulfilled his calling only by performing them. It followed that a man could neither be a good ruler nor a good subject except by doing the things that a ruler or subject was supposed to do, and by the same token a man was justified in doing certain things if he could show that it belonged to his calling to do them. Thus John Winthrop, as governor of Massachusetts, will be found defending certain actions by virtue of the fact that he carried the title of governor and thus had to be guided by the duties of a governor's calling.

Winthrop was not relying simply on his own notions of what a governor should be. A governor was a magistrate, and sixteenth-century Puritan mentors like William Perkins had described the calling of a magistrate with some care. Throughout his tenure of office in Massachusetts Winthrop sought to practice the virtues described in Perkins' treatise on Christian equity. A magistrate was supposed to enforce the laws, but this did not mean an unbending application of the same punishment in every case. This much any fool could do. The calling of a magistrate demanded special talents to fit the punishment to the crime, to bend the law to the particular circumstance. Winthrop earned a good deal of criticism for his "leniency," but he was always ready to defend his practices as proper to his calling.

The social and political implications of the idea of calling were conservative. It had been common in the Middle Ages to think of society as composed of different "estates" into which men were born and lived out their lives. A man was born a husbandman or a yeoman, an artisan, a noble, or a king, and the good order of society demanded that he adhere to the estate in which he was born. The idea of estate lingered on in Puritan times, helping a man to discern his calling; and the two conceptions easily merged in the often repeated Puritan warning that every man, for the good of society, must remain in the place to which God had called him. Winthrop could remind the emigrants to Massachusetts that God had so ordered the condition of mankind that "in all times some must be rich some poore, some highe and eminent in power and dignitie; others meane and in subjeccion," and he was properly shocked when a servant suggested to a master who was unable to pay him that they change places.

Politically, too, the doctrine was conservative. In Massachusetts in the first years, government was entrusted to magistrates who both made the laws and administered them. But in 1634 the magistrates were forced to share their legislative powers with "deputies" whom the freemen sent to represent them in the General Court. Governor Winthrop could not prevent this development, because the royal charter under which the colony was governed gave to freemen the right to participate in the making of laws. But Winthrop refused to recognize the deputies as magistrates. They might assist in the making of laws, as the charter entitled the freemen to do; but the administration of the laws belonged to the calling of the magistrates: it was therefore wrong for the deputies to participate in the General Court when it was engaged in judicial rather than legislative functions. It was wrong too, Winthrop believed, for the laws to prescribe fixed penalties for crimes, because this interfered with the magistrate's exercise of equity in his calling.

The idea of calling also lay behind John Cotton's criticism of democracy, and one can understand the meaning and limits of that criticism only if one bears in mind the idea of calling. When Cotton and other Puritans condemned democracy, they interpreted it as a government in which the people themselves made decisions in a mass meeting, as in a Greek city state. Such a form of government meant in effect that everyone was a magistrate and that either no one or everyone was a subject. This was to confound the two callings of ruler and subject. Hence Cotton's often quoted and usually misunderstood query: "If the people be governors, who shall be governed?" A proper government was one in which a limited number of men, whether one, few, or many, exercised authority over the rest of society. They might be hereditary or elective, but once placed in the office to which God, by whatever means, had called them, it was up to them to do the governing. In Massachusetts they were placed there by annual election, an arrangement that struck many Puritans as unstable and others as highly desirable. Desirable or not, it lasted; and Puritans, until the downfall of the Massachusetts Charter in 1684, had an annual opportunity to change all their rulers. This fact did not, in their eyes, make Massachusetts a democracy; for the actual governing was in the hands of a few men who could bring the requisite wisdom and virtue to their magisterial callings.

The existence of annual elections spared New England Puritans of the seventeenth century from the necessity of thinking about the proper means of removing a ruler who did not fulfill the duties of his calling. He could simply be left out at the next election. But the problem had already received attention from sixteenth-century Puritans in England, who saw that misbehavior in a ruler might affect the calling of a subject. Henry Bullinger, whose writings appealed to Englishmen in the time of Elizabeth I, was cautious in his advice about what a subject's calling demanded in the presence of a tyrant. He suggested that everybody concentrate on reforming religion and pray for God to remove the offender, who was, after all, failing in the task God had assigned him. Calvin had maintained that other, lesser magistrates might have a calling to do the Lord's work in removing a tyrant. Bullinger, too, believed that God sometimes "stirreth up noble captains and valiant men to displace tyrants, and set God's people at liberty; as we see many examples thereof in the books of Judges and Kings." But Bullinger was wary of urging tyrannicide. "Lest any man do fall to abuse those examples," he warned, "let him consider their calling by God [i.e., the calling of the assassins described in *Judges* and *Kings*]: which calling if he have not, or else do prevent, he is so far from doing good in killing the tyrant, that it is to be feared lest he do make the evil double so much as it was before." (See this volume, Document 2.)

Christopher Goodman, who wrote while Elizabeth's

predecessor, Mary Tudor, was burning Protestants, was less hesitant in discerning a call to overthrow tyrants. He and other Protestant spokesmen who had fled to Calvin's Geneva announced the duty of all good subjects to overthrow evil rulers. They, too, worried about the question of who had a proper calling to undertake the task. But their reasoning on the subject and that of later Puritans was less closely tied to the idea of calling than to the second idea we have set out to examine, that of a covenant, or contract, as the source of the ruler's authority.

The Covenant

The transition from medieval to modern times, as has often been suggested, was marked by a transformation in which one man's relationship to another ceased to depend so much on the estate or station in life occupied by each and came to be based more on whatever covenant, that is, contract or agreement, might exist between them. Whether this change owed anything to religious ideas or whether certain religious ideas were themselves the product of the change can never be known, but it is clear that many sixteenth-and seventeenth-century Protestants, and especially Puritans, thought about their relationship with God as though it were based on a covenant.

Cast in these terms, the Christian story told of Adam, created in God's image, who made a covenant (the covenant of works) with his Maker, promising perfect obedience in return for eternal salvation. After Adam broke his covenant, thereby incapacitating his posterity from fulfilling it, God made a new covenant (the covenant of grace) with Abraham, in which Abraham promised only faith that God would save him and his offspring through a redeemer. In return for faith alone, God promised salvation; and since man was hopelessly corrupted by Adam's fall, disabled not only from obedience but even from faith, God would himself grant to his chosen elect the power of faith. Thus God in effect fulfilled both parts of the covenant, but by dealing with man in the form of a covenant he made himself intelligible to man's weak and corrupted reason.

God's promise to Abraham included Abraham's offspring, who became the people of Israel, and until the coming of Christ Israel represented God's chosen people, an elect nation whom he had singled out from all the peoples of the earth for eternal salvation. But with the coming of Christ, God's covenant was opened to all men who believed, and Israel ceased to enjoy any special status. Indeed, since the Jews rejected Christ, they forfeited the covenant; and it was written in the Apocalypse that they would not be recovered until shortly before Christ came on earth again to rule in glory. Meanwhile, every man to whom God gave faith could seize the covenant and look forward to eternal salvation.

According to the Protestant understanding of history, individual Christians had thus been winning salvation ever since the birth of Christ. But what of the nations into which Christians were divided? God did not grant faith to all men but only to a few in any society. Yet He did not wholly neglect those without faith. With every Christian nation He made a covenant, comparable to that which He had made with Israel, though on somewhat different terms.

To every Christian people God promised prosperity and happiness in this world, provided they obeyed His commandments as revealed in the Bible. They were, of course, incapable of perfect obedience. Because of his sinful nature inherited from Adam, every man, even if he had faith, would fail of perfect obedience: while doing the right thing, he would think the wrong thought. But it was possible to maintain at least an outward obedience, and God would prosper the community that showed Him this degree of honor in its actions.

English and Scottish Protestants seem to have been

especially taken with the notion of a national covenant. They tended even to look upon themselves as the successors of Israel, as an elect nation. Though they had to acknowledge that many among them gave no perceptible evidence either of faith or of outward obedience to God's commands, they viewed every failure as a threat to their standing with God. Under Elizabeth they kept hoping for reforms that would assure His continued favor. With the arrival of the Stuarts that hope grew increasingly dim, and preachers warned of the wrath to come upon a people who broke their covenant.

It was fear of God's wrath that prompted many Puritans to leave for the New World before England should suffer the fate of Sodom and Gomorrha. "My dear wife," John Winthrop wrote from London in May, 1629, "I am veryly perswaded, God will bringe some heavye Affliction upon this lande, and that speedylye."[1] In less than a year he was on his way to New England as governor of Massachusetts. On the way he explained to his fellow passengers that the new colony would be in covenant with God, and its success would depend on keeping the covenant. If it failed to do so, he said, "the Lord will surely breake out in wrathe against us be revenged of such a perjured people and make us knowe the price of the breache of such a covenant." (see this volume, Document 5)

For a people in covenant with God, rulers were a necessity. Possibly if Adam had succeeded in paradise, his offspring might have got along without government; but corrupted man was incapable even of outward obedience unless assisted by a ruler's compelling hand. And when a people had bound themselves to God by a covenant, they must enable themselves to keep the covenant by submit-

---

[1]*Winthrop Papers*, II (Boston: Massachusetts Historical Society, 1931), 91.

ting to rulers who would enforce it. Both the subjects's calling to obey and the ruler's to command were directed toward the same object: the fulfillment of the people's covenant with God.

God approved of rulers, called them to office, and endowed them with the sanction of His authority; but He did so, as with other callings, indirectly: He called rulers to office through the consent of their people. It belonged to the people to establish government, define its purposes, place rulers in charge of it, and submit to those rulers as long as they fulfilled their offices properly. To achieve all these ends, the people must engage in a second, subsidiary covenant, not with God but with each other and with their prospective rulers. A French Protestant described the process more explicitly than most Puritans did. "Now we read," said the author of the *Vindiciae contra Tyrannos* "of two sorts of covenants at the inaugurating of kings, the first between God, the king, and the people, that the people might be the people of God. The second, between the king and the people, that the people shall obey faithfully, and the king command justly." The author went on to explain that "the king himself, and all the people should be careful to honor and serve God according to His will revealed in His word, which, if they performed, God would assist and preserve their estates: as in doing the contrary, he would abandon, and exterminate them."[2]

This idea could be productive of radical and even revolutionary attitudes. It might be true that a man should be certain of his calling before raising his hand against a tyrant. But when a ruler failed to enforce obedience to God, when he in fact encouraged or even required disobedience to God, he not only neglected his own calling

---

[2]H. J. Laski, ed., *A Defence of Liberty Against Tyrants* (London: G. Bell & Sons, Ltd., 1924), pp. 71–72.

but violated his covenant with the people and thus forfeited his authority. If he was allowed to continue in office, the people's covenant with God would be broken and the whole community exposed to the wrath of God. It was on this ground that Christopher Goodman called on Englishmen to overthrow Mary Tudor, on this ground that English Puritans did overthrow Charles I, and at least in part on this ground that many New Englanders raised their muskets to overthrow George III.

The idea of a covenant or contract between ruler and people was, of course, not original with the Puritans or peculiar to them; but they gave the idea an importance that few had accorded it hitherto. In England it found expression in the tenuous form of the king's coronation oath; in New England it was annually reenacted in popular elections and expounded by the ministers not only in weekly sermons but also in a special sermon preached on election day. Small wonder that it produced a much more vigilant popular attitude toward government than had been known elsewhere in the world. New Englanders believed that their survival in the wilderness, and later their continued prosperity, depended on a strict enforcement of the terms of the covenant. The representatives of the people indicted their governor not for harshness but for leniency. Every man watched himself and his neighbor for breaches that might invoke God's displeasure. Penitent sinners bewailed the fact that their failings had endangered the public safety. And when a massive Indian attack in 1675 threatened to destroy the English settlements, the first reaction was to search out the "provoking evils," the breaches of covenant that had prompted God to unleash these demons against His people. The General Court did not fail to send men with guns against the enemy but it also undertook long-range measures to win the war by passing laws to correct such errors as pub-crawling and sleeping at sermons.

In New England, then, the idea of the covenant not only retained its radical potentialities, it also prompted the people toward an explicit statement, in the form of legislation, of the terms that God required. The purpose of government was to control human corruption, but Puritans were mindful that governors, too, were men and subject to the same infirmities as themselves. John Winthrop made this point repeatedly in order to warn the people that they must expect mistakes; other Puritans were concerned not only to hold those mistakes to a minimum but also to prevent the burgeoning of corruption that power too often produced in human beings. The corruption of power that Puritans had witnessed in England had often taken the form of assaults on the life, liberty, and property of subjects, and the best defense against it was a recognition throughout the community that the power of government was limited by the rights of subjects. Englishmen had developed this notion further than most peoples, and had established a few specific principles as inviolable. In Massachusetts the Puritans carried the process a step farther: in 1641 they drew up and enacted as legislation a "Body of Liberties" (see this volume, Document 11) defining the rights of subjects more extensively than had ever been done in England. Here the terms of the people's covenant with God and of the ruler's covenant with the people were spelled out in detail.

The Separate Spheres of Church and State

In the Body of Liberties a special section defined "the Liberties the Lord Jesus hath given to the Churches." Among these was the guarantee that "no Injunctions are to be put upon any Church, Church officers or member in point of Doctrine, worship, or Discipline, whether for substance or cercumstance besides the Institutions of the Lord." This was a negative way of stating the positive duty of the magistrate to impose the "Institutions of the Lord." The Puritans who founded Massachusetts had no interest in providing a haven for those who wished to worship as they chose. The covenant that Winthrop and his followers envisaged required them to obey all God's commands, and the most important of these was to have no other gods before Him. They were confident that the God who guided them to Massachusetts had prescribed one and only one religion, one and only one manner of worship. Mary Tudor's adoption of a different religion and worship had made the Reformers call for her head; and the failure of the Stuarts to press the true religion on their subjects threatened the destruction of England. The ruler who failed to punish heresy betrayed his people to the wrath of God as surely as he who failed to punish theft, murder, and adultery.

To the modern reader the assumption of a religious stewardship by the state seems a far cry from the separation of church and state. But the modern American view of this subject was reached by a long and circuitous route, and one of the more notable steps toward it was made by the men who founded Massachusetts. They held that church and state had separate functions; and they believed, with reason, that they had achieved a clearer separation of them than existed in the Old World. In order to understand their views one must look less at what their descendants were to do and more at the situation that they had left behind in Europe.

The Bible was the starting point for the notion that church and state, having separate functions, should employ different officers and different methods. Indeed, the idea is stated or implied so often in the Bible and expounded so insistently in the writings of the Church Fathers that it can scarcely be regarded as a specialty of the Puritans. Pope Gelasius II in the twelfth century had formulated the classic expression of it, and it had received frequent utterance in the sixteenth century by both Catholics and Protestants. The church, it was agreed, represented Christ's kingdom on earth, and its officers held the keys to His kingdom in heaven. Their powers, however, were purely spiritual, for Christ's kingdom was not of this world. The church therefore was not to carry out His will by compulsion but only by the weapons of the spirit: persuasion, admonition, exhortation. Its most severe disciplinary measure was simply expulsion.

The state, on the other hand, representing God's kingly authority, was very much a thing of this world. Its business was to enforce His laws on men whose wills were corrupted by the fall of Adam. Its methods were not spiritual but temporal: the whip, the prison, the gallows, armies, navies, sheriffs, constables, judges. The state, like the church, was a work of God, though by definition a somewhat less significant one; and in spite of their differing functions, church and state met in the state's responsibility for maintaining, among the rest of God's wishes, His true religion. At this juncture arose the question: Who should decide which religion was the true one? Should the church decide or should the state?

In the sixteenth and early seventeenth century, as the Reformation spread through Europe and England, the question became a crucial one. The Pope maintained that as Christ's representative on earth it was up to him to judge whether a ruler was doing his job properly and, in particular, whether he was maintaining true religion. Cardinal Bellarmine, who undertook to explain and defend the position, maintained that the Pope, though not an officer of state, enjoyed an indirect power to judge rulers and could absolve subjects from allegiance to an unworthy king. It went without saying that no Protestant monarch was likely to prove worthy.

In 1570 the Pope excommunicated Queen Elizabeth, and the Spanish Armada of 1588 was sent to restore the true faith by unseating the untrue Queen. But Englishmen had no desire to be freed from allegiance, and their response to the papal judgment was not limited to gunfire. James I undertook to answer Cardinal Bellarmine with an exposition of the divine right of kings. A king, James explained, did not receive his authority through the hands of a pope or of any other church officer, but directly from God himself. Though Puritans preferred to think that power passed to the king from God through the medium of a popular choice and covenant, they applauded James's exclusion of the church from any share in the making of governments. Independent government was the shield that enabled God's true religion to exist in a world once dominated by Antichrist—and both James and the Puritans agreed in identifying the Pope with Antichrist and the Roman Catholic Church with the Whore of Babylon. Only by denying Antichrist could a ruler lead his people to fulfill their covenant with God.

It followed that the ruler must decide what religion was true; though he might properly seek advice from the officers of the church, he was not obliged to follow it. For the church to meddle in this or any other matter of state would not only corrupt the state but also the church. The Roman church had once been a true church, but by seeking and obtaining worldly powers it had betrayed its mission and poisoned itself and all Christendom.

Puritans asserted these principles with more conviction and more consistency than their king could. For the fact was that as the English church retained many relics of its Roman origin, in ceremonies, vestments, and beliefs, so also it retained a Roman identification with the state. At the top, supreme both politically and spiritually, stood the king; in the national legislature the bishops of the church sat in the House of Lords and voted on every act; and at the local level the wardens who managed church property (the spiritual community owned large quantities of temporal goods) were also involved in looking after paupers, discovering the fathers of bastard children, and a host of other secular, governmental matters. In every diocese, church courts made their orders felt. Though they dealt out allegedly spiritual punishments (admonition and excommunication) they charged very temporal fees and fines and extended their jurisdiction over matters that had little to do with the salvation of souls, such as the inheritance of property.

In New England the Puritans did away with what they considered relics of Antichristian practice. The only connection they retained between church and state lay in the provision, adopted in Massachusetts in 1631, that only church members could become freemen and thus be entitled to vote and hold office. At the time, anyone of proper belief and decent behavior could join a church, and the purpose of the provision was simply to exclude heretics and ne'er-do-wells from a hand in the government. As their religious ideas developed, New England Puritans became more exacting in their standards of church membership, demanding proof of religious experience; and after the first few years probably the majority of the population was excluded from membership and thus from participation in colony government. Although some Puritans saw danger in this link between church and state, others, like John Cotton, defended it as the best way to keep the government true to its tasks. The purpose of the requirement was not to give the church, as such, a role in government, for the officers of government were kept distinct and separate from the officers of churches. There were no church courts; the clergy held no place in the legislature; and although no law prevented it, clergymen were not elected to public office.

At the local level, New Englanders avoided the mixture of church and state that existed in the English parish by devising a new and wholly secular institution, the town. The townsmen, regardless of church membership, met in town meeting to regulate local affairs and elected "select-men" to apply the rules. Although the meetings were held in the same building that was used for church services, it was a secular, town building, known as a meetinghouse, not as a church. The church ordinarily owned no property.

The New England churches—strictly speaking there was no such thing as *the* church—did exercise discipline over their members by admonition and excommunication. But the penalties of New England excommunication were genuinely spiritual. In old England, with church membership compulsory for all, a person excommunicated was literally cut off from communication with the rest of society. He lost all political offices he might hold, could not sue in court (but could be sued), and could not speak or have business dealings with other men. If he failed to secure restitution of his church membership (by paying heavy fines), he was imprisoned by the state. In New England, on the other hand, where church membership was a privilege confined to a minority of the population, excommunication simply reduced a man to the status of most of the rest of the population and did not affect his communication with his fellow men. Although he had to be a church member in order to gain political rights, he did not lose them if deprived of membership. The Massachusetts Body of Liberties explicitly provided that "no church censure shall degrade or depose any man from any Civill dignitie, office, or Authoritie he shall have in the Commonwealth." Thus, although a man had to be a church member in order to become an officeholder, it did not follow that he was deprived of office if he lost his church membership.

Governor Winthrop believed that a church had no right to censure officers of government for actions performed in carrying out their duties, but he was unable to establish this view. The majority opinion was that churches could deal with magistrates as they saw fit, provided the churches confined themselves to spiritual methods, while magistrates could likewise deal by temporal methods with churches and church officers, punishing them for any breaches of law. There was, of course, no hostility in New England between church and state. Since both were agencies of the Almighty, there was no need for them to clash; and in practice the magistrates often consulted the ministers about difficult matters of policy. The magistrates never doubted, however, that the ultimate decision in all questions of state lay with them, and not with the ministers. When the ministers offered advice unasked, it was not always welcome.

The whole relationship could be stated in terms of calling. It was part of the magistrate's calling to see true religion established and protected. For that purpose it was entirely appropriate for him to levy taxes in order to support the clergy. On the other hand, it was not part of the clergyman's calling to deal with temporal matters. Winthrop thought that the settlers of Connecticut made a mistake in relying too heavily on clerical advice in political matters. For lack of any substantial number of men qualified to exercise the calling of a magistrate they had to choose men "who had no learning nor judgement, which might fit them for those affairs, though otherwise men holy and religious." As a result, "the main burden for managing of state business fell upon some one or other of their ministers . . . who, though they were men of singular wisdom and godliness, yet, stepping out of their course, their actions wanted that blessing, which otherwise might have been expected."[3] And when the ministers of Massachusetts undertook to comment too freely on a dispute in the Massachusetts General Court, Winthrop noted that they "had done no good offices in this matter, through their misapprehensions both of the intentions of the magistrates, and also of the matters themselves, being affairs of state, which did not belong to their calling."[4]

Thus Massachusetts enjoyed a separation of church and state that had been advocated by Puritans in England but never practiced. Only with this fact in mind can we appreciate the originality and daring of the arguments advanced by Roger Williams for a still wider separation, indeed for a total divorce of religion from government. Williams had a penchant for driving an idea to its logical conclusion, for wringing from it every last shred of implication. In the course of one of these ideological explorations he was led to the conclusion that the magistrate had no calling to protect true religion.

Williams started by examining the Puritan derivation of the state from God's covenant with Israel. All Christians agreed that the example of Israel was not to be taken too literally: some of the laws God prescribed for the Jews did not apply to Christians, for example the prescriptions about meat and drink; and many Jewish ceremonies had only a symbolic significance, as circumcision was symbolic of baptism. Theologians from the time of the Church Fathers had been discovering such symbolic connections and had learned to see events in the Old Testament as prefigurations or prophecies of events in the New Testament. In

---

[3]John Winthrop, *The History of New England*, James Savage, ed. (Boston: Little, Brown & Co., 1853) I, 344.

[4]*Ibid.*, II, 228.

the language of theology the old events were "types" of the new, and the new events were "antitypes" of the old: Jonah entering the belly of the whale, for example, was a type of Christ's descent into Hell, and Christ was Jonah's antitype. Using this conventional typological method, Williams went on to argue that Israel itself was merely a type, a symbol of the Christian church. With the coming of Christ the type came to an end and was succeeded by apostolic churches, small companies of believers gathered by apostles or evangelists to worship God. These were the only antitype of Israel, said Williams. With the ascendancy of Antichrist, i.e., the rise of the papacy, all Christian churches were destroyed. Since then, Williams maintained, there had been no true church; and there could be no true church until Christ returned in glory to start one or authorized apostles to do so.

Having decided that no true church existed, Williams easily concluded that the state had no business professing to protect one. But he could not rest his argument here because it ran squarely counter to the fundamental Puritan belief that the state arose from a covenant with God which obligated it to protect true religion. The state, he decided, was a purely secular association arising solely from an agreement among men. The erroneous view had grown from thinking of the state as the lineal descendant of Israel. It was not. Israel had no successor in the modern world. Israel had indeed been an elect nation in covenant with God, a true church-and-state in combination, wherein the state had been bound to protect religion. But there had been no such combination since Israel's "typical" mission was ended by the coming of Christ. And there never again would be such a combination because Christ did not rule by force. Those who professed to propagate or uphold His kingdom by the sword demonstrated themselves to be false to it.

Williams did not deny that government originated in a covenant, but he did deny that God was a party to the covenant. The magistrate, Williams argued, derived his powers from the people who placed him in office and who covenanted to submit to his government. Unless those people themselves had powers to form churches and protect them with the sword, they could not give such powers to their governors. But God had given power to form churches only to His apostles and evangelists, who no longer existed; even to them He had given no temporal powers, and they had expressly refrained from meddling with government. The state, therefore, was purely a matter of temporal convenience: It should not form churches or support them with taxes, nor should it suppress or prohibit them or exercise any control over religious belief or worship of any kind.

In his own opinion Williams's ideas had conservative implications. If a state was not in covenant with God, there was no reason to fear that God would visit His wrath upon it for violation of His will. Williams acknowledged that government was an ordinance of God in a general way, like marriage, and he favored the suppression and punishment of murder, theft, adultery, and other crimes. But the fact that a government allowed atheism, idolatry, and infidelity of all kinds he regarded as entirely appropriate. There was no excuse, then, for those who cried up rebellion against a king on the ground that he failed to protect true religion. Such men always emphasized the danger of God's wrath against the people who failed to overthrow a heretical king. His own doctrine, Williams claimed, was the one that made men the best subjects.

But Williams was also demanding, of course, a freedom for the subject in religious matters that few governments of his time were willing to grant. In the eighteenth century the descendants of the Puritans arrived at a similar religious freedom, but they got there by a different route from the one that Williams had followed, a route that had more radical implications.

Eighteenth-Century Transformations

During the eighteenth century New Englanders and other Americans continued to think about covenant, calling, and the separation of church and state. But their thoughts were shaped by the changes that passage of time had wrought in the intellectual climate and in the circumstances of life in the New World. The most pervasive intellectual change was the withdrawal of God from His place in the forefront of all thinking. God continued to exert a powerful influence but from a seemingly greater distance. New Englanders of the eighteenth century felt His hand less heavily and less constantly upon them than their fathers had done. They thought more about the way He shook the earth or moved the waters, and less about why He afflicted His chosen people by doing so. And as they became more interested in His handiwork than in His judgments they grew less concerned about their standing with Him. The seventeenth century, overwhelmed with a sense of human depravity, had worried about how to control the corrupt will of the people so as to reduce their offensiveness to God. The eighteenth century was ready, for certain limited purposes at least, to "waive the consideration of man's moral turpitude." In thinking about the state, there was less preoccupation with controlling the depravity of subjects and more with controlling that of rulers; there was less thought of reducing the people's offensiveness to God, more of reducing the ruler's possible offensiveness to the people.

The development of a greater confidence in the virtue and capacities of the people was facilitated among Americans by the manifest success of ordinary men in wringing the comforts of life from a wilderness. By the opening of the eighteenth century it was plain that America was a land of opportunity, not for gentlemen and aristocrats—they fared better in the Old World—but for the man who earned his bread by the sweat of his brow. Work brought high rewards in America, socially and politically as well as economically, and the average eighteenth-century New Englander lived far better than his ancestors or than his counterpart in Europe. Most adults were landowners, earning a modest but secure living from their farms, managing their political affairs in town meetings and through representatives sent to the General Court. They went to church regularly and retained enough familiarity with theology to quarrel with their ministers about it; but they were conspicuously lacking in the Christian virtue of humility and ready to assert themselves not only against ministers but also against their rulers and indeed against anyone who claimed too exalted a station in society.

These new Americans, while adhering to the ideas they had inherited, adapted them to the new intellectual climate and at the same time to their own needs. The most subtle transformation took place in the concept of the calling. In the seventeenth century the word had carried the force of the active verb from which it was derived: It was God who called. And in calling men to different ways of life, He maintained His sense of order by strong admonitions to everyone to work hard at the calling assigned him and to refrain from seeking a more honored position. Thus the idea had served a socially conservative purpose, to curb and discipline all classes of people in subordination to one another and to the government. In the eighteenth century, the voice of God was heard as loud as ever in demanding hard work, but the implication that one man should be subordinate to another was no longer so clear. It simply did not fit the facts of colonial society.

Instead of subordinating people to one another and to the government, the idea of calling was turned to the purpose of keeping government under control of the people. The various offices of government in the seventeenth century had been only loosely differentiated. The General Court of Massachusetts, for instance, had often exercised legislative, judicial, and even executive functions, although even at the beginning Winthrop had tried to distinguish between the powers of deputies and magistrates. In the course of the century, in New England as in old England, the functions of governors, legislators, judges, and other officers became more sharply defined and separated. This distribution and limitation of governmental powers made possible a reorientation of the old doctrine that everyone, in working at his calling, should keep in his place. As ministers at election sermons repeated the familiar admonition to generation after generation they increasingly applied it to the different branches of government and not to the different classes of society. Instead of saying with Winthrop that some must be rich and some poor, a minister might say that "there are different Ranks and Degrees of Men, and accordingly have different Business assign'd them," and then go on at once to apply the idea: "Some are concern'd in *Legislative*, and others in the *Executive* part."[5] In 1762 Abraham Williams could maintain that "various orders and ranks" were necessary to civil society but at the same time insist that men were "naturally equal, as descended from a common Parent, endued with like Faculties and Propensities, having originally equal Rights and Properties." (see this Volume, Document 20) These two apparently contradictory sentiments were reconciled by applying the first one primarily to the various branches of government. A doctrine orig-

[5]Samuel Phillips, *Political Rulers Authoriz'd and Influenced by God* (Boston: John Draper, 1750), p. 8.

inally designed to curb popular aspirations had thus been turned in the opposite direction, to limit the ambition of rulers.

When its hierarchical implications were neutralized by being confined to government, the idea of calling could even be made to foster egalitarianism. The idea had always held latent implications of this kind in its condemnation of idleness and in its insistence on frugality: The rich man was supposed to be as busy and as thrifty as the poor man. In the New World the poor man who kept busy at his calling quickly ceased to be poor; and he also ceased to be humble. Social classes did not disappear, but men in the lower ranks looked toward those in the upper with less and less awe, until aristocracy came to appear almost as archaic as poverty. Benjamin Franklin warned prospective immigrants that eminence in birth was a commodity that could not be carried to a worse market than America. The Americans, said Franklin, did not inquire concerning a stranger, "*What is he?* but, *what can he do?* If he has any useful Art, he is welcome; and if he exercises it, and behaves well, he will be respected by all that know him; but a mere Man of Quality, who, on that Account, wants to live upon the Public, by some Office or Salary, will be despis'd and disregarded. The Husbandman is in honor there, and even the Mechanic, because their employments are useful. The People have a saying, that God Almighty is himself a Mechanic, the greatest in the Univers; and he is respected and admired more for the Variety, Ingenuity, and Utility of his Handyworks, than for the Antiquity of his Family."[6]

By the middle of the eighteenth century Americans heard disturbing reports that the mother country was falling a prey to men of quality, who contended for the spoils of office and wallowed in idleness and luxury. Although

[6]Benjamin Franklin, *Writings*, A. H. Smyth, ed., (New York: The Macmillan Co., 1905–1907) VIII, 606.

the colonists long refrained from allowing these reports to affect their loyalty, they worried about the contagion of British manners, visited the mother country only with trepidation, and did not hesitate to denounce the venal customs officials stationed among them, who seemed to serve no useful, productive purpose (and thus to have no proper callings) but lived in idleness and luxury from the labors of others. When the quarrel with the mother country began, Americans counted on their own industry and frugality to carry the day and admonished themselves not to succumb to the vices of their enemies. Samuel Langdon, calling for resistance to tyranny in 1775, (see this volume, Document 21), denounced luxury as vehemently as he did the British; and the Continental Congress in adopting the Association against trade with Britain, simultaneously exacted of its constitutents a pledge that:

> We will, in our several stations, encourage frugality, economy, and industry, and promote agriculture, arts and the manufactures of this country, especially that of wool; and will discountenance and discourage every species of extravagance and dissipation, especially all horse-racing, and all kinds of gaming, cock-fighting, exhibitions of shews, plays, and other expensive diversions and entertainments; and on the death of any relation or friend, none of us, or any of our families, will go into any further mourning-dress than a black crepe or ribbon on the arm or hat, for gentlemen, and a black ribbon and necklace for ladies, and we will discontinue the giving of gloves and scarves at funerals.[7]

Although the direct object of this resolution was to stop American consumption of British goods, it also aimed at moral reformation of the kind that Langdon and many others were asking for. It demanded that people practice industry, thrift, frugality, the virtues embodied in the doc-

---

[7]W. C. Ford, ed., *Journals of the Continental Congress*, I, 78.

trine of the calling, and its authors probably hoped that these would help to win the favor of the Almighty for the American cause. It may thus have served the same purpose that the Massachusetts General Court had in view a century earlier in its measures against the "provoking evils" that had prompted God to unleash the Indians in King Philip's War. But a change of direction is evident. The measures adopted in 1675 called on the government to suppress, among other things, the pride displayed in immodest and costly fashions. The order of society was upset and God was offended when men and women of a low station wore clothes beyond their means, clothes appropriate only to gentlefolk; and gentlefolk were supposed to set a good example by avoiding vain, giddy, new fashions themselves. The Massachusetts laws against pride in apparel were aimed, in part at least, to maintain a proper order in society, a proper subordination of inferiors to superiors. The measures of 1775, on the other hand, had no such purpose. Industry, economy, and frugality were urged not to suppress popular pride but to foster the success of the American people in their insubordination to the government of England. The doctrine of the calling was harnessed to the cause of revolution.

The idea of covenant underwent a similar transformation and carried with it a new view of the separation of church and state. In the eighteenth century the old sense of New England's covenant with God grew weaker. It did not expire, as is evident from Mayhew's and Langdon's sermons (see this volume, Documents 19 and 21); and it survived into the nineteenth century as the sense of mission that so many observers have found in our history. But the covenant that stood more immediately in the eyes of most Americans by the time of the Revolution was the one between ruler and people. Thinking on this subject had become much more explicit than in the days of Winthrop, thanks largely to the popularity of John Locke's treatises on Civil Government, and of other English and European writings on the subject. These had been so well digested, explained, and disseminated in the writings of men like John Wise and Elisha Williams that eighteenth century Americans could talk of the formation of government without ever recurring to Israel as their model and sometimes without even mentioning God as an initial participant in the covenant.

It required no great effort for them to think of government as arising in the manner Locke described, from a contract or covenant among a group of free individuals, who first joined in a social contract, agreeing to be one people, and then made a second, governmental contract, in which they chose rulers and imposed limits on them. Locke's emphasis on the limitation of the ruler's authority was quite in accord with Puritan practice. Seventeenth-century Massachusetts had had a written body of laws limiting the actions of government and a written charter defining its form and subjecting most of the officers of government to annual election. The only novelty in Locke's explanation of the formation of government was the apparent absence of God from the proceedings, and this omission did not hinder acceptance of his views; for though Locke did not mention God as a participant in either covenant, he did identify God as the author of the laws of nature, which were supposed to prevail even in the absence of government and which government was supposed to enforce. But if God was present in Locke's system, He was well in the background. Government existed not to help the people please God and fend off His wrath but simply to help them protect their lives, liberties, and properties against each other. Such protection had of course been a function of government for the seventeenth-century Puritan too, but for him it had been achieved when his rulers, in performance of their callings, curbed the depravity of his neighbors and thus fulfilled the nation's covenant with God..

As emphasis shifted from the government's obligation to please God to the government's obligation to protect life, liberty, and property, the way was open for the development of a new concept increasingly realized as the century progressed: the government's obligation to please the people. As the godly purpose of the covenant dropped from sight, so did the aura of divinity that had once encompassed rulers. They no longer entered into covenant to perform a godly service with godly assistance, but merely to serve their fellow men. The relative importance in the covenant of the rulers' role and the people's role was thus reversed. Americans looked on their governors less as God's agents than as their own agents, and they concerned themselves more and more with *how* they wanted their rulers to rule.

The Puritans had approached this problem with God's covenant always in mind. They must measure out to rulers whatever authority God allowed, no more, no less. In the Body of Liberties the people of Massachusetts had attempted to do just that. In the eighteenth century, man gave more consideration to what authority he himself was willing to allow. He had come to value certain rights that rulers did not always accord him, and he worked throughout the century to curb and reduce the powers of rulers in order to protect or secure those rights. Locke called them natural rights. They belonged to men—not to governments. According to his formulation, the people in creating a government assigned to their chosen rulers the authority to exercise some of the people's natural rights. But they reserved for themselves sole authority to exercise others. This aspect of Locke's philosophy was as easily grafted upon the Puritan political tradition as the rest: From the vantage point of the eighteenth century, the Body of Liberties could have been interpreted as simply a statement of the people's residual rights and of those they assigned to government.

In limiting the powers of their rulers, men of the eighteenth century were presumably still to be guided by the laws of God and not by their own will alone, because the natural rights at issue were part of the law of nature which God had set forth. But God's law of nature in the eighteenth century guided men to withhold from government certain kinds of authority that God's law in the seventeenth century had required them to assign. When the purpose of government was to satisfy the people's covenant with God by enforcing His laws, it had seemed obvious that the most important of these laws must be the ones concerning His worship. In the attempt to remedy provoking evils in 1675 the Massachusetts General Court had blamed themselves for tolerating Quakers. But in spite of repressive measures, there sprang up a variety of opinion about what was the right way to worship. By the middle of the eighteenth century religion had come to be regarded by many as a private concern, beyond the reach of government. The right to worship God in any way one pleased, men decided, was a natural right, one of those residual natural rights that the people retained when they created a government. It was in fact, as Elisha Williams explained in 1744, an inalienable right, and control over it could not be assigned to government (see this volume, Document 18).

This view is a long way from orthodox Puritanism and very close to the ideas of Roger Williams. But we may perceive something of the change that had overtaken New England if we compare the plea of Roger Williams for religious liberty in 1644 with that of Elisha Williams in 1744. The seventeenth-century Williams denied the state any authority over religion, on the ground that the people, from whom the state derived, did not have the authority from God to create churches and therefore could not endow the state with a power that they did not have, a power that God had reserved to Himself. The eighteenth-century Williams denied the state any authority over religion on the ground that the people, from whom the state derived, had reserved this authority to themselves as an inalienable, residual right that could not be taken from them willingly or unwillingly. The end result was the same in each case, and the difference was one of emphasis, but Roger Williams was more concerned to protect the prerogatives of God, Elisha Williams to protect the rights of the people.

The difference between Elisha Williams and Roger Williams exemplifies once again the lesser preoccupation of the eighteenth century with pleasing God and the greater preoccupation with pleasing the people. This shift, occurring in the Old World as well as the New World, ultimately transformed the authoritarian governments of the seventeenth century into the popular ones of the nineteenth. In England it was heralded by the commonwealth of 1649–1660, which proved abortive. In America widespread ownership of property and popular participation in town, county, and colony government produced an atmosphere more hospitable to the shift and culminated in the American Revolution.

The Revolution, in which the people of America threw off a government that did not please them, greatly increased the confidence of the people in their own powers; and, by compelling them to create new governments, it redirected their attention to the covenant and the importance of their own role in it. The idea of covenant had always implied a capacity in the people to judge in political matters. Although Bullinger had assigned only to "noble captains and valiant men" (see this volume, Document 2) the task of deposing wicked rulers, Goodman (see this volume, Document 1) and other Puritans had insisted that the whole people, every man of them, must sit in judgment on a tyrant, since the whole people would suffer the wrath of God for his wickedness. The New England Puritans, while measuring the ruler's authority by the laws of God, had likewise insisted that the people do the measuring. In the covenant between people and God, God dictated the terms, but in the covenant between people and rulers, the people dictated. And although they must dictate only terms that God approved, the judgment of what He approved was left to the people. It had even been specified by law that the church should have no hand in the matter. No church censure could alter the decisions of the people in the choice of a particular magistrate. They alone must judge whether a ruler was fit to fulfill the nation's covenant with God.

Thus, even when the principal object of government had been to curb the depravity of the people, it had been left to them in the end to make and unmake rulers and to prescribe limits for them. In the American Revolution the people assumed the powers that the Puritans had assigned them. The colonists first attempted to set limits on the British government, and when this proved impossible, they unmade that government and replaced it by covenant with new ones on which they set firm limits. But these were men of the eighteenth century, and the authority they withheld from government they did not retain for God so much as for themselves. In every independent state they adopted a bill of rights defining the areas where they allowed the state no authority, and in every state they prescribed the form of government in a written constitution.

Americans of the Revolutionary generation thus created governments by covenant and by covenant limited their powers; they also by covenant gave to themselves a continuing, active role in the operation of government at all levels. Having observed, as they thought, the degeneration of hereditary monarchy into tyranny, they were no longer content with constitutional limitations on the extent of governmental power but demanded a government in which rulers were continually returned to the people, and in which as many people as possible participated in government. The spread of power among many people, it was believed, would lessen the danger of tyranny and corruption.

This insight took various forms. James Madison applied it to argue for adoption of the United States Constitution (in the *Federalist Papers*) by showing that a large republic, necessarily embracing in its legislature a great variety of interests, must be less susceptible of oppressive government than a small one. Conversely, Antifederalists applied the idea to argue that the Constitution provided for too few persons in the House of Representatives. Ezra Stiles, a New England minister, applied it as early as 1766 to argue for popular elections.[8] Stiles liked to think of himself as a Puritan and considered his political and theological ideas to be in the Puritan tradition. All men were evil, he believed, and might abuse their powers, but it was easier to corrupt a few than many. Therefore, he thought, the wider the electorate the better.

The Revolution accelerated Stiles's thinking, as it did that of other Americans. By 1794 he had progressed to the belief that the common people, in the last analysis, will always judge correctly when properly informed and that even after the establishment of government the people must be allowed to associate freely and extra-legally for the purpose of altering or abolishing government. Only oppressive governments need fear the people. In Stiles's hands the popular role in the covenant has been so

[8]E.S. Morgan, *The Gentle Puritan: A Life of Ezra Stiles* (New Haven: Yale University Press, 1962), pp. 250–251.

magnified as to make government an agency for carrying out the will of the people: Puritanism has been transformed into democracy. (see this volume, Document 22)

The reader will find in the writings that follow a good many ideas relating to politics that have not been touched upon in the Introduction. And anyone who searches other Puritan writings will find still more. Puritanism spurred so much creative thought that no collection can be complete, and no selection is likely to satisfy those who know the subject well. Hopefully, however, these pages will suggest the richness of the Puritan tradition and the debt that modern democracy owes it.

Edmund S. Morgan

New Haven, Connecticut
August, 1965

COLLATERAL READING

The Puritans were perhaps the first English-speaking group to make large-scale use of the printing press for political purposes; and they wrote so much relating in one way or another to politics that a bibliography of relevant original materials would be a great deal longer than this book. A brief selection of titles will be found in Perry Miller and Thomas H. Johnson, *The Puritans* (New York: American Book Company, 1938), pp. 792–796.

The secondary literature about the Puritans is voluminous, and much of it concerns their political thought, although frequently the subject is treated only in the larger context of their religious ideas. Students wishing to acquaint themselves with Puritan origins may profitably begin with M. M. Knappen, *Tudor Puritanism* (Chicago: University of Chicago Press, 1939). The monumental studies of the Elizabethan Parliament by J. E. Neale also furnish valuable background information about Puritan political activities: *The Elizabethan House of Commons* (London: Jonathan Cape, 1949); *Elizabeth I and Her Parliaments* (London: Jonathan Cape, 1953, 1957). More directly concerned with English Puritan thought are the writings of William Haller, all of which present important imaginative insights into the development of English Puritanism: *The Rise of Puritanism* (New York: Columbia University Press, 1938); *Liberty and Reformation in the Puritan Revolution* (New York: Columbia University Press, 1955); *The Elect Nation* (New York: Harper and

Row, 1963). *The Protestant Mind of the English Reformation* by C. H. and Katherine George (Princeton, New Jersey: Princeton University Press, 1961) is a more controversial work, suggesting that the differences between Puritans and Anglicans have been exaggerated.

Another aspect of the English and European background is treated in Charles H. McIlwain's masterly introduction to *The Political Works of James I* (Cambridge, Mass.: Harvard University Press, 1918), which is indispensable for an understanding of Puritan views about the relationship of church and state. George Mosse in *The Holy Pretence* (Oxford: Basil Blackwell, 1957) shows some interesting parallels between Puritan and Catholic political thought. Caroline Robbins in *The Eighteenth-Century Commonwealthman* (Cambridge, Mass.: Harvard University Press, 1959) traces the Puritan political tradition in eighteenth-century England.

Still another facet of Puritan thought is uncovered in Max Weber's famous essay, *The Protestant Ethic and the Spirit of Capitalism*, translated by Talcott Parsons (London: G. Allen and Unwin, Ltd., 1930), which explores some of the implications of the doctrine of calling. Weber's work has been modified in R. H. Tawney's *Religion and the Rise of Capitalism* (London: John Murray, 1926) and challenged in a host of other works, but Weber's perception of the way in which Puritan addiction to work affected society remains one of the great insights of modern scholarship.

American Puritanism has been treated by Perry Miller in a series of books that reach a level of understanding unequaled in any other branch of American intellectual history. The portions of his work that bear most directly on Puritan political thought are *Orthodoxy in Massachusetts* (Cambridge, Mass.: Harvard University Press, 1933), especially pp. 212–313; *The New England Mind: The Seventeenth Century* (New York: Macmillan Company,

1939), especially pp. 365–491; *The New England Mind: From Colony to Province* (Cambridge, Mass.: Harvard University Press, 1953), especially pp. 305–478; and *Errand into the Wilderness* (Cambridge, Mass.: Harvard University Press, 1956), especially pp. 1–98, 141–152.

A number of works treat special aspects of Puritan political thought in New England. George Haskins, *Law and Authority in Early Massachusetts* (New York: Macmillan Company, 1960), is the best study of Puritan legal ideas; it places them in the whole context of Puritanism and Puritan society. In *Puritan Village* (Middletown, Conn.: Wesleyan University Press, 1963), Sumner C. Powell examines the origins of a New England town. B. Katherine Brown's "A Note on the Puritan Concept of Aristocracy," *Mississippi Valley Historical Review*, XLI (1954), 105–112, is essential for an understanding of the way in which Puritans understood the terms "aristocracy" and "democracy." The relationship between church and state is dealt with in A. B. Seidman, "Church and State in the Early Years of the Massachusetts Bay Colony," *New England Quarterly*, XVIII (1945), 211–233. Later developments are covered in Susan M. Reed, *Church and State in Massachusetts, 1691–1740* (Urbana: The University of Illinois, 1914), and Maria L. Greene, *The Development of Religious Liberty in Connecticut* (Boston: Houghton Mifflin and Company, 1905). Carl Bridenbaugh treats New England hostility to Anglican episcopalianism in *Mitre and Sceptre* (New York: Oxford University Press, 1962).

I have examined John Winthrop's political career in *The Puritan Dilemma* (Boston: Little Brown and Company, 1958). Loren Baritz treats Winthrop's political thought in *City on a Hill* (New York: John Wiley and Sons, 1964), pp. 3–45.

Roger Williams has been the subject of many studies. S. H. Brockunier emphasizes his insistence on popular rights in *The Irrepressible Democrat: Roger Williams* (New York: The Ronald Press, 1940). Alan Simpson challenges this and other attributions to Williams of democratic ideas in "How Democratic was Roger Williams?" *William and Mary Quarterly*, third series, XIII (1956), 53–67. Perry Miller's *Roger Willaims: His Contribution to the American Tradition* (Indianapolis: Bobbs-Merrill, 1953) presents selections from Williams' writings and demonstrates his use of typology.

Alice Baldwin explores the assimilation of Lockean political philosophy in *The New England Clergy and the American Revolution* (Durham, N.C.: Duke University Press, 1928). Although Perry Miller did not live to carry his study of the New England mind through the Revolutionary period, he has given us a sketch of the way in which ideas about the covenant were used in that period in "From the Covenant to the Revival," J. W. Smith, ed., *The Shaping of American Religion* (Princeton, N.J.: Princeton University Press, 1961), pp. 322–368.

EDITOR'S NOTE

In transcribing the selections that follow, I have retained the original spelling and punctuation, except that I have transposed "i" and "j" and "u" and "v", wherever appropriate, to correspond to modern usage. I have also silently corrected a few obvious typographical errors. The documents are thus presented in a form approximating that in which they were first published. In cases where a document was published posthumously under the supervision of an editor, for example the writings of John Winthrop, I have not ordinarily included the editor's footnotes. I have, however, introduced footnotes in a few selections where they seemed essential to an understanding of the text. These are numbered and followed by the word "Ed." Footnotes written by the author of a document have been included in their original form.

E.S.M.

Puritan Political Ideas

1558-1794

PART ONE

THE ENGLISH BACKGROUND

---

1. CHRISTOPHER GOODMAN ON RESISTANCE TO TYRANTS

Christopher Goodman (1520–1603) graduated from Oxford in 1541 and remained there in one capacity or another for several years. In 1554, along with many other Protestant divines, he took refuge on the Continent from the rule of Mary Tudor. There, at Geneva, he served with John Knox as pastor to a group of English exiles and wrote the tract from which the following passages have been taken. It was designed to encourage and justify rebellion in England, and it made its points so strenuously that Goodman was not allowed to return for several years after Elizabeth I came to the throne. When he did return, about 1570, Goodman joined the ranks of the Puritans, who found the

---

From Christopher Goodman, *How Superior Powers Ought to be Obeyd of their subjects: and Wherin they may lawfully by Gods Worde be disobeyed and resisted. Wherin also is declared the cause of all this present miserie in England, and the onely way to remedy the same* (Geneva, 1558), pp. 42–47, 58–63, 178–191. Some paragraphing has been supplied in this selection.

Elizabethan church insufficiently reformed. In the first selection that follows, Goodman's starting point is the nineteenth verse of the fourth chapter of Acts, *in which Peter and John answered the rulers of Jerusalem with the words: "Whether it be right in the sight of God to obey you rather than God judge you."*

Now for as muche as we are assured of the trueth and certantie of their answere, wherof none can justlie doute: let us somewhat further consider what thinges are principallie herein conteyned. First we maye hereof justlie conclude, that to obeye man in anie thinge contrary to God, or his precepts thoghe he be in hiest auctoritie, or never so orderly called there unto (as these men, wherof Luke speaketh, were) is no obedience at all, but disobedience.

Secondlie, that it is not a sufficient discharge for us before God, when we denye to accomplyshe their unlawful demandes and threatnings, except we do the contrarie every man in his vocation and office, as occasion is offred, and as his power will serve. Whiche thinges playnlie understande, as they shal geve a clere light in this controversie: so do I not doute by this present answere and facte of Peter and John, to prove moste manifestlie, that althoghe we were destitute of other examples, yet this might appeare sufficient.

As touchinge the firste, that there is no obedience agaynst God which is not playne disobedience: the Apostles say, judge you whither it be right or just in Godds sight to obeye you rather then God: which is as muche as thei would saye, It is not juste nor lawful. Then if it be not lawful and just in Goddes sight, who judgeth things truelie and as thei be in dede, it must nedes folowe that allmaner of obedience agaynst God and his worde, is playne disobedience, and the workers therof likewise condemned as rebells. Why? Bycause it is unjust and unlawfull before God: And all true obedience is lawful, which must not be measured by the will of man, but by the juste Lawes and ordinances of the livinge Lorde. So that after God hathe once pronounced anie thinge that he would have done, either in his Lawe or otherwise: there is no man that may or can dispence therwith, seeme it of never so litle importance in the judgement of men.

He that commandeth the contrarie, is a rebell: and he that obeyeth likewise. Neither dothe this appertayne to the Apostles and ministers onlie in their office, but is a generall argument for all sortes, estates, and degrees of men: for as muche as God hathe like auctoritie of all, and all owe unto him first and principall obedience: and secondly unto men for him, and in him onlie: except they wil be enimies to God, and deny him to be their Lorde. For so muche it is in effecte, when we preferre men to God, obedience to man, before the obedience to God. It is not the auctoritie of the Prince, or the feare of his punishment, that can excuse in his presence: who commandeth his people generalie, high and lowe, riche and poore, man and woman, to heare his voyce, and to observe his statutes. Nether to declyne upon the right hand, nor upon the lefte: nether to adde anie thinge therto, or to take anie thinge from it: but to do that onlie, which the livinge Lorde commandeth. And if we be the shepe of the Lordes foulde, it is not sufficient for us to heare the voyce of our pastor, and to folowe him, except we also deny to heare, muche more to folowe anie other: that is, which calleth not with the voyce of the true pastor. And as there ought to be no creature of like auctoritie amongest us, as our soveraygne Lorde and God, whose creatures we be, and the workemanship of his owne handes: even so, there is none like to him in dignitie, or may be compared to him in power, none like to him in riches, or so able to rewarde his subjectes, beinge Lorde of heaven and earthe, disposer of all things present and to come: distributer not onlie of all corporall and earthlie blessings to those that feare and serve him: but also powreth upon them all spirituall and heavenlie graces in great aboundance.

Moreover, as by his auctoritie, power, dignitie, riches and liberalitie, he maye of right demande of us obedience: so must we persuade our selves in not rendring the same to him willinglie, that none can deliver us from his horrible punishementes and destruction, whiche he threatneth upon all such as wilfully transgresse his holie preceptes, and declyne from his Lawes. Nether wil he regarde by what means, or by whose commandement we transgresse his lawes. For that can be no excuse for us, thoghe he be Kinge, Quene, or Emperour that commandeth or threatneth us. For what is kinge, Quene, or Emperour compared to God? Is the punishement of earthe, ashes, of vile man, whose breath is in his nostrilles, more to be feared then the plages of God, who hath power both of body and soule to destroye them everlastingly? Was it any earthly power that broght the waters upon the universall worlde, and drowned all mankinde for synne, viii persons excepted? Did man destroye Sodome and Gomorrhe with fier and brymstone? Came the plages of Egypt, the drowninge of Pharao, the overtrow of the Cananites, the subversion of Jerusalem, by the power of man? If these be the workes of man and not of God, feare man and not God: but if there be none of these evells which cometh upon anie Citie, or contrie, wherof the Lorde is not the worker: beware that the feare of mans punishment, cause thee not to fall in to the handes of this mightie revenger, whiche is an horrible thinge, as the Apostle writeth.

Princes therfore, and all powers upon thee arth, are not

to be compared unto God, whose Lieutenants onlie they shuld be, and are no longer then he wil, in whose handes their hartes are, to move and turne at his pleasure. And for that cause it is their duetie to seke all means possible, wherbie the glorie of God might be advanced, by whom they are them selves so highlie exalted above their brethern, and in no cause to minister occasion of rebellion agaynst his mightie Majestie: but rather to be examples to others (over whom they are constitute) of all Godlie liffe and lawfull obedience. . . . .

Of the whiche we may justlie conclude, that by the ordinance of God, no other kinges or Rulers, oght to be chosen to rule over us, but suche as will seeke his honor and glorie, and will commaunde and do nothing contrarie to his Lawe. Wherewith they are no lesse, ye much more charged, then the common people: because their charge is double: that is, not onelie to feare God them selves, but to see that their people feare him also, to whom they owe in that case all humble obedience and reverence. For they be (as was sayed) Goddes subjectes and Lieutenantes, for whose cause they must be reverenced, doinge their duetie.

But if they will abuse his power, liftinge them selves above God and above their brethern, to drawe them to idolatrie, and to oppresse them, and their contrie: then are they nomore to be obeyed in any commandements tending to that ende: but to be contemned as vile Sergeantes in comparison of the high Judge and Magistrate, who oght to do nothing, but as he is commaunded to do by the Judge and superior power according to the lawe. Other wise, if he lift him selfe above the chief Judge, lokyng to be honored and obeyed more then he: who would not abhorre suche a Sergeant, and not onelie to withstande his commandement, but to accuse him as a rebellious traytor, and banishe him from amongest them? And yet here is but rebellion agaynst man, who is but mortall. What oght we then to do unto that kinge or Prince, that lifteth him selfe up agaynst the Majestie of God, who is immortal, to whome belongeth all power, dominion and honor? Is he anie more in comparison of God, then the Sergeant in respecte of the judge? Shall the Sergeant be punished as a traytor, and this man honored as a kinge, which doth no parte of the office therunto belonginge? Or rather is not his crime and treason greater, and deservith so muche more, as God is more excellent, compared to anie worldlie power, then is anie kinge or Prince compared to the moste vileste Sergeant?

Moreover, whence hathe he this honor? Of him selfe? Is anie man naturallie borne a kinge, Or hathe he it of God? And if of God, wherto, but to use it with God, and not agaynste him. Seing then it is not juste in Goddes sight to obeye man rather then God: neither that their is anie dispensacion of man that can dispence with his holie commandements, neither the auctoritie of Prince, nor feare of punishment can excuse us. Seing also, that kinges are institute to rule in Goddes feare and Lawes, as subjectes and Sergeants to God, and not agaynste his Lawes, and above him: it must nedes followe (as we firste sayed) that all obedience geven to suche, wicked Princes agaynste God, is playne rebellion in his judgemente. And in that case to obeye God, and disobeye man, is true obedience, how so ever the worlde judgeth. For as none will condemne Peter and John of disobedience, because they woulde not herein obeye their ordynarie Magistrates: nomore will anie which have right judgement, condemne the like resistance in others, which alike is lawfull to all.

Or ells shulde the Israelites be excused, by cause they obeyed their wicked kinge Jereboam in worshippinge his calves in Dan, and Bethel.

Then shuld that cruell butcher Doeg, in killinge Ahimalech with LXXXV Priests or Levites, and the whole towne of Nob, at the commandement of ungodlie kinge Saul, have bene preferred to the reste of all his servantes and souldiars. And the souldiars also of cruell Herode shuld be blamelesse in murthering and sheading the bloude of so many infantes in Bethlehem at Herods commandement. Then shulde the wicked Jewes be gyltlesse of Christes deathe and his Prophets, whom they consented to murther by the parsuasion of their Rulers. And the counterfayte Christians this day, which everie where (but especiallie in our miserable countrie) imprison, famishe, murther, hange, and burne their owne countriemen, and deare children of God, at the commandement of furious Jesabel, and her false Priestes and Prophetes, the blouddie Bishopps and shavelynges, shulde be giltlesse in all their doinges. But all these doth God (who is a Jelious and righteous God, and cannot abide his honor to be geven to any other, nor suffer the bloude of the innocent longe to crie unto him for vengeance) condemne as blasphemers, idolatres, and cruell murtherers: which saithe: Thou shalt have no other Goddes but me. Thou shalt not kill. And if God dothe make this, disobedience (as thou mayst playnely see) what commandement of man can aulter his sentence, before whom there is no obedience in evil thinges? Yea, if the whole multitude, from the hiest to the lowest, wolde agree and consent to do evel, yet muste not thou followe them saith the Lorde. For if thou do (notwithstanding the commandement of thy Prince, or example of all others) thou art with them a rebell, and a rebell agaynst thy Lorde and God: from whose wrathe and heavie indignation, no man can defende thee in the dreadfull daie of his visitacion, which is at hande. . . . .

Wel, the day of the Lorde will come, when you shal fele what it is to fight for your Masse, and to betraye the Gospell, to rise and rebell agaynste your lawfull Prince, and to obeye and defende a bastarde, and open enimie to God, an utter destruction of the whole realme: to murther and banishe your naturall countriemen and loving brethern, to honor and receave strangers Gods expresse adversaries: a cruell people, a prowde nation: a people of a farre and of a strange langage, whose tongue ye shall not understande, an impudent nation, and hard harted people, with out all pitie and mercie, which nether will be moved with the lamentable voyce of the mothers, nor shewe anie compassion for the pittiful crye of their sucklinges and infantes. And whi? because ye have chosen to obeye vile man, yea a raginge and madd woman, rather then the almightie and mercifull God. Repent, repent, o ye people of England, for your destruction is at hande. Forsake with spede the unlawfull obedience of fleshe and bloude, and learne to geve honor in tyme to the living Lorde, that he maye staye his hande, and drawe to him agayne his stretched out arme, that you may fynde mercie, and that the bothom of your cupp be not turned upwarde.

Alas saye you, what is this we heare? Be not the people, of them selves as sheepe without a pastor? If the Magistrates and other officers contemne their duetie in defending Gods glorie and the Lawes committed to their charge, lieth it in our power to remedie it? Shall we that are subjectes take the sworde in our handes? It is in dede as you say, a great discouraging to the people when they are not stirred up to godlynesse by the good example of all sortes of Superiors, Magistrates and officers in the faithefull executing of their office: and so muche more when they are not defended by them in their right and title, as wel concerning religion, as the freedome of their naturall countrie: but moste of all when they, which shuld be ther guydes and Capitayns, are become instrumentes to inforce them to wicked impietie. Nevertheles, all this can be no excuse for you, seing, that evill doinges of others, whether they be Lordes, Dukes, Barons, knights or any inferior officers, may not excuse you in evil. And thoghe you had no man of power upon your parte: yet, it is a sufficient assurance for you, to have the warrant of Godds worde upon your side, and God him self to be your Capitayne who willeth not onely the Magistrates and officers to roote out evil from amongest them, be it, idolatrie, blasphemie or open injurie, but the whole multitude are therwith charged also, to whom a portion of the sworde of justice is committed, to execute the judgementes which the Magistrates lawfully commande. And therfore if the Magistrates would whollye despice and betraye the justice and Lawes of God, you which are subjectes with them shall be condemned except you mayntayne and defend the same Lawes agaynst them, and all others to the uttermoste of your powers, that is, with all your strength, with all your harte and with all your soule, for this hath God required of you, and this have you promised unto him not under condition (if the Rulers will) but without all exceptions to do what so ever your Lorde and God shall commande you.

As touching idolatrie, it is worthie to be considered what Moyses wrytethe, or rather the Spirite of God by him, how the Lorde in that place chargeth the whole people to stone to death without mercy the false Prophet or dreamer, when anie shulde rise up amongest them, yea thoghe the thinges came to passe which he before spake, if that therby he soght to perswade them or drawe them to idolatrie. And also howe he suffred such amongest his people to try and prove them, whether they woulde love him with all their harte and with all their soule, meaning (as every man may well perceave) that if they shulde yelde for all their signes and wonders to idolatrie, and not punishe such false Prophetes and dreamers as God had raysed up: that then they loved him not, yea that they had playnly forsaken and denied him, for that he commanded expreslye that everie such Prophet shuld be put to death, and therfore chargeth to take the evill from amongest them. Which commandement as it is not geven onely to the Rulers and Governors (thoghe I confesse it chieflie apperteyneth to their office to see it executed, for which cause they are made Rulers) but also is comon to all the people, who are likewise bownde to the observation of the same: evenso is the punishment appoynted of God, belonging to allmaner of persons without exception, being found transgressors. For the Lorde is a just punisher, with whom there is no respecte of persons, who willeth his people to be like him in their judgementes. In judgemente (saithe the Lorde) comitte no unrighteousnes, nether respect the face of the poore, nether be you afrayde at the contenaunce of the mightie, but judge uprightly to your neghbour.

Moreover that every persone both high and lowe is charged of God with this Lawe, and none freede from the punishment, it is evident in the same Chapter folowing [Deuteronomy, xiii]: Where God doth not permit somuche as privie whispering in thy eare, tending to idolatrie, unpunished, no not of thy dearest frende or kinsman, sayng: Yf thine owne naturall brother, sonne, daughter, or the wyffe of thine owne bosome, or thy neghboure whom thou loveste as thine owne liffe, secreatly provoke thee to idolatrie, to serve strange Gods, either farre or neare, geve not place to him, nether heare him, nether let thine eye have pitie upon him, nether shalt thou pardon him, or hide him, but shalt utterly sley him: thy hande shall first be upon such a one to kill him, and then the handes of all the people &c.

The like commandement is also geven in the 17. and 18. Chap. of the same boke, charging all the people of God in generall, to see idolatrie punished without mercie, and that in all persones. Wherfore we may moste certaynely conclude, that if the Rulers and Magistrates in this case, woulde not execute the Lawes of God where with they are so straightly charged, that then the people are not discharged, excepte they put it in execution to take the evil from amongest them, to whom it also belongeth. Next, that no persone is exempted by any Lawe of God from this punishment, be he kinge, Quene or Emperour, that is, either openly or prively knowne to be an idolatrer be he never so neare or deare unto us, he must dye the death. For God hath not placed them above others to transgresse his Lawes as they liste, but to be subjecte unto them as well as others, over whom they governe. And if they be subjecte unto his Lawes, they muste be subject to the punishment also, when they be fownd disobedient transgressors: yea, so muche the more as their example is more daungerous. For looke what wickednesse reigneth in the Magistrates, the subjectes comonly take incouragement therby to imitate the same, as we see in the examples of jeroboam. Achab and wicked Manasses, who being suffred in the beginninge to commit idolatrie, and to erecte idoles, made the same likewise laufull to all their subjectes. For the same cause God commanded Moyses to hange up all the capitaynes and heads of the people, for that by their example they made the people idolatrers also: he had no respect to their auctoritie, because they were Rulers, but so muche the rather woulde he have them so sharplie punished, that is, hanged agaynst the sunne without mercy: which judgement, thoghe it was done at Gods commandment firste, and after at Moyses, yet were the people executors of the same, and all did understand that it was juste: and not for that tyme onely, but to be a perpetuall example for ever, and a sure admonition of their duetie in the like defection from God, to hange up such Rulers as shulde drawe them from him.

And thoghe it appeare at the firste sight a great disordre, that the people shulde take unto them the punishment of transgression, yet, when the Magistrates and other officers cease to do their duetie, they are as it were, without officers, yea, worse then if they had none at all, and then God geveth the sworde in to the peoples hande, and he him self is become immediatly their head (Yf they will seeke the accomplishment of his Lawes) and hath promised to defende them and blesse them.

And althogh the rebellion of the people, their ingratitude and contempte of Godes Lawes hath bene such at all tymes, that it is a rare thinge to shewe their duetie in this behalf, by anye example: yet is there one facte of the Isralites worthie memorie, and appertayning, to this purpose, whiche is written in the boke of the Judges, at what tyme they had no lawfull Magistrate in all Israell. Who notwithstandinge rose up whollie together agaynst the Tribe of Benjamin in Gabaa (because of that shamefull vilanie, which the sonnes of Belial had done to the Levites wiffe) and sayed or agreed amongest them selves, that none shuld departe to their houses or tentes, before they were revenged of their owne brethern the Benjamites, to slea those detestable persons, which had so shamefully abused the Levites wiffe, albeit she was an harlot, and they without a guide or Capitayne: not knowing when they came to the felde who shulde be their governour to leade them, and geve the onset, before they had consulted with God, who appoynted unto them Juda. Here do we see the eleven Tribes, to whome the Levite made his complaynt, in sendinge to every Tribe a portion of his wiffe, did not excuse them selves to shew justice, bicause they wanted a lawfull Magistrate to governe them, nor thoght them selves discharged for that they were as sheeppe without a pastor: except they did thus arme them selves againste the sonnes of Belial the ungodly Benjamites to see the Judgementes of God executed accordinge to his Law (and as they saide them selves) to cut of the evil from amongest, then demandinge in the end the wicked men that had committed that vilanie.

But you wil say: It is an other matter for the people to enterprice such an acte being without a Ruler, and when they have a Ruler appoynted unto them, without whom they may do nothing. To this I answered before, that it is all one to be without a Ruler, and to have such as will not rule in Gods feare. Yea it is much better to be destitut altogether, then to have a tyrant and murtherer. For then are they nomore publik persons, contemning their publik auctoritie in usinge it agaynst the Lawes, but are to be taken of all men, as private persones, and so examyned and punished. Never the lesse, to the intent ye may understande, that the governour oght not to take away all right from the people, nether discharge them utterly, from the execution of justice: let us consider a like example of the peoples zele under the worthie Capitayne Josua, who when they but harde [i.e., heard] that the Sonnes of Ruben, the Sonnes of Gad, and the half Tribe of Manasses, had erected up an Altar in their portion, which God had geven them beyonde Jordane, thinking that they had so done, to have sacrificed theron, and so to have fallen from God: assembled them selves together wholly, agaynst the Rubenytes, Gaddites and half Tribe of Manasses to revenge that defection from God (as they tooke it) thoghe afterwarde they proved it to be nothing so. Which facte, as it declared an earnest true zele in the people for the defence of Gods glorye, and his religion: so Josua their Capitayne, nether did nor ought to have reproved them: yea, happie might Josua thinke him self, that had his people so readie to mayntayne of their owne accorde the Lawes of God, which before in the dayes of Moyses were so stubburne and rebellious.

And if this redinesse was commendable, having a worthie Magistrat and godly Capitayne: how necessary is it to be used amongest the people when they have ungodly and wicked Princes, who seke by all means to drawe them rather from the Lawe of God, then to incourage them to mayntayne the same? Wherfore this zele to defend Gods Lawes and preceptes, wherewith, all sortes of men are charged, it is not onely prayse worthie in all, but requyred of all, not onely in abstayninge from the transgression of the sayed Lawes, but to see the judgementes therof executed upon all maner of persones with out exception. And that if it be not done by the consent and ayed of the Superiours, it is lawfull for the people, yea it is their duetie to do it them selves, as well upon their owne rulers and Magistrat, as upon other of their bretheren, having the worde of God for their warrant, to which all are subjecte, and by the same charged to cast forthe all evill from them, and to cut of every rotten membre, for feare of infecting the whole body, how deare or pretious so ever it be. If death be deserved, death: if other punishmentes, to see they be executed in all.

For this cause have you promised obedience to your Superiors, that they might herein helpe you: and for the same intent have they taken it upon them. If they will so do, and keepe promisse with you accordinge to their office, then do you owe unto them all humble obedience: If not, you are discharged, and no obedience belongeth to them: because they are not obedient to God, nor be his ministers to punishe the evell, and to defend the good. And therfore your studie in this case, oght to be, to seeke how you may dispose and punishe according to the Lawes, such rebells agaynst God, and oppressers of your selves and your countrie: and not how to please them, obeye them, and flatter them as you do in their impietie. Which is not the waye to obtayne peace, and quietnesse, but to fall in to the handes of the allmightie God, and to be subjecte to his fearefull plagues and punishmentes.

2. HENRY BULLINGER ON THE DUTIES OF RULERS AND SUBJECTS

Henry Bullinger (1504–1575), a successor of Zwingli at Zurich, became acquainted with many leading English Protestants during their exile on the Continent during the reign of Mary Tudor (1553–1558). He maintained an active correspondence with the exiles after their return to England and influenced Puritan thought through the publication in English of his magnum opus, The Decades, *which appeared in several editions in the 1570's and 1580's. The following passages from this work, concerning the functions of government, were probably acceptable to most English Protestants, Puritan and Anglican alike.*

. . . Touching the magistrate and his office, I mean to speak of them in another place: so much as it is necessarily requisite for this present time St Peter uttereth, where he saith, "Fear God, honour the king." Let us therefore acknowledge and confess, that the magistrate's office is ordained of God for men's commodity, and that God by the magistrate doth frankly bestow on us very many and great commodities. The peers do watch for the common people, if they do rightly discharge their office, not shewing themselves to be detestable tyrants; they judge the people, they

---

From Henry Bullinger, *The Decades*, edited for the Parker Society by Thomas Harding, Parker Society, *Publications*, vols, VII–X (Cambridge, England, 1849), vol. VII, 279–281, 314–318, 323–328, 337–344.

take up controversies, they keep justice in punishing the guilty and defending innocents, and, lastly, they fight for the people. And for the excellency of their office, which is both the chiefest and the most necessary, God doth attribute to the magistrate the use of his own name, and calleth the princes and senators of the people gods, to the intent that they by the very name should be put in mind of their duty, and that the subjects might thereby learn to have them in reverence. God is just, good, righteous, and one which hath no respect of persons: and such an one ought the good judge or magistrate to be. Monks and heremites do praise their profession or solitary life, extolling it above the skies; but I think verily, that there is more true virtue in one politic man, who governeth the commonweal and doth his duty truly, than in many thousands of monks and heremites, who have not so much as one word expressed in the holy scriptures for the defence of their vocation and vowed order of living: yea, I am ashamed that I have compared the holy office of magistrates with that kind of people, in whom there is nothing found worthy to be compared with them, insomuch as they fly from the labour and ordinance that God hath made profitable for their people and countrymen. Truly, if the prince do faithfully discharge his office in the commonweal, he heapeth up to himself a number of very good works and praise that never shall be ended. Therefore the magistrate must be obeyed, and all his good and upright laws. No sedition or conspiracies ought in any case to be moved against him. We must not curse or speak evil of the magistrate. For God himself in his law doth charge us, saying: "Thou shalt not speak evil of the gods, nor curse the prince of the people." If he chance at any time to sin, let us behave ourselves toward him as to our father; of whom I have spoken a little before.

It happeneth oftentimes, that magistrates have a good

mind to promote religion, to advance common justice, to defend the laws, and to favour honesty; and yet notwithstanding, they are troubled with their infirmities, yea, sometime with grievous offences: howbeit, the people ought not therefore to despise them and thrust them beside their dignity. David had his infirmities, albeit otherwise a very good prince. By his adultery he endamaged much his people and kingdom: and, for to make his trouble the more, Absolon sinned grievously, and went about to put him beside his crown and kingdom. So likewise in other princes there are no small number of vices, which nevertheless neither move nor ought to move godly people to rebellious sedition, so long as justice is maintained and good laws and public peace defended. We ought to pray earnestly and continually for the magistrate's welfare. We must aid him with our help and counsel, so oft as need shall serve and occasion be given. We must not deny him our riches or bodies to assist him withal. The saints did gather their substance in common to help the magistrate, so oft as public safeguard did so require. The Israelites of all ages did always fight for their judges, for their kings and other magistrates; and so did all other people upon good advice taken: and likewise, on the other side, did the princes fight for the people. I would therefore that those offices of godly naturalness were of force and did flourish even at this day in all kingdoms, cities, and commonweals. Let every nation give to his magistrate that which by law, or by custom, or by necessity, it oweth him. For Paul the apostle saith: "Give to every one that which ye owe; tribute to whom tribute belongeth, custom to whom custom, fear to whom fear, and honour to whom honour is due." (Rom. xiii). . . .

. . . Now many there are which will have the magistrate to be of two sorts, to wit, either good or bad. The good magistrate is he who, being lawfully ordained, doth lawfully execute his office and duty. The evil magistrate is he which, when he hath by evil means got the authority, doth turn and dispose it as himself lusteth. And hereupon the question is wont to be demanded: Whether an evil, that is, a tyrannical, magistrate, be of God or no? To this I answer, that God is the author of good, and not of evil. For God by nature is good, and all his purposes are good, being directed to the health and preservation, not to the destruction, of us men. Therefore the good and healthful ordaining of the magistrate, without all doubt, is of God himself, who is the author of all goodness.

But here it is requisite, that we make a difference betwixt the office which is the good ordinance of God, and the evil person that doth not rightly execute that good office. If therefore in the magistrate evil be found, and not the good for which he was ordained, that cometh of other causes, and the fault thereof is in the men and persons, which neglect God and corrupt the ordinance of God, and not in God, nor in his ordinance: for either the evil prince, seduced by the devil, corrupteth the ways of God, and by his own fault and naughtiness transgresseth God's ordinance, so far, that he doth worthily deserve the name of devilish power, and not divine authority;—(we have an example hereof in the magistrate of Jerusalem: for although he were able to refer the beginning of his power by degrees unto Moses, and so unto God himself who did ordain it; yet, for because he taketh the Saviour in the garden and bindeth him, to his servants it is said, "Ye are come out as it were to a thief with swords and staves; when I was daily with you in the temple, ye stretched not forth your hands against me; but this is even your hour, and the power of darkness." Lo, here he calleth the ordinary magistrate the power of the devil, when he abuseth his power. What could be more evidently spoken? But here ye must mark, that the reproach was in the person, and not in the office.

Likewise also the Roman empire was ordained by God, as by the visions of Daniel it is clearly evident: and yet, when Nero, not without God's ordinance, bare the sway in the empire, whatsoever he did as king and emperor, contrary to the office of a good king, that did he not of God, but of the devil: for whereas he hung up and beheaded the apostles of Christ, moving a bloody persecution against the church, that sprang not from elsewhere than from the devil, the father of murder. So then, verily, we ought not at any time to defend the tyrannical power, and say that it is of God: for tyranny is not a divine, but a devilish, kind of government; and tyrants themselves are properly the servants of the devil, and not of God:) or else otherwise, some people do deserve by their wicked deeds to have, not a king, but a tyrant. So then the people's sin is another cause that evil magistrates are found in commonweals. In the meanwhile, the king is of the Lord, and sometimes he makes an hypocrite reign. Wherefore the evil magistrate is of God, even as also seditions, wars, plagues, hail, frost, and other miseries of mankind come from the Lord, as punishment of sin and wickedness, which the Lord hath appointed to be executed, as he himself saith: "I will give them children to be their kings, and infants shall rule them; because their tongue and heart hath been against the Lord." Likewise the Lord stirred up the cruel kings of Assyria and Babylon against his city and own peculiar people, whose living was not agreeable to their profession.

But now, how and after what sort subjects ought to be affected toward such hard, cruel, and tyrannical princes, we learn partly by the example of David, and partly by the doctrine of Jeremy and the apostles. David was not ignorant what kind of man Saul was, a wicked and merciless fellow: yet, notwithstanding, he fled to escape his hands; and when he had occasion given him once or twice to kill him, he slew him not, but spared the tyrant and reverenced him as though he had been his father. Jeremias prayed for Joachim and Zedechias, wicked kings both, and obeyed them until they came to matters flatly contrary to God's religion. For where I spake touching the honour due to parents, there did I by the scriptures prove, that we ought not to obey the wicked commandments of godless magistrates, because it is not permitted to magistrates to ordain or appoint any thing contrary to God's law, or the law of nature. Now the Acts of the Apostles teach us in what sort the apostles did behave themselves in dealing with tyrannical magistrates. Let them, therefore, that are vexed with tyrants, and oppressed with wicked magistrates, take this advice to follow in that perplexity. First, let them call to remembrance, and consider, what and how great their sins of idolatry and uncleanness are, which have already deserved the revenging anger of their jealous God: and then let them think, that God will not withdraw his scourge, unless he see that they redress their corrupt manners and evil religion. So then first, they must go about and bring to pass a full reformation of matters in religion, and perfect amendment of manners amiss: then must they pray continually that God will vouchsafe to pull and draw his oppressed people out of the mire of mischief, wherein they stick fast. For that counsel did the Lord himself, in the eighteenth after Luke, give to those that are oppressed, promising therewithal assured aid and present delivery. But what and how the oppressed must pray, there are examples extant in the ninth of Daniel, and in the fourth chapter of the Acts of the Apostles. Let them also, whose minds are vexed, call to remembrance the sayings of Peter and Paul, the chief of the apostles. "The Lord," saith Peter, "knoweth how to deliver his from temptation, as he delivered Lot." Paul saith: "God is faithful, and will not suffer his to be tempted above their strength; yea, he will turn their temptations unto the best." Let them call to mind the captivity of Israel, wherein God's people were detained at Babylon by the space of seventy years: and therewithal let them think upon the goodly comfort of the captives, which Esay hath expressed from his fortieth chapter unto his forty-ninth. Let us persuade ourselves, that God is good, merciful, and omnipotent, so that he can, when he will, at ease deliver us. He hath many ways and means to set us at liberty. Let us have a regard only, that our impenitent, filthy, and wicked life do not provoke the Lord to augment and prolong the tyrants' cruelty. The Lord is able, upon the sudden, to change the hearts of princes (for "the hearts of kings are in the hands of the Lord, as the rivers of water, to turn them which way he will"), and to make them, which have been hitherto most cruelly set against us, to be our friends and favourable to us; and them which have heretofore most bloodily persecuted the true religion, to embrace the same most ardently, and with a burning zeal to promote it so far as they may. We have evident examples hereof in the books of the Kings, of Esdras, and Nehemias, and in the volume of Daniel's prophecy. Nabuchodonosor, whose purpose was to toast with fire and utterly to destroy the martyrs of God for true religion, was immediately after compelled to praise God, because he saw the martyrs preserved: and he himself doth by edicts given out publicly proclaim and set forth the only true God and his true religion. Darius, the son of Assuerus, suffereth Daniel to be cast into the lions' den: but straightway he draweth him out again, and shutteth up Daniel's enemies in the same den, to be torn in pieces by the famishing beasts. Cyrus, the puissant king of Persia, advanceth true religion: Darius, son of Hystaspes, whose surname was Artaxerxes, did by all means possible aid and set forward the godly intent of God's people in building up again their city and temple. Let us not doubt therefore of God's aid and helping hand. For God sometime doth utterly destroy, and sometime he chasteneth, untoward tyrants with some horrible and sudden disease: as it is evident that it happened to Antiochus, Herod the Great, and to his nephew, Herod Agrippa, to Maxentius also, and other enemies of God and tyrants over men. Sometime he stirreth up noble captains and valiant men to displace tyrants, and set God's people at liberty; as we see many examples thereof in the books of Judges and Kings. But lest any man do fall to abuse those examples, let him consider their calling by God: which calling if he have not, or else do prevent, he is so far from doing good in killing the tyrant, that it is to be feared lest he do make the evil double so much as it was before. . . .

. . . I see many that are of opinion, that the care and ordering of religion doth belong to bishops alone, and that kings, princes, and senators ought not to meddle therewith.

But the catholic verity teacheth, that the care of religion doth especially belong to the magistrate; and that it is not in his power only, but his office and duty also, to dispose and advance religion. For among them of old their kings were priests; I mean, masters and overseers of religion. Melchizedech, that holy and wise prince of the Canaanitish people who bare the type or figure of Christ our Lord, is wonderfully commended in the holy scriptures: now he was both king and priest together. Moreover, in the book of Numbers, to Josue, newly ordained and lately consecrated, are the laws belonging to religion given up and delivered. The kings of Juda also, and the elect people of God, have for the well ordering of religion (as I will by examples anon declare unto you) obtained very great praise: and again, as many as were slack in looking to religion are noted with the mark of perpetual reproach. Who is ignorant, that the magistrate's especial care ought to be to keep the commonweal in safeguard and prosperity? Which undoubtedly he cannot do, unless he provide to have the word of God preached to his people, and cause them to be taught the true worship of God, by that means making himself, as it were, the minister of true religion. In Leviticus and Deuteronomy the Lord doth largely set down the good prepared for men that are religious and zealous indeed; and reckoneth up, on the other side, the evil appointed for the contemners of true religion. But the good magistrate is commanded to retain and keep prosperity among his people, and to repel all kind of adversity. Let us hear also what the wise man, Salomon, saith in his Proverbs: "Godliness and truth preserve the king, and in godliness his seat is holden up." "When the just are multiplied, the people rejoice; and when the wicked ruleth, the people lamenteth. The king by judgment stablisheth his dominion, but a tyrant overthroweth it. When the wicked increase, iniquity is multiplied, and the just shall see their decay. Where the word of God is not preached, the people decay; but happy is he that keepeth the law. Whereby we gather, that they, which would not have the care of religion to appertain to princes, do seek and bring in the confusion of all things, the dissolution of princes and their people, and lastly, the neglecting and oppression of the poor.

Furthermore, the Lord commandeth the magistrate to make trial of doctrines, and to kill those that do stubbornly teach against the scriptures, and draw the people from the true God. The place is to be seen in the thirteenth of Deut. God also forbade the magistrate to plant groves, or erect images: as is to be seen in the seventeenth of Deut. And by those particularities he did insinuate things general; forbidding to ordain, to nourish, and set forth superstition or idolatry; wherefore he commanded to advance true religion: and so consequently it followeth, that the care of religion belongeth to the magistrate. What may be thought of that moreover, that the most excellent princes and friends of God among God's people did challenge to themselves the care of religion as belonging to themselves; insomuch that they exercised and took the charge thereof, even as if they had been ministers of the holy things? Josue in the mount Hebal caused an altar to be builded, and fulfilled all the worship of God, as it was commanded of God by the mouth of Moses. David, in bringing in and bestowing the ark of God in his place, and in ordering the worship of God, was so diligent, that it is wonder to tell. So likewise was Salomon, David's son. Neither do I think that any man knoweth not how much Abia, Josaphat, Ezechias, and Josias, laboured in the reformation of religion, which in their times was corrupted and utterly defaced. The very heathen kings and princes are praised, because, when they knew the truth, they gave out edicts for the confirmation of true religion against blasphemous mouths. Nabuchodonozor, the Chaldean, the most mighty monarch of all the world, than who I doubt whether any more great and mighty did reign in the world, publisheth a decree, that he should be torn in pieces, and his house made a jakes, whosoever spake reproachfully against the true God which made both heaven and earth. The place is extant in the third chapter of Daniel's prophecy. Darius Medus, the son of Assuerus, king Cyrus his uncle, saith: "I have decreed that all men in the whole dominion of my kingdom do fear the God of Daniel:" as is to be seen in the sixth of Daniel. Cyrus, king of Persia, looseth the Jews from bondage, and giveth them in charge to repair the temple, and restore their holy rites again. Darius Persa, the son of Hystaspes, saith: "I have decreed for every man which changeth any thing of my determination touching the reparation of the temple, and the restoring of the worship of God, that a beam be taken out of his house, and set up, and he hanged thereon, and his house to be made a jakes"

The very same Darius again, who was also called Artaxerxes, saith: "Whosoever will not do the law of thy God (Esdras), and the law of the king, let judgment straightway pass upon him, either to death, or to utter rooting out, or to confiscation of his goods, or imprisonment." All this we find in the book of Esdras.

The men, which are persuaded that the care and ordering of religion doth belong to bishops alone, do make an objection, and say, that these examples, which I have alleged, do nothing appertain to us which are Christians, because they are examples of the Jewish people. To whom mine answer is: The men of this opinion ought to prove, that the Lord Jesus and his apostles did translate the care of religion from the magistrate unto bishops alone: which they shall never be able to do. But we, on the other side, will briefly shew, that those ancient princes of God's people, Josue, David, and the rest, were Christians verily and indeed; and that therefore the examples which are derived from them and applied to christian princes, both are and ought to be of force and effect among us at this day. I will in the end add also the prophecy of the prophet Esay, whereby it may appear, that even now also kings have in the church at this day the same office that those ancient kings had in that congregation which they call the Jewish church. There is no doubt but that they ought to be accounted true Christians, which, being anointed with the Spirit of Christ, do believe in Christ, and are in the sacraments made partakers of Christ. For Christ (if ye interpret the very word) is as much to say as "anointed." Christians therefore, according to the etymology of their name, are anointed. That anointing, according to the apostle's interpretation, is the Spirit of God, or the gift of the Holy Ghost. But St Peter testifieth, that the Spirit of Christ was in the kings and prophets. And Paul affirmeth flatly, that we have the very same Spirit of faith that they of old had;

and doth moreover communicate our sacraments with them, where he saith, that they were baptized under the cloud, and that they all drank of the spiritual rock that followed them, which rock was Christ.

Since then the case is so, the examples, truly, which are derived from the words and works of those ancient kings, for the confirmation of faith and charity, both are and ought to be of force with us. And yet I know that every thing doth not consequently follow upon the gathering of examples. But here we have, for the making good of our argument, an evident prophecy of Esay, who foretelleth that kings and princes, after the times of Christ and the revealing of the gospel, should have a diligent care of the church, and should by that means become the feeders and nurses of the faithful. Now it is evident what it is to feed and to nourish; for it is all one as if he should have said, that they should be the fathers and mothers of the church. But he could not have said that rightly, if the care of religion did not belong to princes, but to bishops alone. The words of Esay are these: "Behold, I will stretch out my hand unto the Gentiles, and set up my token to the people; and they shall bring thee thy sons in their laps, and thy daughters on their shoulders. And kings shall be thy nursing fathers, and queens thy nursing mothers; they shall fall before thee with their faces flat upon the earth, and lick up the dust of thy feet," &c. Shall not we say, that all this is fully performed in some christian princes? Among whom the first was the holy emperor Constantine, who, by calling a general council, did determine to establish true and sincere doctrine in the church of Christ, with a settled purpose utterly to root out all false and heretical phantasies and opinions. And when the bishops did not go rightly to work by the true rule and touchstone of the gospel and of charity, he blamed them, upbraiding them with tyrannical cruelty, and declaring therewithal what peace the

Lord had granted by his means to the churches: adding moreover, that it were a detestable thing, if the bishops, forgetting to thank God for his gifts of peace, should go on among themselves to bait one another with mutual reproaches and taunting libels, thereby giving occasion of delight and laughter to wicked idolaters; when as of duty they ought rather to handle and treat of matters of religion. For (saith he) the books of the evangelists, apostles, and oracles of the ancient prophets, are they which must instruct us in the understanding of God's holy law. Let us expel, therefore, this quarrelling strife, and think upon the questions proposed, to resolve them by the words of scripture inspired from above. After him again, the holy emperors, Gratian, Valentinian, and Theodosius, make a decree, and give out the edict in these very words: "We will and command all people, that are subject to our gracious empire, to be of that religion, which the very religion, taught and conveyed from Peter till now, doth declare that the holy apostle Peter did teach to the Romans." And so forward.

By this, dearly beloved, ye perceive how kings and princes, among the people of the new Testament, have been the foster-fathers and nourishers of the church; being persuaded that the care of religion did first of all and especially belong to themselves. . . .

. . . Here followeth now the second part of the magistrates' ordinance, which consisteth in making good laws for the preservation of honesty, justice, and public peace; which is likewise accomplished in good and upright laws. But some there are who think it mere tyranny to lay laws on free men's backs, as it were a yoke upon necks not used to labour; supposing that every one ought rather to be left to his own will and discretion. The apostle indeed did say, "The law is not given for the just, but for the unjust:" but the cause, why the law is not given to the just, is because he is just; for the just worketh justice, and doth of his own accord the thing which the law exacteth of every mortal man. Wherefore the law is not troublesome to the just man, because it is agreeable to the mind and thoughts of upright livers, who do embrace it with all their hearts. But the unjust desireth nothing more than to live as he lusteth: he is not conformable in any point to the law, and therefore must he by the law be kept under, and bridled from marring himself and hurting other. So then, since to good men the laws are no troublesome burden but an acceptable pleasure, which are also necessary for the unjust, as ordained for the bridling of lawless and unruly people; it followeth consequently, that they are good and profitable for all men, and not to be rejected of any man. What may be said of that, moreover, that God himself, who did foresee the disposition of us men, what we would be, and hath still favoured the true liberty which he desired always to have preserved among his people, as one that ever meant them good, and never did ordain the thing that should turn to their hinderance or discommodity; that God himself (I say) was their lawgiver, and hath not suffered any age at any time to live as people without a law? Yea too, those commonweals have been happy always, that have admitted laws, and submitted themselves to be governed by laws; when as, contrarily, those kingdoms have of all other been most miserable, and torn in pieces by civil dissensions and foreign enemies, which, having banished upright laws, did strive to maintain their own kind of freedom, their uncontrolled dealing and licentious liberty, that is, their beastly lust and uncivil rudeness. Good laws therefore are for the health and preservation of the people, and necessary for the peace and safeguard of commonweals and kingdoms.

Wherefore it is a wonder to see the folly of some Christians, since the very heathens have given so honest report of laws and lawgivers. They took their lawgivers for gods, confessing thereby that good laws are the gift of God. But the gift of God cannot be superfluous and unprofitable. Plutarch called laws the life of cities. Demosthenes did expressly confess that laws are the gifts of God. Cicero named laws the bonds of the city (because without laws it is loosed and dispersed), the foundation of liberty, and the well-spring of justice and perfect honesty. For laws undoubtedly are the strongest sinews of the commonweal, and life of the magistrates: so that neither the magistrates can without the laws conveniently live and rule the weal public, nor the laws without the magistrates shew forth their strength and lively force. The magistrate therefore is the living law, and the law is the dumb magistrate. By executing and applying the law, the law is made to live and speak: which those princes do not consider that are wont to say, *Wir sind das recht,* "We are the right, we are the law." For they suppose that they at their pleasure may command what they list, and that all men by and by must take it for law. But that kind of ruling, without all doubt, is extreme tyranny. The saying of the poet is very well known, which representeth the very words of a tyrant:

> I say, and it shall be so;
> My lust shall be the law.

The prince, indeed, is the living law, if his mind obey the written laws, and square not from the law of nature. Power and authority, therefore, is subject unto laws; for unless the prince in his heart agree with the law, in his breast do write the law, and in his words and deeds express the law, he is not worthy to be called a good man, much less a prince. Again, a good prince and magistrate hath power over the law, and is master of the laws, not that they may turn, put out, undo, make and unmake, them as they list at their pleasure; but because he may put them in practice among the people, apply them to the necessity of the state, and attemper their interpretation to the meaning of the maker.

They therefore are deceived as far as heaven is wide, which think for a few privileges, of emperors and kings granted to the magistrate to add, diminish, or change some point of the law, that therefore they may utterly abolish good laws, and live against all law and seemliness. For, as no emperors or kings are permitted to grant any privileges contrary to justice, goodness, and honesty; so, if they do grant any such privilege, it ought not to be received or taken of good subjects for a good turn or benefit, but to be counted rather (as it is indeed) their utter destruction and clean overthrow. Among all men, at all times and of all ages, the meaning and substance of the laws touching honesty, justice, and public peace, is kept inviolable: if change be made, it is in circumstances, and the law is interpreted as the case requireth, according to justice and a good end. The law saith, "Let no man kill another: let him that killeth another be killed himself." That law remaineth for ever unchangeable, neither is it lawful for any man at any time to put it out or wipe it away. And yet the rigour of the law may be diminished, and the law itself favourably interpreted: as, for example, if a man kill one whom he loveth entirely well, and kill him by chance, and not of set purpose or pretended malice, so that, when he hath done, he is sorry for it at the very heart, and would (if it were possible) buy his life again with whatsoever he hath to give for it; in such a case the killer ought not to be killed, and therein the magistrate may dispense with the rigour of the law. Another beareth a deadly and continual grudge to one, whom he killeth, and goeth about to colour the matter under the pretence of hap and misfortune: for he sought occasion, that he might for himself have a shew of chance-medley. In such a case as this the magistrate cannot change any jot of the law, but must needs kill him whom the meaning of the law commandeth to kill. I could allege more examples like unto these; but my care is, of purpose, so much as I may, not to be too tedious unto you with too long a discourse. By this that I have spoken it is apparently evident, that laws are good and not to be broken, and how far forth they do admit the prince's ἐπιείκειαν, that is, the prince's moderation, interpretation, limitation, or dispensation, lest peradventure that old and accustomed proverb be rightly applied unto them, "Law with extremity is extreme injury."

Hitherto I have declared that laws are good, profitable, necessary, and not to be broken: it remaineth now to tell what and what kind of laws the magistrate ought most chiefly to use for the ordering and maintaining of honesty, justice, and public peace, according to his office. Some there are whose opinion is, that the magistrate ought not to use any written laws, but that he should rather give sentence as he thought best according to natural equity, as the circumstances of place, time, persons, and cases do seem to require. Other some there are that do their endeavour to thrust into all kingdoms and commonweals the judicial laws of Moses. And some there are which, having once rejected the law of Moses, will have no judgment given in law, but what is derived out of the laws of heathen princes. But since they that have the pre-eminence and magistrate's authority are men either good or bad; and since that, even in the best men, covetousness, anger, hatred, favour, grief, fear, and other affections, are rife to be found; to whom, I pray you, have they committed the commonweal, which, rejecting all written statutes and certain laws, would have every man that is a magistrate to give judgment as he himself thinketh best? Have they not committed their commonweal to the rule of a beast? But what shall I say then of evil men that are in authority, since in the best men things are so amiss? As good were a kingdom subject to the furies of hell, as bound to the judgments of naughty men. But we will (say they) have them give judgment according to the equity of nature's law, and not after the lust of their corrupt affection. Mine answer is to that; that they will give judgment as affection leadeth them without controlment, and say that they judged by natural equity. They cannot, they will say, judge otherwise, nor otherwise understand the pith of the matter. They think that best which they have determined, and nothing is done contrary to conscience; and thou for thy labour shalt be called *Coram nobis* for daring find fault with their sentence in judgment. And so shall the just man perish, barbarous affections shall have the upper hand, and naughty men rule all the roost. Yea, and admit we grant all men are good that are called to be magistrates; yet diversity of opinions, that will rise in giving of judgment, will stir up among them endless brawls and continual troubles. If all things therefore be well considered, the best way by a great deal is to put written laws in ure.

Let us learn this by the example of our eternal, wise, excellent, and mighty God, who gave to the Jews, his peculiar people, such laws as at his commandment were set down in writing. The magistrate hath otherwise business enough to judge, that is, to apply and confer the causes with the laws; to see how far and wherein they agree or disagree; and to judge who hath offended against the law, and who have not transgressed the law.

Now it is to be marked, that in Moses' judicial law there are many things proper and peculiar to the Jewish nation, and so ordained, according to the state of the place, time, and persons, that, if we should go about to thrust on and apply them all to other nations, we should seem to shew ourselves more than half mad. And to what end should we bring back and set up again among the people of God the offscourings of the heathen that were cast out a great while ago? The apostles of our Lord Jesus Christ did bind or burden no man with the laws of Moses; they never condemned good laws of the heathens, nor commended to any man naughty laws of the Gentiles; but left the laws, with the use and free choice of them, for the saints to use as they thought good. But therewithal they ceased not most diligently to beat into all men's heads the fear of God, faith, charity, justice, and temperance; because they knew that they, in whose hearts those virtues were settled, can either easily make good laws themselves, or pick and choose out the best of those which other men make. For it maketh no matter whether the magistrate pick out of Moses' Jewish laws, or out of the allowable laws of the heathen, sufficient laws for him and his countrymen, or else do keep still the old and accustomed laws which have before been used in his country, so that he have an eye to cut off such wicked, unjust, and lawless laws, as are found to be thrust in among the better sort. For I suppose that upright magistrates ought to take off curiosity and new invented novelties. "Seldom," saith the proverb, "is the crow's eye picked out without troublesome stirs:" and curious men's new laws are for the most part worse than the old, that are broken by them and utterly abolished.

Furthermore, all laws are given for ordering of religion or outward worship of God, or else for the outward conversation of life and civil behaviour. Touching the laws of religion, I have spoken of them before. For civil and politic laws, I add thus much, and say, that those seem to be the best laws, which, according to the circumstance of every place, person, state, and time, do come nearest unto the precepts of the ten commandments and the rule of charity, not having in them any spot of iniquity, licentious liberty, or shameless dishonesty. Let them, moreover, be brief and short, not stretched out beyond measure, and wrapped in with many expositions: let them have a full respect to the matter whereto they are directed, and not be frivolous and of no effect.

Now mark, that politic laws do for the most part consist in three especial and principal points—honesty, justice, and peace. Let laws therefore tend to this end, that discipline and honesty may be planted and maintained in the commonweal, and that no unseemly, licentious, and filthy act be therein committed. Let law forbid all uncleanness, wantonness, lightness, sensuality, and riotousness, in apparel, in building, in bibbing and banquetting. Let wedlock be commanded by law to be kept holy. Let stews and brothel-houses be banished the realm. Let adulteries, whoredoms, rapes, and incests, be put to exile. Let moderate feastings be allowed and admitted. Let thriftiness be used, which is the greatest revenue that a man can enjoy. Briefly, whatsoever is contrary to honesty and seemliness, let it by law be driven out and rejected.

Let justice by laws be strongly fortified. Let it by laws be provided, that neither citizen nor foreigner be hurt or hindered in fame, in goods, in body, or life. Let upright laws be made for the obtaining of legacies and inheritances, for the performing of contracts and bargains, for covenants and agreements, for suretiships, for buying and selling, for weights and measures, for leases and things let to hire, for lending and borrowing, for pawns in mortgage, for use, commodity, and usury of money. Let order be taken for maintenance of peace between the father and his children, betwixt man and wife, betwixt the master and the servant; and, to be short, that every man may have his own. For my meaning is not here to reckon up particularly every several point and tittle of the law.

Lastly, means must be made by giving of laws, that peace may be established, whereby every man may enjoy his own. All violent robberies and injuries must be expelled; privy grudges and close conspiracies must not be thought of. And war must be quieted by wisdom, or else undertaken and finished with manly fortitude.

But, that we may have such a magistrate and such a life,

the apostle commanded us earnestly to pray, where he saith: "I exhort you that, first of all, prayers, supplications, intercessions, and giving of thanks, be made for all men; for kings and for all that are in authority, that we may live a quiet and peaceable life in all godliness and honesty."

---

3. WILLIAM PERKINS ON CALLINGS

William Perkins (1558–1602) attended Cambridge University and remained there as a fellow of Christ's College until 1594, when he married. No other English divine was more admired by Puritans. His writings, which were always lucid and well-organized, went through numerous editions after his death and influenced all subsequent Puritans. The first selection, below, describes the doctrine of "calling" and is taken from "A Treatise of the Vocations or Callings of men, with sorts and kinds of them, and the right use thereof."

1. COR. 7 . VERSE 20.

Let every man abide in that calling, wherein hee was called.

From the 17. verse of this chapt. to the 25. there are two questions handled. First, whether a man beeing called to Christianity uncircumcised, must bee circumcised after his calling. The second is, whether beeing a bondman when he is called, hee must then leave his calling. Now the sum

---

From *The Workes of that Famous and Worthy Minister of Christ in the Universitie of Cambridge, Mr. William Perkins* (London: I. Legatt, 1626–31, 3 vols.), II, 750–759.

of the Apostles answer to them both, is laid downe in this 20. verse: as if hee should say; let every man continue in that calling, wherein hee was called unto Christ: that is, wherein hee walked and lived when it pleased God by the ministery of his Gospel, to cal him unto the profession of Christian religion. The cause why I have chosen to speake of these words, is, because I meane to intreate of this point of vocation or calling; considering few men rightly know how to live and goe on in their callings, so as they may please God. Therefore to proceede in order, in speaking of this point; First, I will shew what *Vocation* or *Calling* is. Secondly, I. will set downe the *parts* and *kindes* thereof. Thirdly, the holy & lawfull use of every mans particular calling: all which are in some sort touched in the words of my text.

For the first: *A vocation or calling, is a certain kind of life, ordained and imposed on man by God, for the common good.* First of all I say, it is a *certaine condition or kind of life:* that is, a certaine manner of leading our lives in this world. For example, the life of a king is to spend his time in the governing of his subjects, and that is his calling: and the life of a subject is to live in obedience to the Magistrate, and that is his calling. The state and condition of a Minister is, to leade his life in preaching of the Gospell and word of God, and that is his calling. A master of a family, is to leade his life in the government of his family, and that is his calling, In a word, that particular and honest manner of conversation, whereunto every man is called and set apart, that is (I say) his calling.

Now in every calling we must consider two causes. First, the efficient and author thereof. Secondly, the finall and proper end. The author of every calling, is God himselfe: and therefore *Paul* saith; *As God hath called every man, let him walke,* vers. 17. And for this cause, the order & manner of living in this world, is called a *Vocation*; because every man is to live as he is called of God. For looke as in the campe, the Generall appointeth to every man his place and standing; one place for the horse-man, & another for the foot-man, and to every particular souldier likewise, his office and standing, in which hee is to abide against the enemie, and therein to live and die: even so it is in humane societies: God is the Generall, appointing to every man his particular calling and as it were his standing: and in that calling he assignes unto him his particular office; in performance whereof he is to live & die. And as in a campe, no souldier can depart his standing, without the leave of the Generall; no more may any man leave his calling, except he receive liberty from God. Againe, in a clocke, made by the art and handy-worke of man, there be many wheeles, and every one hath his severall motion, some turne this way, some that way, some goe softly, some apace: and they are all ordered by the motion of the watch. Behold here a notable resemblance of Gods speciall providence over mankinde, which is the watch of the great world, allotting to every man his motion and calling: and in that calling, his particular office and function. Therefore it is true that I say, that God himselfe is the author and beginning of callings.

This overthroweth the heathenish opinion of men; which thinke that the particular condition and state of man in this life comes by chance: or by the bare will & pleasure of man himself. Secondly, by this which hath bin said, we learn, that many perswading themselves of their callings, have for all this, no calling at al. As for example, such as live by usury, by carding and dicing, by maintaining houses of gaming, by plaics and such like: For God is the author of every lawfull calling: but these and such miserable courses of living, are either against the word of God, or else are not grounded thereupon. And therefore are no callings or vocations, but avocations from God and his waies.

Now as God is the author of every calling, so he hath

two actions therein. First, he ordaineth the calling itself. And secondly, he imposeth it on man called: & therfore I say, *vocation is a certen kind of life, ordained & imposed by God.* For the first, God ordaineth a calling, when he prescribeth and commandeth the same, in, and by his word: and those callings and states of life, which have no warrant from Gods word, are unlawfull. Now God in his word, ordaineth callings two waies. First by commanding and prescribing them particularly, as hee doth the most weightie callings in the family, Church, or common-wealth. Secondly, by appointing and setting down certain lawes and commandements, generally; whereby we may easily gather, that he doth either approove, or not approove of them, though they bee not particularly prescribed in the word.

The second action of God, which is the imposition of callings, is, when he doth particularly set apart any man, to any particular calling: and this must be understood of all callings in the world. Now God doth this two waies. First by himselfe immediately, without the helpe of any creature. Thus in the beginning was *Adam* called & appointed to dresse the garden of Eden. Thus *Abraham* was called from the idolatrie of his fore-fathers, and received into the covenant of grace. Thus was *Moses* called to bee a Prince over the Israelites, to guide them out of Egypt, into the promised land. And in the new Testament, thus were the Apostles called to preach the Gospel. Secondly, God cals mediately by meanes, which be of two sorts; men and angels. By an angel was Philip, being a Deacon, called to be an Evangelist: and the set or appointed callings in Church and common-wealth, are ordinarily disposed by men, who are in this matter the instruments of God. And therefore men lawfully called by them, are truely called of God. Thus the Elders of Ephesus, called by the Apostles, and the rest of the Church, are said to be called by the holy Ghost. And thus we see how God is the author of every calling.

The finall cause or end of every calling, I note in the last words of the description; *For the common good:* that is, for the benefite and good estate of mankinde. In mans body there be sundry parts and members, and every one hath his severall use and office, which it performeth not for it selfe, but for the good of the whole bodie; as the office of the eye, is to see, of the eare to heare, and the foote to goe. Now all societies of men, are bodies, a family is a bodie, and so is every particular Church a bodie, and the common-wealth also: and in these bodies there be severall members which are men walking in severall callings and offices, the execution whereof, must tend to the happy and good estate of the rest; yea of all men every where, as much as possible is. The common good of men stands in this, not onely that they live, but that they live well, in righteousnes and holines, and consequently in true happinesse. And for the attainement hereunto, God hath ordained and disposed all callings, and in his providence designed the persons to beare them. Here then we must in generall know, that he abuseth his calling, whosoever he be that against the end thereof, imployes it for himselfe, seeking wholly his own, and not the common good. And that common saying, *Every man for himselfe, and God for us all,* is wicked, and is directly against the end of every calling or honest kinde of life.

Thus much of the description of *Vocation* in generall. Now before I come particularly to intreate of the speciall kindes of callings, there are two generall rules to bee learned of all, which belong to every calling.

The first: whatsoever any man enterprizeth or doth, either in word or deede, he must doe it by vertue of his calling, and he must keepe himselfe within the compasse, limits, or precincts thereof. This rule is laid downe in these wordes of the Apostles: *Let every man abide in that calling, wherein he was called:* the drift wherof is, to binde men to their calling, & to teach them to performe all their actions by warrant thereof. It is said, *Hebr. 11.6. Without faith it is impossible to please God*: and *Whatsoever is not of faith, is sinne.* Whatsoever is not done within the compasse of a calling, is not of faith, because a man must first have some warrant and word of God to assure him of his calling, to do this or that thing, before he can do it in faith. When the two brethren that strove about their inheritance came to Christ: & willed him to make agreement betweene them, Christ answered, *Luk. 12.14. Who made me a Judge or devider betweene you?* as if hee should say, it is not within the compasse of my calling: for I came to accomplish the worke of mans redemption, and not to devide inheritances: hereby giving us to understand, that every thing to bee done must be done by warrant of some calling: and so long as men keepe themselves in their callings, they have a promise of protection from God, *Psal. 91.11. Hee shall give his Angels charge over thee, to keepe thee in all thy waies:* that is so long as thou keepest thy selfe within the waies of thy calling, so long shall my Angels preserve thee. The example of *David* is worthy our considering, for hee depending on the providence of God, & walking in his calling, had the protection of God, when *Saul* smote twice at him with a speare: when he was made a captain of a thousand that he might bee slaine of the Philistims: when *Michol* was promised to be his wife for an hundred foreskins of the Philistims: when *Saul* commanded his own servants to kill him, when he smot againe at him with a speare: when he fought to take him in his owne house: when he followed him ta *Naioth* in Ramah: when he was absent from the Solemne feast made by *Saul:* when the priests of *Nob* were slaine, 85. persons, and all the inhabitants of the place: when *Saul* persecuted him in the desart of *Mahon*. Contrariwise, when any man is without the compasse of his calling, he is out of the way, and by this meanes hee bereaves himselfe of the protection of the Almighty; and lies open and naked to al the punishments & plagues of God. And if we marke it well, the word of God shews evidently to what dangers they are subject, that doe any thing either without or against their callings. *Sampson s* strength lay not in his haire (as men commonly thinke) but because hee went out of his calling, by breaking the vow of a Nazarite, when he gave occasion to *Dalilah* to cut off his haire, therfore he lost his strength; for God promiseth strength, but with a commandement, that he should bee a Nazarite to the end, *Iud.* 13.5. When *Saul* was commanded to slay the Amalekites, against his calling he spared *Agag* upon a foolish pitty, and the best things; and thereupon *Samuel* reprooved him of rebellion against God, which was as the sin of witchcraft, and for this very cause was he rejected of God from being king over Israel. *Jonas* being called to preach at Ninivie, went about by flight to shake off the calling of God, but when he comes to the sea, he is tossed by a tempest, and cast out of the ship, and swallowed by a fish that God hath prepared for this purpose. When *Peter* beyond the limits of his calling, would needes warme him at the high Priests fire, it cost him the breach of his conscience; for at the very voice of a Damosel he denied Christ with cursing and banning. And the Exorcists in the Acts, that without sufficient calling, tooke on them to conjure evill spirits in the name of Jesus, were overcome by the same spirits, & were faine to flie away naked & wounded. In a word, looke what judgements befall men, marke well the time and circumstance thereof, it shall be found, that they are cast upon them by the hand of God, when they are forth of their callings, which God hath prescribed them to keepe. Therefore this must alwaies be remembered & practised carefully; that we doe take nothing in hand, unles we have first ranked our selves within the precincts of our callings.

The second generall rule which must bee remembred, is this: That *Every man must doe the duties of his calling with diligence:* & therfore *Salomon* saith, *Eccl.* 9.10. *Whatsoever is in thine hand to do, do it with al thy power.* S. *Paul* bids him that ruleth, rule with diligence; and every man to wait on his office, *Rom.* 12.8. And *Jeremy* saith, *Jer.* 48.10 *Cursed is he that doth the work of the Lord negligently.* That which Christ saith of the worke of our redemption, *It is meate and drinke for me to do my Fathers will:* the same must every man say in like sort of his particular calling. Of this diligence there be two reasons: first of al, the end why God bestowes his gifts upon us, is, that they might be imployed in his service, and to his glory, and that in this life. Therefore *Paul* saith, *Redeeme the time:* and Christ, *Walke while ye have light.* And againe, *I must do his work while it is day:* For we see trades men and travellers rise early to their businesse, lest night overtake them. Secondly to them which imploy their gifts; more is given, and from them which imploy them not, is taken that which they have: and labour in a calling is as pretious as gold or silver. Hereupon hee that maimes a man, & disables him to doe the worke of his calling, by Gods law is bound to give him the value of his labour, *Exod.* 21.19. And to like purpose our people have a common saying, that an occupation is as good as land, because land may be lost; but skill and labour in a good occupation is profitable to the end, because it will helpe at neede, when land and all things faile. And on the other side, wee must take heede of two damnable sinnes that are contrary to this diligence. The first is idlenesse, whereby: the duties of our callings, and the occasions of glorifying God, are neglected or omitted. The second is slouthfulnes, whereby they are performed slackly and carelesly. God in the Parable of the hus-bandman, cals them that are idle into his vineyard, saying, *Why stand ye idle all the day? Mat. 20.6.* And the servant that had received but one talent, is called an evill servant, because he was slouthfull in the use of it: for so it is said. *Thou evill servant and slouthful, Mat. 25.26. S. Paul* gives this rule to the Thessalonians, *He that would not labour, must not eate:* yet such a one hee would have to bee noted by a letter, as walked inordinately. And this he sheweth, that slouth and negligence in the duties of our callings, are a disorder against that comly order which God hath set in the societies of mankind, both in church and common-wealth. And indeed, idlenes and slouth are the causes of many damnable sinnes. The idle bodie, and the idle braine, is the shop of the divell. The sea, if it mooved not, could not but putrifie, and the body, if it be not stirred and mooved, breedeth diseases. Now the idle and slouthful person is a sea of corruption; and when he is most idle, Satan is least idle; for then is he most busie to draw him to manifold sinnes.

Thus much of the two general rules. Now follow the parts and kindes of Vocations: and they are of two sorts: Generall, or Particular. The generall calling is the calling of Christianity, which is common to all that live in the Church of God. The particular, is that special calling that belongs to some particular men: as the calling of a Magistrate, the calling of a Minister, the calling of a Master, of a father, of a childe, of a servant, of a subject, or any other calling that is common to all. And *Paul* acknowledging this distinction of *Callings*, when he saith, *Let every man abide in that calling, wherin he is called,* that is, in that particular and personall calling, in which he was called to bee a Christian. Of these two in order.

The generall Calling is that wherby a man is called out

of the world to bee a child of God, a member of Christ, & heire of the kingdome of heaven. This calling belongs to every one within the compasse of the Church, not any one accepted. Here I have just occasion to make a long discourse touching the calling of men to Christ and Christian Religion, but I wil only touch the maine duties thereof, which are especially foure. The first is, the invocation of the name of God in Christ. When as *Saul* got letters from the high Priests to persecute the Church, it is said by *S. Luk. Act.* 9.14. that he received authoritie to *bind all that call upon the name of God. Paul* writing to the Church of Corinth, calleth the members thereof *Saints: and such as call on the name of the Lord Jesus, 1. Cor. 1.2.* By both which places the holy Ghost would give us to understand, that invocation is a maine duty which every Christian man is to performe continually; and it containes both prayer and thanksgiving in the name and mediation of Jesus Christ. And indeed by this action a Christian is distinguished and severed from all other sorts of men in the world, that pretend devotion or religion. By this it appeareth, howsoever al men do desire to beare this name, & take unto them this generall calling, yet very few are indeed true and sound Christians: for not one of an hundred can rightly invocate the name of God, though they can indeede repeate the words of prayer, yet they want the spirit of grace, & supplications, wherby they should aske grace in Christs name, and give thanks for benefits received. Thus many bearing in shew the name of Christ, want the power thereof. Nay which is more, not to call on the name of God is made by the Prophet *David*, the note and marke of an Atheist, that *saith in his heart there is no God, Psal. 14.9.*

The second duty is, as much as possibly we can, to further the good estate of the true Church of God. It is indeede principally the dutie of the Minister, and yet generally it appertaines to all; for as in mans body, the eye by seeing, the eare by hearing, the tongue by speaking, and every part by his proper office doth further the good of the whole body: Even so, all that are called to bee members of Christ, must as much as in them lyeth, procure the good of the whole mistical body of Christ. *David* in the name of the whole Church saith, *Psal.* 122. 69. *I will procure thy wealth, and pray for the peace of Jerusalem, they shall prosper that love thee.* And after hee had humbled himselfe for the two grievous sins of adultery and murther, in the end he praies to God to build the walles of Jerusalem. For the building of the tabernacle, the Jews brought free-will offerings according to their ability. Some brought gold and precious stones, others silver and silke, & such as had no better thing, brought rammes skins, and badgers skins: even so, in the building of Gods Church his spiritual tabernacle, every Christian must bring a free-wil offering, he must doe something even to the utmost of his power, to the building of Gods Church, though his service be but meane. Though men (as I have said) fondly imagine, that this dutie is proper to the ministers of the word; yet the truth is, it belongs not onely unto them, but to every one that professeth himselfe to bee a member of the body of Christ: in which respect he must, so much as he can, procure and further the good of the whole.

Here then wee are to consider the meanes whereby this dutie may bee done. They are especially three. The first is prayer, not onely for our selves, but for the good estate of the whole Church of God on earth. To this effect spake Christ to his disciples, when he saw the Jewes like scattered sheepe without a shepheard; *Pray to the Lord of the harvest, that hee would thrust forth labourers into the harvest, Mat.* 9.38. And in that prayer, commonly called the Lords prayer, we are taught to say, *Let thy kingdome come*: where by *kingdome* is not onely meant the kingdome of glory in heaven, but the kingdome of grace, which is the happy and blessed condition of Gods Church on earth. And therefore *Paul* biddeth the Thessalonians pray, that Gods word may have free passage and be glorified, 2. *Thess.* 3.1.

The second meanes is, the worke of edification, which *Paul* enjoynes the Thessalonians: *Edifie one another, I. Thess.* 5.1 1. And Saint *Judo v.* 20. *Edifie your selves upon your most holy faith.* The Church of God is a Temple made without hands, the foundation is Christ; and every member of Christ with all that appertaine to Gods election, are living stones: the builders of this temple principally, are Pastours and teachers, and not onely they, but all Christian persons generally. The case stands here as it did in the building of the materiall temple, the principall builders whereof were such as cut and laid stones, and wrought curious workes; besides whom, there were many others, which though they could neither cut nor frame, yet did they further the building, either by carrying of burthens, or making of mortar: even so in the building of Gods spirituall Church, though all cannot square stones like Masons, nor build as the Minister doth, yet all without exception pertaining to the Church of God, must put their helping hands to further this building. And this may bee done two waies: first, by using all good means, whereby we may draw our kindred, friends, & neighbors to the love and obedience of true religion. This duty *Paul* propoundeth to the Corinthians in his owne example, saying: *He pleased all men in al things,not seeking his own profit, but the profit of many, that they might be saved,* 1. *Cor.* 10.33. Secondly, this thing is done by confirming those which are called, by often admonitions, exhortations, consolations, and all other like duties that serve to this end. And by these duties may the meanest person in the Church of God, build or edifie.

Heere I may justly complaine of the neglect of this duty:

for the case stands thus in the barren and fruitlesse age of the world: men are so farre from the duties of edification, that they use all meanes, rather to pull downe then to build. For he that gives himselfe but to learne the duties of religion, and in some sort to live accordingly, is made a signe and a by-word among the common people, & also a wonder. And this shewes, that the practise of this duty of edification lies dead, whereto neverthelesse we are bound, by vertue of generall calling.

The third meanes of furthering the good of Gods Church, is, to conferre the temporall blessings that God hath bestowed upon us according to our abilitie, to the good thereof. *Honour God with thy riches,* saith *Salomon*, Proverb. 3.9. and that is done especially, when they are employed to the maintaining and furthering of true religion, and the worshippe of God. There be other ends for which God hath given riches, but this of all is the principall. Yet alas, this dutie is but slenderly practised of such as carry the name of Christ: for many of the richer sort spend a great part of their increase upon hawkes, buls, beares, dogs, or riotously mispend the same in some sporting or gaming: and disable themselves to doe that good they should unto the Church of God. And the meaner sort nowadaies spend that they get in fine apparell, and good cheere: and by this meanes the house of God is lesse regarded: for every common man nowadaies must be a gentleman, and it is very hard sometimes for a stranger to discerne the master from the servant: and there is such excesse in all degrees, that now for daily attire, the noblest are the plainest. To this dutie I may also adde, that every Christian parent, by vertue of his generall calling, is to dedicate some of his male children, as much as possible is, to the service of the ministerie; if so be they have gifts and inclinations of nature fit for that calling. And in this case the example of *Anna* may bee a good direction for us to follow, who did before-hand consecrate *Samuel* her first borne to the Lord. By this meanes the ministery shall be continued, Gods Church and religion maintained, and his Gospell published from age to age to the end of the world.

The third generall dutie of Christianitie, is, that every man should become a servant to his brother in all the duties of love. A Christian is the freest of all men in the world. For in that respect he is the childe of God in Christ, he is truly freed from hel, death, and condemnation; yea, and in part from sinne and Satan, and that in this life: and yet for al this, he must be a servant unto every man. But how? by all the duties of love, as occasion shall be offered, and that for the common good of all men. Marke well the words of Saint *Paul, 1. Cor.* 9.19. *Though I bee free from all men, yet have I made my selfe servant to all, that I might winne the more.* If it bee said, this dutie appertaines to an Apostle, I answer, that *Paul* enjoynes it indifferently to every man, *Galat.* 5.13. *Doe ye service one to another in love.* And for this cause the servants of God are said to bee *trees of righteousnesse*, whose leaves serve for medicine, and their fruit for meate, not for themselves, but for others. Let us therefore in the feare of God bee careful to learne this dutie: for the practise of it is the speciall ornament of Christs holy Gospel.

The last generall duty is set downe by Saint *Paul, Eph.* 4.1. *Walke worthy that calling wherto God hath called you.* Againe, *Titus* 2.10. he biddeth servants so to carry themselves toward their masters, that they may adorne the Gospel of God in all things: and he sets downe in the words following, how men may adorne religion by their profession: namely, by *denying ungodlinesse and worldly lusts*, by living soberly, righteously, and godly in this present world. In a word, this calling of Christianitie is the most excellent calling in the world, and hee walketh worthy the same that keepeth a good conscience before God, and is unblameable before all men.

This dutie I commend to the meditation and practise of all men whatsoever; we were once baptized, and therin gave up our names to God and Christ; and wee are content to heare the word, and receive the Supper of the Lord as a pledge of his mercy and love. Wee must therefore walke as they to whom the mercy and love of God pertaines. Christ pronounceth a *woe to them that give offence, Matth. 18.7.* And indeed it were better for any man to be as farre under the earth, as he is above it, then by a bad and loose conversation to slander the name of God, whose professed servant hee is: and as Christ saith, *It were better a milstone were hanged about his necke, and hee were throwne into the bottome of the sea.* As *David* prayeth, *Psal.* 119.39. *Lord, take from me rebuke and shame, which I do feare, because thy judgements are good:* So must we pray, Lord take from me rebuke & shame, for thy Gospel is good. And that wee may evermore walke worthy of this calling, wee first of all must depend by faith on the providence and mercy of God at all times. Secondly, wee must daily turne unto him, by a continuall renewing of our repentance. Thirdly, wee must indeavour to performe new obedience in respect of all his commandements.

Thus much of the generall calling common to all men as they are Christians. Now followeth the second kinde of calling, and that is personall. A personall calling is the execution of some particular office; arising of that distinction which God makes betweene man and man in every societie. First I say, it is *the execution of some particular office;* as for example, the calling of a magistrate is to execute the office of government over his subjects, the office of a minister is to execute the duty of teaching his people, the calling of a master, is to execute the office of authority and government over his servants: the office of a Physition, is to put in practise the good means whereby life and health are preserved. In a word, in every estate the practise and execution of that particular office, wherein any man is placed, is his personall calling.

Secondly I adde, that it ariseth from that distinction which God maketh betweene man and man in every society: to shew what is the foundation and ground of all personall callings. And it is a point to bee considered of us, which I thus explaine: God in his word hath ordained the societie of man with man, partly in the Common-wealth, partly in the Church, and partly in the family: and it is not the will of God that man should live and converse alone by himselfe. Now for the maintaining of society, he hath ordained a certaine bond to linke men together, which Saint *Paul* calleth *the bond of peace, and the bond of perfection*, namely, love. And howsoever hee hath ordained societies, and the bond of them all, yet hath he appointed that there should stil remaine a distinction betweene man and man, not onely in regard of person, but also in other respects: for as the whole bodie is not the hand, nor the foote, nor the eye, but the hand one part, the foot another, and the eye another: and howsoever in the bodie one part is linked to another, yet there is a distinction betwixt the members, whereby it commeth to passe, that the hand is the hand, not the foot, and the foote, the foote, not the hand, nor the eye: so it is in societies; there is a disntinction in the members thereof, and that in two respects: first, in regard of the inward gifts which God bestowed on every man, giving to severall men severall gifts according to his good pleasure. Of this distinction in regard of inward gifts, *Paul* intreates at large, *1. Cor. 12.* through the whole chapter, where he sheweth the diversity of gifts that God bestowes on his Church, and so proportionally in every society. Now looke as the inward gifts of men are severed, so are the persons distinguished in their societies accordingly. Secondly, persons are distinguished by order, whereby God hath appointed, that in every society one person should bee above or under another; not making all equall, as though the bodie should bee all head and nothing else: but even in degree and order, hee hath set a distinction, that one should be above another. And by reason of this distinction of men, partly in respect of gifts, partly, in respect of order, come personall callings. For if all men had the same gifts, and all were in the same degree and order, then should all have one and the same calling: but in asmuch as God giveth diversitie of gifts inwardly, and distinction of order outwardly, hence proceede diversitie of personall callings, and therefore I added, that personall callings arise from that distinction which God maketh betweene man and man in every societie. And thus wee see what is a personall calling. Now before I come to intreate of the parts thereof, there bee other generall rules to bee learned, which concerne all personall callings whatsoever.

1. Rule. Every person of every degree, state, sexe, or condition without exception, must have some personall and particular calling to walke in. This appeareth plainly by the whole word of God. *Adam* so soone as he was created, even in his integrity had a personall calling assigned him by God: which was, to dresse and keepe the garden. And after *Adams* fall, the Lord giveth a particular commandement to him and all his posterity, which bindeth all men to walke in some calling, either in the Church or Commonwealth, saying, *Gen.* 3.19. *In the sweate of thy browes shalt thou eate thy bread.* Againe, in the renewing of the law in mount Sinai, the fourth commaundement doth not onely permit labour on sixe daies, but also injoynes the same (as I take it) to us all. For Gods example is there propounded for us to follow, that as he rested the seventh day, so must also we: and consequently, as hee spent sixe dayes in the worke of creation, so should wee in our personall callings. And S. *Paul* giveth this rule, *Eph. 4.28. Let him that stole steale no more, but let him rather worke with his hands the thing that is good, that hee may have to give to him that needeth.* Christ the head of men, lived with *Joseph* in the calling of a Carpenter, till the time of his baptisme, and hereupon it was that the Jewes said, *Is not this the carpenter the sonne of Mary?* and after he was baptized, and was as it were solemnly admitted into the office of a Mediatour, the worke of our redemption was then his calling, in which he both lived and died. Yea the Angels of God have their particular callings, in that they doe his *commandements in obeying the voyce of his word.* And therefore all that descend of *Adam* must needes have some calling to walke in, either publike, or private, whether it be in the Church, or Common-wealth, or family.

Hence we may learne sundry points of instruction; first of all, that it is a foule disorder in any Common-wealth, that there should bee suffered rogues, beggars, vagabonds; for such kind of persons commonly are of no civill societie or corporation, nor of any particular Church: and are as rotten legges, and armes that drop from the body. Againe, to wander up and downe from yeere to yeere to this end, to seeke and procure bodily maintenance, is no calling, but the life of a beast: and consequently a condition or state of life flat against the rule; That every one must have a particular calling. And therefore the Statute made the last Parliament for the restraining of beggars and rogues, is an excellent Statute, and being in substance the very law of God, is never to be repealed.

Againe, hereby is otherthrowen the condition of Monkes and Friars: who challenge to themselves that they live in a state of perfection, because they live apart from the societies of men in fasting and prayer: but contrariwise, this

Monkish kind of living is damnable; for besides the generall duties of fasting and praier, which appertaine to al Christians, every man must have a particular & personal calling, that he may bee a good and profitable member of some society and body. And the auncient Church condemned all Monkes for theeves and robbers, that besides the generall duties of prayer and fasting, did not withal imploy themselves in some other calling for their better maintenance.

Thirdly, we learne by this, that miserable and damnable is the estate of those that beeing enriched with great livings and revenewes, do spend their daies in eating and drinking, in sports and pastimes, not imploying themselves in service for Church or Common-wealth. It may be haply thought, that such gentlemen have happy lives; but it is farre otherwise: considering every one, rich or poore, man or woman, is bound to have a personall calling, in which they must performe some duties for the common good, according to the measure of the gifts that God hath bestowed upon them.

Fourthly, hereby also it is required that such as we commonly call serving men, should have, beside the office of waiting, some other particular calling, unlesse they tend on men of great place and state: for onely to waite, and give attendance, is not a sufficient calling, as common experience telleth: for waiting servants, by reason they spend the most of their time in eating and drinking, sleeping and gaming after dinner and after supper, do proove the most unprofitable members both in Church and Common-wealth. For when either their good masters die, or they be turned out of their office for some misdemeanour, they are fit for no calling, being unable to labour; and thus they give themselves either to begge or steale. The waiting man of *Cornelius* that Centurion, was also by calling a souldier: and it were to be wished now adaies, that gentlemen would make choice of such servants that might not onely tend on their persons, but also tend upon some other convenient office. It is good for every man to have two strings to his bow.

II. Rule. Every man must judge that particular calling, in which God hath placed him, to be the best of all callings for him: I say not simply best, but best for him. This rule is set forth unto us in the example of *Paul, I have learned* (saith he) *in whatsoever state I am, to bee content and well pleased.* The practise of this dutie is the stay & foundation of the good estate both of Church and Common-wealth: for it maketh every man to keepe his owne standing, and to imploy himselfe painefully within his calling; but when we begin to mislike the wise disposition of God, and to thinke other mens callings better for us then our owne, then followes confusion and disorder in every society. When *Absalom* a child, and subject of king *David,* was not content with his estate, but sought his fathers kingdome, and said, *O that I were judge among you:* many contentions and hurliburlies followed in the Commonwealth of the Jewes all his daies. And the sonnes of *Zebedeus* not contenting themselves with the calling of Disciples, but being inflamed with desire of honour and dignity, sought two principal offices in Christ his kingdom, which (as they deemed) should be a civill and worldly kingdome. Hence arose envy and heart burning among the desciples, and further evils would have insued, unlesse the wisedome of our Saviour Christ had cut them off. The Bishops of the Church of Rome, not contented with their Ecclesiasticall estate, affected the honour of the Empire: and by this meanes brought havocke and ruine upon the whole Church: yea, the very first family that ever was in the world, felt the smart of this evill. *Cain,* because he feared the losse of his primacy, whereby he was to be a Priest, Prophet, & ruler in *Adams* house, after his decease, slew his brother *Abel.* And this may well bee gathered by the words of the text, where when *Cain* began to be angry, the Lord said; *If thou dost well, there is remission; if not, sin lies at the doore.* Now *Cain* might haply reply & say; this is well, but my griefe remaines, that I must loose my right & dignity. To this God answereth thus, in the next words; *And his appetite shall be to thee, and thou shalt rule over him;* namely, *if thou doe well.* And from time to time, the greatest discords that have fallen out in the Church of God, have issued from this fountaine. And the same is also true in the Common-wealth: hence come treacheries, treasons, and seditions, when men, not content with their own estate and honors, seeke higher places: and being disappointed, grow to discontentments, & so forward to all mischiefe. Therfore in a word, the good estate of the Church and common-wealth, is when every person keepes himselfe to his owne calling. And this wil undoubtedly come to passe, if we consider what be our callings; and that we are placed in them of God; and therefore judge them to be the best callings of all for us.

III. Rule. Every man must joyne the practise of his personall calling, with the practice of the generall calling of Christianity, before described. More plainely: Every particular calling must be practised in, & with the generall calling of a Christian. It is not sufficient for a man in the congregation, and in common conversation, to bee a Christian, but in his very personall calling, he must shew himselfe to be so. As for example. A Magistrate must not onely in generall be a Christian, as every man is, but he must be a Christian Magistrate, in executing the office of a Magistrate in bearing the sword. A master of a family, must not onely be a Christian abroad in the towne, and in the congregation, in the sight of strangers, but also in the administration and regiment of his particular family, towards wife, children, and servants. It is not enough for a woman to be vertuous openly to strangers; but her vertue must privately shew it selfe in her subjection and obedience to her owne husband. A Schoolemaster must not onely be a Christian in the assembly, when hee heareth the word, and receiveth the Sacraments, but he must also shew himselfe to bee a Christian in the office of teaching. And thus must every man behave himselfe in his particular calling: because the particular calling & practise of the duties thereof, severed from the foresaid generall calling, is nothing else but a practise of injustice and profanenes. And the generall calling of Christianitie, without the practise of some particular calling, is nothing els, but the forme of godlinesse, without the power thereof: And therefore both callings must be joyned, as body and soule are joyned in a living man. And that wee may the better joyne both our callings together, wee must consider the maine end of our lives, and that is, to serve God in the serving of men in the workes of our callings. God, as he made man, so can he preserve man, without the helpe of man: but his pleasure is, that men should be his instruments, for the good of one another. For this cause hath he ordained the excellent office of Magistrates & Ministers, and almost an infinite variety of trades of life, all tending to preserve the body or soule, or both. Thus God manifests his fatherly care over us, by the imployment of men in his service, according to their severall vocations, for our good: and there is not so much as the vassall or bond-man; but he must serve God by serving his master: as *Paul* teacheth; And by this one point, wee may learne two things. The first, that they profane their lives & callings that imploy them to get honours, pleasures, profits, worldly commodities, &c. for thus wee live to another end then God hath appointed, and thus we serve our selves, & consequently, neither God, nor man. Some man will say perchance; What, must we not labour in our callings, to maintaine our families? I answer; this must be done: but this is not the scope and end of our lives. The true end of our lives is, to do service to God, in serving of man: and for a recompence of this service, God sends his blessings on mens travailes, and he allowes them to take for their labours. Secondly, by this we learne, how men of meane place & calling, may comfort themselves. Let them consider, that in serving of men, by performance of poore and base duties they serve God: and therefore that their service is not base in his sight: & though their reward from men be little, yet the reward at Gods hand, shall not be wanting. For seeing they serve God in serving of men, they may justly looke for reward from both. And thus may we reape marveilous contentation in any kind of calling, though it be but to sweepe the house, or keepe sheepe, if we can thus in practise, unite our callings.

By this rule may any man rightly judge of himselfe & others. For wheresoever these two callings are severed, whatsoever is in shew, there is nothing in substance. And by this also we may discerne a common fault in the lives of many men, who shew themselves ready and willing to heare the word of God; yea, they approove it, receive the Sacraments, and professe themselves to bee members of Christ: and all these bee good duties of the first and generall calling: but goe on further, and looke into their particular callings, there shall you find nothing lesse, there is al out of order; some bee usurers and oppressours, some ingrossers, some use false weights and measures, some lying and swearing, some are loose & lascivious. It may be, such persons resolve themselves that all is well, when they doe some duties of their generall calling: but whereas they neglect the performance of the said duties, in their particular callings, they are farre out of order; yea, they leade a dangerous and lamentable course of life. For though they be indued with excellent gifts, and bee able to speake well, conceive prayer, and with some reverence to heare the Word, and receive the Sacraments, yet if they practise not the duties of godlinesse within their own callings, al is but hypocrisie. And therefore, unlesse they repent the greater their gifts are, the more shal they make to their deeper condemnation at the day of judgment.

Againe, this rule serveth to teach all men the right way to reforme their lives. If thou wouldst leade a life unblameable both before God & man, thou must first of all bethinke thy selfe, what is thy particular calling, and then proceede to practise duties of the morall law, and all other duties of Christianity, in that very calling. And if thou wouldest have signes and tokens of thy election and salvation, thou must fetch them from the constant practise of thy two callings joyntly together: Sever them in thy life, and thou shalt finde no comfort, but rather shame and confusion of face, unlesse thou repent.

IV. Rule. Such as beare publike callings, must first reforme themselves in private. When *Moses* went from Midian to Egypt, to be a governour of the Israelites, the Lord withstood him in the way, by reason of a fault in his private family, that his child was not circumcised according to the law of God. How shal he order publike matters for the common good, that cannot order his owne private estate?

V. Rule. A particular calling must give place to the generall calling of a Christian, when they cannot both stand together. As for example: a servant is bound to his master to obey him, either because he is a vassall, or at the least because he is hired to serve for wages: the said master being a zealous Papist, threatneth his servant, being a Protestant, that unlesse he condescend to heare Masse, he shall either burne at a stake, or carry a faggot. Now the servant seeing the malicious purpose of his master, and not finding himselfe able to beare the brunt of a triall, in this case, he departs & withdrawes himselfe for a time: And the question is, whether he doth wel or no? The answer is, he doth: and in such a case, he may lawfully flie from his master: for a servant that by personall calling is bound to an earthly master, is further by a generall calling, bound unto God. And the particular calling of any man, is inferiour to the generall calling of a Christian: and when they cannot both stand together, the particular calling must give place; because we are bound unto God in the first place, and unto man, under God: and so farre onely as we may withall, keepe our bond with God. And thus much of the five generall rules, that are to be practised in every particular calling. . . .

---

4. WILLIAM PERKINS ON CHRISTIAN EQUITY

One of the most vexing questions for the Christian magistrate was the application of God's absolute laws to man's feeble and corrupt condition. The problem was one that particularly troubled Governor John Winthrop of Massachusetts, who sometimes found himself in difficulties with his zealous subjects for following the kind of advice that Perkins gave in "EPIEKEIA, or a Treatise of Christian Equity and Moderation," from which the following selection is taken.

Publike Equity is that, which is practised in publike meetings and assemblies of men, as in Courts of justice, Assises, Sessions, Counsels, Parliaments, and such like.

From William Perkins, *Workes*, II, 437–441.

The matter whereabout this publike Equity is conversant, is the right and convenient, and the moderate and discreet *execution of the lawes of men.*

Lawes of men, made by lawfull authority according to Gods Law, and for the common good, are, and are to be esteemed, bones and sinewes to hold together, props, and pillars, to uphold the common wealth, and all societies. God therefore hath given to Kings, and to their lawfull deputies, power and authority, not only to command & execute his owne lawes, commanded in his Word: but also to ordaine and enact other good and profitable lawes of their owne, for the more particular government of their people, and to bee helps for the better executing of Gods lawes. And also to annexe a punishment and penalty to the said lawes: which penalty is to be according to the quality of the fault, greater or lesse: insomuch that they may in many cases (if the common good so require) inflict even death itselfe. And further, God hath given these gods upon earth, a power, as to make these lawes, and annexe these punishments: so also upon mens defaults and breaches, hath he given them authority to execute the law so made, and to inflict upon the offender the punishment annexed.

Now because this point is of great moment in a commonwealth; & the true knowledge and due practice thereof, is the glory and beauty of a kingdome: therefore for the better direction herein, both of Prince and people, Magistrate and people governed; let us enter further into the consideration thereof.

In the lawes of Common wealths, two things are to be considered, the sight whereof wil give great light, to know more perfectly what this *publike equity is.*

These are 1. the extremity of the law: 2. the mitigation of the law.

Both these are put into the hand of the Magistrate by

God himselfe, to bee ordered according to his discretion, and as the circumstance requireth: and of them in order. The *extremitie of the law,* is, when any law of man, is urged and executed straightly & precisely, according to the literall sense, & strict forme of the words, and the exactest meaning that can be made out of the words, without any manner of relaxation, at that time, when there is good and convenient cause of mitigation, in regard of the person offending.

The point cannot wel be expressed in fewer words.

The principall and most materiall clause in this description of *extremity,* is in those words: *At that time, when there is just cause of mitigation, in regard of the person offending.* For if there be no good cause of mitigation, then it is not called extremity, but justice of the law: but when there is good cause, why in a Christian consideration of some circumstances, this justice should be mitigated, and yet is not; but contrariwise is extremely urged, and pressed to the furthest, then it is extremity: Now this extremity of the law, is in this case so farre from justice, as indeed it is flat injustice. And herein is the proverbe true; *summum jus, summa injuria*: that is, the extremitie of the law, is extreme injury. And of this doth the holy Ghost meane, *Eccles. 7.7.Bee not over just*, that is, presse not justice too far, nor urge it too extremely in all cases, lest sometimes you make the name of justice, a cover for cruelty.

Now besides this, there is a second thing in the hand of the Magistrate, namely, the *moderation, relaxation, or mitigation of this extremity:* and that is, when the proper forme of the words, and the strictest meaning of the law is not urged, and the punishment prescribed in the law, is moderated, or lessened, or deferred, or (it may be) remitted, upon good and sufficient reason; and in such cases as whereof the law speakes not directly, nor the law-maker did purposely aime at. The ground of this mitigation is, because no law makers being men, can foresee, or set downe all cases that may fall out. Therefore when the case altereth, then must the discretion of the law-maker shew it selfe, & doe that which the law cannot doe.

This mitigation is in the hand of the Magistrate, as well as the extremity: nay, it is a part of his duty as well as the former; and he offends as well, that neglects to *mitigate the extremity*, when just occasion is, as hee that neglects to *execute the extremity*, when there is need. As therefore, hee is no way fit to bee a Judge, who hath no knowledge or care to execute the law: so he is but halfe a Judge, who can doe nothing but urge the law, & the plain words of the law, and is not able also to mitigate the rigour of the law, when need so requireth. Therefore every Magistrate is to practise this with the other, and not to separate those things which God hath joyned.

But now lest this moderation, and mitigation of mans lawes, (which is the practice of publike equity) should turne to the maintenance of malefactours, the abolishing of lawes, the despising or weakening of authority, (which in these daies little needs) wee must therefore now remember this caution, *That there must be no mitigation, but honest, profitable, and convenient.* If any man aske, when it is so? I answer in three cases.

First, when the mitigation stands with the law of nature.

Secondly, when it agreeth with the morall law, or any part of the written word.

Thirdly, when an inferiour law is overruled, or countermanded by a higher law.

In these three cases, the moderation of mens lawes, and the mitigation of the punishment due, by the extremitie of these lawes, is honest and good, and may, and ought to bee practised.

But if it be contrary, and not warranted by some of these:

then that mitigation is flat injustice, and a manifest wrong unto the law.

That the difference of these two, the *extremity,* and *mitigation,* may better bee discerned, let us consider it in some examples.

It is the law of England, and many other countries, that the theefe shall die.

Now though the word of God hath not the same punishment in plaine tearmes: yet is the law good and warrantable, as shall appeare in the sequell, and I thinke is doubted of by none.

The drift of this law is, to represse that common and generall sinne of theevery, a prevailing sinne, as any other, and so far prevailing, as the rigour of good lawes is necessarily required, for the repressing of it: so that this law was made, for the cutting off of such rotten members as doe but corrupt others, and of whose amendment there is no hope.

Now, suppose a young boy pinched with hunger, cold, and poverty, steales meate, apparell, and other things for reliefe, being pressed to it by want, and not having knowledge, or grace to use better meanes: to put this person to death for the fact, is the *extremity of the law,* in respect of the circumstances of the person, who did it, being a childe: and of the end for which he did it, to relieve his wants.

Now the moderation in this case is, when upon these considerations, that first, he is nor an olde, nor a practised theefe, but young and corrigible, one that being reformed, may live long, and prove a good member in the commonwealth: and secondly, that his theft was not hainous, but the things he stole were of small value: and thirdly, that he did it not upon a malicious, cruell, and injurious intent but to releeve his hunger and want. *The equity or moderation,* I say in this case, is not to inflict death, (for that were extremity,) but to determine a punishment, lesse than death: yet such a one as shall be sufficient to reforme the party from this sinne, to punish the fault, to terrifie others, and to satisfie the law.

Thus in this example it appeares manifestly what this moderation is, and what is extremity, which is contrary to it: and the same might we see in many more.

Now having thus considered these two together, hereupon we may see what this publike equity is, namely nothing else, but a moderation and mitigation of the extremity of a law, upon honest and convenient reasons, and in such cases, as were not directly intended in the law. The observation and due practice of this equity, is the glory, credit, and honor of all publike assemblies, as assises, sessions, and all courts of justice; and without the observation of this, when neede is, all that they doe is flat injustice in that case. For they lame and maime the law, they fulfill but the one part of the law: for in every law there are these two things: *the extremity in plaine termes, and the mitigation implied,* and these two together make the law perfect: and the glory of the law stands as well in practising of the mitigation, as in the execution of extremity; nay, sometime it stands in the mitigation, and not in the extremity, insomuch as the moderation is then the equity of the law, and the extremity is meere injustice. And as this is the glory of the law, so is it the glory of Judges and Magistrates, thus to execute the Lawes, and to temper them with such discretion, as neither too much mitigation, doe abolish the law, nor too much extremitie leave no place for mitigation. Therefore (to make an end of this point) two sorts of men are here reproveable. First, such men (as by a certaine foolish kinde of pity, are so carried away,) that would have nothing but mercy, mercy, and would have all punishments, forfeitures, penalties, either quite taken away, & remitted, or at least lessened, and moderated, they would also have the extremity of the law executed on no man. This is the highway to abolish lawes, and consequently to pull downe authority, and so in the end to open a doore to all confusion, disorder, and to all licentiousnesse of life. But I need not to say much herein, for there are but few that offend in this kinde, mans nature being generally inclined rather to cruelty than to mercy. This fault proceedes, either from a weaknesse of wit, and an effeminatenesse of minde; and then a man is unfit to be a Judge: or else from vaine glory, and a base and affected popularity, and such a man is unworthy to be a Judge.

But in the second place, this doctrine and the very scope of this text, condemnes another sort of men, which are more combersome; that is to say, some men have nothing in their mouthes but the *law, the law;* and *justice, justice*; in the meane time forgetting, that justice alwayes shakes hands with her sister mercy, and that all lawes allow a mitigation. The causes of this evill are two.

1. The generall corruption of mans nature, which is alwayes ready to deale too hardly with other men: as also too mildly with themselves, and partially in their owne causes.

2. And secondly, for the most part, such men doe gaine more by law, than by equity, more by extremity, than by mitigation: as the souldier lives better by warre, than by peace; and as the flesh flie feedes on the wound, that cannot feede on the sound flesh: so these men gaine by law, that which they can never get by equity: for equity and moderation breed unity, and if all men were at unity, what should become of them? but extremitie breeds variance for (in reason) one extremitie drawes on an other, & so in mens variances, they are set on worke: and the more the better for them. These men therefore, sticke so precisely on their points, and on the very tricks and trifles of the law, as (so the law be kept, and that in the very extremitie of it,) they care not, though equitie were troden under foote: and that law may reigne upon the earth, & they by

it; they care not, though mercie take her to her wings, and flie to heaven. These men (for all their goodly shewes) are the decayers of our estate, and enemies to all good government. For though they have nothing in their mouthes, but *Justice, Justice,* and have banished mercy, yet let them knowe, that Justice will not stay where mercy is not. They are sisters, & goe alwaies hand in hand: they are the two pillars, that uphold the throne of the Prince: as you cannot hold mercy, where justice is banished, so cannot you keepe justice where mercy is exiled: and as mercy without justice, is foolish pittie, so justice without mercy, is crueltie. So that as these men have banished mercy, so within a short time, they will send justice after her, and crueltie and oppression will come in their roomes, which are the very overthrow of all states.

These men, when they are made practisers of the law, Judges, or Magistrates, are to learne this lesson, which the holy Ghost here teacheth, *Let your equitie be knowne to all men:* and let all Magistrates thinke it their honour, to be counted *mercifull Judges:* let them rejoyce, as well to shew mercy when there is cause, as to execute extremitie when there is desert: and let them labour for that Christian wisedome and discretion, whereby they may be able to discerne, when *mercy* and *mitigation* should take place, and when *extremitie* should bee executed. If inferiour judges or Magistrates bee negligent herein, then must we have recourse to the Prince, the highest Judge on earth, and under God the first Fountaine of Justice and mercy: whose care must bee, that as justice and mercy (not one of them, but both together) doe uphold his throne, & fasten the Crowne upon his head: so he likewise see them both maintained, and take order, that in the execution of his owne lawes, there bee alwaies a roome as well for mercy and mitigation, as for justice and extremity. This must he doe, because his lawes cannot be as Gods lawes are, Gods lawes are *perfect* and *absolute,* and of such an universall righteousnesse, as that at all times, and in all places, they are of equall strength, and of the same equitie in all cases: and therefore are to be executed without dispensation, relaxation, or any mitigation, which cannot be offered unto them, but with injurie and violation. But mens lawes, comming from their owne wits, are *imperfect,* and so in all cases, they doe not hold the same equitie, and therfore must needs bee executed with a discret and wise moderation. This moderation is publike equity, and this publike *Equity,* is the scope of this text, and the due practice of it in the execution of mans lawes, is the glory of all Christian Common-wealths.

Hitherto of the first and principall branch of *Publike Equity.*

To proceede further. As this publike *Equitie* principally stands in the moderation of the lawes of men; so it descends more specially even to all the publike actions of a mans life: so that by the rule and direction of this Equity, thus described, men may know how to guide themselves, *in suing bonds, and taking forfeitures*: and how men may with good conscience, carie themselves in *surety-ships, in taking of fines, in letting of leases,* and in all manner of mutuall bargaines, betwixt man and man. By vertue of this, a man may see how to frame all these and such like actions, in such sort, as himselfe shall reape credit, and gaine enough, and his neighbour helpe and succour by him.

For in forfeitures of bonds, forfeitures of lands, or leases, in surety-ships, in rents, in fines, and all other dealings of men together, there are these two things.

First, *the extremitie,* that is, that which the law will afford a man in that case: and there is secondly, the *moderation* of the extremity, upon good and convenient reasons: let us consider of them in some few examples.

A man is bound to another, in an hundreth pound, to pay

fifty at a day. The same man, not by negligence, but by some necessitie, breakes his day, and afterwards brings the principall debt: now to take the *forfeiture,* is in this case, *extremitie:* though the law doth yeeld it. And if a man stand upon this extremitie, hee deales *not honestly and equally, but hardly and extreamely* with his neighbour: and the law cannot free him in this case, from manifest injustice.

What is then the *moderation* in this case? Even this, to take thine owne, and remit the forefeiture: the reason is, because the cause and ground of appointing a forfeiture, was not for advanntage, but only for the better security of the principall: which seeing thou hast, thou hast that the law did intend thee.

Againe, his breach was not wilfull, or with purpose to hurt thee, but against his will. If therefore thou beest directly damnified by his missing thy day, (without all equivocation) then take thy reasonable dammages out of his forfeiture, if not, then remit the whole forfeiture; *and this moderation is publike equity.* And without this, there can bee no buying nor selling, borrowing nor lending, betwixt man and man. See another example. One takes a lease of thee, for yeares, to pay thee such a rent; and for not payment of that rent, his lease to be void. The poore man misseth his rent day: now what saith the law? his lease is forfeited: but to take this advantage, is the *extremitie* of the law: the moderation is, to remit the same forefeiture, in part, or in whole, as thou shalt see the reason in equity and conscience: *This moderation is in this case, Publike equitie,* and without this, there can be no letting of lands, betwixt man and man.

So for fines and rents, the law saith, *Thou maiest make the most of thine owne:* If thou stretch this law as farre as the very words will beare, then maiest thou make such fines and rents, as may grinde the faces of the poore, so as no man shall live under thee: but thus to doe, is *Extremitie,* and beyond the purpose of the law.

The moderation in this case is, not to take all thou maiest get, but so to fine and rent thy lands, as he that takes them, may live of them: The reason of this *Mitigation* is, because envie and hatred; may often make many men offer more for a farme, then it is worth, to crosse and hurt their neghbour, or to get all into their owne hand. Here therefore, though the law doth yeeld thee all that, which a man doth willingly offer, yet must thine own conscience bee a law unto thee, to make thee a moderatour of that extremitie.

Let these three examples serve for many. Now in these and all other publike dealings betwixt men in the world; a man observes *Publike equitie* when hee dealeth not with his neighbour, according to that *extremitie,* which the strickt words of the law will beare: but according to that *Moderation*, which good conscience requireth; and which the law itselfe in some cases doth admit. By the knowledge of these two, a man that hath any conscience, may see how to carie himselfe, in all these civill affaires, in an even, upright, and equall course, and warrantable not onely by the law of the land, but even by the law and word of God.

And I make this distinction of the law of the land, and the word of God, because wee are to know this for a rule: *That every extremitie, which a law in the strictest acception doth afford, is not warrantable to bee urged by the word of God: and yet notwithstanding it is good, convenient, and requisit, that the extremitiee bee warranted by the law, because in some cases, it must needs be executed.* The lawes of men, may ordaine and appoint extremities: but the law of God must tell us, when to urge them, and when to moderate them: So then when a man takes the extremitie, hee doth that, that is alwaies warrantable by the law, but in some cases not warrantable by Gods word, which commandeth a *Mitigation,* when there is good reason for it. But he that taketh the *extremitie,* when there is no just cause of mitigating it and againe doth mitigate it, when there is cause, his course is not onely warrantable by the lawes of men, but even by the lawes of God also. For it is the duty of every Christian man, to remember in all his bargaines & dealings, that his manner of dealing must not onely be warranted by the lawes of the land, but even by Gods word also: & this is to be knowne and taken for a generall rule in all this treatise. And he that will duly consider the true difference of *extremitie* and *moderation,* as they are here described, may see how to carie himselfe in all his dealings, so as they may bee warrantable: both by our owne lawes, and by the word of God.

To returne then to the matter, and to end this point of publike equitie: If any man shall object, that this *moderation* is a wrong to the law: I answer, it is not: for it is neither *against the law,* nor altogether *besides the law,* but onely *besides the strictest meaning of the law.* Nay it is included in the law, as wel as the extremity is, though not in the same maner: for the *extremity* is warrented by the law, *mitigation* is but tolerated: the law alloweth *extremitie,* but it onely admitteth a *mitigation.* So then, both *extremitie* and *mitigation* are within the law, but it is in the hand principally of the Magistrate, and in some cases of other men also, to discerne the severall circumstances, when the one is to bee executed, and when the other: for sometime one is the justice of the law, and sometime the other; and according as these two are justly and wisely executed or neglected, so is the justice of the law executed or neglected.

The want of this equitie in mens publike actions, is the cause of much cruelty, oppression, and inequalitie in dealings betwixt man and man: because *extremitie* is for the most part onely regarded, and *mitigation* is banished out of all bargaines. And it is impossible, to keepe good conscience in forfeitures of bonds, and in forfeiture of lands, surety-ships, fines, rents, and such kinde of actions, unlesse there be due regard had to the practice of this publike equity. Men therefore must consider that they are Christians, and live in a Christian Commonwealth; And they must not stand onely upon the law, and the advantage that the law gives. As they are men, they have a law of the country, which may allow extremitie; but as they are Christians, they live under a law of God, the eternal law which must judge them at the last day; the righteous law, which no creature shall ever bee able to blame of injustice, or of extremitie; and men must know, that God himselfe commands this equitie of one man to another.

But if men, for the feare of God, will not deale *equally and moderately*, with them that are in their power; but stand strictly upon forfeitures and other extremities; then must the godly Magistrate exercise his power, and by the force of his authoritie, cause them to mitigate their extremitie, and to put in practice that equitie which becommeth Christians. And let every Judge and Magistrate know, that by the law of the everlasting God, hee not onely may, but is bound thus to doe to them who will not doe it of themselves. It may bee therefore good counsell to all men rather to practise this Christian *Equitie* of themselves, then to bee compelled to it by authoritie: for every vertue and good worke, the more free and voluntarie it is, the more acceptable is it to God, and more commendable before men: and let all men remember, that whereas the strict words of mens lawes, seeme to give them leave to urge the extremitie, yet cannot that excuse them, nor free them from the danger of Gods law, which commands them to practise *Christian equitie and moderation.*

Now before we make an end of this Publike equity, one point is necessary to be handled in few words. Some may object, if moderation be intended, and included in our law; as well, as extremity *why then is extremity only mentioned in the law,* and *not this mitigation;* which they doe so much urge unto us? The answer is ready, The law expresseth and urgeth *the extremitie,* to fray men thereby, from comming within the danger of the extremitie; and concealeth the *mitigation,* lest it should bee an encouragement to offend: yet intending it as well as the extremitie, and leaving it in the hand of the Magistrate, to put in practise, when just occasion is offered, as well as the extremitie. Herein appeareth the great wisedome of the law-makers, our ancient forefathers, who well and wisely foresaw, that though *mitigation* be as necessarie as extremitie, and oftentimes more: yet because of the ill consciences of the most men, and the readinesse of all men to offend, thought it fitter to expresse *the extremitie* in plaine tearmes; thereby to keep ill men within the compasse of obedience, and closely to leave the *mitigation* to the discretion of the Magistrate. So then our law-givers concealed the mitigation, and expressed it not in their laws, in good policie, and to good purpose. If we therefore doe onely take *the extremity,* wee take onely one part of their intent, and shew our selves unwise and shallow witted, who cannot see the wisedome, which they closely concealed, in wise and Christian policie.

He is not worthy the name of a lawyer, at least of a Christian lawyer, much lesse worthy the place and seate of a Judge, who knoweth not this. For if the law contained not both these, it were unrighteous; and so no law, For *mitigation* is for the good man, and *extremitie* for the evill, the carelesse and unconscionable man: if there were no extremitie, how could the evill man be kept within compasse? and how should the poore honest man live, if there were no mitigation? So then, it is warrantable by the word of God, and good conscience, that *extremitie* should be in force, and should stand by the law, but so as it alwaies admit of *mitigation,* when need is.

Let therefore our conclusion be, to exhort every man, into whose hands is put the execution of lawes, to shew himselfe as wise, in executing them, as were our forefathers in the making of them: that is, as well to regard *the Mitigation which is concealed, as the Extremity which is expressed*: so shall the law-makers wise intent be performed, publike equitie preserved: and much Injustice *and hard dealing prevented.*

Now in regard of this, that hath beene delivered touching publike Equitie, lawyers must not thinke, that I have gone beyond the compasse of my calling, and encroched upon their liberties. For they are to know, that the lawes of men, are policie, but Equity is Christianitie. Now Christianitie was, before there were any lawes of men: & therfore they must bee ordered according to the rules of Christianitie. Againe, Divines must take lawyers advice, concerning *Extremitie* and *the letter of the law:* good reason then that lawyers take the Divines advice, touching *Equity which is the intent of the law.* Moreover, their law is but the ministery of *equity;* but our law *the word of God* is the fountaine of Equity: therefore the principall rules of Equitie, must they fetch from our law: considering that law without *equitie,* is plaine tyrannie. Lastly, in the first Christian Commonwealth that ever was, namely, the Jewes, the Divines, that is, the Priests of those dayes, were the only lawyers: for their positive lawes were the judiciall laws, given by God himselfe, whose interpreters were the Priests and Levites. If therefore; once the Divines had so much to doe with positive lawes, it may not now bee thought amiss, if they give advice out of the word of God, touching the equall execution of the lawes of men.

And so much touching the doctrine of publike Equitie, grounded upon the word of God. . . .

PART TWO

THE NEW ENGLAND PURITANS

5. A MODEL OF CHRISTIAN CHARITY BY JOHN WINTHROP

More than any other individual, John Winthrop (1588–1649) was responsible for the political success of the Puritan experiment in New England. Leaving a comfortable living and extensive lands in the Old World, he brought to New England a sense of high mission and the charter of the Massachusetts Bay Company. He had been elected Governor of the Company before his departure from England, and he was reelected annually during most of his lifetime by the freemen of the colony, to whom he and his colleagues had extended the privileges that the charter had conferred on the Company. In the following speech or sermon, written and probably delivered to his fellow passengers on the voyage across the Atlantic in 1630, Winthrop explained to them what they were doing.

From *Winthrop Papers*, II, 282–295. Reprinted with the permission of the Massachusetts Historical Society.

Written
On Boarde the Arrabella,
On the Attlantick Ocean.
By the Honorable JOHN WINTHROP *Esquire.*
In His passage, (with the great Company of Religious people, of which Christian Tribes he was the Brave Leader and famous Governor;) from the Island of Great Brittaine, to New-England in the North America. Anno 1630.

CHRISTIAN CHARITIE.
A MODELL HEREOF.

God Almightie in his most holy and wise providence hath soe disposed of the Condicion of mankinde, as in all times some must be rich some poore, some highe and eminent in power and dignitie; others meane and in subjeccion.

THE REASON HEREOF.

1. REAS: *First,* to hold conformity with the rest of his workes, being delighted to shewe forthe the glory of his wisdome in the variety and differance of the Creatures and the glory of his power, in ordering all these differences for the preservacion and good of the whole, and the glory of his greatnes that as it is the glory of princes to have many officers, soe this great King will have many Stewards counting himselfe more honoured in dispenceing his guifts to man by man, then if hee did it by his owne immediate hand.

2. REAS: *Secondly,* That he might have the more occasion to manifest the worke of his Spirit: first, upon the wicked in moderateing and restraineing them: soe that the riche and mighty should not eate upp the poore, nor the poore, and dispised rise upp against theire superiours, and shake off theire yoake; 2ly in the regenerate in exerciseing

his graces in them, as in the greate ones, theire love mercy, gentlenes, temperance etc., in the poore and inferiour sorte, theire faithe patience, obedience etc:

3. REAS: Thirdly, That every man might have need of other, and from hence they might be all knitt more nearly together in the Bond of brotherly affeccion: from hence it appeares plainely that noe man is made more honourable then another or more wealthy etc., out of any perticuler and singuler respect to himselfe but for the glory of his Creator and the Common good of the Creature, Man; Therefore God still reserves the propperty of these guifts to himselfe as Ezek: 16. 17. he there calls wealthe his gold and his silver etc. Prov: 3. 9. he claimes theire service as his due honour the Lord with thy riches etc. All men being thus (by divine providence) rancked into two sortes, riche and poore; under the first, are comprehended all such as are able to live comfortably by theire owne meanes duely improved; and all others are poore according to the former distribution. There are two rules whereby wee are to walke one towards another: JUSTICE and MERCY. These are allwayes distinguished in theire Act and in theire object, yet may they both concurre in the same Subject in eache respect; as sometimes there may be an occasion of shewing mercy to a rich man, in some sudden danger of distresse, and allsoe doeing of meere Justice to a poor man in regard of some perticuler contract etc. There is likewise a double Lawe by which wee are regulated in our conversacion one towardes another: in both the former respects, the lawe of nature and the lawe of grace, or the morrall lawe or the lawe of the gospell, to omitt the rule of Justice as not propperly belonging to this purpose otherwise then it may fall into consideracion in some perticuler Cases: By the first of these lawes man as he was enabled soe withall [is] commaunded to love his neighbour as himselfe upon this ground stands all the precepts of the morrall lawe, which

concernes our dealings with men. To apply this to the works of mercy this lawe requires two things first that every man afford his help to another in every want or distresse Secondly, That hee performe this out of the same affeccion, which makes him carefull of his owne good according to that of our Saviour Math: [7.12] Whatsoever ye would that men should doe to you. This was practised by Abraham and Lott in entertaineing the Angells and the old man of Gibea.

The Lawe of Grace or the Gospell hath some differance from the former as in these respectes first the lawe of nature was given to man in the estate of innocency; this of the gospell in the estate of regeneracy: 2ly, the former propounds one man to another, as the same fleshe and Image of god, this as a brother in Christ allsoe, and in the Communion of the same spirit and soe teacheth us to put a difference betweene Christians and others. Doe good to all especially to the household of faith; upon this ground the Israelites were to putt a difference betweene the brethren of such as were strangers though not of the Canaanites. 3ly. The Lawe of nature could give noe rules for dealeing with enemies for all are to be considered as freinds in the estate of innocency, but the Gospell commaunds love to an enemy. proofe. If thine Enemie hunger feede him; Love your Enemies doe good to them that hate you Math: 5. 44.

This Lawe of the Gospell propoundes likewise a difference of seasons and occasions there is a time when a christian must sell all and give to the poore as they did in the Apostles times. There is a tyme allsoe when a christian (though they give not all yet) must give beyond theire abillity, as they of Macedonia. Cor: 2. 6. likewise community of perills calls for extraordinary liberallity and soe doth Community in some speciall service for the Churche. Lastly, when there is noe other meanes whereby our Christian brother may be releived in this distresse, wee must help him beyond our ability, rather then tempt God, in putting him upon help by miraculous or extraordinary meanes.

This duty of mercy is exercised in the kindes, Giveing, lending, and forgiveing.

QUEST. What rule shall a man observe in giveing in respect of the measure?

ANS. If the time and occasion be ordinary he is to give out of his aboundance—let him lay aside, as god hath blessed him. If the time and occasion be extraordinary he must be ruled by them; takeing this withall, that then a man cannot likely doe too much especially, if he may leave himselfe and his family under probable meanes of comfortable subsistance.

OBJECTION. A man must lay upp for posterity, the fathers lay upp for posterity and children and he is worse than an Infidell that provideth not for his owne.

ANS. For the first, it is plaine, that it being spoken by way of Comparison it must be meant of the ordinary and usuall course of fathers and cannot extend to times and occasions extraordinary; for the other place the Apostle speakes against such as walked inordinately, and it is without question, that he is worse then an Infidell whoe throughe his owne Sloathe and voluptuousnes shall neglect to provide for his family.

OBJECTION. The wise mans Eies are in his head (saith Salomon) and foreseeth the plague, therefore wee must forecast and lay upp against evill times when hee or his may stand in need of all he can gather.

ANS: This very Argument Salomon useth to perswade to liberallity. Eccle: [11. 1.] cast thy bread upon the waters etc.: for thou knowest not what evill may come upon the land Luke 16. make you freinds of the riches of Iniquity; you will aske how this shall be? very well. for first he that gives to the poore lends to the lord, and he will repay him even in this life an hundred fold to him or his. The righteous is ever mercifull and lendeth and his seed enjoyeth the blessing; and besides wee know what advantage it will be to us in the day of account, when many such Witnesses shall stand forthe for us to witnesse the improvement of our Tallent. And I would knowe of those whoe pleade soe much for layeing up for time to come, whether they hold that to be Gospell Math: 16. 19. Lay not upp for yourselves Treasures upon Earth etc. if they acknowledge it what extent will they allowe it; if onely to those primitive times lett them consider the reason whereupon our Saviour groundes it, the first is that they are subject to the moathe, the rust the Theife. Secondly, They will steale away the hearte, where the treasure is there will the heart be allsoe. The reasons are of like force at all times therefore the exhortacion must be generall and perpetuall which [applies] allwayes in respect of the love and affeccion to riches and in regard of the things themselves when any speciall service for the churche or perticuler distresse of our brother doe call for the use of them; otherwise it is not onely lawfull but necessary to lay upp as Joseph did to have ready uppon such occasions, as the Lord (whose stewards wee are of them) shall call for them from us: Christ gives us an Instance of the first, when hee sent his disciples for the Asse, and bidds them answer the owner thus, the Lord hath need of him; soe when the Tabernacle was to be builte his [servant] sends to his people to call for their silver and gold etc.; and yeildes them noe other reason but that it was for his worke, when Elisha comes to the widowe of Sareptah and findes her prepareing to make ready her pittance for herselfe and family, he bids her first provide for him, he challengeth first gods parte which shee must first give before shee must serve her owne family, all these teache us that the lord lookes that when hee is pleased to call for his right in any thing wee have, our owne Interest wee have must stand aside, till his turne be served, for the other wee need looke noe further then to that of John 1. he whoe hath this worlds goodes and seeth his brother to neede, and shutts upp his Compassion from him, how dwelleth the love of god in him, which comes punctually to this Conclusion: if thy brother be in want and thou canst help him, thou needst not make doubt, what thou shouldst doe, if thou lovest god thou must help him.

QUEST: What rule must wee observe in lending?

ANS: Thou must observe whether thy brother hath present or probable, or possible meanes of repayeing thee, if ther be none of these, thou must give him according to his necessity, rather than lend him as hee requires; if he hath present meanes of repayeing thee, thou art to looke at him, not as an Act of mercy, but by way of Commerce, wherein thou arte to walke by the rule of Justice, but, if his meanes of repayeing thee be onely probable or possible then is hee an object of thy mercy thou must lend him, though there be danger of looseing it Deut: 15. 7. If any of thy brethren be poore etc. thou shalt lend him sufficient that men might not shift off this duty by the apparant hazzard, he tells them that though the Yeare of Jubile were at hand (when he must remitt it, if hee were not able to repay it before) yet he must lend him and that chearefully: it may not greive thee to give him (saith hee) and because some might object, why soe I should soone impoverishe my selfe and my family, he adds with all thy Worke etc. for our Saviour Math: 5. 42. From him that would borrow of thee turne not away.

QUEST: What rule must wee observe in forgiveing?

ANS: Whether thou didst lend by way of Commerce or in mercy, if he have noething to pay thee [thou] must forgive him (except in cause where thou hast a surety or a lawfull pleadge) Deut. 15. 2. Every seaventh yeare the

Creditor was to quitt that which hee lent to his brother if hee were poore as appeares ver: 8[4]: save when there shall be noe poore with thee. In all these and like Cases Christ was a generall rule Math: 7. 22. Whatsoever ye would that men should doe to you doe yee the same to them allsoe.

QUEST: What rule must wee observe and walke by in cause of Community of perill?

ANS: The same as before, but with more enlargement towardes others and lesse respect towards our selves, and our owne right hence it was that in the primitive Churche they sold all had all things in Common, neither did any man say that that which he possessed was his owne likewise in theire returne out of the Captivity, because the worke was greate for the restoreing of the church and the danger of enemies was Common to all Nehemiah exhortes the Jewes to liberallity and readines in remitting theire debtes to theire brethren, and disposeth liberally of his owne to such as wanted and stands not upon his owne due, which hee might have demaunded of them, thus did some of our forefathers in times of persecucion here in England, and soe did many of the faithful in other Churches whereof wee keepe an honourable remembrance of them, and it is to be observed that both in Scriptures and latter stories of the Churches that such as have beene most bountifull to the poore Saintes especially in these extraordinary times and occasions god hath left them highly Commended to posterity, as Zacheus, Cornelius, Dorcas, Bishop Hooper, the Cuttler of Brussells and divers others observe againe that the scripture gives noe causion to restraine any from being over liberall this way; but all men to the liberall and cherefull practise hereof by the sweetest promises as to instance one for many, Isaiah 58. 6: Is not this the fast that I have chosen to loose the bonds of wickednes, to take off the heavy burdens to lett the oppressed goe free and to breake every Yoake, to deale thy bread to the hungry and to bring the poore that wander into thy house, when thou seest the naked to cover them etc. then shall thy light breake forthe as the morneing, and thy healthe shall growe speedily, thy righteousnes shall goe before thee, and the glory of the lord shall embrace thee, then thou shalt call and the lord shall Answer thee etc. 2. 10: If thou power out thy soule to the hungry, then shall thy light spring out in darknes, and the lord shall guide thee continually, and satisfie thy Soule in draught, and make fatt thy bones, thou shalt be like a watered Garden, and they shall be of thee that shall build the old wast places etc. on the contrary most heavy cursses are layd upon such as are straightened towards the Lord and his people Judg: 5. [23] Cursse ye Meroshe because the [y] came not to help the Lord etc. Pro: [21. 13] Hee whoe shutteth his eares from hearing the cry of the poore, he shall cry and shall not be heard: Math: 25. [41] Goe ye cursssed into everlasting fire etc. [42.] I was hungry and ye fedd mee not. Cor: 2. 9. 16. [6.] He that soweth spareingly shall reape spareingly.

Haveing allready sett forth the practise of mercy according to the rule of gods lawe, it will be usefull to lay open the groundes of it allsoe being the other parte of the Commaundement and that is the affeccion from which this exercise of mercy must arise, the Apostle tells us that this love is the fullfilling of the lawe, not that it is enough to love our brother and soe noe further but in regard of the excellency of his partes giveing any motion to the other as the Soule to the body and the power it hath to sett all the faculties on worke in the outward exercise of this duty as when wee bid one make the clocke strike he doth not lay hand on the hammer which is the immediate instrument of the sound but setts on worke the first mover or maine wheele, knoweing that will certainely produce the sound which hee intends; soe the way to drawe men to the workes of mercy is not by force of Argument from the goodnes or necessity of the worke, for though this course may enforce a rationall minde to some present Act of mercy as is frequent in experience, yet it cannot worke such a habit in a Soule as shall make it prompt upon all occasions to produce the same effect but by frameing these affeccions of love in the hearte which will as natively bring forthe the other, as any cause doth produce the effect.

The diffinition which the Scripture gives us of love is this Love is the bond of perfection. First, it is a bond, or ligament. 2ly, it makes the worke perfect. There is noe body but consistes of partes and that which knitts these partes together gives the body its perfeccion, because it makes eache parte soe contiguous to other as thereby they doe mutually participate with eache other, both in strengthe and infirmity in pleasure and paine, to instance in the most perfect of all bodies, Christ and his church make one body: the severall partes of this body considered aparte before they were united were as disproportionate and as much disordering as soe many contrary quallities or elements but when christ comes and by his spirit and love knitts all these partes to himselfe and each to other, it is become the most perfect and best proportioned body in the world Eph: 4. 16. "Christ by whome all the body being knitt together by every joynt for the furniture thereof according to the effectuall power which is in the measure of every perfeccion of partes a glorious body without spott or wrinckle the ligaments hereof being Christ or his love for Christ is love 1 John: 4. 8. Soe this definition is right Love is the bond of perfeccion.

From hence wee may frame these Conclusions.

1 first all true Christians are of one body in Christ 1. Cor. 12. 12. 13. 17. [27.] Ye are the body of Christ and members of [your?] parte.

2ly. The ligamentes of this body which knitt together are love.

3ly. Noe body can be perfect which wants its propper ligamentes.

4ly. All the partes of this body being thus united are made soe contiguous in a speciall relacion as they must needes partake of each others strength and infirmity, joy, and sorrowe, weale and woe. 1 Cor: 12. 26. If one member suffers all suffer with it, if one be in honour, all rejoyce with it.

5ly. This sensiblenes and Sympathy of each others Condicions will necessarily infuse into each parte a native desire and endeavour, to strengthen defend preserve and comfort the other.

To insist a little on this Conclusion being the product of all the former the truthe hereof will appeare both by precept and patterne i. John. 3. 10. yee ought to lay downe your lives for the brethren Gal: 6. 2. beare ye one anothers burthens and soe fulfill the lawe of Christ.

For patterns wee have that first of our Saviour whoe out of his good will in obedience to his father, becomeing a parte of this body, and being knitt with it in the bond of love, found such a native sensiblenes of our infirmities and sorrowes as hee willingly yeilded himselfe to deathe to ease the infirmities of the rest of his body and soe heale theire sorrowes: from the like Sympathy of partes did the Apostles and many thousands of the Saintes lay downe theire lives for Christ againe, the like wee may see in the members of this body among themselves. 1. Rom. 9. Paule could have beene contented to have beene seperated from Christ that the Jewes might not be cutt off from the body: It is very observable which hee professeth of his affectionate part[ak]eing with every member: whoe is weake (saith hee) and I am not weake? whoe is offended and I burne not; and againe. 2 Cor: 7. 13. therefore wee are comforted because yee were comforted. of Epaphroditus he speaketh Phil: 2. 30. that he regarded not his owne life to [do] him service soe Phebe. and others are called the servantes of the Churche, now it is apparant that they served not for wages or by Constrainte but out of love, the like wee shall finde in the histories of the churche in all ages the sweete Sympathie of affeccions which was in the members of this body one towardes another, theire chearfullnes in serveing and suffering together how liberall they were without repineing harbourers without grudgeing and helpfull without reproacheing and all from hence they had fervent love amongst them which onely make [s] the practise of mercy constant and easie.

The next consideracion is how this love comes to be wrought; Adam in his first estate was a perfect modell of mankinde in all theire generacions, and in him this love was perfected in regard of the habit, but Adam Rent in himselfe from his Creator, rent all his posterity allsoe one from another, whence it comes that every man is borne with this principle in him, to love and seeke himselfe onely and thus a man continueth till Christ comes and takes possession of the soule, and infuseth another principle love to God and our brother. And this latter haveing continuall supply from Christ, as the head and roote by which hee is united get the predominency in the soule, soe by little and little expells the former 1 John 4. 7. love cometh of god and every one that loveth is borne of god, soe that this love is the fruite of the new birthe, and none can have it but the new Creature, now when this quallity is thus formed in the soules of men it workes like the Spirit upon the drie bones Ezek. 37. [7] bone came to bone, it gathers together the scattered bones or perfect old man Adam and knitts them into one body againe in Christ whereby a man is become againe a liveing soule.

The third Consideracion is concerning the exercise of

this love, which is twofold, inward or outward, the outward hath beene handled in the former preface of this discourse, for unfolding the other wee must take in our way that maxime of philosophy, Simile simili gaudet or like will to like; for as it is things which are carved with disafeccion to eache other, the ground of it is from a dissimilitude or [*blank*] ariseing from the contrary or different nature of the things themselves, soe the ground of love is an apprehension of some resemblance in the things loved to that which affectes it, this is the cause why the Lord loves the Creature, soe farre as it hath any of his Image in it, he loves his elect because they are like himselfe, he beholds them in his beloved sonne: soe a mother loves her childe, because shee throughly conceives a resemblance of herselfe in it. Thus it is betweene the members of Christ, each discernes by the worke of the spirit his owne Image and resemblance in another, and therefore cannot but love him as he loves himselfe: Now when the soule which is of a sociable nature findes any thing like to it selfe, it is like Adam when Eve was brought to him, shee must have it one with herselfe this is fleshe of my fleshe (saith shee) and bone of my bone shee conceives a great delighte in it, therefore shee desires nearenes and familiarity with it: shee hath a greate propensity to doe it good and receives such content in it, as feareing the miscarriage of her beloved shee bestowes it in the inmost closett of her heart, shee will not endure that it shall want any good which shee can give it, if by occasion shee be withdrawne from the Company of it, shee is still lookeing towardes the place where shee left her beloved, if shee heare it groane shee is with it presently, if shee finde it sadd and disconsolate shee sighes and mournes with it, shee hath noe such joy, as to see her beloved merry and thriveing, if shee see it wronged, shee cannot beare it without passion, shee setts noe boundes of her affeccions, nor hath any thought of reward, shee findes recompence enoughe in the exercise of her love towardes it, wee may see this Acted to life in Jonathan and David. Jonathan a valiant man endued with the spirit of Christ, soe soone as hee Discovers the same spirit in David had presently his hearte knitt to him by this linement of love, soe that it is said he loved him as his owne soule, he takes soe great pleasure in him that hee stripps himselfe to adorne his beloved, his fathers kingdome was not soe precious to him as his beloved David, David shall have it with all his hearte, himselfe desires noe more but that hee may be neare to him to rejoyce in his good hee chooseth to converse with him in the wildernesse even to the hazzard of his owne life, rather then with the greate Courtiers in his fathers Pallace; when hee sees danger towards him, hee spares neither care paines, nor perill to divert it, when Injury was offered his beloved David, hee could not beare it, though from his owne father, and when they must parte for a Season onely, they thought theire heartes would have broake for sorrowe, had not theire affeccions found vent by aboundance of Teares: other instances might be brought to shewe the nature of this affeccion as of Ruthe and Naomi and many others, but this truthe is cleared enough. If any shall object that it is not possible that love should be bred or upheld without hope of requitall, it is graunted but that is not our cause, for this love is allwayes under reward it never gives, but it allwayes receives with advantage: first, in regard that among the members of the same body, love and affection are reciprocall in a most equall and sweete kinde of Commerce. 2ly [3ly], in regard of the pleasure and content that the exercise of love carries with it as wee may see in the naturall body the mouth is at all the paines to receive, and mince the foode which serves for the nourishment of all the other partes of the body, yet it hath noe cause to complaine; for first, the other partes send backe by secret passages a due proporcion of the same nourishment in a better forme for the strengthening and comforteing the mouthe. 2ly the labour of the mouthe is accompanied with such pleasure and content as farre exceedes the paines it takes: soe is it in all the labour of love, among christians, the partie loveing, reapes love againe as was shewed before, which the soule covetts more than all the wealthe in the world. 2ly [4ly]. noething yeildes more pleasure and content to the soule then when it findes that which it may love fervently, for to love and live beloved is the soules paradice, both heare and in heaven: In the State of Wedlock there be many comfortes to beare out the troubles of that Condicion; but let such as have tryed the most, say if there be any sweetnes in that Condicion comparable to the exercise of mutuall love.

From the former Consideracions ariseth these Conclusions.

1 First, This love among Christians is a reall thing not Imaginarie.

2ly. This love is as absolutely necessary to the being of the body of Christ, as the sinewes and other ligaments of a naturall body are to the being of that body.

3ly. This love is a divine spirituall nature free, active strong Couragious permanent under valueing all things beneathe its proper object, and of all the graces this makes us nearer to resemble the virtues of our heavenly father.

4ly. It restes in the love and wellfare of its beloved, for the full and certaine knowledge of these truthes concerning the nature use, [and] excellency of this grace, that which the holy ghost hath left recorded 1. Cor. 13. may give full satisfaccion which is needfull for every true member of this lovely body of the Lord Jesus, to worke upon theire heartes, by prayer meditacion continuall exercise at least of the speciall [power] of this grace till Christ be formed in them and they in him all in eache other knitt together by this bond of love.

It rests now to make some applicacion of this discourse

by the present designe which gave the occasion of writeing of it. Herein are 4 things to be propounded: first the persons, 2ly, the worke, 3ly, the end, 4ly the meanes.

1. For the persons, wee are a Company professing our selves fellow members of Christ, In which respect onely though wee were absent from eache other many miles, and had our imploymentes as farre distant, yet wee ought to account our selves knitt together by this bond of love, and live in the excercise of it, if wee would have comforte of our being in Christ, this was notorious in the practise of the Christians in former times, as is testified of the Waldenses from the mouth of one of the adversaries Aeneas Sylvius, mutuo [solent amare] penè antequam norint, they use to love any of theire owne religion even before they were acquainted with them.

2ly. for the worke wee have in hand, it is by a mutuall consent through a speciall overruleing providence, and a more then an ordinary approbation of the Churches of Christ to seeke out a place of Cohabitation and Consorteshipp under a due forme of Government both civill and ecclesiasticall. In such cases as this the care of the publique must oversway all private respects, by which not onely conscience, but meare Civill pollicy doth binde us; for it is a true rule that perticuler estates cannott subsist in the ruine of the publique.

3ly. The end is to improve our lives to doe more service to the Lord the comforte and encrease of the body of christe whereof wee are members that our selves and posterity may be the better preserved from the Common corrupcions of this evill world to serve the Lord and worke out our Salvacion under the power and purity of his holy Ordinances.

4ly for the meanes whereby this must bee effected, they are 2fold, a Conformity with the worke and end wee aime at, these wee see are extraordinary, therefore wee must not content our selves with usuall ordinary meanes whatsoever wee did or ought to have done when wee lived in England, the same must wee doe and more allsoe where wee goe: That which the most in theire Churches maineteine as a truthe in profession onely, wee must bring into familiar and constant practise, as in this duty of love wee must love brotherly without dissimulation, wee must love one another with a pure hearte fervently wee must beare one anothers burthens, wee must not looke onely on our owne things, but allsoe on the things of our brethren, neither must wee think that the lord will beare with such faileings at our hands as hee dothe from those among whome we have lived, and that for 3 Reasons.

1. In regard of the more neare bond of mariage, betweene him and us, wherein he hath taken us to be his after a most strickt and peculiar manner which will make him the more Jealous of our love and obedience soe he tells the people of Israell, you onely have I knowne of all the families of the Earthe therefore will I punishe you for your Transgressions.

2ly, because the lord will be sanctified in them that come neare him. Wee know that there were many that corrupted the service of the Lord some setting upp Alters before his owne, others offering both strange fire and strange Sacrifices allsoe; yet there came noe fire from heaven, or other sudden Judgement upon them as did upon Nadab and Abihu whoe yet wee may thinke did not sinne presumptuously.

3ly When God gives a speciall Commission he lookes to have it stricktly observed in every Article, when hee gave Saule a Commission to destroy Amaleck hee indented with him upon certaine Articles and because hee failed in one of the least, and that upon a faire pretence, it lost him the kingdome, which should have beene his reward, if hee had observed his Commission: Thus stands the cause betweene God and us, wee are entered into Covenant with him for this worke, wee have taken out a Commission, the Lord hath given us leave to drawe our owne Articles wee have professed to enterprise these Accions upon these and these ends, wee have hereupon besought him of favour and blessing: Now if the Lord shall please to heare us, and bring us in peace to the place wee desire, then hath hee ratified this Covenant and sealed our Commission, [and] will expect a strickt performance of the Articles contained in it, but if wee shall neglect the observacion of these Articles which are the ends wee have propounded, and dissembling with our God, shall fall to embrace this present world and prosecute our carnall intencions, seekeing greate things for our selves and our posterity, the Lord will surely breake out in wrathe against us be revenged of such a perjured people and make us knowe the price of the breache of such a Covenant.

Now the onely way to avoyde this shipwracke and to provide for our posterity is to followe the Counsell of Micah, to doe Justly, to love mercy, to walke humbly with our God, for this end, wee must be knitt together in this worke as one man, wee must entertaine each other in brotherly Affeccion, wee must be willing to abridge our selves of our superfluities, for the supply of others necessities, wee must uphold a familiar Commerce together in all meekenes, gentlenes, patience and liberallity, wee must delight in eache other, make others Condicions our owne rejoyce together, mourne together, labour, and suffer together, allwayes haveing before our eyes our Commission and Community in the worke, our Community as members of the same body, soe shall wee keepe the unitie of the spirit in the bond of peace, the Lord will be our God and delight to dwell among us, as his owne people and will commaund a blessing upon us in all our wayes, soe that wee shall see much more of his wisdome power goodnes and truthe then formerly wee have beene acquainted with, wee shall finde that the God of Israell is among us, when tenn of us shall be able to resist a thousand of our enemies, when hee shall make us a prayse and glory, that men shall say of succeeding plantacions: the lord make it like that of New England: for wee must Consider that wee shall be as a Citty upon a Hill, the eies of all people are uppon us; soe that if wee shall deale falsely with our god in this worke wee have undertaken and soe cause him to withdrawe his present help from us, wee shall be made a story and a by-word through the world, wee shall open the mouthes of enemies to speake evill of the wayes of god and all professours for Gods sake; wee shall shame the faces of many of gods worthy servants, and cause theire prayers to be turned into Cursses upon us till wee be consumed out of the good land whether wee are goeing: And to shutt upp this discourse with that exhortacion of Moses that faithfull servant of the Lord in his last farewell to Israell Deut. 30. Beloved there is now sett before us life, and good, deathe and evill in that wee are Commaunded this day to love the Lord our God, and to love one another to walke in his wayes and to keepe his Commaundements and his Ordinance, and his lawes, and the Articles of our Covenant with him that wee may live and be multiplyed, and that the Lord our God may blesse us in the land whether wee goe to possesse it: But if our heartes shall turne away soe that wee will not obey, but shall be seduced and worshipp [serve *cancelled*] other Gods our pleasures, and proffitts, and serve them; it is propounded unto us this day, wee shall surely perishe out of the good Land whether wee passe over this vast Sea to possesse it;

Therefore lett us choose life,
that wee, and our Seede,
may live; by obeyeing his
voyce, and cleaveing to him,
for hee is our life, and
our prosperity.

6. THE JOURNAL OF JOHN WINTHROP

Governor Winthrop believed in Massachusetts. After he stepped aboard the Arbella *to sail there, he began to keep a journal, and he continued to make entries in it for the rest of his life. It was intended to be a record, not of the growth of his soul in grace, but of the works of God in Massachusetts. In it Winthrop spoke of himself in the third person and described political disputes with remarkable impartiality, occasionally explaining why the governor or the deputy governor (when he held that position) thought as he did. The passages selected for publication here by no means exhaust the riches of this great document for the study of Puritan political thought, but they give some idea of the author's thinking and of the problems encountered by Puritans in putting their political ideas into practice.*

In Massachusetts, not the least of those problems arose from the circumstances under which the government was formed. The colony was founded under authority granted in a royal charter, or "patent," to the Massachusetts Bay Company in 1629. The charter empowered the Company to govern the colony in any way it saw fit, provided the laws were in conformity with those of England, but it prescribed in detail the government of the Company itself. The freemen (stockholders) of the Company were to meet four times a year in a "General Court," to make laws for both Company and colony. Once a year, at the Court held in May, the freemen were to elect a governor, deputy governor, and eighteen assistants, who could meet monthly to

---

From John Winthrop, *The History of New England from 1630 to 1649*, James Savage, ed. (Boston, 1853, 2 vol.), *passim*.

when they get to the US social distinctions dissappear, because opportunity is afforded to everyone, a middle class society forms liberty is also easy to come by, people can just move 5 miles away and stop following strict laws *manage the Company's affairs when the General Court was not in session.*

At first the Company met in London and governed the colony through an appointed governor, John Endecott. But in 1630 the meetings of the Company were transferred to Massachusetts; Winthrop and several other freemen went there, bringing the charter with them. Henceforth the government of the colony was identical with that of the Company.

Two important changes served to adapt the government of a trading company to that of a Puritan commonwealth. First, by an order of May, 1631, freemanship, carrying the right to vote and hold office, ceased to be related to stockholding and was opened to members of orthodox Puritan churches in the colony. Secondly, the direct participation of freemen in legislation ceased. In October, 1630, the General Court agreed to transfer legislative functions to the assistants, but in 1634, as recorded in some of the selections that follow, the freemen of the various settlements began appointing "deputies" to sit in the General Court in their places and make laws. Although the freemen elected the governor, deputy governor, and assistants (known collectively as "magistrates") annually, the deputies evidently considered themselves to be the special agents of the people, and a contest for power ensued between deputies and magistrates. Several selections deal with episodes in this contest, in which, it should be remembered, neither side was less or more Puritan than the other.

Among the selections have also been included several passages relating to Roger Williams before his banishment from Massachusetts, because Winthrop's Journal is virtually the only contemporary record of Williams's political and religious opinions at the time. Williams's own published writings were written several years later, and his few surviving letters reveal very little about his political ideas.

[April 12, 1631] At a court[1] holden at Boston, (upon information to the governour, that they of Salem had called Mr. Williams to the office of a teacher,) a letter was written from the court to Mr. Endecott to this effect: That whereas Mr. Williams had refused to join with the congregation at Boston, because they would not make a public declaration of their repentance for having communion with the churches of England, while they lived there; and, besides, had declared his opinion, that the magistrate might not punish the breach of the Sabbath, nor any other offence, as it was a breach of the first table;[2] therefore, they marvelled they would choose him without advising with the council; and withal desiring him, that they would forbear to proceed till they had conferred about it.

[February 17, 1631–2] The governour and assistants called before them, at Boston, divers of Watertown; the pastor and elder[3] by letter, and the others by warrant. The occasion was, for that a warrant being sent to Watertown

---

[1]One of the monthly meetings of the Assistants with the Governor and Deputy Governor. [Ed.]

[2]The first four of the Ten Commandments were known as the First Table, the last six as the Second Table. [Ed.]

[3]By the "elder" Winthrop here means the ruling elder, a lay officer chosen by the church to preside over the moral behavior of the members. But Winthrop also uses the word to apply to all church officers in general, as in the selection that follows, where he speaks of the "elders and brethren." [Ed.]

for levying of £8, part of a rate of £60, ordered for the fortifying of the new town, the pastor and elder, etc., assembled the people and delivered their opinions, that it was not safe to pay moneys after that sort, for fear of bringing themselves and posterity into bondage. Being come before the governour and council, after much debate, they acknowledged their fault, confessing freely, that they were in an error, and made a retractation and submission under their hands, and were enjoined to read it in the assembly the next Lord's day. The ground of their error was, for that they took this government to be no other but as of a mayor and aldermen, who have not power to make laws or raise taxations without the people; but understanding that this government was rather in the nature of a parliament, and that no assistant could be chosen but by the freemen, who had power likewise to remove the assistants and put in others, and therefore at every general court (which was to be held once every year) they had free liberty to consider and propound anything concerning the same, and to declare their grievances, without being subject to question, or, etc., they were fully satisfied; and so their submission was accepted, and their offence pardoned.

[July, 1632] The congregation at Boston wrote to the elders and brethren of the churches of Plimouth, Salem, etc., for their advice in three questions: 1. Whether one person might be a civil magistrate and a ruling elder at the same time? 2. If not, then which should be laid down? 3. Whether there might be divers pastors in the same church?—The 1st was agreed by all negatively; the 2d doubtfully; the 3d doubtful also.

[Dec. 27, 1633] The governour and assistants met at Boston, and took into consideration a treatise, which Mr. Williams (then of Salem) had sent to them, and which he had formerly written to the governour and council of Plimouth, wherein, among other things, he disputes their right to the lands they possessed here, and concluded that, claiming by the king's grant, they could have no title, nor otherwise, except they compounded with the natives. For this, taking advice with some of the most judicious ministers, (who much condemned Mr. Williams's error and presumption,) they gave order, that he should be convented at the next court, to be censured, etc. There were three passages chiefly whereat they were much offended: 1, for that he chargeth King James to have told a solemn public lie, because in his patent he blessed God that he was the first Christian prince that had discovered this land: 2, for that he chargeth him and others with blasphemy for calling Europe Christendom, or the Christian world: 3, for that he did personally apply to our present king, Charles, these three places in the Revelations, viz., [*blank*].

Mr. Endecott being absent, the governour wrote to him to let him know what was done, and withal added divers arguments to confute the said errors, wishing him to deal with Mr. Williams to retract the same, etc. Whereto he returned a very modest and discreet answer. Mr. Williams also wrote to the governour, and also to him and the rest of the council, very submissively, professing his intent to have been only to have written for the private satisfaction of the governour etc., of Plimouth, without any purpose to have stirred any further in it, if the governour here had not required a copy of him; withal offering his book, or any part of it, to be burnt.

At the next court he appeared penitently, and gave satisfaction of his intention and loyalty. So it was left, and nothing done in it.

[January 24, 1633–4] The governour and council met again at Boston, to consider of Mr. Williams's letter, etc., when, with the advice of Mr. Cotton and Mr. Wilson, and weighing his letter, and further considering of the aforesaid offensive passages in his book, (which, being written in very obscure and implicative phrases, might well admit of doubtful interpretation,) they found the matters not to be so evil as at first they seemed. Whereupon they agreed, that, upon his retractation, etc., or taking an oath of allegiance to the king, etc., it should be passed over.

[April 1, 1634] Order was taken for ministering an oath to all house keepers and sojourners, being twenty years of age and not freemen, and for making a survey of the houses and lands of all freemen.

Notice being sent out of the general court to be held the 14th day of the third month, called May, the freemen deputed two of each town to meet and consider of such matters as they were to take order in at the same general court; who, having met, desired a sight of the patent, and, conceiving thereby that all their laws should be made at the general court, repaired to the governour to advise with him about it, and about the abrogating of some orders formerly made, as for killing of swine in corn, etc. He told them, that, when the patent was granted, the number of freemen was supposed to be (as in like corporations) so few, as they might well join in making laws; but now they were grown to so great a body, as it was not possible for them to make or execute laws, but they must choose others for that purpose: and that howsoever it would be necessary hereafter to have a select company to intend that work, yet for the present they were not furnished with a sufficient number of men qualified for such a business, neither could the commonwealth bear the loss of time of so many as must intend it. Yet this they might do at present, viz., they might, at the general court, make an order, that, once in the year, a certain number should be appointed (upon summons from the governour) to revise all laws, etc., and to reform what they found amiss therein; but not to make any new laws, but prefer their grievances to the court of assistants; and that no assessment should be laid upon the country without the consent of such a committee, nor any lands disposed of.

[May 14, 1634] At the general court, Mr. Cotton preached,[4] and delivered this doctrine, that a magistrate ought not to be turned into the condition of a private man without just cause, and to be publicly convict, no more than the magistrates may not turn a private man out of his freehold, etc., without like public trial, etc. This falling in question in the court, and the opinion of the rest of the ministers being asked, it was referred to further consideration.

The court chose a new governour, viz., Thomas Dudley, Esq., the former deputy; and Mr. Ludlow was chosen deputy; and John Haines, Esq., an assistant, and all the rest of the assistants chosen again.

At this court it was ordered, that four general courts should be kept every year, and that the whole body of the freemen should be present only at the court of election of magistrates, etc., and that, at the other three, every town should send their deputies, who should assist in making laws, disposing lands, etc. Many good orders were made this court. It held three days, and all things were carried very peaceably, notwithstanding that some of the assistants were questioned by the freemen for some errors in their government, and some fines imposed, but remitted again before the court brake up. The court was kept in the

---

[4]The practice thus begun, of having one of the colony's leading ministers preach a sermon before the annual election, was continued to the nineteenth century. [Ed.]

meeting-house at Boston, and the new governour and the assistants were together entertained at the house of the old governour, as before.

[Nov. 27, 1634] It was likewise informed, that Mr. Williams of Salem had broken his promise to us, in teaching publickly against the king's patent, and our great sin in claiming right thereby to this country, etc. and for usual terming the churches of England antichristian. We granted summons to him for his appearance at the next court.

[April 30, 1635] The governour and assistants sent for Mr. Williams. The occasion was, for that he had taught publicly, that a magistrate ought not to tender an oath to an unregenerate man, for that we thereby have communion with a wicked man in the worship of God, and cause him to take the name of God in vain. He was heard before all the ministers, and very clearly confuted. Mr. Endecott was at first of the same opinion, but he gave place to the truth.

[May 6, 1635] The deputies having conceived great danger to our state, in regard that our magistrates, for want of positive laws, in many cases, might proceed according to their discretions, it was agreed that some men should be appointed to frame a body of grounds of laws, in resemblance to a Magna Charta, which, being allowed by some of the ministers, and the general court, should be received for fundamental laws.

[July 8, 1635] At the general court, Mr. Williams of Salem was summoned, and did appear. It was laid to his charge, that, being under question before the magistracy and churches for divers dangerous opinions, viz. 1, that the magistrate ought not to punish the breach of the first table, otherwise than in such cases as did disturb the civil peace; 2, that he ought not to tender an oath to an unregenerate man; 3, that a man ought not to pray with such, though wife, child, etc.; 4, that a man ought not to give thanks after the sacrament nor after meat, etc.; and that the other churches were about to write to the church of Salem to admonish him of these errors; notwithstanding the church had since called him to [the] office of a teacher. Much debate was about these things. The said opinions were adjudged by all, magistrates and ministers, (who were desired to be present,) to be erroneous, and very dangerous, and the calling of him to office, at that time, was judged a great contempt of authority. So, in fine, time was given to him and the church of Salem to consider of these things till the next general court, and then either to give satisfaction to the court, or else to expect the sentence; it being professedly declared by the ministers, (at the request of the court to give their advice,) that he who should obstinately maintain such opinions, (whereby a church might run into heresy, apostacy, or tyranny, and yet the civil magistrate could not intermeddle,) were to be removed, and that the other churches ought to request the magistrates so to do.

[July 12, 1635] Salem men had preferred a petition, at the last general court, for some land in Marblehead Neck, which they did challenge as belonging to their town; but, because they had chosen Mr. Williams their teacher, while he stood under question of authority, and so offered contempt to the magistrates, etc., their petition was refused till, etc. Upon this the church of Salem write to other churches, to admonish the magistrates of this as a heinous sin, and likewise the deputies; for which, at the next general court, their deputies were not received until they should give satisfaction about the letter.

[August, 1635] Mr. Williams, pastor of Salem, being sick and not able to speak, wrote to his church a protestation, that he could not communicate with the churches in the bay; neither would he communicate with them, except they would refuse communion with the rest; but the whole church was grieved herewith.

[October, 1635] At this general court, Mr. Williams, the teacher at Salem, was again convented, and all the ministers in the bay being desired to be present, he was charged with the said two letters,—that to the churches, complaining of the magistrates for injustice, extreme oppression, etc., and the other to his own church, to persuade them to renounce communion with all the churches in the bay, as full of antichristian pollution, etc. He justified both these letters, and maintained all his opinions; and, being offered further conference or disputation, and a month's respite, he chose to dispute presently. So Mr. Hooker was appointed to dispute with him, but could not reduce him from any of his errors. So, the next morning, the court sentenced him to depart out of our jurisdiction within six weeks, all the ministers, save one, approving the sentence; and his own church had him under question also for the same cause; and he, at his return home, refused communion with his own church, who openly disclaimed his errors, and wrote an humble submission to the magistrates, acknowledging their fault in joining with Mr. Williams in that letter to the churches against them, etc.

[January, 1635–6] The governour and assistants met at Boston to consider about Mr. Williams, for that they were credibly informed, that, notwithstanding the injunction laid upon him (upon the liberty granted him to stay till the spring) not to go about to draw others to his opinions, he did use to entertain company in his house, and to preach to them, even of such points as he had been censured for; and it was agreed to send him into England by a ship then ready to depart. The reason was, because he had drawn above twenty persons to his opinion, and they were intended to erect a plantation about the Naragansett Bay, from whence the infection would easily spread into these churches, (the people being, many of them, much taken with the apprehension of his godliness). Whereupon a warrant was sent to him to come presently to Boston, to be shipped, etc. He returned answer, (and divers of Salem came with it,) that he could not come without hazard of his life, etc. Whereupon a pinnace was sent with commission to Capt. Underhill, etc., to apprehend him, and carry him aboard the ship, (which then rode at Natascutt;) but, when they came at his house, they found he had been gone three days before; but whither they could not learn.

He had so far prevailed at Salem, as many there (especially of devout women) did embrace his opinions, and separated from the churches, for this cause, that some of their members, going into England, did hear the ministers there, and when they came home the churches here held communion with them.

[January 18, 1635–6] Mr. Vane and Mr. Peter, finding some distraction in the commonwealth, arising from some difference in judgment, and withal some alienation of affection among the magistrates and some other persons of quality, and that hereby factions began to grow among the people, some adhering more to the old governour, Mr. Winthrop, and others to the late governour, Mr. Dudley,—the former carrying matters with more lenity, and the latter with more severity,—they procured a meeting, at Boston, of the governour, deputy, Mr. Cotton, Mr. Hooker, Mr. Wilson, and there was present Mr. Winthrop,

Mr. Dudley, and themselves; where, after the Lord had been sought, Mr. Vane declared the occasion of this meeting, (as is before noted,) and the fruit aimed at, viz. a more firm and friendly uniting of minds, etc., especially of the said Mr. Dudley and Mr. Winthrop, as those upon whom the weight of the affairs did lie, etc., and therefore desired all present to take up a resolution to deal freely and openly with the parties, and they each with other, that nothing might be left in their breasts, which might break out to any jar or difference hereafter, (which they promised to do). Then Mr. Winthrop spake to this effect: that when it pleased Mr. Vane to acquaint him with what he had observed, of the dispositions of men's minds inclining to the said faction, etc., it was very strange to him, professing solemnly that he knew not of any breach between his brother Dudley and himself, since they were reconciled long since, neither did he suspect any alienation of affection in him or others from himself, save that, of late, he had observed, that some new comers had estranged themselves from him, since they went to dwell at Newtown; and so desired all the company, that, if they had seen any thing amiss in his government or otherwise, they would deal freely and faithfully with him, and for his part he promised to take it in good part, and would endeavor, by God's grace, to amend it. Then Mr. Dudley spake to this effect: that for his part he came thither a mere patient, not with any intent to charge his brother Winthrop with any thing; for though there had been formerly some differences and breaches between them, yet they had been healed, and, for his part, he was not willing to renew them again; and so left it to others to utter their own complaints. Whereupon the governour, Mr. Haynes, spake to this effect: that Mr. Winthrop and himself had been always in good terms, etc.; therefore he was loath to give any offence to him, and he hoped that, considering what the end of this meeting was, he would take it in good part, if he did deal openly and freely, as his manner ever was. Then he spake of one or two passages, wherein he conceived, that [he] dealt too remissly in point of justice; to which Mr. Winthrop answered, that his speeches and carriage had been in part mistaken; but withal professed, that it was his judgment, that in the infancy of plantation, justice should be administered with more lenity than in a settled state, because people were then more apt to transgress, partly of ignorance of new laws and orders, partly through oppression of business and other straits; but, if it might be made clear to him, that it was an error, he would be ready to take up a stricter course. Then the ministers were desired to consider of the question by the next morning, and to set down a rule in the case. The next morning, they delivered their several reasons, which all sorted to this conclusion, that strict discipline, both in criminal offences and in martial affairs, was more needful in plantations than in a settled state, as tending to the honor and safety of the gospel. Whereupon Mr. Winthrop acknowledged that he was convinced, that he had failed in over much lenity and remissness, and would endeavor (by God's assistance) to take a more strict course hereafter. Whereupon there was a renewal of love amongst them, and articles drawn to this effect:—

1. That there should be more strictness used in civil government and military discipline.

2. That the magistrates should (as far as might be) ripen their consultations beforehand, that their vote in public might bear (as the voice of God).

3. That, in meetings out of court, the magistrates should not discuss the business of parties in their presence, nor deliver their opinions, etc.

4. That trivial things, etc., should be ended in towns, etc.

5. If differences fall out among them in public meetings, they shall observe these rules:—

1. Not to touch any person differing, but speak to the cause.

2. To express their difference in all modesty and due respect to the court and such as differ, etc.

3. Or to propound their difference by way of question.

4. Or to desire a deferring of the cause to further time.

5. After sentence, (if all have agreed,) none shall intimate his dislike privately; or, if one dissent, he shall sit down, without showing any further distaste, publicly or privately.

6. The magistrates shall be more familiar and open each to other, and more frequent in visitations, and shall, in tenderness and love, admonish one another, (without reserving any secret grudge,) and shall avoid all jealousies and suspicions, each seeking the honor of another, and all, of the court, not opening the nakedness of one another to private persons; in all things seeking the safety and credit of the gospel.

7. To honor the governour in submitting to him the main direction and ordering the business of the court.

8. One assistant shall not seem to gratify any man in undoing or crossing another's proceedings, without due advice with him.

9. They shall grace and strengthen their under officers in their places, etc.

10. All contempts against the court, or any of the magistrates, shall be specially noted and punished; and the magistrates shall appear more solemnly in public, with attendance, apparel, and open notice of their entrance into the court.

[October, 1636] Mr. Cotton, being requested by the general court, with some other ministers, to assist some of the magistrates in compiling a body of fundametal laws, did this court, present a model of Moses his judicials, compiled in an exact method, which were taken into further consideration till the next general court.

[March 9, 1636–7] The ministers, being called to give advice about the authority of the court in things concerning the churches, etc., did all agree of these two things: 1. That no member of the court ought to be publicly questioned by a church for any speech in the court, without the license of the court. The reason was, because the court may have sufficient reason that may excuse the sin, which yet may not be fit to acquaint the church with, being a secret of state. The second thing was, that, in all such heresies or errors of any church members as are manifest and dangerous to the state, the court may proceed without tarrying for the church; but if the opinions be doubtful, etc., they are first to refer them to the church, etc.

[June 3, 1637] Upon the news from Mr. Williams, that the Pequods were dispersed, and some come in and submitted to the Naragansetts, (who would not receive them before he had sent to know our mind,) the governour and council thought it needless to send so many men, and therefore sent out warrants only for one half of the two hundred; but some of the people liked not of it, and came to the governour to have all sent. He took it ill; and though three of the ministers came with them to debate the matter, he told them, that if any one, discerning an error in the proceedings of the council, had come, in a private manner, to acquaint him therewith, etc., it had been well done; but to come, so many of them, in a public and popular way, was not well, and would bring authority into contempt.

This they took well at his hands, and excused their intentions. So it was thought fit to send about forty men more, which was yielded rather to satisfy the people, than for any need that appeared.

[November, 1637] After this,[5] many of the church of Boston, being highly offended with the governour for this proceeding, were earnest with the elders to have him called to account for it; but they were not forward in it, and himself, understanding their intent, thought fit to prevent such a public disorder, and so took occasion to speak to the congregation to this effect:—

1. That if he had been called, etc., he would have desired, first, to have advised with the elders, whether the church had power to call in question the proceedings of the civil court.

2. He would have consulted with the rest of the court, whether he might discover the counsels of the court to this assembly.

3. Though he knew, that the elders and some others did know, that the church could not inquire into the justice and proceedings of the court, etc.; yet, for the satisfaction of such as did not, and were willing to be satisfied, he would declare his mind herein.

4. He showed, that, if the church had such power, they must have it from Christ, but Christ had disclaimed it in his practice and by rule, as Luke [*blank*], Matt. [*blank*]; and the scripture holds not out any rule or example for it; and though Christ's kingly power be in his church, yet that is not that kingly power whereby he is King of kings and Lord of lords, for by that kings reign and princes, etc. It is true, indeed, that magistrates, as they are church members,

[5]Winthrop had just described the measures taken by the General Court in November, 1637 against Anne Hutchinson and her followers, who were either banished or disarmed. [Ed.]

are accountable to the church for their failings, but that is when they are out of their calling; for we have examples of the highest magistrates in the same kind, as Uzzia, when he would go offer incense in the temple, the officers of the church called him to account, and withstood him. But when Asa put a prophet in prison, and when Salam put out Abiathar from the priesthood, (the one being a good act and the other ill,) yet the officers of the church did not call either of them to account for it. If a magistrate shall, in a private way, take away a man's goods or his servants, etc., the church may call him to account for it; but if he doth thus in pursuing a course of justice, (though the thing be unjust,) yet he is not accountable, etc.

5. For himself, he did nothing in the cases of the brethren, but by the advice and direction of our teacher and other of the elders. For in the oath, which was administered to him and the rest, etc., there was inserted, by his advice, this clause,—In all causes wherein you are to give your vote, etc., you are to give your vote as in your judgment and conscience you shall see to be most for the public good, etc.; and so for his part he was persuaded, that it would be most for the glory of God, and the public good, to pass sentence as they did.

6. He would give them one reason, which was a ground for his judgment, and that was, for that he saw, that those brethren, etc., were so divided from the rest of the country in their judgment and practice, as it could not stand with the public peace, that they should continue amongst us. So, by the example of Lot in Abraham's family, and after Hagar and Ishmael, he saw they must be sent away.

[May 22, 1639] The court of elections was; at which time there was a small eclipse of the sun. Mr. Winthrop was chosen governour again, though some laboring had been, by some of the elders and others to have changed, not out of any dislike of him, (for they all loved and esteemed him,) but out of their fear lest it might make way for having a governour for life, which some had propounded as most agreeable to God's institution and the practice of all well ordered states. But neither the governour nor any other attempted the thing; though some jealousies arose which were increased by two occasions. The first was, there being want of assistants, the governour and other magistrates thought fit (in the warrant for the court) to propound three, amongst which Mr. Downing, the governour's brother-in-law, was one, which they conceived to be done to strengthen his party, and therefore, though he were known to be a very able man, etc., and one who had done many good offices for the country for these ten years, yet the people would not choose him. Another occasion of their jealousy was, the court, finding the number of deputies to be much increased by the addition of new plantations, thought fit, for the ease both of the country and the court, to reduce all towns to two deputies. This occasioned some to fear, that the magistrates intended to make themselves stronger, and the deputies weaker, and so, in time, to bring all power into the hands of the magistrates; so as the people in some towns were much displeased with their deputies for yielding to such an order. Whereupon, at the next session, it was propounded to have the number of deputies restored; and allegations were made, that it was an infringement of their liberty; so as, after much debate, and such reasons given for diminishing the number of deputies, and clearly proved that their liberty consisted not in the number, but in the thing, divers of the deputies, who came with intent to reverse the last order, were, by force of reason, brought to uphold it; so that, when it was put to the vote, the last order for two deputies only was confirmed. Yet, the next day, a petition was brought to the court from the freemen of Roxbury, to have the third deputy restored. Whereupon the reasons of the court's proceedings were set down in writing, and all objections answered, and sent to such towns as were unsatisfied with this advice, that, if any could take away those reasons, or bring us better for what they did desire, we should be ready, at the next court, to repeal the said order.

The hands of some of the elders (learned and godly men) were to this petition, though suddenly drawn in, and without due consideration, for the lawfulness of it may well be questioned: for when the people have chosen men to be their rulers, and to make their laws, and bound themselves by oath to submit thereto, now to combine together (a lesser part of them) in a public petition to have any order repealed, which is not repugnant to the law of God, savors of resisting an ordinance of God; for the people, having deputed others, have no power to make or alter laws, but are to be subject; and if any such order seem unlawful or inconvenient, they were better prefer some reasons, etc., to the court, with manifestation of their desire to move them to a review, then peremptorily to petition to have it repealed, which amounts to a plain reproof of those whom God hath set over them, and putting dishonor upon them, against the tenor of the fifth commandment.

There fell out at this court another occasion of increasing the people's jealousy of their magistrates, viz.: One of the elders, being present with those of his church, when they were to prepare their votes for the election, declared his judgment, that a governour ought to be for his life, alleging for his authority the practice of all the best commonwealths in Europe, and especially that of Israel by God's own ordinance. But this was opposed by some other of the elders with much zeal, and so notice was taken of it by the people, not as a matter of dispute, but as if there had been some plot to put it in practice, which did occasion the deputies, at the next session of this court, to deliver in an order drawn to this effect: That, whereas our sovereign lord, King Charles, etc., had, by his patent, established a governour, deputy and assistants, that therefore no person, chosen a counsellor for life,[6] should have any authority as a magistrate, except he were chosen in the annual elections to one of the said places of magistracy established by the patent. This being thus bluntly tendered, (no mention being made thereof before,) the governour took time to consider of it, before he would put it to vote. So, when the court was risen, the magistrates advised of it, and drew up another order to this effect: That whereas, at the court in [*blank*], it was ordered, that a certain number of magistrates should be chosen to be a standing council for life, etc., whereupon some had gathered that we had erected a new order of magistrates not warranted by our patent, this court doth therefore declare, that the intent of the order was, that the standing council should always be chosen out of the magistrates, etc.; and therefore it is now ordered, that no such counsellor shall have any power as a magistrate, nor shall do any act as a magistrate, etc., except he be annually chosen, etc., according to the patent; and this order was after passed by vote. That which led those of the council to yield to this desire of the deputies was, because it concerned themselves, and they did more study to remove these jealousies out of the people's heads, than to preserve any power or dignity to themselves above others; for till this court those of the council, viz., Mr. Endecott, had stood and executed as a magistrate, without any annual election, and so they had been reputed by the elders and all the people till this present. But the order was

[6]In March, 1636, the General Court had established a standing council of magistrates to serve for life terms and exercise broad executive powers. [Ed.]

drawn up in this form, that it might be of less observation and freer from any note of injury to make this alteration rather by way of explanation of the fundamental order, than without any cause shown to repeal that which had been established by serious advice of the elders, and had been in practice two or three years without any inconvenience. And here may be observed, how strictly the people would seem to stick to their patent, where they think it makes for their advantage, but are content to decline it, where it will not warrant such liberties as they have taken up without warrant from thence, as appears in their strife for three deputies, etc., when as the patent allows them none at all, but only by inference, etc., voting by proxies, etc.

[September, 1639] The people had long desired a body of laws, and thought their condition very unsafe, while so much power rested in the discretion of magistrates. Divers attempts had been made at former courts, and the matter referred to some of the magistrates and some of the elders; but still it came to no effect; for, being committed to the care of many, whatsoever was done by some, was still disliked or neglected by others. At last it was referred to Mr. Cotton and Mr. Nathaniel Warde, etc., and each of them framed a model, which were presented to this general court, and by them committed to the governour and deputy and some others to consider of, and so prepare it for the court in the 3d month next. Two great reasons there were, which caused most of the magistrates and some of the elders not to be very forward in this matter. One was, want of sufficient experience of the nature and disposition of the people, considered with the condition of the country and other circumstances, which made them conceive, that such laws would be fittest for us, which should arise pro re nata upon occasions, etc., and so the laws of England and other states grew, and therefore the fundamental laws of England are called customs, consuetudines. 2. For that it would professedly transgress the limits of our charter, which provide, we shall made no laws repugnant to the laws of England, and that we were assured we must do. But to raise up laws by practice and custom had been no transgression; as in our church discipline, and in matters of marriage, to make a law, that marriages should not be solemnized by ministers, is repugnant to the laws of England; but to bring it to a custom by practice for the magistrates to perform it, is no law made repugnant, etc. At length (to satisfy the people) it proceeded, and the two models were digested with divers alterations and additions, and abbreviated and sent to every town, (12,) to be considered of first by the magistrates and elders, and then to be published by the constables to all the people, that if any man should think fit, that any thing therein ought to be altered, he might acquaint some of the deputies therewith against the next court.

[December 3, 1639] There were so many lectures now in the country, and many poor persons would usually resort to two or three in the week, to the great neglect of their affairs, and the damage of the public. The assemblies also were (in divers churches) held till night, and sometimes within the night, so as such as dwelt far off could not get home in due season, and many weak bodies could not endure so long, in the extremity of the heat or cold, without great trouble, and hazard of their health. Whereupon the general court ordered, that the elders should be desired to give a meeting to the magistrates and deputies, to consider about the length and frequency of church assemblies, and to make return to the court of their determinations, etc. This was taken in ill part by most of the elders and other of the churches, so as that those who should have met at Salem, did not meet, and those in the bay, when they met with the magistrates, etc., at Boston, expressed much dislike of such a course, alleging their tenderness of the church's liberties, (as if such a precedent might enthrall them to the civil power, and as if it would cast a blemish upon the elders, which would remain to posterity, that they should need to be regulated by the civil magistrate, and also raise an ill savour of the people's coldness, that would complain of much preaching, etc., —when as liberty for the ordinances was the main end (professed) of our coming hither). To which it was answered, 1. That the order was framed with as much tenderness and respect as might be in general words, without mentioning sermons or lectures, so as it might as well be taken for meetings upon other occasions of the churches, which were known to be very frequent. 2. It carried no command, but only an expression of a desire. 3. It concluded nothing, but only to confer and consider. 4. The record of such an order will be rather an argument of the zeal and forwardness of the elders and churches, as it was of the Israelites', when they offered so liberally to the service of the tabernacle, as Moses was forced to restrain them. Upon this interpretation of the court's intent, the elders were reasonably satisfied, and the magistrates finding how hardly such propositions would be digested, and that, if matters should be further pushed, it might make some breach, or disturbance at least, (for the elders had great power in the people's hearts, which was needful to be upheld, lest the people should break their bonds through abuse of liberty, which divers, having surfeited of, were very forward to incite others to raise mutinies and foment dangerous and groundless jealousies of the magistrates, etc., which the wisdom and care of the elders did still prevail against; and indeed the people themselves, generally, through the churches, were of that understanding and moderation, as they would easily be guided in their way by any rule from scripture or sound reason:) in this consideration, the magistrates and deputies, which were then met, thought it not fit to enter any dispute or conference with the elders about the number of lectures, or for appointing any certain time for the continuance of the assemblies, but rested satisfied with their affirmative answer to these two propositions: 1. That their church assemblies might ordinarily break up in such season, as people that dwell a mile or two off might get home by daylight. 2. That, if they were not satisfied in the declaration of our intentions in this order of court, that nothing was attempted herein against the church's liberties, etc., they would truly acquaint us with the reasons of their unsatisfiedness; or, if we heard not from them before the next court, we should take it for granted, that they were fully satisfied. They desired, that the order might be taken off the record: but for that it was answered, that it might not be done without consent of the general court; only it was agreed unto, that the secretary might defer to enter it in the book till the mind of the court might be known.

[October, 1640] The elders had moved at a general court before, that the distinction between the two jurisdictions might be set down, that the churches might know their power, and the civil magistrate his. The same had been moved by the magistrates formerly, and now at this court they presented a writing to that effect, to be considered by the court, wherein they declared that the civil magistrate should not proceed against a church member before the church had dealt with him, with some other restraints which the court did not allow of. So the matter was referred to further consideration, and it appeared, indeed, that divers of the elders did not agree in those points.

At this court Mr. Ezekiel Rogers, pastor of the church in

Rowley, being not kindly dealt with, nor justly, as he alleged, concerning the limits of their town, moved for further enlargement for taking in a neck of land upon Merrimack near Cochitawit, for which end they desired their line might run square from Ipswich line. This line was granted, and he said it should satisfy, but within an hour after it was discovered that he was mistaken, and that such a line would not reach the neck, whereupon he came again and confessed his mistake, and still demanded the neck. The court was very doubtful what to do in it, having formerly granted a plantation at Cochitawit, and did not yield his request. Whereupon he pleaded justice, upon some promises of large accommodations, etc., when we desired his sitting down with us, and grew into some passion, so as in departing from the court, he said he would acquaint the elders with it. This behaviour, being menacing, as it was taken, gave just cause of offence to the court, so as he was sent for, not by the officer, but by one of Rowley deputies. Before he came, he wrote to the governour, wherein he confessed his passionate distemper, declared his meaning in those offensive speeches, as that his meaning was that he would propound the case to the elders for advice only about the equity of it, which he still defended. This would not be accepted, but the court would have him appear and answer: only they left him to take his own time, so the next day he came, not accompanied with any other of the elders, though many were then in town, and did freely and humbly blame himself for his passionate distemper; and the court knowing that he would not yield from the justice of his cause, (as he apprehended it,) they would not put him upon any temptation, but accepted his satisfaction, and freely granted what he formerly desired.

[June, 1641] I must here return to supply what was omitted concerning the proceedings of the last court of elections. There had been much laboring to have Mr. Bellingham chosen, and when the votes were numbered he had six more than the others; but there were divers who had not given in their votes, who now came into the court and desired their liberty, which was denied by some of the magistrates, because they had not given them in at the doors. But others thought it was an injury, yet were silent, because it concerned themselves, for the order of giving in their votes at the door was no order of court, but only direction of some of the magistrates; and without question, if any freeman tender his vote before the election be passed and published, it ought to be received.

Some of the freemen, without the consent of the magistrates or governour, had chosen Mr. Nathaniel Ward to preach at this court, pretending that it was a part of their liberty. The governour (whose right indeed it is, for till the court be assembled the freemen are but private persons) would not strive about it, for though it did not belong to them, yet if they would have it, there was reason to yield it to them. Yet they had no great reason to choose him, though otherwise very able, seeing he had cast off his pastor's place at Ipswich, and was now no minister by the received determination of our churches. In his sermon he delivered many useful things, but in a moral and political discourse, grounding his propositions much upon the old Roman and Grecian governments, which sure is an error, for if religion and the word of God makes men wiser than their neighbors, and these times have the advantage of all that have gone before us in experience and observation, it is probable that by all these helps, we may better frame rules of government for ourselves than to receive others upon the bare authority of the wisdom, justice, etc. of those heathen commonwealths. Among other things, he advised the people to keep all their magistrates in an equal rank, and not give more honor or power to one than to another, which is easier to advise than to prove, seeing it is against the practice of Israel (where some were rulers of thousands, and some but of tens) and of all nations known or recorded. Another advice he gave, that magistrates should not give private advice, and take knowledge of any man's cause before it came to public hearing. This was debated after in the general court, where some of the deputies moved to have it ordered. But it was opposed by some of the magistrates upon these reasons: 1. Because we must then provide lawyers to direct men in their causes. 2. The magistrates must not grant out original process, as now they do, for to what end are they betrusted with this, but that they should take notice of the cause of the action, that they might either divert the suit, if the cause be unjust, or direct it in a right course, if it be good. 3. By this occasion the magistrate hath opportunity to end many differences in a friendly way, without charge to the parties, or trouble to the court. 4. It prevents many difficulties and tediousness to the court to understand the cause aright (no advocate being allowed, and the parties being not able, for the most part, to open the cause fully and clearly, especially in public). 5. It is allowed in criminal causes, and why not in civil. 6. Whereas it is objected that such magistrate is in danger to be prejudiced, answer, if the thing be lawful and useful, it must not be laid aside for the temptations which are incident to it, for in the least duties men are exposed to great temptations.

Mrs. Hutchinson and those of Aquiday island broached new heresies every year. Divers of them turned professed anabaptists, and would not wear any arms, and denied all magistracy among christians, and maintained that there were no churches since those founded by the apostles and evangelists, nor could any be, nor any pastors ordained, nor seals administered but by such, and that the church was to want these all the time she continued in the wilderness, as yet she was. Her son Francis and her son-in-law Mr. Collins (who was driven from Barbadoes where he had preached a time and done some good, but so soon as he came to her was infected with her heresies) came to Boston, and were there sent for to come before the governour and council. But they refused to come, except they were brought; so the officer led him, and being come (there were divers of the elders present) he was charged with a letter he had written to some in our jurisdiction, wherein he charged all our churches and ministers to be antichristian, and many other reproachful speeches, terming our king, king of Babylon, and sought to possess the people's hearts with evil thoughts of our government and of our churches, etc. He acknowledged the letter, and maintained what he had written, yet sought to evade by confessing there was a true magistracy in the world, and that christians must be subject to it. He maintained also that there were no gentile churches (as he termed them) since the apostles' times, and that none now could ordain ministers, etc. Francis Hutchinson did agree with him in some of these, but not resolutely in all; but he had reviled the church of Boston (being then a member of it) calling her a strumpet. They were both committed to prison; and it fell out that one Stoddard, being then one of the constables of Boston, was required to take Francis Hutchinson into his custody till the afternoon, and said withal to the governour, Sir, I came to observe what you did, that if you should proceed with a brother otherwise than you ought, I might deal with you in a church way. For this insolent behavior he was committed, but being dealt with by the elders and others, he came to see his error, which was that he did conceive that the magistrate ought not to deal with a member of the church before the church had proceeded with him. So the next Lord's day in the open assembly, he did freely and very affectionately confess his error and his contempt of authority, and being bound to appear at the next court, he did the like there to the satisfaction of all. Yet for example's sake he was fined 20*s*., which though some of the magistrates would have had it much less, or rather remitted, seeing his clear repentance and satisfaction in public left no poison or danger in his example, nor had the commonweath or any person sustained danger by it.

[December, 1641] This session continued three weeks, and established 100 laws, which were called the Body of Liberties. They had been composed by Mr. Nathaniel Ward, (sometime pastor of the church of Ipswich: he had been a minister in England, and formerly a student and practiser in the course of the common law,) and had been revised and altered by the court, and sent forth into every town to be further considered of, and now again in this court, they were revised, amended, and presented, and so established for three years, by that experience to have them fully amended and established to be perpetual.

Mr. Hathorn and some others were very earnest to have some certain penalty set upon lying, swearing, etc., which the deputy and some other of the magistrates opposed, (not disliking to have laws made against these or any other offences, but in respect of the certain punishment,) whereupon Mr. Hathorn charged him with seeking to have the government arbitrary, etc., and the matter grew to some heat, for the deputy[7] was a wise and a stout gentleman, and knew Mr. Hathorn his neighbor well, but the strife soon fell, and there was no more spoken of it that court. Yet this gave occasion to some of the magistrates to prepare some arguments against the course intended, of bringing all

[7]The deputy governor, John Endecott. [Ed.]

punishments to a certainty. The scope of these reasons was to make good this proposition, viz. All punishments, except such as are made certain in the law of God, or are not subject to variation by merit of circumstances, ought to be left arbitrary to the wisdom of the judges.

Reason 1. God hath left a pattern hereof in his word, where so few penalties are prescribed, and so many referred to the judges; and God himself varieth the punishments of the same offences, as the offences vary in their circumstances; as in manslaughter, in the case of a riotous son proving incorrigible, in the same sin aggravated by presumption, theft, etc., which are not only rules in these particular cases, but to guide the judges by proportion in all other cases: as upon the law of adultery, it may be a question whether Bathsheba ought to die by that law, in regard to the great temptation, and the command and power of the kings of Israel. So that which was capital in the men of Jabesh Gilead, Judges [*xxi. 10*] in not coming up to the princes upon proclamation, was but confiscation of goods, etc., in Ezra 10. 8. See 2d Sam. 14. 6. 11.

Reason 2. All punishments ought to be just, and, offences varying so much in their merit by occasion of circumstances, it would be unjust to inflict the same punishment upon the least as upon the greatest.

3. Justice requireth that every cause should be heard before it be judged, which cannot be when the sentence and punishment is determined before hand.

4. Such parts and gifts, as the word of God requires in a judge, were not so necessary, if all punishments were determined beforehand.

5. God hath not confined all wisdom, etc., to any one generation, that they should set rules for all others to walk by.

6. It is against reason that some men should better judge

of the merit of a cause in the bare theory thereof, than others (as wise and godly) should be able to discern of it pro re nata.

7. Difference of times, places, etc., may aggravate or extenuate some offences.

8. We must trust God, who can and will provide as wise and righteous judgment for his people in time to come, as in the present or forepassed times; and we should not attempt the limiting of his providence, and frustrating the gifts of others, by determining all punishments, etc.

Objection. In theft and some other cases, as cases capital, God hath prescribed a certain punishment.

Ans. 1. In theft, etc., the law respects the damage and injury of the party, which is still one and the same, though circumstances may aggravate or extenuate the sin. 2. In capital cases death is appointed as the highest degree of punishment which man's justice can reach.

Objection. Then we might as well leave all laws arbitrary at the discretion of the judge.

Ans. 1. The reason is not like. 1. God gave a certain law where he left the punishment arbitrary, so as we have a clear rule to guide the law where the punishment may be uncertain. The varying of the offence in the circumstances doth not vary the ground or equity of the law, nor the nature of the guilt, as it doth the measure of the reward. He is as fully guilty of theft who steals a loaf of bread for his hunger, as he that steals an horse for his pleasure.

Objection. The statutes in England set down a certain penalty for most offences.

Ans. 1. We are not bound to make such examples ourselves. 2. The penalty, commonly, is not so much as the least degree of that offence deserves: 12*d.* for an oath, 5*s.* for drunkenness, etc.

[May 10, 1643] Our court of elections was held, when Mr. Ezekiel Rogers, pastor of the church in Rowley, preached. He was called to it by a company of freemen, whereof the most were deputies chosen for the court, appointed, by order of the last court, to meet at Salem about nomination of some to be put to the vote for the new magistrates. Mr. Rogers, hearing what exception was taken to this call, as unwarrantable, wrote to the governour for advice, etc., who returned him answer: That he did account his calling not to be sufficient, yet the magistrates were not minded to strive with the deputies about it, but seeing it was noised in the country, and the people would expect him, and that he had advised with the magistrates about it, he wished him to go on. In his sermon he described how the man ought to be qualified whom they should choose for their governour, yet dissuaded them earnestly from choosing the same man twice together, and expressed his dislike of that with such vehemency as gave offence. But when it came to trial, the former governour, Mr. Winthrop, was chosen again, and two new magistrates, Mr. William Hibbins and Mr. Samuel Simons.

[March 21, 1643–4] At the same court in the first month, upon the motion of the deputies, it was ordered that the court should be divided in their consultations, the magistrates by themselves, and the deputies by themselves, what the one agreed upon they should send to the other, and if both agreed, then to pass, etc. This order determined the great contention about the negative voice.

[June, 1644] At this court there arose some troubles by this occasion. Those of Essex had procured at the court before, that the deputies of the several shires should meet before this court to prepare business, etc., which accordingly they did, and propounded divers things which they agitated and concluded among themselves, without communicating them to the other shires, who conceived they had been only such things as had concerned the commonwealth, but when they came now to be put to this court, it appeared that their chief intent was to advantage their own shire. As, 1. By drawing the government thither. 2. By drawing the courts thither. 3. By drawing a good part of the country stock thither. 4. By procuring four of those parts to be joined in commission with the magistrates. And for this end they had made so strong a party among the deputies of the smaller towns (being most of them mean men, and such as had small understanding in affairs of state) as they easily carried all these among the deputies. But when the two bills came to the magistrates, they discerning the plot, and finding them hurtful to the commonwealth, refused to pass them, and a committee of both being appointed to consider the reasons of both sides, those of the magistrates prevailed.

But the great difference was about a commission, which the deputies sent up, whereby power was given to seven of the magistrates and three of the deputies and Mr. Ward (some time pastor of Ipswich, and still a preacher) to order all affairs of the commonwealth in the vacancy of the general court, which the magistrates returned with this answer: That they conceived such commission did tend to the overthrow of the foundation of our government, and of the freemen's liberty, and therefore desired the deputies to consider of a way how this danger might be avoided, and the liberty of the freemen preserved inviolable, otherwise they could not comfortably proceed in other affairs.

Upon this return all the deputies came to confer with the magistrates. The exceptions the magistrates took were these. 1. That this court should create general officers which the freemen had reserved to the court of elections.

2. That they should put out four of the magistrates from that power and trust which the freemen had committed to them. 3. At the commission itself, seeing they ought not to accept that power by commission which did belong to them by the patent and by their election. They had little to answer to this, yet they alleged a precedent or two where this court had ordered some of the magistrates and some others to be a council of war, and that we had varied from our patent in some other things, and therefore were not bound to it in this.

But they chiefly stood upon this, that the governour and assistants had no power out of court but what was given them by the general court. To this the magistrates replied: 1. That such examples as were against rules or common right were errors and no precedents. 2. That council was for one particular case only, and not of general extent. 3. In those things wherein we had varied from our patent we did not touch the foundation of our government. To the last it was said, that the governour and assistants had power of government before we had any written laws or had kept any courts; and to make a man a governour over a people, gives him, by necessary consequence, power to govern that people, otherwise there were no power in any commonwealth to order, dispose, or punish in any case where it might fall out, that there were no positive law declared in.

It was consented to that this court had authority to order and direct the power of these magistrates for time, place, persons, etc., for the common good, but not wholly to deprive them of it, their office continuing: so as these being chosen by the people, by virtue of the patent to govern the people, a chief part whereof consists in counsel, they are the standing council of the commonwealth, and therefore in the vacancy of this court, may act in all the affairs thereof without any commission.

Upon this they withdrew, and after a few hours came again, and then they tendered a commission for war only, and none of the magistrates to be left out. But the magistrates refused to accept of any commission, but they would consent the same should pass by order so as the true power of the magistrates might be declared in it: or to a commission of association, to add three or four others to the magistrates in that council: or to continue the court a week longer, and send for the elders to take their advice in it; but none of these would be accepted. But they then moved, that we would consent that nothing might be done till the court met again, which was before agreed to be adjourned to the 28th of (8). To this was answered, that, if occasion required, they must act according to the power and trust committed to them; to which their speaker replied—You will not be obeyed.

[May, 1644] A fourth matter then in consideration was upon a speech, which the governour[8] made to this effect, viz. 1. That he could not but bewail the great differences and jarrings which were upon all occasions, among the magistrates, and between them and the deputies; that the ground of this was jealousies and misreports; and thereupon some elders siding, etc., but not dealing with any of them in a way of God; but hearing them reproached and passing it in silence: also their authority questioned, as if they had none out of court but what must be granted them by commission from the general court, etc.,—and the way to redress hereof was, that the place and power of magistrates and deputies might be known; and so the elders were desired (which they willingly assented to) to be mediators of a thorough reconciliation, and to go about it presently, and to meet at Boston two or three days before

[8]John Endecott. [Ed.]

the next court to perfect the same. But indeed the magistrates did all agree very well together, except two only, viz., Mr. Bellingham and Mr. Saltonstall, who took part with the deputies against the other ten magistrates about their power, and in other cases where any difference was. And some of the elders had done no good offices in this matter, through their misapprehensions both of the intentions of the magistrates, and also of the matters themselves, being affairs of state, which did not belong to their calling.

[Oct. 30, 1644] The general court assembled again, and all the elders were sent for, to reconcile the differences between the magistrates and deputies. When they were come, the first question put to them was that which was stated by consent the last session, viz.

Whether the magistrates are, by patent and election of the people, the standing council of this commonwealth in the vacancy of the general court, and have power accordingly to act in all cases subject to government, according to the said patent and the laws of this jurisdiction; and when any necessary occasions call for action from authority, in cases where there is no particular express law provided, there to be guided by the word of God, till the general court give particular rules in such cases.

The elders, having received the question, withdrew themselves for consultation about it, and the next day sent to know, when we would appoint a time that they might attend the court with their answer. The magistrates and deputies agreed upon an hour, but the deputies came not all, but sent a committee of four (which was not well, nor respectively, that when all the elders had taken so much pains at their request, some having come thirty miles, they would not vouchsafe their presence to receive their answer). Their answer was affirmative on the magistrates' behalf, in the very words of the question, with some reasons thereof. It was delivered in writing by Mr. Cotton in the name of them all, they being all present, and not one dissentient.

Upon the return of this answer, the deputies prepared other questions to be propounded to the elders, and sent them to the magistrates to take view of. Likewise the magistrates prepared four questions, and sent them also to the deputies.

The magistrates' questions, with the elders' answers, were:—

1. Whether the deputies in the general court have judicial and magistratical authority?

2. Whether by patent the general court, consisting of magistrates and deputies, (as a general court) have judicial and magistratical authority?

3. Whether we may warrantably prescribe certain penalties to offences, which may probably admit variable degrees of guilt?

4. Whether a judge be bound to pronounce such sentence as a positive law prescribes, in case it be apparently above or beneath the merit of the offence?

The elders answer to the two first.

1. The patent, in express words, giveth full power and authority, as to the governour and assistants, so to the freemen also assembled in general court.

2. Whereas there is a threefold power of magistratical authority, viz., legislative, judicial, and consultative or directive of the public affairs of the country for provision and protection. The first of these, viz., legislative is expressly given to the freemen, jointly with the governour and assistants. Consultative or directive power, etc., is also granted by the patent as the other. But now for power of judicature, (if we speak of the constant and usual administration thereof,) we do not find that it is granted to the

freemen, or deputies, in the general court, either by the patent, or the elections of the people, or by any law of the country. But if we speak of the occassional administration thereof, we find power of judicature administrable by the freemen, jointly with the governour and assistants upon a double occasion. 1, In case of defect or delinquency of a magistrate, the whole court, consisting, etc., may remove him. 2, If by the law of the country there lie any appeal to the general court, or any special causes be reserved to their judgment, it will necessarily infer, that, in such cases, by such laws, the freemen, jointly with the governour and assistants, have power of judicature, touching the appellant's cause of appeal and those reserved cases. What we speak of the power of freemen by patent, the same may be said of the deputies, so far forth as the power of the freemen is delegated to them by order of law.

To the third and fourth questions the elders answer.

1. Certain penalties may and ought to be prescribed to capital crimes, although they may admit variable degrees of guilt; as in case of murder upon prepensed malice, and upon sudden provocation, there is prescribed the same death in both, though murder upon prepensed malice be of a far greater guilt than upon sudden provocation, Numb. 35. 16. 18 with 20. 21. Also in crimes of less guilt, as in theft, though some theft may be of greater guilt than other, (as for some man to steal a sheep, who hath less need, is of greater guilt, than for another, who hath more need,) the Lord prescribed the same measure of restitution to both.

2. In case that variable circumstances of an offence do so much vary the degrees of guilt, as that the offence is raised to an higher nature, there the penalty must be varied to an higher answerable proportion. The striking of a neighbor may be punished with some pecuniary mulct, when the striking of a father may be punished with death. So any sin committed with an high hand, as the gathering of

sticks on the Sabbath day, may be punished with death, when a lesser punishment may serve for gathering sticks privily, and in some need.

3. In case circumstances do so vary a sin, as that many sins are complicated or wrapped up in it, the penalty is to be varied, according to the penalties of those several sins. A single lie may be punished with a less mulct, than if it be told before the judgment seat, or elsewhere, to the damage of any person, whether in his good name, by slander, or in his estate, by detriment in his commerce; in which case, a lie aggravated by circumstances is to be punished with respect both to a lie and to a slander and to the detriment which another sustaineth thereby.

4. In case that the circumstances, which vary the degrees of guilt, concern only the person of the offender, (as whether it were the first offence, or customary, whether he were enticed thereto, or the enticer, whether he were principal or accessory, whether unadvised, or witting or willing, etc.) there it were meet the penalty should be expressed with a latitude, whereof the lowest degree to be expressed (suppose five shillings, or, as the case may be, five stripes) and the highest degree, twenty shillings or, etc., or stripes more or less; within which compass or latitude it may be free to a magistrate to aggravate or mitigate the penalty, etc. Yet even here also care would be taken, that a magistrate attend, in his sentence, as much as may be, to a certain rule in these circumstances, lest some persons, whose sins be alike circumstanced with others, if their punishment be not equal, etc., may think themselves more unequally dealt withal than others.

5. In those cases wherein the judge is persuaded in conscience, that a crime deserveth a greater punishment than the law inflicteth, he may lawfully pronounce sentence according to the prescript penalty, etc., because he hath no power committed to him by law to go higher. But

where the law may seem to the conscience of the judge to inflict a greater penalty than the offence deserveth, it is his part to suspend his sentence, till by conference with the lawgivers, he find liberty, either to inflict the sentence, or to mitigate it.

6. The penalties of great crimes may sometimes be mitigated by such as are in chief power, out of respect to the public good service which the delinquent hath done to the state in former times, as Solomon did by Abiathar, 1 Kings 2. 26. 27.

Questions propounded to the elders by the deputies.

1. Whether the governour and assistants have any power by patent to dispense justice in the vacancy of the general court, without some law or order of the same to declare the rule?

The elders' answer was negative; and further, they conceived it meet, the rule should be express for the regulating of all particulars, as far as may be, and where such cannot be had, to be supplied by general rules.

2. Quest. Whether any general court hath not power by patent, in particular cases, to choose any commissioners, (either assistants or freemen,) exempting all others, to give them commission, to set forth their power and places? By "any particular case" we mean in all things, and in the choice of all officers, that the commonwealth stands in need of between election and election; not taking away the people's liberty in elections, nor turning out any officer so elected by them, without showing cause.

The elders answer.

1. If the terms, "all things," imply or intend all cases of constant judicature and counsel, we answer negatively, etc., because then it would follow, that the magistrates might be excluded from all cases of constant judicature and counsel, which are their principal work, whereby also the end of the people's election would be made frustrate.

2. But if these terms, "all things," imply or intend cases (whether occasional or others) belonging neither to constant judicature nor counsel, we answer affirmatively, etc., which yet we understand with this distinction, viz., that if the affairs committed to such officers and commissioners be of general concernment, we conceive the freemen, according to patent, are to choose them, the general court to set forth their power and places; but if they be of merely particular concernment, then we conceive the general court may choose them, and set forth their power and places. Whereas we give cases of constant judicature and council to the magistrates, we thus interpret the word "counsel." Counsel consists of care and action. In respect of care, the magistrates are not limited; in respect of action, they are to be limited by the general court, or by the supreme council. Finally, it is our humble request, that in case any difference grow in the general court, between magistrates and deputies, either in these, or any like weighty cases, which cannot be presently issued with mutual peace, that both parties will be pleased to defer the same to further deliberation for the honor of God and of the court.

Upon other propositions made by the deputies, the elders gave this further answer, viz.

That the general court, consisting of magistrates and deputies, is the chief civil power of this commonwealth, and may act in all things belonging to such a power, both concerning counsel, in consulting about the weighty affairs of the commonwealth, and concerning making of laws, also concerning judicatures, in orderly impeaching, removing, and sentencing any officers, even the highest, according to law, likewise in receiving appeals, whether touching civil or criminal causes, wherein appeals are or shall be allowed by the general court; provided that all such appeals proceed orderly from an inferior court to the court of assistants, and from thence to the general court; or if the case were first depending in the court of assistants, then to proceed from thence to the general court, in all such cases as are appealable, "as in cases judged evidently against law, or in cases "wherein the subject is sentenced to banishment, loss of "limb, or life, without an express law, or in cases weighty "and difficult, (not admitting small matters, the pursuit "whereof would be more burdensome to the court and "country, than behoveful to the appellant, nor needlessly "interrupting the ordinary course of justice in the court of "assistants, or other inferior courts;) provided also, that if it "do appear, that the appeal proceed not out of regard of "right, but from delay of justice, or out of contention, that "a due and just punishment be by law ordained, and in-"flicted upon such appellant."

That no magistrate hath power to vary from the penalty of any law, etc., without consulting with the general court.

3. Quest. Whether the titles of governour, deputy, and assistants do necessarily imply magistratical authority, in the patent?

The elders' answer was affirmative.

4. Quest. Whether the magistratical power be not given by the patent to the people or general court, and by them to the governour, etc.

The elders answer, the magistratical power is given to the governour, etc., by the patent. To the people is given, by the same patent, to design the persons to those places of government; and to the general court power is given to make laws, as the rules of their administration.

These resolutions of the elders were after put to vote, and were allowed to be received, except those in the last page marked in the margin thus, " ". Most of the deputies were now well satisfied concerning the authority of the magistrates, etc., but some few leading men (who had drawn on the rest) were still fixed upon their own opinions. So hard a matter it is, to draw men (even wise and godly) from the love of the fruit of their own inventions.

There fell out at this court another occasion of further trouble. The deputy governour[9] having formerly, and from time to time, opposed the deputies' claim of judicial authority, and the prescribing of set penalties in cases which may admit variable degrees of guilt, which occasioned them to suspect, that he, and some others of the magistrates, did affect an arbitrary government, he now wrote a small treatise about these points, showing what arbitrary government was, and that our government (in the state it now stood) was not arbitrary, neither in the ground and foundation of it, nor in the exercise and administration thereof. And because it is of public, and (for the most part) of general concernment, and being a subject not formerly handled by any that I have met with, so as it may be of use to stir up some of more experience and more able parts to bestow their pains herein, I have therefore made bold to set down the whole discourse, with the proceedings which happened about it, in a treatise by itself, with some small alterations and additions (not in the substance of the matter) for clearer evidence of the question. And I must apologize this to the reader, that I do not condemn all prescript penalties, although the argument seem to hold forth so much, but only so far as they cross with the rules of justice, and prudence, and mercy; also, in such cases of smaller concernment, as wherein there may be lawful liberty allowed to judges to use admonition, or to respite an offender to further trial of reformation, etc.

[May, 1645] I suppose something may be expected from me, upon this charge that is befallen me, which moves me

[9]Winthrop. [Ed.]

to speak now to you; yet I intend not to intermeddle in the proceedings of the court, or with any of the persons concerned therein [10] Only I bless God, that I see an issue of this troublesome business. I also acknowledge the justice of the court, and, for mine own part, I am well satisfied, I was publicly charged, and I am publicly and legally acquitted, which is all I did expect or desire. And though this be sufficient for my justification before men, yet not so before the God, who hath seen so much amiss in my dispensations (and even in this affair) as calls me to be humble. For to be publicly and criminally charged in this court, is matter of humiliation, (and I desire to make a right use of it,) notwithstanding I be thus acquitted. If her father had spit in her face, (saith the Lord concerning Miriam,) should she not have been ashamed seven days? Shame had lien upon her, whatever the occasion had been. I am unwilling to stay you from your urgent affairs, yet give me leave (upon this special occasion) to speak a little more to this assembly. It may be of some good use, to inform and rectify the judgments of some of the people, and may prevent such distempers as have arisen amongst us. The great questions that have troubled the country, are about the authority of the magistrates and the liberty of the people. It is yourselves who have called us to this office, and being called by you, we have our authority from God, in way of an ordinance, such as hath the image of God eminently stamped upon it, the contempt and violation whereof hath been vindicated with examples of divine vengeance. I entreat you to consider, that when you choose magistrates, you take them from among yourselves, men subject to like

[10]Winthrop, at this time deputy governor, had been describing a long and complicated dispute relating to the militia officers of the town of Hingham. Accused of acting arbitrarily, he had left his seat among the magistrates to plead his cause before the court and be judged. Upon his acquittal he delivered this "little speech." [Ed.]

passions as you are. Therefore when you see infirmities in us, you should reflect upon your own, and that would make you bear the more with us, and not be severe censurers of the failings of your magistrates, when you have continual experience of the like infirmities in yourselves and others. We account him a good servant, who breaks not his covenant. The covenant between you and us is the oath you have taken of us, which is to this purpose, that we shall govern you and judge your causes by the rules of God's laws and our own, according to our best skill. When you agree with a workman to build you a ship or house, etc., he undertakes as well for his skill as for his faithfulness, for it is his profession, and you pay him for both. But when you call one to be a magistrate, he doth not profess nor undertake to have sufficient skill for that office, nor can you furnish him with gifts, etc., therefore you must run the hazard of his skill and ability. But if he fail in faithfulness, which by his oath he is bound unto, that he must answer for. If it fall out that the case be clear to common apprehension, and the rule clear also, if he transgress here, the error is not in the skill, but in the evil of the will: it must be required of him. But if the case be doubtful, or the rule doubtful, to men of such understanding and parts as your magistrates are, if your magistrates should err here, yourselves must bear it.

For the other point concerning liberty, I observe a great mistake in the country about that. There is a twofold liberty, natural (I mean as our nature is now corrupt) and civil or federal. The first is common to man with beasts and other creatures. By this, man, as he stands in relation to man simply, hath liberty to do what he lists; it is a liberty to evil as well as to good. This liberty is incompatible and inconsistent with authority, and cannot endure the least restraint of the most just authority. The exercise and maintaining of this liberty makes men grow more evil, and in time to be worse than brute beasts: omnes sumus licentia deteriores. This is that great enemy of truth and peace, that wild beast, which all the ordinances of God are bent against, to restrain and subdue it. The other kind of liberty I call civil or federal, it may also be termed moral, in reference to the covenant between God and man, in the moral law, and the politic covenants and constitutions, amongst men themselves. This liberty is the proper end and object of authority, and cannot subsist without it; and it is a liberty to that only which is good, just, and honest. This liberty you are to stand for, with the hazard (not only of your goods, but) of your lives, if need be. Whatsoever crosseth this, is not authority, but a distemper thereof. This liberty is maintained and exercised in a way of subjection to authority; it is of the same kind of liberty wherewith Christ hath made us free. The woman's own choice makes such a man her husband; yet being so chosen, he is her lord, and she is to be subject to him, yet in a way of liberty, not of bondage; and a true wife accounts her subjection her honor and freedom, and would not think her condition safe and free, but in her subjection to her husband's authority. Such is the liberty of the church under the authority of Christ, her king and husband; his yoke is so easy and sweet to her as a bride's ornaments; and if through frowardness or wantonness, etc., she shake it off, at any time, she is at no rest in her spirit, until she take it up again; and whether her lord smiles upon her, and embraceth her in his arms, or whether he frowns, or rebukes, or smites her, she apprehends the sweetness of his love in all, and is refreshed, supported, and instructed by every such dispensation of his authority over her. On the other side, ye know who they are that complain of this yoke and say, let us break their bands, etc., we will not have this man to rule over us. Even so, brethren, it will be between you and your magistrates. If you stand for your natural corrupt liberties, and will do what is good in your own eyes, you will not endure the least weight of authority, but will murmur, and oppose, and be always striving to shake off that yoke; but if you will be satisfied to enjoy such civil and lawful liberties, such as Christ allows you, then will you quietly and cheerfully submit unto that authority which is set over you, in all the administrations of it, for your good. Wherein, if we fail at any time, we hope we shall be willing (by God's assistance) to hearken to good advice from any of you, or in any other way of God; so shall your liberties be preserved, in upholding the honor and power of authority amongst you.

The deputy governour having ended his speech, the court arose, and the magistrates and deputies retired to attend their other affairs. Many things were observable in the agitation and proceedings about this case. It may be of use to leave a memorial of some of the most material, that our posterity and others may behold the workings of satan to ruin the colonies and churches of Christ in New England, and into what distempers a wise and godly people may fall in times of temptation; and when such have entertained some false and plausible principles, what deformed superstructures they will raise thereupon, and with what unreasonable obstinacy they will maintain them.

Some of the deputies had seriously conceived, that the magistrates affected an arbitrary government, and that they had (or sought to have) an unlimited power to do what they pleased without control, and that, for this end, they did strive so much to keep their negative power in the general court. This caused them to interpret all the magistrates' actions and speeches (not complying exactly with their own principles) as tending that way, by which occasions their fears and jealousies increased daily. For prevention whereof they judged it not unlawful to use even extrema remedia, as if salus populi had been now the transcendant rule to walk by, and that magistracy must be no other, in effect, than a ministerial office, and all authority, both legislative, consultative, and judicial, must be exercised by the people in their body representative. Hereupon they labored, equis et velis, to take away the negative vote. Failing of that, they pleaded that the magistrates had no power out of the general court, but what must be derived from the general court; and so they would have put upon them commissions, for what was to be done in the vacancy of the general court, and some of themselves to be joined with the magistrates, and some of the magistrates left out. This not being yielded unto, recourse was had to the elders for advice, and the case stated, with incredible wariness; but the elders casting the cause against them, (as is before declared,) they yet believed, (or at least would that others should,) that the elders' advice was as much for them in their sense as for the magistrates, (and if it were, they had no cause to shun the advice of the elders, as they have seemed to do ever since). This project not prevailing, the next is, for such a body of laws, with prescript penalties in all cases, as nothing might be left to the discretion of the magistrates, (while in the mean time there is no fear of any danger in reserving a liberty for their own discretion in every case,) many laws are agreed upon, some are not assented unto by the magistrates not finding them just. Then is it given out, that the magistrates would have no laws, etc. This gave occasion to the deputy governour to write that treatise about arbitrary government, which he first tendered to the deputies in a model, and finding it approved by some, and silence in others, he drew it up more at large, and having advised with most of the magistrates and elders about it, he intended to have presented it orderly to the court. But to prevent that, the first day of the court, the deputies had gotten a copy, which was presently read amongst them as a dangerous libel of some unknown author, and a committee was presently appointed to examine it, many false and dangerous things were collected out of it, all agreed and voted by them, and sent up to the magistrates for their assent, not seeming all this time to take any notice of the author, nor once moving to have his answer about it, for they feared that his place in the council would have excused him from censure, as well as the like had done Mr. Saltonstall for his book against the standing council not long before. But if they could have prevailed to have had the book censured, this would have weakened his reputation with the people; and so if one of their opposite had been removed, it would somewhat have facilitated their way to what they intended; but this not succeeding as they expected, they kept it in deposito till some fitter season. In this time divers occasions falling out, wherein the magistrates had to do in the vacancy of the general court, as the French business, the seizure of the Bristol ship by Captain Stagg, and of the Dartmouth ship by ourselves, as is before related, and other affairs, they would still declare their judgments contrary to the magistrates' practice; and if the event did not answer the counsel, (though it had been interrupted by themselves or others,) there needed no other ground to condemn the counsel; all which tended still to weaken the authority of the magistrates, and their reputation with the people.

[October 29, 1645] There came hither to Boston at the same time out of England one Captain Partridge, who had served the parliament, but in the ship he broached and zealously maintained divers points of antinomianism and familism, for which he was called before the magistrates and charged with the said opinions, to which he refused to give any answer. But before he departed, he was willing to confer with Mr. Cotton, which accordingly he did, and Mr. Cotton reported to the magistrates, that he found him corrupt in his judgment, but ignorant of those points which he had maintained, so as he perceived he had been but lately taken with them, and that upon argument he was come off from some of the worst of them, and he had good hope to reclaim him wholly; but some of the magistrates requiring a present renouncing of all under his hand, he the said captain was not willing to that before he were clearly convinced of his error in them. It was moved by some of the magistrates, in regard he had made so hopeful a beginning, and that winter was now at hand, and it would be very hard to expose his wife and family to such hardships, etc., to permit him to stay here till the spring, but the major part (by one or two) voting the contrary, he was forced to depart, and so went to Rhode Island. This strictness was offensive to many, though approved of by others. But sure the rule of hospitality to strangers, and of seeking to pluck out of the fire such as there may be hope of to be reduced out of error and the snare of the devil, do seem to require more moderation and indulgence of human infirmity where there appears not obstinacy against the clear truth.

---

7. JOHN WINTHROP ON RESTRICTION OF IMMIGRATION

In 1637, Anne Hutchinson was banished from Massachusetts because of her "antinomian" claim to a direct revelation from God. During the controversy that preceded the sentence against her, the General Court became alarmed

---

From *Winthrop Papers,* III, 422–426. Reprinted with the permission of the Massachusetts Historical Society.

that persons of similar belief might come to the colony from England. To forestall such a development, the Court passed an order forbidding anyone to entertain strangers for more than three weeks without consent of some of the magistrates (i.e., the governor, deputy governor, and assistants). The order aroused such controversy that Winthrop was moved to write the following defense of it. Here one may see that the idea of a covenant or social contract could be put to conservative, as well as radical uses.

A DECLARATION IN DEFENSE OF AN ORDER OF COURT MADE IN MAY, 1637

A Declaration of the Intent and Equitye of the Order made at the last Court, to this effect, that none should be received to inhabite within this Jurisdiction but such as should be allowed by some of the Magistrates

For clearing of such scruples as have arisen about this order, it is to be considered, first, what is the essentiall forme of a common weale or body politic such as this is, which I conceive to be this—The consent of a certaine companie of people, to cohabite together, under one government for their mutual safety and welfare.

In this description all these things doe concurre to the well being of such a body, 1 Persons, 2 Place, 3 Consent, 4 Government or Order, 5 Wellfare.

It is clearely agreed, by all, that the care of safety and wellfare was the original cause or occasion of common weales and of many familyes subjecting themselves to rulers and laws; for no man hath lawfull power over another, but by birth or consent, so likewise, by the law of proprietye, no man can have just interest in that which belongeth to another, without his consent.

From the premises will arise these conclusions.

1. No common weale can be founded but by free consent.

2. The persons so incorporating have a public and relative interest each in other, and in the place of their cohabitation and goods, and laws etc. and in all the means of their wellfare so as none other can claime priviledge with them but by free consent.

3. The nature of such an incorporation tyes every member thereof to seeke out and entertaine all means that may conduce to the wellfare of the bodye, and to keepe off whatsoever doth appeare to tend to theire damage.

4. The wellfare of the whole is [not] to be put to apparent hazard for the advantage of any particular members.

From these conclusions I thus reason.

1. If we heere be a corporation established by free consent, if the place of our cohabitation be our owne, then no man hath right to come into us etc. without our consent.

2. If no man hath right to our lands, our government priviledges etc., but by our consent, then it is reason we should take notice of before we conferre any such upon them.

3. If we are bound to keepe off whatsoever appears to tend to our ruine or damage, then we may lawfully refuse to receive such whose dispositions suite not with ours and whose society (we know) will be hurtfull to us, and therefore it is lawfull to take knowledge of all men before we receive them.

4. The churches take liberty (as lawfully they may) to receive or reject at their discretion; yea particular towns make orders to the like effect; why then should the common weale be denied the like liberty, and the whole more restrained than any parte?

5. If it be sinne in us to deny some men place etc. amongst us, then it is because of some right they have to this place etc. for to deny a man that which he hath no right unto, is neither sinne nor injury.

6. If strangers have right to our houses or lands etc., then it is either of justice or of mercye; if of justice let them plead it, and we shall know what to answer: but if it be only in way of mercye, or by the rule of hospitality etc., then I answer 1st a man is not a fit object of mercye except he be in miserye. 2d. We are not bound to exercise mercye to others to the ruine of ourselves. 3d. There are few that stand in neede of mercye at their first coming hither. As for hospitality, that rule doth not bind further than for some present occasion, not for continual residence.

7. A family is a little common wealth, and a common wealth is a greate family. Now as a family is not bound to entertaine all comers, no not every good man (otherwise than by way of hospitality) no more is a common wealth.

8. It is a generall received rule, *turpius ejicitur quam non admittitur hospes,* it is worse to receive a man whom we must cast out againe, than to denye him admittance.

9. The rule of the Apostle, John 2. 10. is, that such as come and bring not the true doctrine with them should not be received to house, and by the same reason not into the common weale.

10. Seeing it must be granted that there may come such persons (suppose Jesuits etc.) which by consent of all ought to be rejected, it will follow that by this law (being only for notice to be taken of all that come to us, without which we cannot avoyd such as indeed are to be kept out) is no other but just and needfull, and if any should be rejected that ought to be received, that is not to be imputed to the law, but to those who are betrusted with the execution of it. And herein is to be considered, what the intent of the law is, and by consequence, by what rule they

are to walke, who are betrusted with the keeping of it. The intent of the law is to preserve the wellfare of the body; and for this ende to have none received into any fellowship with it who are likely to disturbe the same, and this intent (I am sure) is lawful and good. Now then, if such to whom the keeping of this law is committed, be persuaded in theire judgments that such a man is likely to disturbe and hinder the publick weale, but some others who are not in the same trust, judge otherwise, yet they are to follow their owne judgments, rather than the judgments of others who are not alike interested: As in tryall of an offender by jury; the twelve men are satisfied in their consciences, upon the evidence given, that the party deserves death: but there are 20 or 40 standers by, who conceive otherwise, yet is the jury bound to condemn him according to their owne consciences, and not to acquit him upon the different opinion of other men, except theire reasons can convince them of the errour of their consciences, and this is according to the rule of the Apostle. Rom. 14. 5. Let every man be fully persuaded in his own mynde.

If it be objected, that some prophane persons are received and others who are religious are rejected, I answer 1st, It is not knowne that any such thinge has as yet fallen out. 2. Such a practice may be justifiable as the case may be, for younger persons (even prophane ones) may be of lesse danger to the common weale (and to the churches also) than some older persons, though professors of religion: for our Saviour Christ when he conversed with publicans etc. sayeth that such were nearer the Kingdom of heaven than the religious pharisees, and one that is of large parts and confirmed in some erroneous way, is likely to doe more harme to church and common weale, and is of lesse hope to be reclaymed, than 10 prophane persons, who have not yet become hardened, in the contempt of the meanes of grace.

Lastly, Whereas it is objected that by this law, we reject good christians and so consequently Christ himselfe: I answer 1st. It is not knowne that any christian man hath been rejected. 2. a man that is a true christian, may be denyed residence among us, in some cases, without rejecting Christ, as admitt a true christian should come over, and should maintain community of goods, or that magistrates ought not to punish the breakers of the first table, or the members of churches for criminal offences: or that no man were bound to be subject to those lawes or magistrates to which they should not give an explicite consent, etc. I hope no man will say, that not to receive such an one were to reject Christ; for such opinions (though being maintained in simple ignorance, they might stand with a state of grace yet) they may be so dangerous to the publick weale in many respects, as it would be our sinne and unfaithfullness to receive such among us, except it were for tryall of theire reformation. I would demand then in the case in question (for it is bootlesse curiosity to refrayne openesse in things publick) whereas it is sayd that this law was made of purpose to keepe away such as are of Mr. Wheelwright his judgment (admitt it were so which yet I cannot confesse) where is the evill of it? If we conceive and finde by sadd experience that his opinions are such, as by his own profession cannot stand with externall peace, may we not provide for our peace, by keeping of [f] such as would strengthen him and infect others with such dangerous tenets? and if we finde his opinions such as will cause divisions, and make people looke at their magistrates, ministers and brethren as enemies to Christ and Antichrists etc., were it not sinne and unfaithfullness in us, to receive more of those opinions, which we already finde the evill fruite of: Nay, why doe not those who now complayne joyne with us in keeping out of such, as well as formerly they did in expelling Mr. Williams for the like, though lesse dangerous? Where this change of theire judgments should arise I leave them to themselves to examine, and I earnestly entreat them so to doe, and for this law let the equally mynded judge, what evill they finde in it, or in the practice of those who are betrusted with the execution if it (*ca.* June, 1637).

---

8. JOHN WINTHROP ON ARBITRARY GOVERNMENT

With the adoption of the Body of Liberties in 1641, the deputies had achieved specific guarantees against infringement of popular rights, but they wished to see fixed penalties prescribed for all offenses. Winthrop, still devoted to the Christian equity described by William Perkins (see this volume, Document 4), believed that the magistrate should have a wide discretion in applying the law. In 1644 Winthrop set forth his views under circumstances described in his journal entry for October 30, 1644 (see this volume, Document 6). The following passage is from the treatise referred to there.

. . . Justice ought to render to every man accordinge to his deservinge, eye for eye, hand for hande etc: and Luk: 12: 47: the servant, who transgressed against knowledge was to be beaten with more stripes then he who trans-

---

From *Winthrop Papers*, IV, 468–482. Reprinted with the permission of the Massachusetts Historical Society.

gressed of Ignorance: If we had a Lawe, that every lye should be punished 40*s* and 2 offendors should be Convicte at the same tyme: the one a youthe of Honest Conversation, never known to lye before: and now suddainly surprized, with feare of some discredit, had tould a lye, wherin was no danger of harme to any other: The other, an olde notorious lyer: and his lye contrived of purpose, for a pernitious ende: It were not Juste, to punish both these alike: As 40*s* were too little for the one, soe it were too muche for the other. Besides penaltyes (we knowe) comminge of pœna, should cause paine or greife to the offenders. It must be an Affliction: yet not a destruction, except in Capitall, or other haynous Crimes: but in prescript penaltyes Aut[horit]ye shoots at adventure: if the same penalty hitts a Riche man, it paines him not, it is no Affliction to him, but if it lights upon a poore man, it breakes his backe.

Everye Lawe must be Just in everye parte of it, but if the penaltye annexed be unjust, how can it be held forthe as a Just Lawe? To prescribe a penaltye, must be by some Rule, otherwise, it is an usurpation of Gods prerogative: but where the Lawe makers, or Declarers canot finde a Rule for prescribinge a penaltye, if it come before the Judges pro re nata, there it is determinable by a certaine Rule, viz: by an ordinance sett up of God for that purpose, which hathe a sure promise of divine Assistance, Exo: 21: 22, Deut: 16: 18: Judges and Officers shalt thou make etc: and they shall Judge the people with Just Judgment: Deut: 25: 1: 2: and 17: 9: 10: 11. If a Lawe were made that if any man were found drunken he should be punished by the Judges accordinge to the meritt of his offence: this is a just Lawe, because it is warranted by a Rule: but if a certaine penaltye were prescribed, this would not be just, because it wants a Rule, but when suche a Case is brought before the Judges, and the qualitye of the person and other circumstances considered, they shall finde a Rule to Judge by; as if Naball, and Uriah, and one of the stronge drunkards of Ephraim were all 3 togither accused before the Judges for drunkennesse, they could so proportion their severall sentences, accordinge to the severall natures and degrees of their offences, as a Just and divine sentence might appeare in them all: for a divine sentence is in the lipps of the Kinge his mouth transgresseth not in Judgment Pro: 16: but no suche promise was ever made to a paper Sentence of humane Aut[horit]ye or Invention. He who hathe promised his servants to teach them what to Answeare, even in that houer, when they shalbe brought before Judgments seats, etc: will allso teach his ministers the Judges, what sentence to pronounce, if they will allso observe his worde, and trust in him. Care not for the morrowe etc. is a Rule of generall extent, to all Cases where our providence may either crosse with some Rule or Ordinance of his, or may occasion us to relye more upon our owne strengthe and meanes, then upon his grace and blessing. In the sentence which Solomon gave betweene the 2 Harlotts: 1: Kings: 3: 28, It is sayd All Israell heard of the Judgment which the Kinge had Judged: and they feared the Kinge, for they sawe that the wisedome of God was in him to doe Judgment. see heer, how the wisdome of God was glorified, and the Aut[horit]ye of the Judge strengthned, by this sentence: whereas in mens prescript sentences, neither of these can be attained, but if the Sentence hitt right, all is ascribed to the wisdome of our Ancestors, if otherwise, it is endured as a necessary evill, since it may not be altered.

Prescript penaltyes take away the use of Admonition, which is allso a divine sentence and an Ordinance of God, warranted by Scripture: as appeares in Solomons Admonition to Adonijah and Nehemiahs to those that brake the Sabbaoth: Eccl: 12: 11: 12: The Words of the wise are as goads, and as nayles fastened by the masters of Assemblys—by these (my sonne) be admonished, Pro: 29: 1: Isay. 11: 4: Pro. 17: 10: A Reproofe entereth more into a wise man, then 100 stripes into a foole.

Judges are Gods upon earthe: therefore, in their Administrations, they are to holde forthe the wisdome and mercye of God, (which are his Attributes) as well as his Justice: as occasion shall require, either in respecte of the qualitye of the person, or for a more generall good: or evident repentance, in some cases of less publ[ic] consequence, or avoydinge imminent danger to the state, and such like prevalent Considerations. Exo: 22: 8: 9: for thefte and other like Trespasses, double restitution was appointed by the Lawe: but Lev: 6: 2: 5: in such cases, if the partye Confessed his sinne, and brought his offeringe, he should onely restore the principall, and adde a fifthe parte thereto. Adultery and incest deserved deathe, by the Lawe, in Jacobs tyme (as appeares by Juda his sentence, in the case of Thamar): yet Ruben was punished onely with losse of his Birthright, because he was a Patriark. David his life was not taken awaye for his Adulterye and murder, (but he was otherwise punished) in respect of publ[ic] interest and advantage, he was valued at 10000 common men: Bathsheba was not putt to deathe for her Adulterye, because the Kinges desire, had with her, the force of a Lawe. Abiathar was not putt to deathe for his Treason, because of his former good service and faithfullnesse. Shemei was Reprived for a tyme, and had his pardon in his owne power, because of his profession of Repentance in such a season. Those which brake the Sabbaothe in Nehemiah his tyme, were not putt to deathe but first admonished, because the state was not setled etc. Joab was not putt to deathe for his murders, in Davids tyme, for avoydinge imminent publ[ic] danger, the sonnes of Zeruiah had the advantage of David, by their interest in the men of Warre: and the Com[mon] w[ealth] could not yet spare them. But if Judges be tyed to a prescript punishment, and no libertye lefte for dispensation or mitigation in any Case, heer is no place lefte for wisdome or mercye: whereas Sol[omon] saythe Pro: 20: 28: mercy and trueth preserve the Kinge; and his Throne is upholden by mercye.

I would knowe by what Rule we may take upon us, to prescribe penaltyes, where God prescribes none. If it be Answ: from Gods example, I must Replye 1: God prescribes none except Capitall, but onely in suche Cases as are betweene party and party, and that is rather in a waye of satisfaction to the partye wronged, then to Justice and intention. 2. Gods examples are not warrants for us, to goe against Gods Rules; our Rule is to give a Just Sentence, which we cant doe (in most Cases) before the Offence is committed etc. 5*s* now may be more than 20*s* heerafter and e contra. if examples in Scripture be warrant for us to proceed against Rule, then we may passe by Murders, Adulteryes, Idolatryes, etc: without Capitall punishments: then we might putt the Children to deathe for parents offences etc:

If we should enq[uire] allso of the ende of prescribing penaltyes, it can be no other but this, to prevent oppression of the people, by unjust Sentences; and then I am again to seeke of a Rule, to weaken the power and Justice of an Ordinance of God, through distrust of his providence: and promise of Assistance in his owne Ordinance: who must give the Lawe makers wisdome etc. to prescribe sentences? must not God? and may we not then trust him, to give as muche wisdome etc: to suche Judges, as he shall sett up after us? it is said when they had Judges by Gods appointment, God was with the Judge. so may we still believe, that if our posterity shall choose Judges accordinge to God, he wilbe with our Judges in tyme to come, as well as with the present.

It may be further demanded, what power we have over

the persons and estates of the succeedinge generations? If we should now prescribe, where our posteritye etc. should dwell, what quantityes of land they should till: what places they should tende unto: what diet they should use, what Clothes they should weare etc: by what Rule could we challenge this power? yet we have example for some of these in Scripture, as of Jonadab the sonne of Rechab: etc: but no man will take these as warrant for us to laye suche injunctions upon those which come after us, because they are to have the same interest, and freedome in their estates and persons that we have in ours.

And for preventinge of oppression, etc: is there no waye to helpe that, but by breache of Rule? shall we runne into manifest injustice, for feare of I know not what future danger of it? is there not a cleare waye of helpe in suche cases, by Appeal, or Petition, to the highest Aut[horit] ye? If this will not releive, in a partic[ular] case, we shall then be in a very ill Case, for all our prescript penaltyes. Besides, there may be such a generall Lawe made (as in magna Charta) that may prevent the overthrowinge of mens estates, or lands, etc: by Fines, etc: (and I think it as needfull, as any Lawe or Libertye we have) whereby the Judges may be restrayned, within certaine limitts, which (if occasion should require to exceede) may be referred to the Generall Court. And in Corp[ora]l punishments, a Libertye in suche and suche Cases, to redeeme them at a certaine rate: This would sufficiently assure the proper persons and estates, from any great oppression, if withall, our Courts of Judicature, were kept but by 3 or 5 magistrates at most, which may well be ordered, without any deviation from our Patent. and so the greater number of magistrates should be free from ingagement in any Case, which might come to a review upon Appeal or Petition.

It is an error so to conceive of Lawes, as if they could not be perfecte without penaltyes annexed, for they are as truely distinct as light and darknesse: Lawe was Created with and in man, and so is naturall to him: but penaltye is positive and accidentall. Lawe is bonum simpliciter, but poena is simpliciter malum in subjecto: therefore Lawes may be declared and given, without any penaltyes annexed.

Isay. 10: 1: Woe to them that Decree unrighteous Decrees: and write greivousnesse, which they have prescribed: so that where the penaltye proves greiveous by the unrighteousnesse of a prescript Decree, it will drawe a woe after it, as well as unrighteous sentence: Deut: 25: 15: thou shalt have a perfect and a just weight and measure: If God be so stricte in Commutative Justice, that every Acte therein must be by a just and perfecte Rule, what warrant have we, to thinke that we maye dispence distributive or vindictive Justice to our brethren by gesse, when we prescribe a certaine measure to an incertaine meritt.

But it wilbe objected: volenti non fit iniuria: the people givinge us power to make lawes to binde them, they doe implicitly give their Consent to them. To this it may be Answeared: that where they putt themselves into our power to binde them to Lawes and penalties, they can intende no other but suche as are just and righteous: and althoughe their implicit Consent may binde them to outward obedience, yet it neither tyes them to satisfaction, nor frees suche Lawmakers from unrighteousnesse, nor the Law it self from injustice; nor will suche a Lawe be a sufficient warrant to the Conscience of the Judge, to pronounce suche a sentence, as he knowes to be apparently disproportionable to the offence brought before him.

Althoughe my Arguments conclude against prescript penaltyes indefinitely, yet I doe not deny but, they may be lawfull in some Cases: for an universall affirmative proposition may be true, though it comprehend not every partic[ular], as when we say All the Country was Rated to such a charge, no man will conceive that everye person and every woman etc, was rated; and when we saye suche an one was cast out by the wholl churche, this is a true speeche (to common intendment) though every partic[ular] member did not consent. Where any penalty may be prescribed by a Rule, so as the Judge may pronounce a Just sentence, I have formerly, and shall still joyne in it.

We will now Answeare such objections, as are made, against the libertye required to be lefte to Judges, in their Sentences.

1 ob: Judges are subject to Temptations, if their sentences be not prescribed.

Answ. 1: We may not transgresse Rules, to avoyde Temptations: for God will have his servants exercised with temptations, that the power of his grace may be made manifest in mans Infirmitye: A master will not sende his servant about his businesse in a darke night, to avoyde Temptations of ill companye or the like, which he may possibly meet with in the daye tyme: nor will any Christian man take in his Corne or haye before it be readye, for avoyding a Temptation of takinge it in upon the Sabbaothe: we doe not forbidd wine to be brought to us, though we knowe it is a great occasion of Temptation to sinne.

2: Those, who make Lawes, and prescribe penaltyes, are also men subjecte to Temptations: and may allso miscarrye through Ignorance, heedlessnesse, or sinister respects: and it is not hard, to prove, that the Lawe makers, in all States, have Committed more and more pernitious errors then the Judges: as 40 tymes greater then the law of God [*illegible*] and [*illegible*] as much [*illegible*] to the ruin of a mans estate [*illegible*] and there is good reason for it: 1: they supposinge themselves tyed to no Rule, nor lyable to any accompt, are in the more danger of being misledd: 2: he who prescribes a punishment in a Case, wherein no person stands before him to be judged, cannot be so warye of sheddinge innocent blood, or sparinge a guilty person, or committinge other injustice, as the Judge who hathe the person and Cause before him: when Saule prescribed that Capitall sentence against suche as should tast ought before night if Jonathans case had then been before him, he would have Judged otherwise. Dangers more remote are ever lesse heeded. 3: Lawe makers have not so cleare a Callinge, in prescribinge penaltyes, as Judges have in passinge sentences, and therefore, there cannot be expected the like blessinge of Assistance from God. Judges are necessarylye tyed to give sentence in a Cause before them but Lawe makers are not so bounde to prescribe sentences.

3: If a Judge should sometymes erre in his Sentence, through misprision, or Temptation: the error or fault is his owne: and the injurye or damage extends not farr: but an error in the Lawe, resteth upon the Ordinance it selfe, and the hurte of it may reache far, even to posteritye. there is more unrighteousnesse, and dishonor, in one unjust Lawe, then in many unjust Sentences.

2 ob: God prescribed some certaine penaltyes: and that in Cases where offences doe usually vary in their degree and meritt:

Answ: 1: We have shewed before how God might doe it, in regard of his absolute soveraintye.

2: It is no Injustice in him, because the least degree of the smalest offence, (before his Judgment seate) deserves the highest degree of punishment.

3: In some of these (as in Thefte) he variethe the punishment according to the measure and nature of the offence. In others as deathe, perpetuall servitude, etc: beinge the Just Reward of suche offences in their simple nature, they have not a fitt Subjecte, for an increace of punishment to take place upon: he who is putt to deathe for Adulterye, cannot dye againe for Incest concurringe therewith and he who is adjudged to perpetuall servitude for stealinge 100*li* cannot be capeable of a further sentence for batterye.

4: In all, or most of those Offences, the penaltye was in waye of satisfaction, to such as were damnified thereby and in such cases, Justice will not allowe a Judge any Libertye to alter or remitt any thinge: nor can any circumstance leade to qualification: a Riche man hath the same right to satisfaction for his goods stollen from him, as a poore man: and the poorest mans life is the life of man, as well as a Princes:

5: These Presedents were given to the Judges, not with direction to prescribe penaltyes to other Lawes that had none: but with Commandment to give Judgement in all Cases, by the equitye of these: (there are some formes of prayer and sermons in scripture, but this dothe not prove ergo all etc.)

3 ob: If the determination of the Lawe were lefte to the Judges, that were Arbitrary Government: and is it not in reason the same, if the punishment of the Transgression of the Lawe, be committed to them?

Answ: The Reason is not alike in bothe Cases.

1: The determination of Lawe belonges properly to God: he is the onely Lawgiver: but he hathe given power and gifts to men to interprett his Lawes: and this belonges principally to the highest Aut[horit]ye in a Com[mon] W[ealth] and subordinately to other magistrates and Judges accordinge to their severall places.

2: The Lawe is allwayes the same, and not changeable by any circumstances of aggravation, or extenuation, as the penaltye is: and therefore drawes a certaine guilt upon every Transgressor whither he sinne of Ignorance, or against Knowledge, or presumptuously: and therefore Lawes or the Interpretation of them, may be prescribed, without any danger, because no event can alter the Reason, or Justice of them: as it may of punishments.

3: The Lawe is more generall and lyeth as a burden, upon all persons and at all tymes: but the penaltye reaches to none, but transgressors and to suche, onely when they are brought under sentence, and not before.

4: It is needfull that all men should knowe the Lawes, and their true meaninges, because they are bound to them, and the safety and wellfare of the Com[mon] W[ealth] consists in the observation of them: therefore it is needfull they should be stated and declared, as soone as is possible; but there is not the like necessitye or use of declaringe their penaltyes before hande, for they who are godly and vertuous, will observe them, for Conscience, and Vertues sake: and for suche as must be helde in by feare of punishment, it is better they should be kept in feare of a greater punishment then to take libertye to transgresse, through the Contempt of a smaller.

4 ob: It is safe for the Com[mon] W[ealth] to have penaltyes prescribed, because we know not what magistrates or Judges we may have heerafter.

Answ: 1: God foresawe, that there would be corrupt Judges in Israell, yet he lefte most penaltyes, to their determination.

2: There is no wisdome of any State can so provide, but that in many thinges of greatest concernment, they must confide in some men: and so it is in all humane Affaires: the wisest merchants, and the most warye, are forced to repose great trust in the wisdome and faithfullnesse of their servants, Factors, masters of their Shipps, etc. All States, in their generalls of warre, Admiralls, Embassadors, Treasurers, etc: and these are Causes of more publ[ic] Consequence, then the Sentence of a Judge in matters of misdemeanor, or other smaler offences.

3: When we have provided against all common, and

probable events, we may and ought to trust God for safety from suche dangers, as are onely possible, but not likely, to come upon us: especially when our strivinge to prevent suche possible dangers, may hazard the deprivation, or weakninge of a present good; or may drawe those, or other evills, neerer upon us.

This discourse is runne out to more length then was intended: the Conclusion is this: The Goverment of the Massachusetts consists of Magistrates and Freemen: in the one is placed the Aut[horit]ye, in the other the Libertye of the Com[mon] W[ealth] either hath power to Acte, both alone, and both togither, yet by a distinct power, the one of Libertye, the other of Aut[horit]ye: the Freemen Act of them selves in Electinge their magistrates and Officers: the magistrates Acte alone in all occurrences out of Court: and both Acte togither in the Generall Court: yet all limited by certaine Rules, bothe in the greater and smaller affaires: so as the Government is Regular in a mixt Aristocratie, and no waye Arbitrary.

---

9. JOHN COTTON ON CHURCH AND STATE

John Cotton (1584–1652) a graduate of Trinity College, Cambridge University, had already earned a reputation as minister of Boston (Lincolnshire), England, when he crossed the ocean to become minister of Boston, Massachusetts. There, in spite of some initial disagreements with other ministers over theological questions, he came to be regarded as one of the principal spokesmen of New England

---

From Thomas Hutchinson, *The History of the Colony of Massachusett's Bay* (London: M. Richardson, 2nd ed., 1765), pp. 490–501.

Puritanism. When a number of English noblemen with Puritan leanings proposed to settle in Massachusetts, provided that the colony revamp the government to their liking, Cotton was deputed to answer them. He did so, after consulting other leading New Englanders, and sent the answer with an accompanying letter to Lord Say and Seal (one of the noblemen). Both documents are included here.

The reader may note that Cotton's rejection of democracy and defense of theocracy are based on definitions of those words quite different from the ones in general use today. The Standing Council to which he refers, of which the members were elected for life, was an abortive institution that was never given significant powers. The "negative voyce" for freemen on the one hand and for governor and assistants on the other, eventuated in the splitting of the General Court of Massachusetts into a bicameral legislature in 1644.

CERTAIN PROPOSALS MADE BY LORD SAY, LORD BROOKE, AND OTHER PERSONS OF QUALITY, AS CONDITIONS OF THEIR REMOVING TO NEW-ENGLAND, WITH THE ANSWERS THERETO.

DEMAND 1. That the common-wealth should consist of two distinct ranks of men, whereof the one should be for them and their heirs, gentlemen of the country, the other for them and their heirs, freeholders.

ANSWER. Two distinct ranks we willingly acknowledge, from the light of nature and scripture; the one of them called Princes, or Nobles, or Elders (amongst whom gentlemen have their place) the other the people. Hereditary dignity or honours we willingly allow to the former, unless by the scandalous and base conversation of any of them, they become degenerate. Hereditary liberty, or estate of freemen, we willingly allow to the other, unless they also, by some unworthy and slavish carriage, do disfranchize themselves.

DEM. 2. That in these gentlemen and freeholders, assembled together, the chief power of the common-wealth shall be placed, both for making and repealing laws.

ANS. So it is with us.

DEM. 3. That each of these two ranks should, in all public assemblies, have a negative voice, so as without a mutual consent nothing should be established.

ANS. So it is agreed among us.

DEM. 4. That the first rank, consisting of gentlemen, should have power, for them and their heirs, to come to the parliaments or public assemblies, and there to give their free votes personally; the second rank of freeholders should have the same power for them and their heirs of meeting and voting, but by their deputies.

ANS. Thus far this demand is practised among us. The freemen meet and vote by their deputies; the other rank give their votes personally, only with this difference, there be no more of the gentlemen that give their votes personally, but such as are chosen to places of office, either governors, deputy governors, councellors, or assistants. All gentlemen in England have not that honour to meet and vote personally in Parliament, much less all their heirs. But of this more fully, in an answer to the ninth and tenth demand.

DEM. 5. That for facilitating and dispatch of business,

and other reasons, the gentlemen and freeholders should sit and hold their meetings in two distinct houses.

ANS. We willingly approve the motion, only as yet it is not so practised among us, but in time, the variety and discrepancy of sundry occurrences will put them upon a necessity of sitting apart.

DEM. 6. That there shall be set times for these meetings, annually or half yearly, or as shall be thought fit by common consent, which meetings should have a set time for their continuance, but should be adjourned or broken off at the discretion of both houses.

ANS. Public meetings, in general courts, are by charter appointed to be quarterly, which, in this infancy of the colony, wherein many things frequently occur which need settling, hath been of good use, but when things are more fully settled in due order, it is likely that yearly or half yearly meetings will be sufficient. For the continuance or breaking up of these courts, nothing is done but with the joint consent of both branches.

DEM. 7. That it shall be in the power of this parliament, thus constituted and assembled, to call the governor and all publick officers to account, to create new officers, and to determine them already set up: and, the better to stop the way to insolence and ambition, it may be ordered that all offices and fees of office shall, every parliament, determine, unless they be new confirmed the last day of every session.

ANS. This power to call governors and all officers to account, and to create new and determine the old, is settled already in the general court or parliament, only it is not put forth but once in the year, viz. at the great and general court in May, when the governor is chosen.

DEM. 8. That the governor shall ever be chosen out of the rank of gentlemen.

ANS. We never practice otherwise, chusing the governor either out of the assistants, which is our ordinary course, or out of approved known gentlemen, as this year[1] Mr. Vane.

DEM. 9. That, for the present, the Right Honorable the Lord Viscount Say and Seale, the Lord Brooke, who have already been at great disbursements for the public works in New-England, and such other gentlemen of approved sincerity and worth, as they, before their personal remove, shall take into their number, should be admitted for them and their heirs, gentlemen of the country. But, for the future, none shall be admitted into this rank but by the consent of both houses.

ANS. The great disbursements of these noble personages and worthy gentlemen we thankfully acknowledge, because the safety and presence of our brethren at Connecticut is no small blessing and comfort to us. But, though that charge had never been disbursed, the worth of the honorable persons named is so well known to all, and our need of such supports and guides is so sensible to ourselves, that we do not doubt the country would thankfully accept it, as a singular favor from God and from them, if he should bow their hearts to come into this wilderness and help us. As for accepting them and their heirs into the number of gentlemen of the country, the custom of this country is, and readily would be, to receive and acknowledge, not only all such eminent persons as themselves and the gentlemen they speak of, but others of meaner estate, so be it is of some eminency, to be for them and their heirs, gentlemen of the country. Only, thus standeth our case. Though we receive them with honor and allow them pre-eminence and accommodations according to their condition, yet we do not, ordinarily, call them forth to the power of election, or administration of magistracy, until they be received as members into some of our churches, a privilege, which we doubt not religious gentlemen will

[1] 1636.

willingly desire (as David did in Psal. xxvii. 4.) and christian churches will as readily impart to such desirable persons. Hereditary honors both nature and scripture doth acknowledge (Eccles. xix. 17.) but hereditary authority and power standeth only by the civil laws of some commonwealths, and yet, even amongst them, the authority and power of the father is no where communicated, together with his honors, unto all his posterity. Where God blesseth any branch of any noble or generous family, with a spirit and gifts fit for government, it would be a taking of God's name in vain to put such a talent under a bushel, and a sin against the honor of magistracy to neglect such in our public elections. But if God should not delight to furnish some of their posterity with gifts fit for magistracy, we should expose them rather to reproach and prejudice, and the commonwealth with them, than exalt them to honor, if we should call them forth, when God doth not, to public authority.

DEM. 10. That the rank of freeholders shall be made up of such, as shall have so much personal estate there, as shall be thought fit for men of that condition, and have contributed, some fit proportion, to the public charge of the country, either by their disbursements or labors.

ANS. We must confess our ordinary practice to be otherwise. For, excepting the old planters, i.e. Mr. Humphry, who himself was admitted an assistant at London, and all of them freemen, before the churches here were established, none are admitted freemen of this commonwealth but such as are first admitted members of some church or other in this country, and, of such, none are excluded from the liberty of freemen. And out of such only, I mean the more eminent sort of such, it is that our magistrates are chosen. Both which points we should willingly persuade our people to change, if we could make it appear to them, that such a change might be made according to God; for, to give you a true account of the grounds of our proceedings herein, it seemeth to them, and also to us, to be a divine ordinance (and moral) that none should be appointed and chosen by the people of God, magistrates over them, but men fearing God (Ex. xviii. 21.) chosen out of their brethren (Deut. xvii. 15.) saints (1 Cor. vi. 1.) Yea, the apostle maketh it a shame to the church, if it be not able to afford wise men from out of themselves, which shall be able to judge all civil matters between their brethren (ver. 5.) And Solomon maketh it the joy of a commonwealth, when the righteous are in authority, and the calamity thereof, when the wicked bear rule. Prov. xxix. 2.

OBJ. If it be said, there may be many carnal men whom God hath invested with sundry eminent gifts of wisdom, courage, justice, fit for government.

ANS. Such may be fit to be consulted with and employed by governors, according to the quality and use of their gifts and parts, but yet are men not fit to be trusted with place of standing power or settled authority. Ahitophel's wisdom may be fit to be heard (as an oracle of God) but not fit to be trusted with power of settled magistracy, lest he at last call for 12000 men to lead them forth against David, 2 Sam. xvii. 1, 2, 3. The best gifts and parts, under a covenant of works (under which all carnal men and hypocrites be) will at length turn aside by crooked ways, to depart from God, and, finally, to fight against God, and are therefore, herein, opposed to good men and upright in heart, Psal. cxxv. 4, 5.

OBJ. If it be said again, that then the church estate could not be compatible with any commonwealth under heaven.

ANS. It is one thing for the church or members of the church, loyally to submit unto any form of government, when it is above their calling to reform it, another thing to chuse a form of government and governors discrepant from the rule. Now, if it be a divine truth, that none are to be trusted with public permanent authority but godly men, who are fit materials for church fellowship, then from the same grounds it will appear, that none are so fit to be trusted with the liberties of the commonwealth as church members. For, the liberties of the freemen of this commonwealth are such, as require men of faithful integrity to God and the state, to preserve the same. Their liberties, among others, are chiefly these. 1. To chuse all magistrates, and to call them to account at their general courts. 2. To chuse such burgesses, every general court, as with the magistrates shall make or repeal all laws. Now both these liberties are such, as carry along much power with them, either to establish or subvert the commonwealth, and therewith the church, which power, if it be committed to men not according to their godliness, which maketh them fit for church fellowship, but according to their wealth, which, as such, makes them no better than worldly men, then, in case worldly men should prove the major part, as soon they might do, they would as readily set over us magistrates like themselves, such as might hate us according to the curse, Levit. xxvi. 17. and turn the edge of all authority and laws against the church and the members thereof, the maintenance of whose peace is the chief end which God aimed at in the institution of Magistracy. 1 Tim. ii. 1. 2.

COPY OF A LETTER FROM MR. COTTON TO LORD SAY AND SEAL IN THE YEAR 1636.

RIGHT HONOURABLE,

What your Lordship writeth of Dr. Twisse his works *de scientiâ mediâ*, and of the sabbath, it did refresh me to reade, that his labors of such arguments were like to come to light; and it would refresh me much more to see them here: though (for my owne particular) till I gett some release from some constant labors here (which the church is desirous to procure) I can get litle, or noe oppertunity to reade any thing, or attend to any thing, but the dayly occurrences which presse in upon me continually, much beyond my strength either of body or minde. Your Lordships advertisement touching the civill state of this colony, as they doe breath forth your singular wisdome, and faithfulness, and tender care of the peace, so wee have noe reason to misinterprite, or undervalue your Lordships eyther directions, or intentions therein. I know noe man under heaven (I speake in Gods feare without flattery) whose counsell I should rather depend upon, for the wise administration of a civill state according to God, than upon your Lordship, and such confidence have I (not in you) but in the Lords presence in Christ with you, that I should never feare to betrust a greater commonwealth than this (as much as in us lyeth) under such a *perpetuâ dictaturâ* as your Lordship should prescribe. For I nothing doubt, but that eyther your Lordship would prescribe all things according to the rule, or be willing to examine againe, and againe, all things according to it. I am very apt to believe, what Mr. Perkins hath, in one of his prefatory pages to his golden chaine, that the word, and scriptures of God doe conteyne a short *upoluposis*, or platforme, not onely of theology, but also of other sacred sciences, (as he calleth them) attendants, and handmaids thereunto, which he maketh ethicks, eoconomicks, politicks, church-government, prophecy, academy. It is very suitable to Gods all-sufficient wisdome, and to the fulnes and perfection of Holy Scriptures, not only to prescribe perfect rules for the right ordering of a private mans soule to everlasting blessednes with himselfe, but also for the right ordering of a mans family, yea, of the commonwealth too, so farre as both of them are subordinate to spiritual ends, and yet avoide both the churches usurpation upon civill jurisdictions, *in ordine ad spiritualia,* and the commonwealths invasion upon ecclesiasticall administrations, *in ordine* to civill peace, and conformity to the civill state. Gods institutions (such as the government of church and of commonwealth be) may be close and compact, and co-ordinate one to another, and yet not confounded. God hath so framed the state of church government and ordinances, that they may be compatible to any common-wealth, though never so much disordered in his frame. But yet when a commonwealth hath liberty to mould his owne frame (*scripturæ plenitudinem adoro*) I conceyve the scripture hath given full direction for the right ordering of the same, and that, in such sort as may best mainteyne the *euexia* of the church. Mr. Hooker doth often quote a saying out of Mr. Cartwright (though I have not read it in him) that noe man fashioneth his house to his hangings, but his hangings to his house. It is better that the commonwealth be fashioned to the setting forth of Gods house, which is his church: than to accommodate the church frame to the civill state. Democracy, I do not conceyve that ever God did ordeyne as a fitt government eyther for church or commonwealth. If the people be governors, who shall be governed? As for monarchy, and aristocracy, they are both of them clearely approoved, and directed in scripture, yet so as referreth the soveraigntie to himselfe, and setteth up Theocracy in both, as the best forme of government in the commonwealth, as well as in the church.

The law, which your Lordship instanceth in [that none shall be chosen to magistracy among us but a church member] was made and enacted before I came into the country; but I have hitherto wanted sufficient light to plead against it. 1st. The rule that directeth the choice of supreame governors, is of like aequitie and weight in all magistrates, that one of their brethren (not a stranger) should be set over them, Deut. 17. 15. and Jethroes counsell to Moses was approved of God, that the judges, and officers to be set over the people, should be men fearing God, Exod. 18. 21. and Solomon maketh it the joy of a commonwealth, when the righteous are in authority, and their mourning when the wicked rule, Prov. 29. 21. Jab 34. 30. Your Lordship's feare, that this will bring in papal excommunication, is just, and pious: but let your Lordship be pleased againe to consider whether the consequence be necessary. *Turpius ejicitur quam non admittitur:* non-membership may be a just cause of non-admission to the place of magistracy, but yet, ejection out of his membership will not be a just cause of ejecting him out of his magistracy. A godly woman, being to make choice of an husband, may justly refuse a man that is eyther cast out of church fellowship, or is not yet receyved into it, but yet, when shee is once given to him, shee may not reject him then, for such defect. Mr. Humfrey was chosen for an assistant (as I heare) before the colony came over hither: and, though he be not as yet joyned into church fellowship (by reason of the unsetlednes of the congregation where he liveth) yet the commonwealth doe still continue his magistracy to him, as knowing he waiteth for oppertunity of enjoying church fellowship shortly.

When your Lordship doubteth, that this corse will draw all things under the determination of the church, *in ordine ad spiritualia* (seeing the church is to determine who shall be members, and none but a member may have to doe in the government of a commonwealth) be pleased (I pray you) to conceyve, that magistrates are neyther chosen to office in the church, nor doe governe by directions from the church, but by civill lawes, and those enacted in generall corts, and executed in corts of justice, by the governors and assistants. In all which, the church (as the church) hath nothing to doe: onely, it prepareth fitt instruments both to rule, and to choose rulers, which is no ambition in the church, nor dishonor to the commonwealth, the apostle, on the contrary, thought it a great dishonor and reproach to the church of Christ, if it were not able to yield able judges to heare and determine all causes amongst their brethren, 1 Cor. 6. 1. to 5. which place alone seemeth to me fully to decide this question: for it plainely holdeth forth this argument: It is a shame to the church to want able judges of civill matters (as v. 5.) and an audacious act in any church member voluntarily to go for judgment, otherwhere than before the saints (as v. 1.) then it will be noe arrogance nor folly in church members, nor prejudice to the commonwealth, if voluntarily they never choose any civill judges, but from amongst the saints, such as church members are called to be. But the former is cleare: and how then can the latter be avoyded. If this therefore be (as your Lordship rightly conceyveth one of the maine objections if not the onely one) which hindereth this commonwealth from the entertainment of the propositions of those worthy gentlemen, wee intreate them, in the name of the Lord Jesus, to consider, in meeknes of wisdome, it is not any conceite or will of ours, but the holy counsell and will of the Lord Jesus (whom they seeke to serve as well as wee) that overruleth us in this case: and we trust will overrule them also, that the Lord onely may be exalted amongst all his servants. What pittie and griefe were it, that the observance of the will of Christ should hinder good things from us!

But your Lordship doubteth, that if such a rule were necessary, then the church estate and the best ordered commonwealth in the world were not compatible. But let not our Lordship so conceyve. For, the church submitteth itselfe to all the lawes and ordinances of men, in what commonwealth soever they come to dwell. But it is one thing, to submit unto what they have noe calling to reforme: another thing, voluntarily to ordeyne a forme of government, which to the best discerning of many of us (for I speake not of myselfe) is expressly contrary to rule. Nor neede your Lordship feare (which yet I speake with submission to your Lordships better judgment) that this corse will lay such a foundation, as nothing but a mere democracy can be built upon it. Bodine confesseth, that though it be *status popularis*, where a people choose their owne governors; yet the government is not a democracy, if it be administred, not by the people, but by the governors, whether one (for then it is a monarchy, though elective) or by many, for then (as you know) it is aristocracy. In which respect it is, that church government is justly denyed (even by Mr. Robinson) to be democratical, though the people choose their owne officers and rulers.

Nor neede wee feare, that this course will, in time, cast the commonwealth into distractions, and popular confusions. For (under correction) these three things doe not undermine, but doe mutually and strongly mainteyne one another (even those three which wee principally aime at) authority in magistrates, liberty in people, purity in the church. Purity, preserved in the church, will preserve well ordered liberty in the people, and both of them establish well-ballanced authority in the magistrates. God is the author of all these three, and neyther is himselfe the God of confusion, nor are his wayes the wayes of confusion, but of peace.

What our brethren (magistrates or ministers, or leading freeholders) will answer to the rest of the propositions, I shall better understand before the gentlemans returne from Connecticutt, who brought them over. Mean while two of the principall of them, the generall cort hath already condescended unto. 1. In establishing a standing councell, who, during their lives, should assist the governor in managing the chiefest affayres of this little state. They have chosen, for the present, onely two (Mr. Winthrope and Mr.

Dudley) not willing to choose more, till they see what further better choyse the Lord will send over to them, that so they may keep an open doore, for such desireable gentlemen as your Lordship mentioneth. 2. They have graunted the governor and assistants a negative voyce, and reserved to the freemen the like liberty also. Touching other things, I hope to give your Lordship further account, when the gentleman returneth.

He being now returned, I have delivered to him an answer to the rest of your demands, according to the mindes of such leading men amongst us, as I thought meete to consult withall, concealing your name from any, except 2 or 3, who alike doe concurr in a joynt desire of yeilding to any such propositions, as your Lordship demandeth, so farre as with allowance from the word they may, beyond which I know your Lordship would not require any thing.

Now the Lord Jesus Christ (the prince of peace) keepe and bless your Lordship, and dispose of all your times and talents to his best advantage: and let the covenant of his grace and peace rest upon your honourable family and posterity throughout all generations.

Thus, humbly craving pardon for my boldnesse and length, I take leave and rest,

Your Honours to serve in Christ Jesus,

J. C.

---

10. JOHN COTTON ON LIMITATION OF GOVERNMENT

John Cotton was a conservative in politics—he once argued that magistrates should enjoy a lifetime tenure

---

From John Cotton, *An Exposition upon the Thirteenth Chapter of the Revelation* (London: Livewel Chapman, 1655), pp. 71–73.

—but he held no brief for arbitrary government. In the following passage from a set of sermons explaining a part of the Apocalypse (not published until after his death) he spells out the importance of setting limits on rulers.

. . . This may serve to teach us the danger of allowing to any mortall man an inordinate measure of power to speak great things, to allow to any man uncontrollableness of speech, you see the desperate danger of it: Let all the world learn to give mortall men no greater power then they are content they shall use, for use it they will: and unlesse they be better taught of God, they will use it ever and anon, it may be make it the passage of their proceeding to speake what they will: And they that have liberty to speak great things, you will finde it to be true, they will speak great blasphemies. No man would think what desperate deceit and wickednesse there is in the hearts of men: And that was the reason why the Beast did speak such great things, hee might speak, and no body might controll him: What, saith the Lord in *Jer.* 3. 5. *Thou hast spoken and done evill things as thou couldst.* If a Church or head of a Church could have done worse, he would have done it: This is one of the straines of nature, it affects boundlesse liberty, and to runne to the utmost extent: What ever power he hath received, he hath a corrupt nature that will improve it in one thing or other; if he have liberty, he will think why may he not use it. Set up the Pope as Lord Paramount over Kings and Princes, and they shall know that he hath power over them, he will take liberty to depose one, and set up another. Give him power to make Laws, and he will approve, and disprove as he list; what he approves is Canonicall, what hee disproves is rejected: Give him that power, and he will so order it at length, he will make such a State of Religion, that he that so lives and dyes shall never be saved, and all this springs from the vast power that is given to him, and from the deep depravation of nature. Hee will open his mouth, *His tongue is his owne, who is Lord over him,* Psal. 12. 3, 4. It is therefore most wholsome for Magistrates and Officers in Church and Common-wealth, never to affect more liberty and authority then will do them good, and the People good; for what ever transcendant power is given, will certainly over-run those that give it, and those that receive it: There is a straine in a mans heart that will sometime or other runne out to excesse, unlesse the Lord restraine it, but it is not good to venture it: It is necessary therefore, that all power that is on earth be limited, Church-power or other: If there be power given to speak great things, then look for great blasphemies, look for a licentious abuse of it. It is counted a matter of danger to the State to limit Prerogatives; but it is a further danger, not to have them limited: They will be like a Tempest, if they be not limited: A Prince himselfe cannot tell where hee will confine himselfe, nor can the people tell: But if he have liberty to speak great things, then he will make and unmake, say and unsay, and undertake such things as are neither for his owne honour, nor for the safety of the State. It is therefore fit for every man to be studious of the bounds which the Lord hath set: and for the People, in whom fundamentally all power lyes, to give as much power as God in his word gives to men: And it is meet that Magistrates in the Common-wealth, and so Officers in Churches should desire to know the utmost bounds of their own power, and it is safe for both: All intrenchment upon the bounds which God hath not given, they are not enlargements, but burdens and snares; They will certainly lead the spirit of a man out of his way sooner or later. It is wholsome and safe to be dealt withall as God deales with the vast Sea; *Hitherto shalt thou come, but there shalt thou stay thy proud waves:* and therefore if they be but banks of simple sand, they will be good enough to check the vast roaring Sea. And so for Imperiall Monarchies, it is safe to know how far their power extends; and then if it be but banks of sand, which is most slippery, it will serve, as well as any brazen wall. If you pinch the Sea of its liberty, though it be walls of stone or brasse, it will beate them downe: So it is with Magistrates, stint them where God hath not stinted them, and if they were walls of brasse, they would beate them downe, and it is meet they should: but give them the liberty God allows, and if it be but a wall of sand it will keep them: As this liquid Ayre in which we breath, God hath set it for the waters of the Clouds to the Earth; It is a Firmament, it is the Clouds, yet it stands firme enough, because it keeps the Climate where they are, it shall stand like walls of brasse: So let there be due bounds set, and I may apply it to Families; it is good for the Wife to acknowledge all power and authority to the Husband, and for the Husband to acknowledg honour to the Wife, but still give them that which God hath given them, and no more nor lesse: Give them the full latitude that God hath given, else you will finde you dig pits, and lay snares, and cumber their spirits, if you give them lesse: there is never peace where full liberty is not given, nor never stable peace where more then full liberty is granted: Let them be duely observed, and give men no more liberty then God doth, nor women, for they will abuse it: The Devill will draw them, and Gods providence leade them thereunto, therefore give them no more than God gives. And so for children; and servants, or any others you are to deale with, give them the liberty and authority you would have them use, and beyond that stretch not the tether, it will not tend to their good nor yours: And also from hence gather, and goe home with this meditation; That certainly here is this distemper in our natures, that we cannot tell how to use liberty, but wee shall very readily corrupt our selves: Oh the bottomlesse depth of sandy earth! of a corrupt spirit, that breaks over all bounds, and loves inordinate vastnesse; that is it we ought to be careful of. . . .

---

11. THE MASSACHUSETTS BODY OF LIBERTIES

The freemen of Massachusetts wished to be governed by laws that were publicly known and announced. The charter of the Massachusetts Bay Company endowed them with the power to make such laws in the General Court; and the colony had scarcely become established before they began to think about enacting, not simply a few laws as the occasion arose, but an entire code. Governor Winthrop, as can be seen in the selections from his diary, feared that such a code would prevent adaptation of the settlement to the unforeseen contingencies of life in the wilderness and that it would also expose the colony to interference from England, because it would present that government with clear evidence that Massachusetts was violating the requirement of the charter that all laws conform with those of England. The General Court nevertheless appointed a series of committees, beginning in 1635, to draft a code of laws. As Winthrop was usually a member, the committees made slow progress.

The first concrete result came in October 1636, when

From William H. Witmore, ed., *The Colonial Laws of Massachusetts Reprinted from the Edition of 1660, with the Supplement of 1672. Containing also the Body of Liberties of 1641* (Boston: City Council of Boston, 1889), pp. 32–61.

the Reverend John Cotton, a member of one of the committees (although not a member of the General Court) presented "a model of Moses his Judicials." This adaptation of Mosaic Law to New England apparently did not satisfy the General Court (although it later became the basic code of the New Haven Colony), and it was 1639 before another committee presented another draft. The author this time was Nathaniel Ward, who had served for two years as pastor of Ipswich and who had also had ten years' legal training and practice in London. Ward cast his code in a form that would later have been labeled a bill of rights. He had no more love for popular government than John Cotton, but like Cotton he believed that governments must be limited, and he thought the best form of limitation was a public statement of the rights of subjects.

Ward's draft was sent to the various towns for discussion (a procedure that the author considered improper); and in 1641, after further discussion in the General Court, the Body of Liberties was enacted into law. Many of the provisions embodied practices already in existence, but they set down popular rights in black and white for all to see.

A COPPIE OF THE LIBERTIES OF THE MASSACHUSETS COLONIE IN NEW ENGLAND.

The free fruition of such liberties Immunities and priveledges as humanitie, Civilitie, and Christianitie call for as due to every man in his place and proportion without impeachment and Infringement hath ever bene and ever will be the tranquillitie and Stabilitie of Churches and Commonwealths. And the deniall or deprivall thereof, the disturbance if not the ruine of both.

We hould it therefore our dutie and safetie whilst we are about the further establishing of this Government to collect and expresse all such freedomes as for present we foresee may concerne us, and our posteritie after us, And to ratify them with our sollemne consent.

We doe therefore this day religiously and unanimously decree and confirme these following Rites, liberties and priveledges concerneing our Churches, and Civill State to be respectively impartiallie and inviolably enjoyed and observed throughout our Jurisdiction for ever.

1. No mans life shall be taken away, no mans honour or good name shall be stayned, no mans person shall be arested, restrayned, banished, dismembred, nor any wayes punished, no man shall be deprived of his wife or children, no mans goods or estaite shall be taken away from him, nor any way indammaged under coulor of law or Countenance of Authoritie, unlesse it be by vertue or equitie of some expresse law of the Country waranting the same, established by a generall Court and sufficiently published, or in case of the defect of a law in any parteculer case by the word of god. And in Capitall cases, or in cases concerning dismembring or banishment, according to that word to be judged by the Generall Court.

2. Every person within this Jurisdiction, whether Inhabitant or forreiner shall enjoy the same justice and law, that is generall for the plantation, which we constitute and execute one towards another without partialitie or delay.

3. No man shall be urged to take any oath or subscribe any articles, covenants or remonstrance, of a publique and

Civill nature, but such as the Generall Court hath considered, allowed, and required.

4. No man shall be punished for not appearing at or before any Civill Assembly, Court, Councell, Magistrate, or Officer, nor for the omission of any office or service, if he shall be necessarily hindred by any apparent Act or providence of God, which he could neither foresee nor avoid. Provided that this law shall not prejudice any person of his just cost or damage, in any civill action.

5. No man shall be compelled to any publique worke or service unlesse the presse be grounded upon some act of the generall Court, and have reasonable allowance therefore.

6. No man shall be pressed in person to any office, worke, warres or other publique service, that is necessarily and sufficiently exempted by any naturall or personall impediment, as by want of yeares, greatnes of age, defect of minde, fayling of sences, or impotencie of Lymbes.

7. No man shall be compelled to goe out of the limits of this plantation upon any offensive warres which this Commonwealth or any of our freinds or confederats shall volentarily undertake. But onely upon such vindictive and defensive warres in our owne behalfe or the behalfe of our freinds and confederats as shall be enterprized by the Counsell and consent of a Court generall, or by Authority derived from the same.

8. No mans Cattel or goods of what kinde soever shall be pressed or taken for any publique use or service, unlesse it be by warrant grounded upon some act of the generall Court, nor without such reasonable prices and hire as

the ordinarie rates of the Countrie do afford. And if his Cattle or goods shall perish or suffer damage in such service, the owner shall be suffitiently recompenced.

9. No monopolies shall be granted or allowed amongst us, but of such new Inventions that are profitable to the Countrie, and that for a short time.

10. All our lands and heritages shall be free from all fines and licences upon Alienations, and from all hariotts, wardships, Liveries, Primerseisins, yeare day and wast, Escheates, and forfeitures, upon the deaths of parents or Ancestors, be they naturall, casuall or Juditiall.

11. All persons which are of the age of 21 yeares, and of right understanding and meamories, whether excommunicate or condemned shall have full power and libertie to make there wills and testaments, and other lawfull alienations of theire lands and estates.

12. Every man whether Inhabitant or fforreiner, free or not free shall have libertie to come to any publique Court, Councel, or Towne meeting, and either by speech or writeing to move any lawfull, seasonable, and materiall question, or to present any necessary motion, complaint, petition, Bill or information, whereof that meeting hath proper cognizance, so it be done in convenient time, due order, and respective manner.

13. No man shall be rated here for any estaite or revenue he hath in England, or in any forreine partes till it be transported hither.

14. Any Conveyance or Alienation of land or other estaite what so ever, made by any woman that is married,

any childe under age, Ideott or distracted person, shall be good if it be passed and ratified by the consent of a generall Court.

15. All Counter or fraudulent Alienations or Conveyances of lands, tenements, or any hereditaments, shall be of no validitie to defeate any man from due debts or legacies, or from any just title, clame or possession, of that which is so fraudulently conveyed.

16. Every Inhabitant that is an howse holder shall have free fishing and fowling in any great ponds and Bayes, Coves and Rivers, so farre as the sea ebbes and flowes within the presincts of the towne where they dwell, unlesse the free men of the same Towne or the Generall Court have otherwise appropriated them, provided that this shall not be extended to give leave to any man to come upon others proprietie without there leave.

17. Every man of or within this Jurisdiction shall have free libertie, notwithstanding any Civill power to remove both himselfe, and his familie at their pleasure out of the same, provided there be no legall impediment to the contrarie.

Rites Rules and Liberties concerning Juditiall proceedings.

18. No mans person shall be restrained or imprisoned by any Authority whatsoever, before the law hath sentenced him thereto, If he can put in sufficient securitie, bayle or mainprise, for his appearance, and good behaviour in the meane time, unlesse it be in Crimes Capital, and Contempts in open Court, and in such cases where some expresse act of Court doth allow it.

19. If in a generall Court any miscariage shall be amongst the Assistants when they are by themselves that may deserve an Admonition or fine under 20 sh. it shall be examined and sentenced among themselves, If amongst the Deputies when they are by themselves, It shall be examined and sentenced amongst themselves, If it be when the whole Court is togeather, it shall be judged by the whole Court, and not severallie as before.

20. If any which are to sit as Judges in any other Court shall demeane themselves offensively in the Court, the rest of the Judges present shall have power to censure him for it, if the cause be of a high nature it shall be presented to and censured at the next superior Court.

21. In all cases where the first summons are not served six dayes before the Court, and the cause breifly specified in the warrant, where appearance is to be made by the partie summoned, it shall be at his libertie whether he will appeare or no, except all cases that are to be handled in Courts suddainly called, upon extraordinary occasions, In all cases where there appeares present and urgent cause Any Assistant or officer apointed shal have power to make out Attaichments for the first summons.

22. No man in any suit or action against an other shall falsely pretend great debts or damages to vex his Adversary, if it shall appeare any doth so, The Court shall have power to set a reasonable fine on his head.

23. No man shall be adjudged to pay for detaining any debt from any Crediter above eight pounds in the hundred for one yeare, And not above that rate proportionable for all somes what so ever, neither shall this be a coulour or countenance to allow any usurie amongst us contrarie to the law of god.

24. In all Trespasses or damages done to any man or men, If it can be proved to be done by the meere default of him or them to whome the trespasse is done, It shall be judged no trespasse, nor any damage given for it.

25. No Summons pleading Judgement, or any kinde of proceeding in Court or course of Justice shall be abated, arested or reversed upon any kinde of cercumstantiall errors or mistakes, If the person and cause be rightly understood and intended by the Court.

26. Every man that findeth himselfe unfit to plead his owne cause in any Court shall have Libertie to imploy any man against whom the Court doth not except, to helpe him, Provided he give him noe fee or reward for his paines. This shall not exempt the partie himselfe from Answering such Questions in person as the Court shall thinke meete to demand of him.

27. If any plantife shall give into any Court a declaration of his cause in writeing, The defendant shall also have libertie and time to give in his answer in writeing, And so in all further proceedings betwene partie and partie, So it doth not further hinder the dispach of Justice then the Court shall be willing unto.

28. The plantife in all Actions brought in any Court shall have libertie to withdraw his Action, or to be nonsuited before the Jurie hath given in their verdict, in which case he shall alwaies pay full cost and chardges to the defendant, and may afterwards renew his suite at an other Court if he please.

29. In all Actions at law it shall be the libertie of the plantife and defendant by mutual consent to choose whether they will be tryed by the Bench or by a Jurie,

unlesse it be where the law upon just reason hath otherwise determined. The like libertie shall be granted to all persons in Criminall cases.

30. It shall be in the libertie both of plantife and defendant, and likewise every delinquent (to be judged by a Jurie) to challenge any of the Jurors. And if his challenge be found just and reasonable by the Bench, or the rest of the Jurie, as the challenger shall choose it shall be allowed him, and tales de cercumstantibus impaneled in their room.

31. In all cases where evidence is so obscure or defective that the Jurie cannot clearely and safely give a positive verdict, whether it be a grand or petit Jurie, It shall have libertie to give a non Liquit, or a spetiall verdict, in which last, that is in a spetiall verdict, the Judgement of the cause shall be left to the Court, and all Jurors shall have libertie in matters of fact if they cannot finde the maine issue, yet to finde and present in their verdict so much as they can, If the Bench and Jurors shall so differ at any time about their verdict that either of them cannot proceede with peace of conscience the case shall be referred to the Generall Court, who shall take the question from both and determine it.

32. Every man shall have libertie to replevy his Cattell or goods impounded, distreined, seised, or extended, unlesse it be upon execution after Judgement, and in paiment of fines. Provided he puts in good securitie to prosecute his replevin, And to satisfie such demands as his Adversary shall recover against him in Law.

33. No mans person shall be Arrested, or imprisoned upon execution or judgment for any debt or fine, If the law can finde competent meanes of satisfaction otherwise from

his estaite, and if not his person may be arrested and imprisoned where he shall be kept at his owne charge, not the plantife's till satisfaction be made: unlesse the Court that had cognizance of the cause or some superior Court shall otherwise provide.

34. If any man shall be proved and Judged a commen Barrator vexing others with unjust frequent and endlesse suites, It shall be in the power of Courts both to denie him the benefit of the law, and to punish him for his Barratry.

35. No mans Corne nor hay that is in the feild or upon the Cart, nor his garden stuffe, nor any thing subject to present decay, shall be taken in any distresse, unles he that takes it doth presently bestow it where it may not be imbesled nor suffer spoile or decay, or give securitie to satisfie the worth thereof if it comes to any harme.

36. It shall be in the libertie of every man cast condemned or sentenced in any cause in any Inferior Court, to make their Appeale to the Court of Assistants, provided they tender their appeale and put in securitie to prosecute it before the Court be ended wherein they were condemned, And within six dayes next ensuing put in good securitie before some Assistant to satisfie what his Adversarie shall recover against him; And if the cause be of a Criminall nature, for his good behaviour, and appearance, And everie man shall have libertie to complaine to the Generall Court of any Injustice done him in any Court of Assistants or other.

37. In all cases where it appeares to the Court that the plantife hath willingly and witingly done wronge to the defendant in commenceing and prosecuting any action or

complaint against him, They shall have power to impose upon him a proportionable fine to the use of the defendant, or accused person, for his false complaint or clamor.

38. Everie man shall have libertie to Record in the publique Rolles of any Court any Testimony given upon oath in the same Court, or before two Assistants, or any deede or evidence legally confirmed there to remaine in perpetuam rei memoriam, that is for perpetuall memoriall or evidence upon occasion.

39. In all actions both reall and personall betweene partie and partie, the Court shall have power to respite execution for a convenient time, when in their prudence they see just cause so to doe.

40. No Conveyance, Deede, or promise whatsoever shall be of validitie, If it be gotten by Illegal violence, imprisonment, threatenings, or any kinde of forcible compulsion called Dures.

41. Everie man that is to Answere for any Criminall cause, whether he be in prison or under bayle, his cause shall be heard and determined at the next Court that hath proper Cognizance thereof, And may be done without prejudice of Justice.

42. No man shall be twise sentenced by Civill Justice for one and the same Crime, offence, or Trespasse.

43. No man shall be beaten with above 40 stripes, nor shall any true gentleman, nor any man equall to a gentleman be punished with whipping, unles his crime be very shamefull, and his course of life vitious and profligate.

44. No man condemned to dye shall be put to death within fower dayes next after his condemnation, unles the Court see spetiall cause to the contrary, or in case of martiall law, nor shall the body of any man so put to death be unburied 12 howers, unlesse it be in case of Anatomie.

45. No man shall be forced by Torture to confesse any Crime against himselfe nor any other unlesse it be in some Capitall case where he is first fullie convicted by cleare and suffitient evidence to be guilty, After which if the cause be of that nature, That it is very apparent there be other conspiratours, or confederates with him, Then he may be tortured, yet not with such Tortures as be Barbarous and inhumane.

46. For bodilie punishments we allow amongst us none that are inhumane Barbarous or cruel.

47. No man shall be put to death without the testimony of two or three witnesses or that which is equivalent thereunto.

48. Every Inhabitant of the Country shall have free libertie to search and veewe any Rooles, Records, or Regesters of any Court or office except the Councell, And to have a transcript or exemplification thereof written examined, and signed by the hand of the officer of the office paying the appointed fees therefore.

49. No free man shall be compelled to serve upon Juries above two Courts in a yeare, except grand Jurie men, who shall hould two Courts together at the least.

50. All Jurors shall be chosen continuallie by the freemen of the Towne where they dwell.

51. All Associates selected at any time to Assist the Assistants in Inferior Courts shall be nominated by the Townes belonging to that Court, by orderly agreement amonge themselves.

52. Children, Idiots, Distracted persons, and all that are strangers, or new commers to our plantation, shall have such allowances and dispensations in any Cause whether Criminall or other as religion and reason require.

53. The age of discretion for passing away of lands or such kinde of herediments, or for giveing of votes, verdicts or Sentence in any Civill Courts or causes, shall be one and twentie yeares.

54. Whensoever anything is to be put to vote, any sentence to be pronounced, or any other matter to be proposed, or read in any Court or Assembly, If the president or moderator thereof shall refuse to performe it, the Major parte of the members of that Court or Assembly shall have power to appoint any other meete man of them to do it, And if there be just cause to punish him that should and would not.

55. In all suites or Actions in Any Court, the plantife shall have libertie to make all the titles and claims to that he sues for he can. And the Defendant shall have libertie to plead all the pleas he can in answere to them, and the Court shall judge according to the entire evidence of all.

56. If any man shall behave himselfe offensively at any Towne meeting, the rest of the freemen then present, shall have power to sentence him for his offence. So be it the mulct or penaltie exceede not twentie shilings.

57. Whensoever any person shall come to any very suddaine untimely and unnaturall death, Some assistant, or the Constables of that Towne shall forthwith sumon a Jury of twelve free men to inquire of the cause and manner of their death, and shall present a true verdict thereof to some neere Assistant, or the next Court to be helde for that Towne upon their oath.

Liberties more peculiarlie concerning the free men.

58. Civill Authoritie hath power and libertie to see the peace, ordinances and Rules of Christ observed in every church according to his word. so it be done in a Civill and not in an Ecclesiastical way.

59. Civill Authoritie hath power and libertie to deale with any Church member in a way of Civill Justice, notwithstanding any Church relation, office or interest.

60. No church censure shall degrade or depose any man from any Civill dignitie, office, or Authoritie he shall have in the Commonwealth.

61. No Magestrate, Juror, Officer, or other man shall be bound to informe present or reveale any private crim or offence, wherein there is no perill or danger to this plantation or any member thereof, when any necessarie tye of conscience binds him to secresie grounded upon the word of god, unlesse it be in case of testimony lawfully required.

62. Any Shire or Towne shall have libertie to choose their Deputies whom and where they please for the Gen-

erall Court. So be it they be free men, and have taken there oath of fealtie, and Inhabiting in this Jurisdiction.

63. No Governor, Deputy Governor, Assistant, Associate, or grand Jury man at any Court, nor any Deputie for the Generall Court shall at any time beare his owne chardges at any Court, but their necessary expences shall be defrayed either by the Towne or Shire on whose service they are, or by the Country in generall.

64. Everie Action betweene partie and partie, and proceedings against delinquents in Criminall causes shall be briefly and destinctly entered on the Rolles of every Court by the Recorder thereof. That such actions be not afterwards brought againe to the vexation of any man.

65. No custome or prescription shall ever prevaile amongst us in any morall cause, our meaneing is maintaine anythinge that can be proved to bee morrallie sinfull by the word of god.

66. The Freemen of every Towneship shall have power to make such by laws and constitutions as may concerne the wellfare of their Towne, provided they be not of a Criminall, but onely of a prudentiall nature, And that their penalties exceede not 20 sh. for one offence. And that they be not repugnant to the publique laws and orders of the Countrie. And if any Inhabitant shall neglect or refuse to observe them, they shall have power to levy the appointed penalties by distresse.

67. It is the constant libertie of the free men of this plantation to choose yearly at the Court of Election out of the freemen all the General officers of this Jurisdiction. If they please to dischardge them at the day of Election by

way of vote. They may do it without shewing cause. But if at any other generall Court, we hould it due justice, that the reasons thereof be alleadged and proved. By Generall officers we meane, our Governor, Deputy Governor, Assistants, Treasurer, Generall of our warres. And our Admirall at Sea, and such as are or hereafter may be of the like genrall nature.

68. It is the libertie of the freemen to choose such deputies for the Generall Court out of themselves, either in their owne Townes or elsewhere as they judge fitest. And because we cannot foresee what varietie and weight of occasions may fall into future consideration, And what counsells we may stand in neede of, we decree. That the Deputies (to attend the Generall Court in the behalfe of the Countrie) shall not any time be stated or inacted, but from Court to Court, or at the most but for one yeare, that the Countrie may have an Annuall libertie to do in that case what is most behoofefull for the best welfaire thereof.

69. No Generall Court shall be desolved or adjourned without the consent of the Major parte thereof.

70. All Freemen called to give any advise, vote, verdict, or sentence in any Court, Counsell, or Civill Assembly, shall have full freedome to doe it according to their true Judgements and Consciences, So it be done orderly and inofensively for the manner.

71. The Governor shall have a casting voice whensoever an Equi vote shall fall out in the Court of Assistants, or generall assembly, So shall the presedent or moderator have in all Civill Courts or Assemblies.

72. The Governor and Deputy Governor Joyntly consenting or any three Assistants concurring in consent shall

have power out of Court to reprive a condemned malefactour, till the next quarter or generall Court. The generall Court onely shall have power to pardon a condemned malefactor.

73. The Generall Court hath libertie and Authoritie to send out any member of this Comanwealth of what qualitie, condition or office whatsoever into forreine parts about any publique message or Negotiation. Provided the partie sent be acquainted with the affaire he goeth about, and be willing to undertake the service.

74. The freemen of every Towne or Towneship, shall have full power to choose yearly or for lesse time out of themselves a convenient number of fitt men to order the planting or prudentiall occasions of that Town, according to Instructions given them in writeing, Provided nothing be done by them contrary to the publique laws and orders of the Countrie, provided also the number of such select persons be not above nine.

75. It is and shall be the libertie of any member or members of any Court, Councell or Civill Assembly in cases of makeing or executing any order or law, that properlie concerne religion, or any cause capitall, or warres, or Subscription to any publique Articles or Remonstrance, in case they cannot in Judgement and conscience consent to that way the Major vote or suffrage goes, to make their contra Remonstrance or protestation in speech or writeing, and upon request to have their dissent recorded in the Rolles of that Court. So it be done Christianlie and respectively for the manner. And their dissent onely be entered without the reasons thereof, for the avoiding of tediousness.

76. Whensoever any Jurie of trialls or Jurours are not cleare in their Judgements or consciences conserneing any

cause wherein they are to give their verdict, They shall have libertie in open Court to advise with any man they thinke fitt to resolve or direct them, before they give in their verdict.

77. In all cases wherein any freeman is to give his vote, be it in point of Election, makeing constitutions and orders, or passing sentence in any case of Judicature or the like, if he cannot see reason to give it positively one way or an other, he shall have libertie to be silent, and not pressed to a determined vote.

78. The Generall or publique Treasure or any parte thereof shall never be exspended but by the appointment of a Generall Court, nor any Shire Treasure, but by the appointment of the freemen thereof, nor any Towne Treasurie but by the freemen of that Towneship.

Liberties of Woemen.

79. If any man at his death shall not leave his wife a competent portion of his estaite, upon just complaint made to the Generall Court she shall be relieved.

80. Everie marryed woeman shall be free from bodilie correction or stripes by her husband, unlesse it be in his owne defence upon her assalt. If there be any just cause of correction complaint shall be made to Authoritie assembled in some Court, from which onely she shall receive it.

Liberties of Children.

81. When parents dye intestate, the Elder sonne shall have a doble portion of his whole estate reall and personall, unlesse the Generall Court upon just cause alleadged shall Judge otherwise.

82. When parents dye intestate haveing noe heires males of their bodies their Daughters shall inherit as copartners, unles the Generall Court upon just reason shall judge otherwise.

83. If any parents shall wilfullie and unreasonably deny any childe timely or convenient mariage, or shall exercise any unnaturall severitie towards them, such childeren shall have free libertie to complaine to Authoritie for redresse.

84. No Orphan dureing their minoritie which was not committed to tuition or service by the parents in their life time shall afterwards be absolutely disposed of by any kindred, freind, Executor, Towneship, or Church, nor by themselves without the consent of some Court, wherein two Assistants at least shall be present.

Liberties of Servants

85. If any servants shall flee from the Tiranny and crueltie of their masters to the howse of any freeman of the same Towne, they shall be there protected and susteyned till due order be taken for their relife. Provided due notice thereof be speedily given to their maisters from whom they fled. And the next Assistant or Constable where the partie flying is harboured.

86. No servant shall be put of for above a yeare to any other neither in the life time of their maister nor after their death by their Executors or Administrators unlesse it be by consent of Authoritie assembled in some Court or two Assistants.

87. If any man smite out the eye or tooth of his man-servant, or maid servant, or otherwise mayme or much disfig-

ure him, unlesse it be by meere casualtie, he shall let them goe free from his service. And shall have such further recompense as the Court shall allow him.

88. Servants that have served deligentlie and faithfully to the benefitt of their maisters seaven yeares, shall not be sent away emptie. And if any have bene unfaithfull, negligent or unprofitable in their service, notwithstanding the good usage of their maisters, they shall not be dismissed till they have made satisfaction according to the Judgement of Authoritie.

Liberties of Forreiners and Strangers.

89. If any people of other Nations professing the true Christian Religion shall flee to us from the Tiranny or oppression of their persecutors, or from famyne, warres, or the like necessary and compulsarie cause, They shall be entertayned and succoured amongst us, according to that power and prudence god shall give us.

90. If any ships or other vessels, be it freind or enemy, shall suffer shipwrack upon our Coast, there shall be no violence or wrong offerred to their persons or goods. But their persons shall be harboured, and relieved, and their goods preserved in safety till Authoritie may be certified thereof, and shall take further order therein.

91. There shall never be any bond slaverie, villinage or Captivitie amongst us unles it be lawfull Captives taken in just warres, and such strangers as willingly selle themselves or are sold to us. And these shall have all the liberties and Christian usages which the law of god established in Israell concerning such persons doeth morally require.

This exempts none from servitude who shall be Judged thereto by Authoritie.

Off the Bruite Creature.

92. No man shall exercise any Tirranny or Crueltie towards any bruite Creature which are usuallie kept for mans use.

93. If any man shall have occasion to leade or drive Cattel from place to place that is far of, so that they be weary, or hungry, or fall sick, or lambe, It shall be lawful to rest or refresh them, for a competent time, in any open place that is not Corne, meadow, or inclosed for some peculiar use.

94. *Capitall Laws.*

1.

Dut. 13. 6, 10. Dut. 17. 2, 6. Ex. 22. 20. If any man after legall conviction shall have or worship any other god, but the lord god, he shall be put to death.

2.

Ex. 22. 18. Lev. 20. 27. Dut. 18. 10. If any man or woeman be a witch, (that is hath or consulteth with a familiar spirit,) They shall be put to death.

3.

Lev. 24. 15, 16. If any man shall Blaspheme the name of god, the father, Sonne or Holie ghost, with direct, expresse, presumptuous or high handed blasphemie, or shall curse god in the like manner, he shall be put to death.

4.

Ex. 21. 12. Numb. 35. 13, 14, 30, 31.

If any person committ any wilfull murther, which is manslaughter, committed upon premeditated mallice, hatred, or Crueltie, not in a mans necessarie and just defence, nor by meere casualtie against his will, he shall be put to death.

5.

Numb. 25. 20, 21. Lev. 24. 17.

If any person slayeth an other suddaienly in his anger or Crueltie of passion, he shall be put to death.

6.

Ex. 21. 14.

If any person shall slay an other through guile, either by poysoning or other such divelish practice, he shall be put to death.

7.

Lev. 20. 15, 16.

If any man or woeman shall lye with any beaste or bruite creature by Carnall Copulation, They shall surely be put to death. And the beast shall be slaine and buried and not eaten.

8.

Lev. 20. 13.

If any man lyeth with mankinde as he lyeth with a woeman, both of them have committed abhomination, they both shall surely be put to death.

9.

Lev. 20. 19, and 18, 20. Dut. 22. 23, 24.

If any person committeth Adultery with a maried or espoused wife, the Adulterer and Adulteresse shall surely be put to death.

10.

Ex. 21. 16.

If any man stealeth a man or mankinde, he shall surely be put to death.

11.

Dut. 19. 16, 18, 19. If any man rise up by false witnes, wittingly and of purpose to take away any mans life, he shall be put to death.

12.

If any man shall conspire and attempt any invasion, insurrection, or publique rebellion against our commonwealth, or shall indeavour to surprize any Towne or Townes, fort or forts therein, or shall treacherously and perfediouslie attempt the alteration and subversion of our frame of politie or Government fundamentallie, he shall be put to death.

95. *A Delcaration of the Liberties the Lord Jesus hath given to the Churches.*

1.

All the people of god within this Jurisdiction who are not in a church way, and be orthodox in Judgement, and not scandalous in life, shall have full libertie to gather themselves into a Church Estaite. Provided they doe it in a Christian way, with due observation of the rules of Christ revealed in his word.

2.

Every Church hath full libertie to exercise all the ordinances of god, according to the rules of scripture.

3.

Every Church hath free libertie of Election and ordination of all their officers from time to time, provided they be able, pious and orthodox.

4.

Every Church hath free libertie of Admission, Recommendation, Dismission, and Expulsion, or deposall of their officers and members, upon due cause, with free exercise of the Discipline and Censures of Christ according to the rules of his word.

5.

No Injunctions are to be put upon any Church, Church officers or member in point of Doctrine, worship or Discipline, whether for substance or cercumstance besides the Institutions of the lord.

6.

Every Church of Christ hath freedome to celebrate dayes of fasting and prayer, and of thanksgiveing according to the word of god.

7.

The Elders of Churches have free libertie to meete monthly, Quarterly, or otherwise, in convenient numbers and places, for conferences and consultations about Christian and Church questions and occasions.

8.

All Churches have libertie to deale with any of their members in a church way that are in the hand of Justice. So it be not to retard or hinder the course thereof.

9.

Every Church hath libertie to deale with any magestrate, Deputie of Court or other officer what soe ever that is a member in a church way in case of apparent and just offence given in their places, so it be done with due observance and respect.

10.

Wee allowe private meetings for edification in religion amongst Christians of all sortes of people. So it be without just offence for number, time, place, and other cercumstances.

11.

For the preventing and removeing of errour and offence that may grow and spread in any of the Churches in this Jurisdiction, and for the preserveing of trueith and peace in the several churches within themselves, and for the maintenance and exercise of brotherly communion, amongst all the churches in the Countrie, It is allowed and ratified, by the Authoritie of this Generall Court as a lawfull libertie of the Churches of Christ. That once in every month of the yeare (when the season will beare it) It shall be lawfull for the minesters and Elders, of the Churches neere adjoyneing together, with any other of the breetheren with the consent of the churches to assemble by course in each severall Church one after an other. To the intent after the preaching of the word by such a minister as shall be requested thereto by the Elders of the church where the Assembly is held, The rest of the day may be spent in publique Christian Conference about the discussing and resolveing of any such doubts and cases of conscience concerning matter of doctrine or worship or government of the church as shall be propounded by any of the Breetheren of that church, with leave also to any other Brother to propound his objections or answeres for further satisfaction according to the word of god. Provided that the whole action be guided and moderated by the Elders of the Church where the Assemblie is helde, or by such others as they shall appoint. And that no thing be concluded and imposed by way of Authoritie from one or more Churches upon an other, but onely by way of Brotherly conference and consultations. That the trueth may be searched out to the satisfying of every mans conscience in the sight of god according his worde. And because such an Assembly and the worke theirof can not be duely attended to if other lectures be held in the same weeke. It is therefore agreed with the consent of the Churches. That in that weeke when such an Assembly is held, All the lectures in all the neighbouring Churches for that weeke shall be forborne. That so the publique service of Christ in this more solemne Assembly may be transacted with greater deligence and attention.

96. Howsoever these above specified rites, freedomes, Immunities, Authorities and priveledges, both Civill and Ecclesiastical are expressed onely under the name and title of Liberties, and not in the exact form of Laws or Statutes, yet we do with one consent fullie Authorise, and earnestly intreate all that are and shall be in Authoritie to consider them as laws, and not to faile to inflict condigne and proportionable punishments upon every man impartiallie, that shall infringe or violate any of them.

97. Wee likewise give full power and libertie to any person that shall at any time be denyed or deprived of any of them, to commence and prosecute their suite, Complaint or action against any man that shall so doe in any Court that hath proper Cognizance or judicature thereof.

98. Lastly because our dutie and desire is to do nothing suddainlie which fundamentally concerne us, we decree that these rites and liberties, shall be Audably read and deliberately weighed at every Generall Court that shall be held, within three yeares next insueing, And such of them as shall not be altered or repealed they shall stand so ratified, That no man shall infringe them without due punishment.

And if any Generall Court within these next thre yeares shall faile or forget to reade and consider them as abovesaid. The Governor and Deputy Governor for the time being, and every Assistant present at such Courts shall forfeite 20sh. a man, and everie Deputie 10sh. a man for each neglect, which shall be paid out of their proper estate, and not by the Country or the Townes which choose them, and whensoever there shall arise any question in any Court amonge the Assistants and Associates thereof about the explanation of these Rites and liberties, The Generall Court onely shall have power to interprett them.

---

12. THE BLOUDY TENENT OF PERSECUTION BY ROGER WILLIAMS

Roger Williams (ca. *1603–1683) was not prompted to put his views in writing and publish them until several years after he was expelled from Massachusetts. Williams's style is involved and difficult to follow; a single sentence sometimes stretches out, regardless of punctuation, for several paragraphs before we reach the predicate. Nevertheless, Williams possessed one of the keenest minds in an age that was nothing if not intellectual, and it is worth deciphering his meaning in order to appreciate the originality of his thought.*

The most famous of his writings was The Bloudy Tenent of Persecution for Cause of Conscience *(London, 1644), written in the form of a dialogue between Truth and Peace. It presents a line-by-line refutation of a tract prepared by*

From Narragansett Club, *Publications,* III, 247–254, 412–415.

the Massachusetts ministers, entitled "A Model of Church and Civil Power," which set forth many of the political ideas of orthodox Puritanism. Since no original copy of the Massachusetts tract exists, The Bloudy Tenent *gains an additional interest by virtue of the quotations from it. The two passages that follow are composed of Chapters* 92, 93, *and* 137 *of* The Bloudy Tenent. *Each chapter begins with a quotation from the "Model," which is then refuted.*

CHAP. XCII.

Peace. the 4. head is, The proper meanes of both these Powers to attaine their ends.

"First, the proper meanes whereby the Civill Power "may and should attaine its end, are onely Politicall, and "principally these Five.

"First the erecting and establishing what forme of "Civill Government may seeme in wisedome most meet, "according to generall rules of the Word, and state of the "people.

"Secondly, the making, publishing, and establishing of "wholesome Civill Lawes, not onely such as concerne "Civill Justice, but also the free passage of true Religion: "for, outward Civill Peace ariseth and is maintained from "them both, from the latter as well as from the former:

"Civill peace cannot stand intire, where Religion is "corrupted, 2 *Chron.* 15. 3. 5. 6. *Judg.* 8. And yet such "Lawes, though conversant about Religion, may still be "counted Civill Lawes, as on the contrary, an Oath doth still "remaine Religious, though conversant about Civill matters.

"Thirdly, Election and appointment of Civill officers, to "see execution of those Lawes.

"Fourthly, Civill Punishments and Rewards, of Trans-"gressors and Observers of these Lawes.

"Fifthly, taking up Armes against the Enemies of Civill "Peace.

"Secondly, the meanes whereby the Church may and "should attaine her ends, are only ecclesiasticall, which "are chiefly five.

"First, setting up that forme of Church Government only, "of which Christ hath given them a pattern in his Word.

"Secondly, acknowledging and admitting of no Lawgiver "in the Church, but Christ, and the publishing of his Lawes.

"Thirdly, Electing and ordaining of such officers onely, as "Christ hath appointed in his Word.

"Fourthly, to receive into their fellowship them that are "approved, and inflicting Spirituall censures against them "that offend.

"Fifthly, Prayer and patience in suffering any evill from "them that be without, who disturbe their peace.

"So that Magistrates, as Magistrates, have no power of "setting up the Forme of Church Government, electing "Church officers, punishing with Church censures, but to "see that the Church doth her duty herein. And on the other "side, the Churches as Churches, have no power (though "as members of the Commonweale they may have power) "of erecting or altering formes of Civill Government, "electing of Civill officers, inflicting Civill punishments "(no not on persons excommunicate) as by deposing Magis-"trates from their Civill Authoritie, or withdrawing the "hearts of the people against them, to their Lawes, no more "then to discharge wives, or children, or servants, from "due obedience to their husbands, parents, or masters: or "by taking up armes against their Magistrates, though he "persecute them for Conscience: for though members of "Churches who are publique officers also of the Civill

"State, may suppresse by force the violence of Usurpers, "as *Iehoiada* did *Athaliah,* yet this they doe not as mem-"bers of the Church, but as officers of the Civill State.

Truth. Here are divers considerable *passages* which I shall briefly examine, so far as concernes our *controversie.*

First, whereas they say, that the *Civill Power* may erect and establish what *forme* of *civill Government* may seeme in *wisedome* most meet, I acknowledge the *proposition* to be most true, both in it self, and also considered with the end of it, that a *civill Government* is an *Ordinance* of *God,* to conserve the *civill peace* of people, so farre as concernes their *Bodies* and *Goods,* as formerly hath beene said.

But from this *Grant* I infer, (as before hath been touched) that the *Soveraigne, originall,* and *foundation* of *civill power* lies in the *people,* (whom they must needs meane by the *civill power* distinct from the *Government* set up.) And if so, that a People may erect and establish what *forme* of *Government* seemes to them most meete for their *civill condition:* It is evident that such *Governments* as are by them erected and established, have no more *power,* nor for no longer time, then the *civill power* or people consenting and agreeing shall betrust them with. This is cleere not only in *Reason,* but in the experience of all *commonweales,* where the people are not deprived of their *naturall freedome* by the power of *Tyrants.*

And if so, that the Magistrates receive their power of governing the Church, from the People; undeniably it followes, that a *people,* as a *people,* naturally considered (of what *Nature* or *Nation* soever in *Europe, Asia, Africa* or *America*) have fundamentally and originally, as men, a power to governe the *Church,* to see her doe her *duty,* to correct her, to redresse, reforme, establish, &c. And if this be not to pull *God* and *Christ,* and *Spirit* out of *Heaven,* and subject them unto *naturall,* sinfull, inconstant men, and so consequently to *Sathan* himselfe, by whom all *peoples* naturally are guided, let *Heaven* and *Earth* judge.

Peace. It cannot by their owne *Grant* be denied, but that the *wildest Indians* in *America* ought (and in their kind and severall degrees doe) to agree upon some *formes* of *Government*, some more *civill*, compact in Townes, &c. some lesse. As also that their *civill* and *earthly Governments* be as lawfull and true as any *Governments* in the *World*, and therefore consequently their *Governors* are *Keepers* of the *Church* or both *Tables*, (if any Church of Christ should arise or be amongst them:) and therefore lastly, (if *Christ* have betrusted and charged the *civill* Power with his *Church*) they must judge according to their *Indian* or *American consciences*, for other *consciences* it cannot be supposed they should have.

CHAP. XCIII.

Truth. A Gaine, whereas they say that outward Civill peace cannot stand where *Religion* is corrupted; and quote for it, 2 *Chron.* 15. 3. 5. 6. & *Judges* 8.

I answer with *admiration* how such excellent *spirits* (as these *Authors* are furnished with, not only in heavenly but earthly affaires) should so forget, and be so fast asleep in things so palpably evident, as to say that outward *civill* peace cannot stand, where *Religion* is corrupt. When so many stately *Kingdomes* and *Governments* in the *World* have long and long enjoyed *civill* peace and quiet, notwithstanding their *Religion* is so corrupt, as that there is not the very Name of *Jesus Christ* amongst them: And this every *Historian, Merchant, Traveller,* in *Europe, Asia, Africa, America,* can testifie: for so spake the *Lord Jesus* himselfe, *Joh.* 16. The *world* shall sing and rejoyce.

Secondly, for that Scripture 2 *Chron.* 15. 3. &c. relating the miseries of *Israel* and *Judah*, and *Gods* plagues upon that people for corruption of their *Religion*, it must still have reference to that peculiar state unto which *God* called the seed of one man, *Abraham*, in a *figure*, dealing so with them as he dealt not with any Nation in the World, *Psal. 146. Rom.* 9.

The *Antitype* to this State I have proved to be the *Christian Church*, which consequently hath been and is afflicted with spirituall *plagues*, *desolations* and *captivities*, for corrupting of that *Religion* which hath been revealed unto them. This appeares by the *7 Churches*, and the people of *God*, now so many hundred yeares in wofull *bondage* and slaverie to the mysticall *Babel*, untill the time of their joyfull *deliverance*.

Peace. Yea but they say that such *Lawes* as are conversant about *Religion*, may still be accounted *Civill Lawes*, as on the contrary an Oath doth still remaine *Religious*, though conversant about *Civill* matters.

Truth. Lawes respecting *Religion* are two-fold:

First, such as concerne the *acts* of *Worship* and the *Worship* it self, the *Ministers* of it, their *fitnes* or *unfitnes*, to be suppressed or established: and for such Lawes we find no footing in the New *Testament* of Jesus Christ.

Secondly, *Lawes* respecting *Religion* may be such as meerly concerne the *Civill State*, *Bodies* and *Goods* of such and such persons, professing these and these *Religions*, viz. that such and such persons, notorious for *Mutinies*, *Treasons*, *Rebellions*, *Massacres*, be disarmed: Againe, that no persons *Papists*, *Jewes*, *Turkes*, or *Indians* be disturbed at their *worship*, (a thing which the very *Indians* abhor to practice toward any.) Also that *imanitie* and *freedome* from *Tax* and *Toll* may be granted unto the people of such or such a *Religion*, as the *Magistrate* pleaseth, *Ezra* 7.

These and such as are of this nature, concerning only the *bodies* and *goods* of such and such *Religious persons*, I confesse are meerely Civill.

But now on the other hand, that *Lawes* restraining persons from such and such a *Worship*, because the *Civill state* judgeth it to be false:

That *Laws* constraining to such & such a *worship*, because the *Civill State* judgeth this to be the only true way of worshipping *God:*

That such and such a *Reformation* of *Worship* be submitted unto by all Subjects in such a *Jurisdiction:*

That such and such *Churches, Ministers, Ministries* be pull'd downe, and such and such *Churches, Ministries,* and *Ministrations* set up:

That such *Lawes* properly concerning *Religion, God,* the *Soules* of men, should be *Civill Lawes* and *Constitutions;* is as far from *Reason,* as that the *Commandements* of *Paul,* which he gave the *Churches* concerning *Christs worship* (*1 Cor. 11* & *1 Cor. 14.*) were *Civill* and *Earthly constitutions*: Or that the *Canons* and *Constitutions* of either *ecumenicall* or *Nationall* Synods concerning *Religion,* should be *Civill* and *State-conclusions* and agreements.

To that instance of an *Oath* remaining *religious* though conversant about *civill things;* I answer and acknowledge, an *Oath* may be spirituall, though taken about earthly *businesse,* and accordingly it will prove, and onely prove what before I have said, that a *Law* may be civill though it concerne persons of this and of that *religion,* that is as the *persons* professing it are concerned in *civill respects* of *bodies* or *goods,* as I have opened; whereas if it concerne the soules and religions of men simply so considered in reference to *God,* it must of necessity put on the nature of a *religious* or *spirituall ordinance* or *constitution.*

Beside, it is a most improper and fallacious instance [;] for an *oath,* being an *invocation* of a true or false *God* to judge in a case, is an action of a *spirituall* and *religious nature,* what ever the *subject* matter be about which it is taken, whether *civill* or *religious:* but a *law* or *constitution* may be *civill* or *religious,* as the *subject* about which it is *conversant* is, either *civill* (meerly concerning *bodies* or *goods*) or *religious* concerning *soule* and *worship.*

CHAP. CXXXVII.

Peace. Deare *Truth,* We are now arrived at their last Head: the Title is this, *viz.*

Their power in the Liberties and Priviledges of these Churches.

"First, all Magistrates ought to be chosen out of Church-"members, *Exod.* 18. 21. *Deut.* 17. 15. *Prov.* 29. 2. When "the Righteous rule, the people rejoyce.

"Secondly, that all free men elected, be only Church-"members.

1. Because if none but Church members should rule, "then others should not choose, because they may elect "others beside Church members.

2. From the patterne of *Israel,* where none had power to "choose but only Israel, or such as were joyned to the "people of God.

3. If it shall fall out, that in the Court consisting of "Magistrates and Deputies, there be a dissent between "them which may hinder the common good, that they now "returne for ending the same, to their first principles, "which are the Free men, and let them be consulted with.

Truth. In this *Head* are 2 branches: First concerning the choice of *Magistrates,* that such ought to be chosen as are *Church members:* for which is quoted, *Exod.* 18. 21. *Dut.* 17. 15. *Proverbs* 19. 29.

Unto which I answer: It were to be wished, that since the point is so weighty, as concerning the *Pilots* and *Steeresmen* of *Kingdoms* and *Nations*, &c. on whose *abilitie, care* and *faithfulnesse* depends most commonly the *peace* and *safety* of the *commonweales* they sail in: I say it were to be wished that they had more fully explained what they intend by this *Affirmative*, viz. *Magistrates* ought to be chosen out of *Church members*.

For if they intend by this [*Ought to be chosen*] a *necessitie* of *convenience*, viz. that for the greater advancement of *common utilitie* and *rejoycing* of the people, according to the place quoted *(Prov. 29. 2.)* it were to be desired, prayed for, and peaceably endeavored, then I readily assent unto them.

But if by this [*Ought*] they intend such a *necessitie* as those Scriptures quoted imply, viz. that people shall sin by choosing such for *Magistrates* as are not members of *Churches;* as the *Israelites* should have sinned, if they had not (according to *Jethro's* counsell, *Exod. 18.* and according to the *command* of *God*, Deut 18.) chosen their *Judges* and *Kings* within themselves in *Israel:* then I propose these necessary *Queries*.

First whether those are not lawfull *Civill combinations, societies*, and *communions* of men, *Townes, Cities, States* or *Kingdoms*, where no *Church* of *Christ* is resident, yea where his name was never yet heard of: I adde to this, that Men of no small note, skilfull in the *state* of the *World*, acknowledge, that the *World* divided into 30 parts, 25 of that 30 have never yet heard of the name of *Christ:* If their *Civill polities* and *combinations* be not lawfull, (because they are not *Churches*, and their *Magistrates Church* members) then *disorder, confusion*, and all *unrighteousnes* is lawfull, and pleasing to God.

Secondly, whether in such States or Commonweales,

where a Church or Churches of Christ are resident, such persons may not lawfully succeed to the Crown or Government, in whom the feare of God (according to *Jethroes* councell) cannot be discerned, nor are brethren of the Church, according to *Deut. 17.*) but only are fitted with Civill and Morall abilities, to manage the Civill affaires of the Civill State.

Thirdly, since not many *Wise* and *Noble* are called, but the *poore* receive the *Gospel,* as *God* hath chosen the *poore* of the *World* to be *rich* in *Faith,* 1 Cor. 1. Jam. 2. Whether it may not ordinarily come to passe, that there may not be found in a true *Church* of *Christ* (which sometimes consisteth but of few persons) persons fit to be either *Kings* or *Governours, &c.* whose *civill office* is no lesse difficult then the office of a *Doctor* of *Physick,* a *Master* or *Pilot* of a *Ship,* or a *Captaine* or *Commander* of a *Band* or *Army* of men: for which services, the children of *God* may be no wayes *qualified,* though otherwise excellent for the *feare* of *God,* and the *knowledge* and *Grace* of the *Lord Jesus.*

4. If *Magistrates* ought (that is, ought only) to be chosen out of the *Church,* I demand if they ought not also to be *dethroned* and *deposed,* when they cease to be of the *Church,* either by voluntary departure from it, or by *excommunication* out of it, according to the bloody *tenents* and *practice* of some *Papists,* with whom the *Protestants* (according to their *principles*) although they seeme to abhor it, doe absolutely agree?

5. Therefore lastly, I ask if this be not to turne the *World* upside down, to turne the *World* out of the *World,* to pluck up the *roots* and *foundations* of all *common societie* in the *World?* to turne the *Garden* and *Paradice* of the *Church* and *Saints* into the *Field* of the *Civill State* of the *World,* and to reduce the *World* to the first *chaos* or *confusion.*

13. THE BLOODY TENENT YET MORE BLOODY

John Cotton answered Williams's first attack, with a tract entitled The Bloody Tenent washed and made white in the bloud of the Lambe *(London, 1647). Williams returned to the battle with* The Bloody Tenent yet More Bloody By Mr. Cottons endevour to wash it white in the Blood of the Lambe *(London, 1652). Williams was more concerned to protect religion from interference by the state than he was to protect the state from domination by the church, but some of the conservative implications of his political thought may be discerned in the following passage. It will be noted that if Williams's view of the state is accepted, Christopher Goodman's justification of rebellion (see this volume, Document 1) falls to the ground.*

Truth. I fear Master *Cotton* would create some evil opinion in the *heart* of the *civil Magistrate,* that the discusser is (as the *bloody Jews* told *Pilate*) no friend to *Caesar:* whereas upon a due search it will be found clear as the light, that it is impossible that any that subscribe *ex animo* to the bloody Tenent of persecution, can (*ex animo*) be a *friend* to *Magistracy.* The reason is, all *persecutors,* whether *priests* or *people,* care onely for such *Magistrates* as suite the *end,* the great bloody *end* of *persecution,* of whom they either hope to borrow the *sword,* or whom they hope to make their *executioners.* Their very principles also (*Papist* and *Protestant*) lead them necessarily to dispose

From Narragansett Club, *Publications,* IV, 204–211.

[depose] and kill their *heretical, Apostate, blaspheming Magistrates.*

Peace. But why should Master *Cotton* insinuate any affection in the discusser to that *Tyrant* of all earthly *Tyrants*, the *Pope?*

Truth. To my knowledge Master *Cotton* and others have thought the discusser too zealous against the bloody *beast:* yea, and who knows not this to be the ground of so much sorrowful *difference* between Master *Cotton* and the discusser, to wit, that the discusser grounds his separation from their *churches* upon their not seperating from that man of sin? For Old *England* having compelled all to *church*, compel'd the *Papists* and the *Pope* himself in them: The daughter *New England,* separating from her *mother* in *Old England,* yet maintaines and practises communion with the *Parishes* in *Old.* Who sees not then, but by the *links* of this *mystical chaine, New England Churches* are still fastned to the *Pope* himself?

Peace. Master *Cottons* third *reply* is this, that it is not like that such *Christians* will be faithful to their *prince,* who grow false and disloyal to their *God,* and therefore consequently the *civil Magistrate* must see that the *church degenerate* and apostate not, at least so far as to provoke *Christ* to depart from them.

Truth. This is indeed the down right most bloody and *Popish Tenent* of *persecuting* the *degenerate, heretical* and *Apostate* people: of deposing, yea and killing *Apostatical* and *heretical princes* and *rulers.*

The truth is, the great *Gods* of this world are *God-belly, God-peace, God-wealth, God-honour, God-pleasure* &c. These *Gods* must not be blasphemed, that is, evil spoke of, no not provoked, *&c.* The servants of the living *God* being true to their *Lord* and *Master*, have opposed his *glory, greatness, honour* &c. to these *Gods*, and to such *religions,* *worships*, and *services*, as commonly are made but as a *mask* or *vaile*, or covering of these *Gods*.

Peace. I have long been satisfied, that hence proceeds the *mad cry* of every *Demetrius* and *craftsMaster* of false *worship* in the *world*, *Great* is our *Diana* &c. These men blaspheme our *goddess*, disturbe our *City*, They are false to our *Gods*, how will they be true to us?

Hence that bloody Act of *Parliament* in *Henry* the fifth his dayes made purposely against that true *servant* and *witness* of *God* (in those points of *Christianity* which he knew) and other servants of *God* with him, the Lord *Cobham*, concluding *Lollardy* not only to be *heresie*, (that is, indeed true *Christianity*) but also *treason* against the *Kings person:* whence it followed, that these poor *Lollards* (the *servants* of the most *high God*) were not only to be burnt as *hereticks*, but hanged as *traitors*.

Truth. Accordingly it pleased God to honour that noble Lord *Cobham* both with hanging and burning, as an *heretick* against the *church*, as a *traitor* against the *king:* And hence those divelish accusations and bloody huntings of the poor servants of *God* in the reign of *Francis* the second in *Paris*, because it was said, that their meetings were to consult and act against the *life* of the *king*.

Peace. If this be the *touchstone* of all *obedience*, will it not be the *cut-throat* of all *civil relations*, *unions* and *covenants* between Princes and people, and between the people and people? For may not Master *Cotton* also say, he will not be a faithful *servant*, nor she a faithful *wife*, nor he a faithful *husband*, who grow false and disloyal to their *God?* And indeed what doth this, yea, what hath this truly ranting doctrine (that plucks up all relations) wrought but confusion and combustion all the world over?

Truth. Concerning *faithfulness*, it is most true, that *godliness* is profitable for all things, all *estates*, all *rela-*

tions: yet there is a *civil faithfulness, obedience, honesty, chastity,* &c. even amongst such as own not *God* nor *Christ:* else *Abraham* and *Isaac* dealt foolishly to make *leagues* with ungodly *Princes.* Besides, the whole Scripture commands a continuance in all *Relations* of *government, marriage, service,* notwithstanding that the *grace* of *Christ* had appeared to some, and the rest (it may be an *husband,* a *wife,* a *Magistrate,* a *Master,* a *servant*) were false and disloyal in their several kinds and wayes unto *God,* or wholly ignorant of him.

4. Grant *people* and *Princes* to be like *Julian, Apostate* from the true service of *God,* and consequently to grow less faithful in their places and respective services, yet what ground is there, from the *Testament* of *Christ Jesus,* upon this ground of their *Apostacie,* to prosecute them, as Master *Cotton* saith, The *civil Magistrate* must keep the *church* from *Apostatizing* so, as to cause *Christ* to depart from them.

5. Can the *sword* of *steel* or *arme* of *flesh* make men faithful or loyal to *God?* Or careth *God* for the outward *Loyalty* or *Faithfullness,* when the *inward-man* is *false* and *treacherous?*

Or is there not more danger (in all *matters* of *trust* in this *world*) from an *hyyocrite,* a *dissembler,* a *turncoat* in his *religion* (from the *fear* or *favour* of men) then from a resolved *Jew, Turke* or *Papist,* who holds firme unto his *principles?* &c.

Or lastly, if one *Magistrate, King* or *Parliament* call this or that *heresie, apostacie,* &c. and make men say so will not a stronger *Magistrate, King, Parliament, Army* (that is, a stronger *arm,* or longer and more prosperous *sword*) call that *heresie* and *Apostacie Truth* and *Christianity,* and make men call it so? and do not all *experiences,* and our own most lamentable, in the changes of our *English Religions,* confirme this?

6. Lastly, As carnal policy ever fals into the pit, it digs and trips up its own heels, so I shall end this *passage* with two *paradoxes*, and yet (dear *peace*) thou and I have found them most lamentably true in all ages.

Peace. God delights to befool the *wise* and *high* in their own *conceit* with *paradoxes*, even such as the wisdome of this world thinks *madness:* but I attend to hear them.

Truth. First then, The straining of mens *consciences* by *civil power*, is so far from making men faithful to *God* or man, that it is the ready way to render a man false to both: my ground is this: *civil* and *corporal punishment* do usually cause men to play the *hypocrite*, and dissemble in their *Religion*, to turn and return with the tide, as all *experience* in the *nations* of the *world* doth testifie now.

This *binding* and *rebinding* of *conscience*, contrary or without its own *perswasion*, so weakens and defiles it, that it (as all other *faculties*) loseth its strength, and the very nature of a common honest *conscience:* Hence it is, that even our own histories testifie, that where the *civil sword*, and carnal power, hath made a change upon the *consciences* of men, those *consciences* have been given up, not only to spiritual, but even to *corporal filthiness*, and bloody, and mad oppressing each other, as in the *Marian* bloody times &c.

Peace. Indeed no people [are] so inforced as the *Papists* and the *Mahumetans:* and no people more filthy in soul and body, and no people in the *world* more *bloody* and *persecuting:* but I listen for your second *paradox*.

Truth. Secondly, This *Tenet* of the *Magistrates* keeping the *church* from *Apostatizing*, by practising *civil force* upon the *consciences* of men, is so far from preserving *Religion* pure, that it is a mighty *Bulwark* or *Barricado* to keep out all true *Religion*, yea and all *godly Magistrates* for ever coming into the *World*.

Peace. Doubtless this will seem a hard *riddle*, yet I presume not too hard for the fingers of *time* and *truth* to unty, and render easie.

Truth. Thus I unty it: If the *civil Magistrate* must keep the *church* pure, then all the *people* of the *Cities, Nations*, and *kingdomes* of the *world* must do the same much more, for primarily and fundamentally, they are the *civil Magistrate:* Now the world (saith *John*) lyeth or is situated in *wickedness*, and consequently according to its disposition endures not the *light* of *Christ*, nor his golden *candlestick* the true *Church*, nor easily chooseth a true *Christian* to be her *officer* or *Magistrate*, for she accounts such false to her *Gods* and *Religion*, and suspects their faithfulness &c.

Peace. Hence indeed is it (as I now conceive) that so rarely this *world* admitteth or not long continueth a true servant of *God* in any place of *trust* and *credit*, except some extraordinary hand of *God* over-power, or else his servants by some base *staires* of *Flattery* or worldly *compliance*, ascend the chaire of *Civil-power.*

---

14. LETTERS OF ROGER WILLIAMS

After removing to Providence, Williams carried on a correspondence with several of his old friends in the Bay Colony. A number of these and some later communications between him and the town of Providence have been preserved. The three letters that follow give some interesting sidelights on Williams's political thought. Williams's primary concern was always religious, and where political

---

From Narragansett Club, *Publications*, VI, 3–7.

matters did not touch religious ones, his views were generally conventional.

WILLIAMS TO JOHN WINTHROP

(*Ca.* 1636 or 1637)

For his much honored, Mr. John Winthrop, Deputy Governor these.

[1636 or 1637.]

MUCH HONORED SIR,—

The frequent experience of your loving ear, ready and open toward me (in what your conscience hath permitted) as also of that excellent spirit of wisdom and prudence wherewith the Father of Lights hath endued you, embolden me to request a word of private advise with the soonest convenience, if it may be, by this messenger.

The condition of myself and those few families here planting with me, you know full well: we have no Patent: nor doth the face of Magistracy suit with our present condition. Hitherto, the masters of families have ordinarily met once a fortnight and consulted about our common peace, watch, and planting; and mutual consent have finished all matters with speed and peace.

Now of late some young men, single persons (of whom we had much need) being admitted to freedom of inhabitation, and promising to be subject to the orders made by the consent of the householders, are discontented with their estate, and seek the freedom of vote also, and equality, &c.

Beside, our dangers (in the midst of these dens of lions) now especially, call upon us to be compact in a civil way and power.

I have therefore had thoughts of propounding to my neighbors a double subscription, concerning which I shall humbly crave your help.

The first concerning ourselves, the masters of families: thus,

We whose names are hereunder written, late inhabitants of the Massachusetts, (upon occasion of some difference of conscience,) being permitted to depart from the limits of that Patent, under the which we came over into these parts, and being cast by the Providence of the God of Heaven, remote from others of our countrymen amongst the barbarians in this town of New Providence, do with free and joint consent promise each unto other, that, for our common peace and welfare (until we hear further of the King's royal pleasure concerning ourselves) we will from time to time subject ourselves in active or passive obedience to such orders and agreements, as shall be made by the greater number of the present householders, and such as shall be hereafter admitted by their consent into the same privilege and covenant in our ordinary meeting. In witness whereof we hereunto subscribe, &c.

Concerning those few young men, and any who shall hereafter (by your favorable connivance) desire to plant with us, this,—

We whose names are hereunder written, being desirous to inhabit in this Town of New Providence, do promise to subject ourselves in active or passive obedience to such orders and agreements as shall be made from time to time, by the greater number of the present householders of this Town, and such whom they shall admit into the same fellowship and privilege. In witness whereof, &c.

Hitherto we choose one, (named the officer,) to call the meeting at the appointed time: now it is desired by some of us that the householders by course perform that work, as also gather votes and see the watch go on, &c.

I have not yet mentioned these things to my neighbors, but shall as I see cause upon your loving counsel.

As also since the place I have purchased, secondly, at mine own charge and engagements, the inhabitants paying (by consent thirty shillings a piece as they come, until my charge be out for their particular lots: and thirdly, that I never made any other covenant with any person, but that if I got a place he should plant there with me: my query is this,—

Whither I may not lawfully desire this of my neighbors, that as I freely subject myself to common consent, and shall not bring in any person into the town without their consent: so also that against my consent no person be violently brought in and received.

I desire not to sleep in security and dream of a nest which no hand can reach. I cannot but expect changes, and the change of the last enemy death, yet dare I not despise a liberty, which the Lord seemeth to offer me, if for mine own or others peace: and therefore have I been thus bold to present my thoughts unto you.

The Pequots hear of your preparations, &c., and comfort themselves in this, that a witch amongst them will sink the pinnaces, by diving under water and making holes, &c., as also that they shall now enrich themselves with store of guns, but I hope their dreams (through the mercy of the Lord) shall vanish, and the devil and his lying sorcerers shall be confounded.

You may please, Sir, to take notice that it is of main consequence to take some course with the Wunnashowatuckoogs and Wusquowhananawkits, who are the furthermost Neepnet men, for the Pequots driven from the sea coast with ease, yet there secure and strengthen themselves, and are then brought down so much the nearer to you. Thus with my best respects to your loving self and Mrs. Winthrop, I rest,

Your Worships unfeigned, praying to meet you in this vale of tears or hills of mercy above.

R. WILLIAMS.

WILLIAMS TO THE TOWN OF PROVIDENCE (JANUARY 1655)

To the Town of Providence.

[PROVIDENCE, January, 1654–5.]

That ever I should speak or write a tittle, that tends to such an infinite liberty of conscience, is a mistake, and which I have ever disclaimed and abhorred. To prevent such mistakes, I shall at present only propose this case: There goes many a ship to sea, with many hundred souls in one ship, whose weal and woe is common, and is a true picture of a commonwealth, or a human combination or society. It hath fallen out sometimes, that both papists and protestants, Jews and Turks, may be embarked in one ship; upon which supposal I affirm, that all the liberty of conscience, that ever I pleaded for, turns upon these two hinges—that none of the papists, protestants, Jews, or Turks, be forced to come to the ship's prayers or worship, nor compelled from their own particular prayers or worship, if they practice any. I further add, that I never denied, that notwithstanding this liberty, the commander of this ship ought to command the ship's course, yea, and also command that justice, peace and sobriety, be kept and practiced, both among the seamen and all the passengers. If any of the seamen refuse to perform their services, or

---

From Narragansett Club, *Publications*, VI, 278–279.

passengers to pay their freight; if any refuse to help, in person or purse, towards the common charges or defence; if any refuse to obey the common laws and orders of the ship, concerning their common peace or preservation; if any shall mutiny and rise up against their commanders and officers; if any should preach or write that there ought to be no commanders or officers, because all are equal in Christ, therefore no masters nor officers, no laws nor orders, nor corrections nor punishments;—I say, I never denied, but in such cases, whatever is pretended, the commander or commanders may judge, resist, compel and punish such transgressors, according to their deserts and merits. This if seriously and honestly minded, may, if it so please the Father of lights, let in some light to such as willingly shut not their eyes.

I remain studious of your common peace and liberty.

ROGER WILLIAMS.

WILLIAMS TO DANIEL ABBOT, TOWN CLERK OF PROVIDENCE (JANUARY 15, 1681)

To Mr. Daniel Abbott, Town Clerk of Providence.

PROVIDENCE, 15th January, 1680–81 (so called.)

MY GOOD FRIEND,—

Loving remembrance to you. It has pleased the Most High and Only Wise, to stir up your spirit to be one of the

From Narragansett Club, *Publications,* VI, 401–403.

chiefest stakes in our poor hedge. I, therefore, not being able to come to you, present you with a few thoughts about the great stumbling-block to them that are willing to stumble and trouble themselves, our rates. James Matison had one copy of me, and Thomas Arnold another. This I send to yourself and the town, (for it may be I shall not be able to be at meeting.) I am grieved that you do so much service for so bad recompense; but I am persuaded you shall find cause to say, the Most High God of recompense, who was Abraham's great reward, hath paid me.

CONSIDERATIONS PRESENTED TOUCHING RATES.

1. Government and order in families, towns, &c., is the ordinance of the Most High, Rom. 13, for the peace and and good of mankind. 2. Six things are written in the hearts of all mankind, yea, even in pagans: 1st. That there is a Deity; 2d. That some actions are nought; 3d. That the Deity will punish; 4th. That there is another life; 5th. That marriage is honorable; 6th. That mankind cannot keep together without some government. 3. There is no Englishman in his Majesty dominions or elsewhere, who is not forced to submit to government. 4. There is not a man in the world, except robbers, pirates and rebels, but doth submit to government. 5. Even robbers, pirates and rebels themselves cannot hold together, but by some law among themselves and government. 6. One of these two great laws in the world must prevail, either that of judges and justices of peace in courts of peace, or the law of arms, the sword and blood. 7. If it comes from the courts of trials of peace, to the trial of the sword and blood, the conquered is forced to seek law and government. 8. Till matters come to a settled government, no man is ordinarily sure of his house, goods, lands, cattle, wife, children or life. 9. Hence is that ancient maxim, *It is better to live under a tyrant in peace, than under the sword, or where every man is a*

tyrant. 10. His Majesty sends governors to Barbadoes, Virginia, &c., but to us he shews greater favor in our charter, to choose whom we please. 11. No charters are obtained without great suit, favor or charges. Our first cost a hundred pounds (though I never received it all;) our second about a thousand; Connecticut about six thousand, &c. 12. No government is maintained without tribute, custom, rates, taxes, &c. 13. Our charter excels all in New England, or, *in the world, as to the souls of men.* 14. It pleased God, Rom. 13, to command tribute, custom, and consequently rates, not only for fear, but for conscience sake. 15. Our rates are the least, by far, of any colony in New England. 16. There is no man that hath a vote in town or colony, but *he hath a hand in making the rates by himself or his deputies.* 17. In our colony the General Assembly, Governor, magistrates, deputies, towns, town clerks, raters, constables, &c., have done their duties, the failing lies upon particular persons. 18. It is but folly to resist, (one or more, and if one, why not more?) God hath stirred up the spirit of the Governor, magistrates and officers, driven to it by necessity, to be unanimously resolved to see the matter finished; and it is the duty of every man to maintain, encourage, and strengthen the hand of authority. 19. Black clouds (some years) have hung over Old and New England heads. God hath been wonderfully patient and long suffering to us; but who sees not changes and calamities hanging over us? 20. All men fear, that this blazing herald from heaven[1] denounceth from the Most High, wars, pestilence, famines; it is not then our wisdom to make and keep peace with God and man?

Your old unworthy Servant,

ROGER WILLIAMS.

[1]The comet of 1640. [Ed.]

15. PROVOKING EVILS

In 1675, when New Englanders suffered their first large-scale Indian attack in nearly forty years, they did not hesitate to fight back with every weapon at their disposal. But good Puritans also looked about them for "provoking evils," that is, breaches of their covenant with God, that might have prompted Him to chastise them with so serious a punishment. They discovered several, and in November 1675 the General Court of Massachusetts passed the following measure to correct them. Nowhere in the records of seventeenth-century New England were the basic assumptions of Puritan political thought more explicitly exemplified in practice than in this effort of the government to restore the people to God's favor.

Whereas the most wise & holy God, for severall yeares past, hath not only warned us by his word, but chastized us with his rods, inflicting upon us many generall (though lesser) judgments, but we have neither heard the word nor rod as wee ought, so as to be effectually humbled for our sinns to repent of them, reforme, and amend our wayes; hence it is the righteous God hath heightened our calamity, and given commission to the barbarous heathen to rise up against us, and to become a smart rod and severe scourge to us, in burning & depopulating severall hopefull plantations, murdering many of our people of all sorts, and seeming as it were to cast us off, and putting us to

From N. B. Shurtleff, ed., *Records of the Governor and Company of the Massachusetts Bay in New England* (Boston: William White, 1853–1854) I, 59–63.

shame, and not going forth with our armies, heereby speaking aloud to us to search and try our wayes, and turne againe unto the Lord our God, from whom wee have departed with a great backsliding.

1. The Court, apprehending there is too great a neglect of discipline in the churches, and especially respecting those that are their chil̃dren, through the non acknowledgment of them according to the order of the gospell; in watching over them, as well as chattechising of them, inquireing into theire spirittuall estates, that, being brought to take hold of the covenant, they may acknouledge & be acknouledged according to theire relations to God & to his church, and theire obligations to be the Lords, and to approove themselves so to be by a suiteable profession & conversation; and doe therefore solemnly recommend it unto the respective elders and brethren of the severall churches throughout this jurisdiction to take effectuall course for reformation herein.

2. Whereas there is manifest pride openly appearing amongst us in that long haire, like weomens haire, is worne by some men, either their oune or others haire made into perewiggs, and by some weomen wearing borders of haire, and theire cutting, curling, & immodest laying out theire haire, which practise doeth prevayle & increase, especially amongst the younger sort,—

This Court doeth declare against this ill custome as offencive to them, and divers sober christians amongst us, and therefore doe hereby exhort and advise all persons to use moderation in this respect; and further, doe impower all grand juries to present to the County Court such persons, whither male or female, whom they shall judge to exceede in the premisses; and the County Courts are hereby authorized to proceed against such delinquents either by admonition, fine, or correction, according to theire good discretion.

3. Notwithstanding the wholesome lawes already made by this Court for restreyning excesse in apparrell, yet through corruption in many, and neglect of due execution of those lawes, the evill of pride in apparrell, both for costlines in the poorer sort, & vaine, new, strainge fashions, both in poore & rich, with naked breasts and armes, or, as it were, pinioned with the addition of superstitious ribbons both on haire & apparrell; for redresse whereof, it is ordered by this Court, that the County Courts, from time to time, doe give strict charge to present all such persons as they shall judge to exceede in that kinde, and if the grand jury shall neglect theire duty herein, the County Court shall impose a fine upon them at their discretion.

And it is further ordered, that the County Court, single magistrate, Commissioners Court in Boston, have heereby power to summon all such persons so offending before them, and for the first offence to admonish them, and for each offence of that kinde afterwards to impose a fine of tenn shillings upon them, or, if unable to pay, to inflict such punishment as shall be by them thought most suiteable to the nature of the offence; and the same judges above named are heereby impowred to judge of and execute the lawes already extant against such excesse.

Whereas it may be found amongst us, that mens thresholds are sett up by Gods thresholds, and mans posts besides Gods posts, espeacially in the open meetings of Quakers, whose damnable haeresies, abominable idolatrys, are hereby promoted, embraced, and practised, to the scandall of religion, hazard of souls, and provocation of divine jealousie against this people, for prevention & reformation whereof, it is ordered by this Court and the authority thereof, that every person found at a Quakers meeting shall be apprehended, ex officio, by the constable, and by warrant from a magistrate or commissioner shall be committed to the house of correction, and there to have the discipline of the house applied to them, and to be kept to worke, with bread & water, for three days, and then released, or else shall pay five pounds in money as a fine to the county for such offence; and all constables neglecting their duty in not faithfully executing this order shall incurr the penalty of four pounds, upon conviction, one third whereof to the informer.

And touching the law of importation of Quakers, that it may be more strictly executed, and none transgressing to escape punishment,—

It is heereby ordered, that the penalty to that law averred be in no case abated to lesse than twenty pounds.

5. Whereas there is so mutch profanes amongst us in persons turning their backs upon the publick worship before it be finished and the blessing pronounced,—

It is ordered by this Court, that the officers of the churches, or select-men, shall take care to prevent such disorders, by appointing persons to shutt the meeting house doores, or any other meete way to attaine the end.

6. Whereas there is much disorder & rudenes in youth in many congregations in time of the worship of God, whereby sin & prophaness is greately increased, for reformation whereof,—

It is ordered by this Court, that the select men doe appoint such place or places in the meeting house for children or youth to sit in where they may be most together and in publick veiw, and that the officers of the churches, or select-men, doe appoint some grave & sober person or persons to take a particcular care of and inspection over them, who are heereby required to present a list of the names of such, who, by their oune observance or the information of others, shall be found delinquent, to the next magistrate or Court, who are impowred for the first offence to admonish them, for the second offence to impose a fine of five shillings on theire parents or governnors, or order the children to be whipt, and if incorrigible, to be whipt with ten stripes, or sent to the house of correction for three dayes.

7. Whereas the name of God is prophaned by common swearing and cursing in ordinary communication, which is a sin that growes amongst us, and many heare such oathes and curses, and conceales the same from authority, for reformation whereof, it is ordered by this Court, that the lawes already in force against this sin be vigorously prosecuted; and, as addition thereunto, it is further ordered, that all such persons who shall at any time heare prophane oathes and curses spoken by any person or persons, and shall neglect to disclose the same to some magistrate, commissioner, or constable, such persons shall incurr the same penalty provided in that law against swearers.

8. Whereas the shamefull and scandelous sin of excessive drinking, tipling, & company keeping in tavernes, &c, ordinarys, grows upon us, for reformation whereof,—

It is commended to the care of the respective County Courts not to license any more publick houses then are absolutely necessary in any toune, and to take care that none be licenst but persons of approoved sobriety and fidelity to law and good order; and that licensed houses be regulated in theire improovement for the refreshing & enterteinment of travailers & strangers only, and all toune dwellers are heereby strictly enjoyned & required to forbeare spending their time or estates in such common houses of enterteynment, to drincke & tiple, upon penalty of five shillings for every offence, or, if poore, to be whipt, at the discretion of the judge, not exceeding five stripes; and every ordinary keeper, permitting persons to transgress as above said, shall incurr the penalty of five shillings for each offence in that kinde; and any magistrate, commissioner, or selectmen are impowred & required vigorously to putt the above-said law in execution.

And, ffurther, it is ordered, that all private, unlicensed

houses of enterteinment be diligently searched out, and the penalty of this law strictly imposed; and that all such houses may be the better discovered, the select-men of every toune shall choose some sober and discreete persons, to be authorized from the County Court, each of whom shall take the charge of ten or twelve families of his neighbourhood, and shall diligently inspect them, and present the names of such persons so transgressing to the magistrate, commissioners, or selectmen of the toune, who shall returne the same to be proceeded with by the next County Court as the law directs; and the persons so chosen and authorized, and attending theire duty ffaithfully therein, shall have one third of the fines allowed them; but, if neglect of their duty, and shall be so judged by authority, they shall incurr the same penalty provided against unlicensed houses.

9. Whereas there is a wofull breach of the fifth comandment to be found amongst us, in contempt of authority, civil, ecclesiasticall, and domesticall, this Court doeth declare, that sin is highly provoaking to the Lord, against which he hath borne severe testimony in his word, especially in that remarkeable judgments upon Chorah and his company, and therefore doe strictly require & comand all persons under this goverment to reforme so great an evil, least God from heaven punish offenders heerin by some remarkeable judgments. And it is further ordered, that all County Courts, magistrates, commissioners, selectmen, and grand jurors, according to theire severall capacities, doe take strict care that the lawes already made & provided in this case be duely executed, and particcularly that evil of inferiours absenting themselves out of the families whereunto they belong in the night, and meeting with corrupt company without leave, and against the minde & to the great greife of theire superiours, which evil practise is of a very perrillous nature, and the roote of much disorder.

It is therefore ordered by this Court, that whatever inferiour shallbe legally convicted of such an evil practise, such persons shall be punished with admonition for the first offence, with fine not exceeding ten shillings, or whipping not exceeding five stripes, for all offences of like nature afterwards.

10. Whereas the sin of idlenes (which is a sin of Sodom) doeth greatly increase, notwithstanding the wholesome lawes in force against the same, as an addition to that law,—

This Court doeth order, that the constable, with such other person or persons whom the selectmen shall appoint, shall inspect particcular families, and present a lyst of the names of all idle persons to the selectmen, who are heereby strictly required to proceed with them as already the law directs, and in case of obstinacy, by charging the constable with them, who shall convey them to some magistrate, by him to be committed to the house of correction.

11. Whereas there is oppression in the midst of us, not only by such shopkeepers and merchants who set excessive prizes on their goods, also by mechanicks but *also by mechanicks* and day labourers, who are dayly guilty of that evill, for redress whereoff, & as an adition to the law, title Oppression, itt is ordered by this Court, that any person that judgeth himself oppressed by shopkeepers or merchants in setting excessive prizes on their goods, have heereby liberty to make theire complaint to the grand jurors, or otherwise by petition to the County Court immediately, who shall send to the person accused, and if the Court, upon examination, judge the person complayning injuried, they shall cause the offendor to returne double the overplus, or more then the equall price, to the injured person, and also impose a fine on the offendors at the discretion of the Court; and if any person judge himself oppressed by mechanicks or day labourers, they may make complaint thereof to the selectmen of the toune, who if

upon the examination doe find such complaint just, having respect to the quality of the pay, and the length or shortnes of the day labour, they shall cause the offendor to make double restitution to the party injuried, and pay a fine of double the value exceeding the due price.

12. Whereas there is a loose & sinfull custome of going or riding from toune to toune, and that oft times men & weomen together, upon pretence of going to lecture, but it appeares to be meerely to drincke & revell in ordinarys & tavernes, which is in itself scandalous, and it is to be feared a notable meanes to debauch our youth and hazard the chastity of such as are draune forth thereunto, for prevention whereof,—

It is ordered by this Court, that all single persons who, meerly for their pleasure, take such journeyes, & frequent such ordinaryes, shall be reputed and accounted riotous & unsober persons, and of ill behaviour, and shall be liable to be summoned to appeare before any County Court, magistrate, or commissioner, & being thereof convicted, shall give bond & sufficient sureties for the good behaviour in twenty pounds, and upon refusall so to doe, shall be committed to prison for ten days, or pay a fine of forty shillings for each offence. . . .

---

16. THE PEOPLE OF GOD

Cotton Mather (1663–1728) came of age in the year when Massachusetts lost the royal charter that had given the colony virtual autonomy. In 1686 the whole of New Eng-

---

From Cotton Mather, *The Serviceable Man. A Discourse Made unto the General Court of the Massachusetts Colony, New England, At the Anniversary Election 28d. 3m.* 1690 (Boston: Samuel Green, for Joseph Browning, 1690), pp. 1–10, 27–41.

land was placed under the control of a single, royally appointed governor, Sir Edmund Andros, whose commission empowered and required him to rule without benefit of any representative assembly. Most New Englanders regarded the change as another divine chastisement, comparable to the Indian War of 1675–1676. In 1688, when James II fled from the throne, the people of Boston rose against Andros and shipped him back to England where Cotton Mather's father Increase was working for a res oration of the old charter.

While awaiting this hoped-for event, Massachusetts governed itself in the old way, through a General Court, composed of magistrates and deputies elected annually in May. Part of the traditional procedure at the election was for a leading minister to preach a sermon, discussing the principles of government and the character of good rulers. Cotton Mather was selected for the task in 1690 and delivered a sermon reminding New Englanders of their special destiny and warning their enemies of the fate God had in store for the instruments with which He chastised His chosen people.

NEHEMIAH V. 19.

Think upon me, my God, for Good, according to all that I have done for this People.

THAT you are this Day Assembled for a Revival and a Renewal of your Anniversary *Elections*, is, I suppose, intended by you, as no less a part of your Obedience to their Majesties, who upon the Address of our Convention to Them, Declaring, *That they accepted Government of this People according to the Rules of the Charter*, did in answer thereunto, Order *A Continuance in the Administration thereof:* than it is a part of your Deference to so great and just a Judgment, as that of the *English Nation* Assembled in Parliament, *That the Invasion of our Charters was Illegal and a Grievance, and that they ought to be restored unto us.* But the Word of the Almighty God has been still one usual stroke in our Annual *Solemnities*, and something of that are you now to attend unto.

In the Words now Read, we find not only the *Prayer*, but also the *Picture* of a no less worthy than famous *Magistrate*, and it will be no unprofitable Meditation, to reflect a little upon the occasion of it. The *Truth* and *Manner* of the Return which the *Jews* made out of their *Babylonish Captivity*, had been declared in a Book written by *Ezra*, a great Man greatly concern'd in that Return. But the *Fruit* and *Event* of it is now related, in a Supplement unto that History, written by *Nehemiah* a Renowned Governour of that Restored People; for whom it was no more improper to Record *His own Acts*, than it was for the Great *Julius Caesar* to write his *Commentaries.* This inspired Historian, was doubtless a very *young* man, when he first apply'd himself unto the more open and public service of his Countrey; for the Transactions of more than *fifty* years are comprized in this Narrative of his Administrations; nevertheless God made him a true *Nehemiah* to his Countrey men; that is, *A comforter from the Lord.* The good Providence of God, had made this *Nehemiah*, a blessed Instrument of Rebuilding and Resettling *Jerusalem*, which had been miserably Ruined by *Chaldean* Invasions and Oppressions; from whence, in the twelfth year of his Government, he goes back into *Persia*, where he had been an eminent Officer in the Court of *Artaxerxes Longimanus;* but from thence he soon repeats his Journey of above *nine hundred miles*, and revisits his beloved *Jerusalem*, with a new Commission, by vertue of which he sets himself to

Redress divers Disorders, under which that little Commonwealth was labouring.

The common People at this time were very *Poor* and *Low;* for they had usually many *Children* in their Families that call'd for more *Bread* than their single hands could purchase for them; and yet they had heavy *Taxes* which the Necessity and Calamity of their Affairs *compelled* them to the payment of. The People had no way, but the Borrowing of *Money* to defray all these Charges; but the Rich Lenders took them at this Disadvantage, so as not only to squeeze the cruel Int'rest of *twelve in the Hundred* from them, but also to seize upon their *Lands* which they had Mortgaged for the *Principal:* Yea they hook'd the very persons of their Brethren into Slavery. Very loud complaints were now made, of these oppressions; whereupon the Governour called a *General Court*, and procured the Relaxation of these Difficulties; he seems to erect a *Bank of Credit* among them, and render *Credit* so *passeable*, that the indigent people might still enjoy their Livings, and yet have *Credit* enough to demand from one another what their Exigencies called for. In the Speech which this Honourable Person made upon this occasion, he mentions his own *Exemple* as one *Article*, for the conviction of those who did in this time of Distress Exact upon their Neighbours. They had just before been under a Governour who not only made his Domestick Expences to stand the People in *Five Pounds a Day*, besides large quantities of Provisions, for his Table; but also he had his little creatures about him, whom he used as *Tools* for the getting of *Money*, as often as he or they found a want thereof. But sayes our *Nehemiah: So did not I, because of the fear of God!* No, he would make none of those great Bargains, for which he had an opportunity in the Poverty and Penury of the People; but instead thereof, *He* denied himself of what was his *Right*. He refused the *Salary* which was due unto him as a *Magistrate;* and this, tho' he spent more time than ordinary in the Affairs of the Government: yea, He employed his own *Servants* in those matters for which there seem'd a lack of *Hands*; and He fed many scores above an hundred, of those that were proper Subjects for his Invitations, out of his own Estate. It was not with any *Vanity* that He mentioned these things, but he brought them as a demonstration of his Desire, to ease the People of their *Burdens*.

Our Text, is the *Epiphonema* of this Narrative. No prudent *Magistrate* needs to be told that he ought to be a *Man of Prayer:* They that are to *Act for* God in Government should very much *Be With* God in Devotion. One of the greatest *Magistrates* that ever lived, could give that account of himself, in *Psal.* 109. 4. *I give my self unto Prayer:* but the Words in the Original are so elliptical, as to be only thus much, *I Prayer,* as if he had been all made up of *Prayer*. Such a *Magistrate* was our *Nehemiah* here; every business would he both begin and conclude with *Prayer;* and *Prayer* was like his very Breath, issuing from him with a constant Respiration. Tis one of his *Prayers* that we are now to be entertained with: We will suppose that he *Pray'd in Faith*; and so there are two or three things in the *Prayer*.

First, We have the *Declaration* of a pious Ruler. He says, *I have done for this people;* he had been serviceable to the People of God. What had he *done?* Why, he had *Addressed* the King, on the behalf of his Ruined Country-men; he had undergone a Travel of many *Leagues* to promote their Safety; he had entred upon the Administration of the *Government,* when it would have broke the Heart of any man alive to have medled with it; he had parted with a large portion of his *Riches,* for the use of the Publick; he had born with great *Abuses* from his Enemies; and whatever he saw amiss in *Church* or *State,* he courageously set himself upon the Reformation of it. This had he *done!* But then,

Secondly, We have his joint *Supplication* and *Expectation* thereupon. Sais he, *Think upon me, my God, for Good, according to all this.* That Expression, *Think upon me,* may also be Translated, *Remember me.* And we may not imagine, that any thing is look'd for in a way of *Merit,* but all in a way of *Mercy* here. Hence we have it in those Terms, in Neh. 13. 22. *Remember me, O my God, concerning this, and spare me according to the Greatness of thy Mercy.*

This prayer, is the Result of an observation made, upon that *Goodness,* and *Kindness, Pitty,* which appears in the usual Providence of the most High, towards them that are serviceable to the people of God.

This then is our

DOCTRINE.

The God of Heaven has GOOD THOUGHTS for those men, whose GOOD WORKS render them Serviceable to His People.

I. 'Tis to be taken for granted, as we go along; That our God has, *A People* in the World; and indeed He *ever* had so. The World has always been Blessed with a *People,* who have chosen the Lord Jehovah for their Best Good, and their Last End; *a people* who have chosen the Lord Jesus for the Redeemer of their Souls; *a people* who have Believed and Practised according to the Scriptures of Truth: 'tis the *people,* whose Denomination is that, in Isa. 63. 18. *The people of thy Holiness;* or Gods Holy People. The people of *Israel* was once His people, but upon their Abdication from God; we have now among the *Gentiles*, a *Surrogate Israel.* Such a *people*, and a *Church* of them too, there has been upon Earth, in all Ages *Visible.* If the Existence of such a people were ever to be questioned, it was when the barbarous and horrible Darkness of *Popery*, had covered the face of *Europe*; and yet even then too, we are not at a loss to find such a *people*, in the very Bowels of the *Papal Empire.* The Popish Historians themselves do confess, that the *Waldenses* were a *people* who from the very days of *Constantine* had withdrawn from the conceived Corruptions in the Apostatical Church of *Rome.* Nor were they called *Waldenses*, because *Waldo* was their Father, but because they had their Dwellings in the *Vallies*, that are ever famous for them.

A *People*, implies a *Multitude* of men, and therewithal some *Combination* or *Association* of them. Blessed be our God, there is a Number among the children of men, who by Agreement, may be called, *His.*

II. 'Tis also to be taken for granted, That every man should study to be *Serviceable* unto the people of God. This people, in its Militant Condition here, has many things to be *Done* for it; and our God hath so Disposed of us, as to make us need the Help one of another. The people of God may say unto us, as in Philem. 19. *Thou owest unto me, even thine own self.* We owe the utmost Service unto the Great God, as our *Creator* and *Preserver;* but He has made His People the Receivers of his Rents; they have His Letter of *Atturney* for all the *Goodness* that *we can extend unto them.* The people of God are continually in circumstances, that call for the Assistence of all that are *Well-affected unto the Dust of Zion.* We cannot with any face pretend to be *of them*, if we now withhold, any of that care, or cost, or Time, with which we may be Serviceable to them. They make up, *The Mystical Body of Christ;* and we are worse than silver *Hands*, or wooden *Legs*, in that

Body, if we are not so *sensible* of, as to be *Serviceable* in, their *Difficulties*. It was for the *Good* of this people, that the Son of God, underwent all the Troubles and Sorrows of His deep *Humiliation;* and we are None of *His*, if we count it any *Humiliation* unto our selves, to do any thing that may be for the *Good* of such a people.

* * *

Application.

But it is the Transferring of this Doctrine into the state of *New-England*, that is the *Province* at this time to be served by me; the State of the Countrey is to be as much my Text, as any Verse in the Fifth Chapter of *Nehemiah*. I behold a Representation of this Countrey within these Walls this day, with their Invitation, to speak unto them, in the Name of Him, that we own for *our King, our Lord, our Law-Giver*. But never had any man more cause to suspect his own Ability of speaking unto such an Assembly on such an occasion as is now before me, than that *Son* of yours by whom you are now Addressed. Alas I may make the complaint of the Prophet, in *Jer.* 1. 6. *Behold, I cannot speak;* and add his Reason for it too, with a thousand more: But if I am a *Child*, you know that the little *Stamerings* and *Chatterings* of your *Children* are not heard without your satisfaction in them. Nor while I am thus pressing others to be serviceable, do I dare omit what *Service* may be done by my *Speaking* here: But, *O Lord God of my Master, I pray thee send me good speed this Day!*

There is one *Position* and Three *Deductions* which I now expect your Attention to;

THE POSITION.

The People of *New England* are a *People of God*. There have been very critical and ingenious Attempts made by some Learned men to find *lost Israel* in *America;* tho' it be not easie to find any other Track of them, than this; *that the Tartars are the Ten Tribes,* which Dr. *Fletchers* Dissertations have rendred almost evident; and *the Northern Indians of this mighty Continent are of a Scythian Original* which will be almost as evident unto him, that shall read the Disquisitions of the Learned *Hornius.* But behold, you may see an *Israel* in *America,* by looking upon this Plantation; may *Peace be upon this Israel of God!* It is notorious, That a Settlement in this part of *America,* was first endeavoured by some that had no designs but those of a *Secular Interest:* but the God of Heaven blasted all those Designs, and broke up one Plantation after another by very terrible Frowns of His Holy Providence. Until at length a number of Pious and Worthy men transplanted themselves into this Wilderness, with Designs of practising the *Religion* of the Lord Jesus here, without such *Obstructions* as in *Europe* they feared thereunto; and then, the Great God smil'd upon the undertaking with *Mercies* little short of *Miracles.* Tis the prerogative of *New-England* above all the Countries of the world, *That it is a Plantation for the Christian and Protestant Religion.* You may now see a Land filled with *Churches,* which by solemn and awfull Covenants are *Dedicated* unto the Son of God; there are I suppose, more than an Hundred of those Holy Societies among us, which would, in *Luthers* Judgment, render the *meanest Village* more glorious than an *Ivory palace;* in these *Churches* you may see *Discipline* managed, *Heresy* subdued, *Prophaness* opposed, and *Communion* maintained, with a careful Respect unto the word of God in all; you may see faithful *Ministers,* and sincere *Christians,* and multitudes of Souls Ripening apace for the Kingdom of God; you may see proportionably as much of *God* among them, as in any spot of Ground which the Children of *Adam* walk upon; if our Degeneracies cause you not quickly to loose the *Sight.* By our *Profession* at least, there is *Holiness to the Lord,* written upon all the circumstances of this People; and we *do*, we *may* speak in such a Style, as that in *Isai.* 63. 19. *Lord, we are thine!* We may look upon the Lord, as *the God of our Fathers;* and we still make some claim unto Him. The very *Grandchildren* of the good old Planters here, are every day coming in to lay hold on his Covenant; and they speak after that manner, in *Jer.* 14. 9. *O Lord: we are called by thy Name, Leave us not.*

Well then, *Think upon me, my God, for good, according to all that I have done for this People.*

There are these *Inferences* hence to be insisted on:

DEDUCTION 1.

What will be the *Thoughts* of our God concerning them that shall *Do* all they can *Against* His people here? The man that shall do *Service* for the people of God, has this wish going to Heaven for him, *Remember me, O my God, concerning this.* Well, the man that shall do *mischief* to the people of God, is also to be *Remembred;* it is said in Neh. 13. 29. *Remember them, O my God, because of what they have done.* Believe me, The Almighty God will make those Agents of the Devil know that He'l *Remember* them! those *Tobijahs* and *Sanballats* will not be forgotten.

This people of God, is part of that *Israel*, whereof it may be said, *His Adversaries be round about him.* The Enemies of *New England* have not been few or small; and it is because we are, *A people of God*, that we still have such Enemies. We have indeed been a *persecuted people,* and *Wars* have been made upon us, for our *keeping the Commandments of God, and having the Testimony of Jesus Christ.* Into the List of our present Enemies, who would not put those, who t'other Day, let fall their cursed and cruel Intimations, *That it was convenient this Territory should be possessed by another people!* and those that were so politick as to inform us now and then, *That it was not for the Interest of our Superiours' that we should Thrive!* and those that have had the vanity to publish unto the World in Print, their Proposals, *That the Religion of this people made it unsafe to allow them here.* And with these, who would not reckon those Pagan and Popish Neighbours, that are making the Inroads of a Bloody War upon us? These are our *Declared* Enemies! But in the same *Herd*, you may see many others, whose *Drivers*, have heretofore been in other Countries in former Ages.

Among our worst Enemies, may be Accounted, in short, All that go to *Destroy* or *Frustrate* the Great Ends which this *Plantation* was first erected upon. But what were those *Ends?* The Question was often put unto our Predecessors, in Mat. 11. 7. *What went ye out into the Wilderness to see?* And the Answer to it, is not only too *Excellent*, but also too *Notorious*, to be dissembled. Let all mankind know, That we came into the *Wilderness*, because we would quietly worship God, without that *Episcopacy*, that *Common-Prayer*, and those unwarrantable *Ceremonies*, which the *Land of our Fathers Sepulchres*, has been defiled with, we came, because we would have our Posterity settled under the pure and full *Dispensations* of the Gospel, defended by *Rulers that should be of our selves, and Governours that should proceed from the midst of us.* Hence those are the fatal Enemies of this people, that shall go to Debauch and infect the Rising Generation among us, and corrupt them with evil manners; and learn them to Drink and Drab, and Game, and profane the Sabbath, and *Sin against the Hope of their Fathers;* or, those that shall go to *Decoy* them, and much more *Compel* them, unto those Remainders of *Popery*, which the first Reformers were hindred from sweeping out of the English Nation; among which, I would set a special Remark upon *Super-*

stitious Holy-days, which have too much obtained among our unwary Children. These Enemies do us the worst office in the world; for they do, like *Balaam*, go to make us offend our God, and thereby loose His Presence and His Favour; it was the old *Roman* way of Conquering Cities, they first used Stratagems to get their Gods out of them; a right *Romish* Policy. If the *New-Englanders* once forget their Errand hither, they are immediately deserted by that God, who says, *Wo to them, when I depart from them.*

Unto those Enemies we may Annumerate those *False Accusers*, who are continually misrepresenting of us, in the Court which we have so much Dependence on. There is nothing more easy to be demonstrated, *Than that the people of New-England are the most Loyal People in all the English Dominions;* our greatest pretenders to Loyalty among the Adversaries, we have seen *cursing of their King, and their God, and looking upward*, under not a Tenth part of such inconveniences, which yet never so much as Raised one *Disloyal Thought* in our Selves. *We* that never were any *Charge* unto the *Crown*, unless when our *Charters* were taken from us; have yet approved our selves the most Faithful Subjects of the *Crown*, and been *Earlier* still than any of the *American* Plantations in Testimonies of true Allegiance thereunto. Nevertheless, as of old, when *Cyrus*, who had given the Jews a Charter, was gone off the Stage, and *Cambyses* was Enthroned after him, there were a company of *Samaritans*, who exhibited an Information against that people of God; said they in Ezra 4. 12, 13. *Be it known unto the King, the Jews are Building a Rebellious and a bad City; if it be builded, they will not pay Tribute and Custome, and the Kings Revenue will be Endamaged.* This is one of those Injuries which have been done to *us*. There are some too nearly Related unto the *Accuser of the Brethren*, who are perpetually making against us those groundless and wicked complaints, with which they first put us into *Bear skins*, and then themselves intend to do the *Dogs* part upon us. To pass by the old *Stories*, what Ridiculous and Extravagant Calumnies were the *Last year* published against us, and laid before the High Court of Parliament? by which we had been *undone*, if God had not provided on the Spot, a *Vindicator* for us. And what *Petitions*, what *Remonstrances*, what impudent *Lies*, may still be made against us, is less known to us, than 'tis by *whom* they are made; the men that first *cause* the miscarriages among us, have usually been those that have *Complained* of those miscarriages; and you know whom they take for their *pattern* in doing so. But what would they have? Are they so *Foolish* as to foresee *no* Consequences, or are they so *wicked* as to desire *those* which were t'other day upon us? *Forgive, them, they kno not what they do?* While these *Enemies* are seeking to involve our *Civil Concerns* in Confusion, there are *Sectaries* and *Seducers* that are using their Batt'ring Rams upon our *Sacred* Ones. And among those, the *Quakers* are certainly the most *Malicious*, as well as the most *Pernicious* Enemies. They were once in a ready way to have broken up all the Good Order whether *Civil* or *Sacred*, in the Infancy of this Plantation; which occasioned the Authority whom they would have undermined, then to turn a *Sharp* upon them, by Laws not so severe as those in the Realm of *England* against (their Fathers) the *Jesuites*, on the same Account: yet those *Troublesome Hereticks*, who had no Business here at all, but the overthrowing of our whole Government, would push themselves on the Swords point; and tho' Repeated Banishments with merciful Entreaties to be gone, were first used unto them, nevertheless, two or three of them would rather Dy, than leave the Plantation undisturbed. It is possible a *Bedlam* had been fitter for those Frantic people, than what was inflicted on them; and for my own part, I must profess with regard unto such Hereticks, *Ad Judicium sanguinis Tardus sum;* nor have I the least inclinations to *Hereticide* as a fit way to suppress their Errors; yea, since the Government has been too *safe,* and *strong,* for those Foxes to throw down our wall; we *have* now for many years indulged them an Entire *Liberty of Conscience,* nor is there (nor do I bespeak) the least prospect or intent of giving them interruption in it; but still by *Writing, Railing,* and the *Arts* peculiar to themselves, they are Labouring to *Unchurch* all the Lords people here; they would fain have us give up our whole *Christianity,* for their New Digested and scarce Refined *Paganism,* and have prevailed with some obscure and Remote Nooks of the Country, so to do. Especially *every Shepherd is an Abomination to those Egyptians*: and one of some Figure among them, an Ignorant and Malignant *Apostate,* who has this Mark of the *Unpardonable Sin* upon him, that he calls those *Prayers* of ours, with which the *Holy Spirit* of God, has helped us to vanquish the very *Devils* themselves but so many *Conjurings,* and *Charms,* and *Spells;* this man has vomited more venemous Pamphlets against these Churches, and all the *Ordinances* therein observed, than any that have gone before him; only God has helped some of us lately to furnish our Churches with an *Antidote.* But what will be the *Thoughts* of our God, concerning them that are thus *Doing Against* His people here? I suppose there are some of them now, in this Great Assembly, come with no better Ends, than *he* who of old presented himself among *the Sons of God.* I shall for *their* sake, use the more Freedome, and plainly say; That the *Thoughts* of God about them, are not such as they can have any comfort in. I am to tell you, That *New England* has an *Advocate* in Heaven, who has put in a dreadful Memorial against you all; 'tis that in Neh. 6. 14. *My God, Think thou upon them according to these their works.* Ye Fool hardy men; Do but look into the

Scriptures, and you may know the *Thoughts* of the Omnipotent God concerning you. There are Terrible *Threats* in the Book of God, which will discover the more Terrible *Thoughts* in the Heart of God against men of your Complexion. It is the Thundring voice of the Great God, in Psal. 34. 21. *They that Hate the Righteous shall be Desolate;* and yet the Great Quarrel with *New England* has been, its having so many *Righteous* in it. Some of us may Remember when this very Pulpit had that loud and fair Warning sounded in it, in Zech. 2. 8. *He that touches you, touches the Apple of Gods Eye*; and who of the Auditory then present, quickly and sadly found the Fulfilment of it upon themselves. As, There are *Scripture Menaces*, thus there are *Scripture Exemples* too, to strike Terrour into the Souls of them, who shall go to pull down miseries, upon a *people of the Saints of the most High*. Shall we speak of lesser men? The Jewish Writers tells us, of one *Shebna*, who tho' he Lived in *Jerusalem*, was very deep in the Interests of *Sennacherib*, and a secret Rotten Adversary to the people of God, tho' he were a Professor among them; but God gave that Commission unto His Prophet, in Isa. 22.15. *Go, get thee unto this Treasurer, even unto* Shebna, *and say, Behold, the Lord will violently turn thee, and toss thee like a Ball into a large Countrey, There shalt thou Dy!* Or shall we speak of greater men? *Sennacherib* himself had been a Bloody Adversary to the people of God, and nothing would satisfie him, unless *Jerusalem* too might feel the smart of his Arbitrary Government; but what came on him at last? we read in Isa. 37. 38. *As he was worshipping in the House of his God, his two Sons smote him.* The Jewish Rabbins tell us, That he had vowed to make a Sacrifice of his two Children, unto his False God, which *they* understanding were thus aforehand with him. But why do I descend unto particular instances? All the Bible is full of that vengeance which falls upon the Heads of those that are Enemies to the people of God. We are assured in Psal. 105. 14. *He hath suffered no man to do them wrong, Yea, He has Reproved Kings for their sakes!* What got the *Egyptians* by persuing after the people of God into the *Wilderness*, whither they Retired, that they might worship him? I assure you, *That* was the Thing that fill'd up the measure of all their sins; they were then ripe for the *Last plague* of God upon them. If they that wrong *one Saint* of God, be more undone, than a man thrown into the Sea, with *a milstone about his Neck*, what will be the Fate of him that shall wrong a whole *people* that is *Holy to the Lord.* Some it may be set themselves against the people of God, out of *Revenge;* and this with some shadow of *Reason* and *Justice* on their side; but *This* also will not excuse them. *Achitophel* is deep in the Conspiracy against *David;* why, *David* had abused *Bathsheba*, who was the Grand-child of *Achitophel.* Yet you know what came of him! If they be *Davids*, or a Beloved and Repenting people, which we are prejudic'd against; God will make it a dangerous thing to meddle with them.

But if the *Scriptures* will not affect you; then I pray, look upon your own unhappy *Predecessors*, unto whom God has made this poor People such a *Burdensome Stone*, as to break the Backs of all that have been heaving at it. The Observation has been a thousand times made, by more than ten thousand Persons, That Remarkable and Lamentable *Disasters* have still followed the Adversaries of poor *New-England.* It has been a Countrey of *Witnesses* or *Confessors* for the Lord Jesus; and it is said in *Rev.* 11. 6. *If any man will hurt them, Fire devours them:* one had as good eat *Fire* as go to do such a People any Harm.

What is become of those that have heretofore made their bitter *Invectives* against this innocent People; and *compassed Sea and Land*, with attempts to put a stop unto the Work of the Lord Jesus here? What is become of those that brag'd *Their Arms were long enough to reach us,* and would have *Spoil't* us if they had *Reacht* us with those bloody Popish Arms? Were there never any *Ships broken in Ezion Geber* for us? yea, What is become of whole *Nations* that have taken up Arms for the Distressing of us? their *Captains* and their *Counsellors,* and their *Families,* where are they? *Even so do Thy* (and our) *Enemies perish, O Lord!*

I beseech you to *Read* the History, lest you *make* a part of it. Let me tell you, The people of God in this *Wilderness,* have had many a Dish of *Leviathans* Heads to feed upon; and one would think, none but *Leviathans* or creatures *made without fear,* should follow these: methinks tis a Frenzy to walk in a Track which thus evidently leads down to the *Congregation of the Dead.* The Famous *Mitchel* made no stick of that open and awful protestation, *Wo to that Man, be he Church-member, or No, be he Freeman or No, who shall go about to destroy or basely Betray the Liberties of this people; it were better for him, that he were thrown into the midst of the Sea;* And his Words have not yet proved *Rash.* But what then becomes of them that propound unto themselves no less than our Extirpation? verily, our God will *Think* on them with a *Vengeance.* How far our God may yet *Scourge* us, we cannot say; we have been undutiful enough to be worthy of *Plagues* that shall be *Sore and of long Continuance.* Nevertheless we know what God *Thinks,* to do with the *Rods* after all; they shall be thrown into the *Fire of His Enemies.* But now, *Consider of this;* ye Hardy Fighters against God, *Lest He tear you in peeces, and there be none to Deliver you.*

PART THREE

EIGHTEENTH-CENTURY TRANSFORMATIONS

17. JOHN WISE ON THE PRINCIPLES OF GOVERNMENT

After the fall of Governor Andros Massachusetts never recovered her original charter. Instead she received a new charter that restored her representative assembly but provided for a governor appointed by the King. Under these circumstances it became increasingly difficult to maintain the notion that New Englanders were a chosen people, enjoying a special covenant with God. But, at the same time, the view that government rests on covenant acquired a new popularity in England. In 1688 the King had been deposed by Parliament for breaking his covenant with the nation and had been replaced by a new king. In 1690 John Locke published his Two Treatises of Government, *placing the origin of both society and government in covenant, and in 1703 Basil Kennett published an English translation of Samuel von Pufendorf's* De Jure Naturae et

From John Wise, *A Vindication of the Government of New England Churches* (Boston: J. Allen, for N. Boone, 1717), pp. 32–51.

Gentium. *In such writings the role of God in the forming of society and government was of less importance than it had been for the sixteenth- and seventeenth-century Puritans, but the idea of a covenant as the basis of all human relations remained strong.*

John Wise (1652–1725), as pastor of the church of Ipswich, was not directly concerned with politics or government. But when he wished to defend the congregational form of church government against proposals to establish a more presbyterian form, he turned to the new writings on government in order to lay a foundation for his arguments. In the following passage he leans heavily on Pufendorf. Perhaps few of Wise's contemporaries would have been as willing as he to "wave the Consideration of Mans Moral Turpitude," but through the sermons and writings of ministers like Wise the secularized European conception of covenant came to mingle freely with the old Puritan one.

1. I Shall disclose several Principles of Natural Knowledge; plainly discovering the Law of Nature; or the true sentiments of Natural Reason, with Respect to Mans Being and Government. And in this Essay I shall peculiarly confine the discourse to two heads, *viz.*

1. Of the Natural [in distinction to the Civil] and then,

2. Of the Civil Being of Man. And I shall Principally take Baron *Puffendorff* for my Chief Guide and Spokesman.

1. I shall consider Man in a state of Natural Being, as a Free-Born Subject under the Crown of Heaven, and owing Homage to none but God himself. It is certain Civil Government in General, is a very Admirable Result of Providence, and an Incomparable Benefit to Man-kind, yet must

needs be acknowledged to be the Effect of Humane Free-Compacts and not of Divine Institution; it is the Produce of Mans Reason, of Humane and Rational Combinations, and not from any direct Orders of Infinite Wisdom, in any positive Law wherein is drawn up this or that Scheme of Civil Government. Government [says the Lord *Warrington*] is necessary—in that no Society of Men can subsist without it; and that Particular Form of Government is necessary which best suits the Temper and Inclination of a People. Nothing can be Gods Ordinance, but what he has particularly Declared to be such; there is no particular Form of Civil Government described in Gods Word, neither does Nature prompt it. The Government of the *Jews* was changed five Times. Government is not formed by Nature, as other Births or Productions; If it were, it would be the same in all Countries; because Nature keeps the same Method, in the same thing, in all Climates. If a Common Wealth be changed into a Monarchy, is it Nature that forms, and brings forth the Monarch? Or if a Royal Family be wholly Extinct [as in *Noah's* Case, being not Heir Apparent from Descent from *Adam*] is it Nature that must go to work [with the King Bees, who themselves alone preserve the Royal Race in that Empire] to Breed a Monarch before the People can have a King, or a Government sent over them? And thus we must leave Kings to Resolve which is their best Title to their Crowns, whether Natural Right, or the Constitution of Government settled by Humane Compacts, under the Direction and Conduct of Reason. But to proceed under the head of a State of Natural Being, I shall more distinctly Explain the State of Hùmane Nature in its Original Capacity, as Man is placed on Earth by his Maker, and Cloathed with many Investitures, and Immunities which properly belong to Man separately considered. As,

1. The Prime Immunity in Mans State, is that he is

most properly the Subject of the Law of Nature. He is the Favourite Animal on Earth; in that this Part of Gods Image, *viz.* Reason is Congenate with his Nature, wherein by a Law Immutable, Instampt upon his Frame, God has provided a Rule for Men in all their Actions; obliging each one to the performance of that which is Right, not only as to Justice, but likewise as to all other Moral Vertues, the which is nothing but the Dictate of Right Reason founded in the Soul of Man. *Molloy, De Mao, Praef.* That which is to be drawn from Mans Reason, flowing from the true Current of that Faculty, when unperverted, may be said to be the Law of Nature; on which account, the Holy Scriptures declare it written on Mens hearts. For being indowed with a Soul, you may know from your self, how, and what you ought to act, Rom. 2. 14. *These having not a Law, are a Law to themselves.* So that the meaning is, when we acknowledge the Law of Nature to be the dictate of Right Reason, we must mean that the Understanding of Man is Endowed with such a power, as to be able, from the Contemplation of humane Condition to discover a necessity of Living agreeably with this Law: And likewise to find out some Principle, by which the Precepts of it, may be clearly and solidly Demonstrated. The way to discover the Law of Nature in our own State, is by a narrow Watch, and accurate Contemplation of our Natural Condition, and propensions. Others say this is the way to find out the Law of Nature. *scil.* If a Man any ways doubts, whether what he is going to do to another Man be agreeable to the Law of Nature, then let him suppose himself to be in that other Mans Room; And by this Rule effectually Executed. A Man must be a very dull Scholar to Nature not to make Proficiency in the Knowledge of her Laws. But more Particularly in pursuing our Condition for the discovery of the Law of Nature, this is very obvious to view, *viz.*

1. A Principle of Self-Love, and Self-Preservation, is very predominant in every Mans Being.

2. A Sociable Disposition.

3. An Affection or Love to Man-kind in General. And to give such Sentiments the force of a Law, we must suppose a God who takes care of all Mankind, and has thus obliged each one, as a Subject of higher Principles of Being, then meer Instincts. For that all Law properly considered, supposes a capable Subject, and a Superiour Power; And the Law of God which is Binding, is published by the Dictates of Right Reason as other ways: Therefore says *Plutarch, To follow God and obey Reason is the same thing.* But moreover that God has Established the Law of Nature, as the General Rule of Government, is further Illustrable from the many Sanctions in Providence, and from the Peace and Guilt of Conscience in them that either obey, or violate the Law of Nature. But moreover, the foundation of the Law of Nature with relation to Government, may be thus Discovered. *Scil.* Man is a Creature extreamly desirous of his own Preservation; of himself he is plainly Exposed to many Wants, unable to secure his own safety, and Maintenance without the Assistance of his fellows; and he is also able of returning Kindness by the furtherance of mutual Good; But yet Man is often found to be Malicious, Insolent and easily Provoked, and as powerful in Effecting mischief, as he is ready in designing it. Now that such a Creature may be Preserved, it is necessary that he be Sociable; that is, that he be capable and disposed to unite himself to those of his own species, and to Regulate himself towards them, that they may have no fair Reason to do him harm; but rather incline to promote his Interests, and secure his Rights and Concerns. This then is a Fundamental Law of Nature, that every Man as far as in him lies, do maintain a Sociableness with others, agreeable with the main end and disposition of humane Nature in general. For

this is very apparent, that Reason and Society render Man the most potent of all Creatures. And Finally, from the Principles of Sociableness it follows as a fundamental Law of Nature, that Man is not so Wedded to his own Interest, but that he can make the Common good the mark of his Aim: And hence he becomes Capacitated to enter into a Civil State by the Law of Nature; for without this property in Nature, *viz.* Sociableness, which is for Cementing of parts, every Government would soon moulder and dissolve.

2. The Second Great Immunity of Man is an Orginal Liberty Instampt upon his Rational Nature. He that intrudes upon this Liberty, Violates the Law of Nature. In this Discourse I shall wave the Consideration of Mans Moral Turpitude, but shall view him Physically as a Creature which God has made and furnished essentially with many Enobling Immunities, which render him the most August Animal in the World, and still, whatever has happened since his Creation, he remains at the upper-end of Nature, and as such is a Creature of a very Noble Character. For as to his Dominion, the whole frame of the Lower Part of the Universe is devoted to his use, and at his Command; and his Liberty under the Conduct of Right Reason, is equal with his trust. Which Liberty may be briefly Considered, Internally as to his Mind, and Externally as to his Person.

1. The Internal Native Liberty of Mans Nature in general implies, a faculty of Doing or Omitting things according to the Direction of his Judgment. But in a more special meaning, this Liberty does not consist in a loose and ungovernable Freedom, or in an unbounded Licence of Acting. Such Licence is disagreeing with the condition and dignity of Man, and would make Man of a lower and meaner Constitution than Bruit Creatures; who in all their Liberties are kept under a better and more Ra-

tional Government, by their Instincts. Therefore as *Plutarch* says, *Those Persons only who live in Obedience to Reason, are worthy to be accounted free: They alone live as they* Will, *who have Learnt what they ought to* Will. So that the true Natural Liberty of Man, such as really and truely agrees to him, must be understood, as he is Guided and Restrained by the Tyes of Reason, and Laws of Nature; all the rest is Brutal, if not worse.

2. Mans External Personal, Natural Liberty, Antecedent to all Humane parts, or Alliances must also be considered. And so every Man must be conceived to be perfectly in his own Power and disposal, and not to be controuled by the Authority of any other. And thus every Man, must be acknowledged equal to every Man, since all Subjection and all Command are equally banished on both sides; and considering all Men thus at Liberty, every Man has a Prerogative to Judge for himself, *viz.* What shall be most for his Behoof, Happiness and Well-being.

3. The Third Capital Immunity belonging to Mans Nature, is an equality amongst Men; Which is not to be denyed by the Law of Nature, till Man has Resigned himself with all his Rights for the sake of a Civil State; and then his Personal Liberty and Equality is to be cherished, and preserved to the highest degree, as will consist with all just distinctions amongst Men of Honour, and shall be agreeable with the publick Good. For Man has a high valuation of himself, and the passion seems to lay its first foundation [not in Pride, but] really in the high and admirable Frame and Constitution of Humane Nature. The Word Man, says my Author, is thought to carry somewhat of Dignity in its sound; and we commonly make use of this as the most proper and prevailing Argument against a rude Insulter, *viz. I am not a Beast or a Dog, but am a Man as well as your self.* Since then Humane Nature agrees equally with all persons; and since no one can live a So-

ciable Life with another that does not own or Respect him as a Man; It follows as a Command of the Law of Nature, that every Man Esteem and treat another as one who is naturally his Equal, or who is a Man as well as he. There be many popular, or plausible Reasons that greatly Illustrate this Equality, *viz.* that we all Derive our Being from one stock, the same Common Father of humane Race. On this Consideration *Boethius* checks the pride of the Insulting Nobility.

Quid Genus et Proavos Strepitis?
Si Primordia Vestra,
Auteremque Deum Spectas,
Nullus Degener Extat
Nisi vitiis Pejora Fovens,
Proprium Deserat Orturn.

Fondly our first Descent we Boast;
If whence at first our Breath we Drew,
The common springs of Life we view,
The Airy Notion soon is Lost.

The Almighty made us equal all;
But he that slavishly complyes
To do the Drudgery of Vice,
Denyes his high Original.

And also that our Bodies are Composed of matter, frail, brittle, and lyable to be destroyed by thousand Accidents; we all owe our Existence to the same Method of propagation. The Noblest Mortal in his Entrance on to the Stage of Life, is not distinguished by any pomp or of passage from the lowest of Mankind; and our Life hastens to the same General Mark: Death observes no Ceremony, but Knocks as loud at the Barriers of the Court, as at the Door of the

Cottage. This Equality being admitted, bears a very great force in maintaining Peace and Friendship amongst Men. For that he who would use the Assistance of others, in promoting his own Advantage, ought as freely to be at their service, when they want his help on the like Occasions. *One Good turn Requires another,* is the Common Proverb; for otherwise he must need esteem others unequal to himself, who constantly demands their Aid, and as constantly denies his own. And whoever is of this Insolent Temper, cannot but highly displease those about him, and soon give Occasion of the Breach of the Common Peace. It was a Manly Reproof which *Charactacus* gave the *Romans. Nun Si vos Omnibus etc.* What! because you desire to be Masters of all Men, does it follow therefore that all Men should desire to be your Slaves, for that it is a Command of Natures Law, that no Man that has not obtained a particular and special Right, shall arrogate to himself a Larger share than his fellows, but shall admit others to equal Priviledges with himself. So that the Principle of Equality in a Natural State, is peculiarly transgressed by Pride, which is when a Man without sufficient reason prefers himself to others. And though as *Hensius,* Paraphrases upon *Aristotle's* Politicks to this Purpose. *viz. Nothing is more suitable to Nature, then that those who Excel in Understanding and Prudence, should Rule and Controul those who are less happy in those Advantages,* etc. Yet we must note, that there is room for an Answer, *scil.* That it would be the greatest absurdity to believe, that Nature actually Invests the Wise with a Sovereignity over the weak; or with a Right of forcing them against their Wills; for that no Sovereignty can be Established, unless some Humane Deed, or Covenant Precede: Nor does Natural fitness for Government make a Man presently Governour over another; for that as *Ulpian* says, *by a Natural Right all Men are born free;* and Nature having set all

Men upon a Level and made them Equals, no Servitude or Subjection can be conceived without Inequality; and this cannot be made without Usurpation or Force in others, or Voluntary Compliance in those who Resign their freedom, and give away their degree of Natural Being. And thus we come,

2. To consider Man in a Civil State of Being; wherein we shall observe the great difference betwen a Natural, and Political State; for in the Latter State many Great disproportions appear, or at least many obvious distinctions are soon made amongst Men; which Doctrine is to be laid open under a few heads.

1. Every Man considered in a Natural State, must be allowed to be Free, and at his own dispose; yet to suit Mans Inclinations to Society; And in a peculiar manner to gratify the necessity he is in of publick Rule and Order, he is Impelled to enter into a Civil Community; and Divests himself of his Natural Freedom, and puts himself under Government; which amongst other things Comprehends the Power of Life and Death over Him; together with Authority to Injoyn him some things to which he has an utter Aversation, and to prohibit him other things, for which he may have as strong an Inclination; so that he may be often under this Authority, obliged to Sacrifice his Private, for the Publick Good. So that though Man is inclined to Society, yet he is driven to a Combination by great necessity. For that the true and leading Cause of forming Governments, and yielding up Natural Liberty, and throwing Mans Equality into a Common Pile to be new Cast by the Rules of fellowship; was really and truly to guard themselves against the Injuries Men were lyable to Interchangeably; for none so Good to Man, as Man, and yet none a greater Enemy. So that,

2. The first Humane Subject and Original of Civil Power is the People. For as they have a Power every Man

over himself in a Natural State, so upon a Combination they can and do bequeath this Power unto others; and settle it according as their united discretion shall Determine. For that this is very plain, that when the Subject of Sovereign Power is quite Extinct, that Power returns to the People again. And when they are free, they may set up what species of Government they please; or if they rather incline to it, they may subside into a State of Natural Being, if it be plainly for the best. In the *Eastern* Country of the *Mogul*, we have some resemblance of the Case; for upon the Death of an absolute Monarch, they live so many days without a Civil Head; but in that *Interregnum*, those who survive the Vacancy, are glad to get into a Civil State again; and usually they are in a very Bloody Condition when they return under the Covert of a new Monarch; this project is to indear the People to a Tyranny, from the Experience they have so lately had of an Anarchy.

3. The formal Reason of Government is the Will of a Community, yielded up and surrendred to some other Subject, either of one particular Person, or more, Conveyed in the following manner.

Let us conceive in our Mind a multitude of Men, all Naturally Free and Equal; going about voluntarily, to Erect themselves into a new Common-Wealth. Now their Condition being such, to bring themselves into a Politick Body, they must needs Enter into divers Covenants.

1. They must Interchangeably each Man Covenant to joyn in one lasting Society, that they may be capable to concert the measures of their safety, by a Publick Vote.

2. A Vote or Decree must then nextly pass to set up some Particular speecies of Government over them. And if they are joyned in their first Compact upon absolute Terms, to stand to the Decision of the first Vote concerning the Species of Government: Then all are bound by the Majority to acquiesce in that particular Form thereby set-

tled, though their own private Opinion, incline them to some other Model,

3. After a Decree has specified the Particular form of Government, then there will be need of a New Covenant, whereby those on whom Sovereignty is conferred, engage to take care of the Common Peace, and Welfare. And the Subjects on the other hand, to yield them faithful Obedience. In which Covenant is Included that Submission and Union of Wills, by which a State may be conceived to be but one Person. So that the most proper Definition of a Civil State, is this, *viz.* A Civil State is a Compound Moral Person whose Will [United by those Covenants before passed] is the Will of all; to the end it may Use, and Apply the strength and riches of Private Persons towards maintaining the Common Peace, Security, and Well-being of all. Which may be conceived as tho' the whole State was now become but one Man; in which the aforesaid Covenants may be supposed under Gods Providence, to be the Divine *Fiat*, Pronounced by God, let us make Man. And by way of resemblance the aforesaid Being may be thus Anatomized.

1. The Sovereign Power is the Soul infused, giving Life and Motion to the whole Body.

2. Subordinate Officers are the Joynts by which the Body moves.

3. Wealth and Riches are the Strength.

4. Equity and Laws are the Reason.

5. Councellors the Memory.

6. *Salus Populi*, or the Happiness of the People, is the End of its Being; or main Business to be attended and done.

7. Concord amongst the Members, and all Estates, is the Health.

8. Sedition is Sickness, and Civil War Death.

4. The Parts of Sovereignty may be considered: So,

1. As it Prescribes the Rule of Action: It is rightly termed *Legislative Power.*

2. As it determines the Controversies of Subjects by the Standard of those Rules. So is it justly Termed Judiciary Power.

3. As it Arms the Subjects against Foreigners, or forbids Hostility, so its called the Power of Peace and War.

4. As it takes in Ministers for the discharge of Business, so it is called the Right of Appointing Magistrates. So that all great Officers and Publick Servants, must needs owe their Original to the Creating Power of Sovereignty. So that those whose Right it is to Create, may Dissolve the being of those who are Created, unless they cast them into an Immortal Frame. And yet must needs be dissoluble if they justly forfeit their being to their Creators.

5. The Chief End of Civil Communities, is, that Men thus conjoyned, may be secured against the Injuries, they are lyable to from their own Kind. For if every Man could secure himself singly; It would be great folly for him, to Renounce his Natural Liberty, in which every Man is his own King and Protector.

6. The Sovereign Authority besides that it inheres in every State as in a Common and General Subject. So farther according as it resides in some One Person, or in a Council [consisting of some Select Persons, or of all the Members of a Community] as in a proper and particular Subject, so it produceth different Forms of Commonwealths, *viz.* Such as are either simple and regular, or mixt.

1. The Forms of a Regular State are three only, which Forms arise from the proper and particular Subject, in which the Supream Power Resides, As,

1. A Democracy, which is when the Sovereign Power is Lodged in a Council consisting of all the Mem-

bers, and where every Member has the Priviledge of a Vote. This Form of Government, appears in the greatest part of the World to have been the most Ancient. For that Reason seems to shew it to be most probable, that when Men [being Originally in a condition of Natural Freedom and Equality] had thoughts of joyning in a Civil Body, would without question be inclined to Administer their common Affairs, by their common Judgment, and so must necessarily to gratifie that Inclination establish a Democracy; neither can it be rationally imagined, that Fathers of Families being yet Free and Independent, should in a moment, or little time take off their long delight in governing their own Affairs, and Devolve all upon some single Sovereign Commander; for that it seems to have been thought more Equitable, that what belonged to all, should be managed by all, when all had entered by Compact into one Community. The Original of our Government, says *Plato,* [speaking of the *Athenian* Commonwealth] *was taken from the Equality of our Race. Other States there are composed of different Blood, and of unequal Lines, the Consequence of which are disproportionable Soveraignty, Tyrannical or Oligarchycal Sway; under which men live in such a manner, as to Esteem themselves partly Lords, and partly Slaves to each other. But we and our Country-men, being all Born Brethren of the same Mother, do not look upon our selves, to stand under so hard a Relation, as that of Lords and Slaves; but the Parity of our Descent incline us to keep up the like Parity by our Laws, and to yield the precedency to nothing but to Superiour Vertue, and Wisdom.* And moreover it seems very manifest that most Civil Communities arose at first from the Union of Families, that were nearly allyed in Race and Blood. And though Ancient Story make frequent mention of Kings, yet it appears that most of them were such that had an Influence rather in perswading, then in any Power of Commanding. So *Justin* discribes that Kind of Government, as the most Primitive, which *Aristotle* stiles an Heroical Kingdom. *viz.* Such as is no ways Inconsistent with a Democratical State. *De Princip. Reru.* 1 *L.* 1. *C.*

A democracy is then Erected, when a Number of Free Persons, do Assemble together, in Order to enter into a Covenant for Uniting themselves in a Body: And such a Preparative Assembly hath some appearance already of a Democracy; it is a Democracy in *Embrio* properly in this Respect, that every Man hath the Priviledge freely to deliver his Opinion concerning the Common Affairs. Yet he who dissents from the Vote of the Majority, is not in the least obliged by what they determine, till by a second Covenant, a Popular Form be actually Established; for not before then can we call it a Democratical Government, *viz.* Till the Right of Determining all matters relating to the publick Safety, is actually placed in a General Assembly of the whole People; or by their own Compact and Mutual Agreement, Determine themselves the proper Subject for the Exercise of Sovereign Power. And to compleat this State, and render it capable to Exert its Power to answer the End of a Civil State: These Conditions are necessary.

1. That a certain Time and Place be Assigned for Assembling.

2. That when the Assembly be Orderly met, as to Time and Place, that then the Vote of the Majority must pass for the Vote of the whole Body.

3. That Magistrates be appointed to Exercise the Authority of the whole for the better dispatch of Business, of every days Occurrence; who also may with more Mature diligence, search into more Important Affairs; and if in case any thing happens of greater Consequence, may report it to the Assembly; and be peculiarly Serviceable in putting all Publick Decrees into Execution. Because a large Body of People is almost useless in Respect of the

last Service, and of many others, as to the more Particular Application and Exercise of Power. Therefore it is most agreeable with the Law of Nature, that they Institute their Officers to act in their Name, and Stead.

2. The Second Species of Regular Government, is an Aristocracy; and this is said then to be Constituted when the People, or Assembly United by a first Covenant, and having thereby cast themselves into the first Rudiments of a State; do then by Common Decree, Devolve the Sovereign Power, on a Council consisting of some Select Members; and these having accepted of the Designation, are then properly invested with Sovereign Command; and then an Aristocracy is formed.

3. The Third Species of a Regular Government, is a Monarchy which is settled when the Sovereign Power is confered on some one worthy Person. It differs from the former, because a Monarch who is but one Person in Natural, as well as in Moral account, and so is furnished with an Immediate Power of Exercising Sovereign Command in all Instances of Government; but the fore named must needs have Particular Time and Place assigned; but the Power and Authority is Equal in each.

2. Mixt Governments, which are various and of divers kinds [not now to be Enumerated] yet possibly the fairest in the World is that which has a Regular Monarchy; [in Distinction to what is Dispotick] settled upon a Noble Democracy as its Basis. And each part of the Government is so adjusted by Pacts and Laws that renders the whole Constitution an *Elisium.* It is said of the *British* Empire, *That it is such a Monarchy, as that by the necessary subordinate Concurrence of the Lords and Commons, in the Making and Repealing all Statutes or Acts of Parliament; it hath the main Advantages of an Aristocracy, and of a Democracy, and yet free from the Disadvantages and Evils of either. It is such a Monarchy, as by most Admirable*

Temperament affords very much to the Industry, Liberty, and Happiness of the Subject, and reserves enough for the Majesty and Prerogative of any King, who will own his People as Subjects, not as Slaves. It is a Kingdom, that of all the Kingdoms of the World, is most like to the Kingdom of Jesus Christ, whose Yoke is easie, and Burden light. Present State of *England 1st.* Part 64 *p.*

---

18. THE INALIENABLE RIGHTS OF CONSCIENCE

In 1741 the Great Awakening, a large-scale religious revival, shook the American colonies from New England to Georgia. Itinerant preachers traveled up and down the land, leaving behind them excited, enthusiastic men and women who believed they had felt the Spirit for the first time. Such persons often deserted their old ministers to set up churches where they hoped to sustain the experience that had meant so much to them. Those who had not been awakened viewed these proceedings with horror. To them the whole Awakening appeared to be the work of the devil and his agents, the itinerants. In Connecticut the General Assembly passed a law imposing heavy restrictions on itinerant preachers.

From Elisha Williams, *The essential Rights and Liberties of Protestants. A seasonable Plea for The Liberty of Conscience, and The Right of private Judgment, in Matters of Religion. Without any Controul from human Authority. Being a Letter, from a Gentleman in the Massachusetts-Bay to his Friend in Connecticut* (Boston: S. Kneeland and T. Green, 1744), pp. 1–9, 38–51, 60–65.

Elisha Williams (1694–1755) was no friend of enthusiasm. A graduate of Harvard (1711), he had served as rector of Yale from 1725 to 1739 and had restored to the college the reputation for orthodoxy it had lost when the previous rector defected to the Church of England. But if Williams was orthodox, he was not a bigot, and the Connecticut law shocked him. In response to it he wrote the most powerful plea for liberty of conscience to appear in New England in the first half of the eighteenth century.

SIR,

I Now give you my Thoughts on the *Questions* you lately sent me. As you set me the Task, you must take the Performance as it is without any Apology for its Defects. I have wrote with the usual Freedom of a Friend, aiming at nothing but Truth, and to express my self so as to be understood. In order to *answer your main Enquiry* concerning the *Extent* of the *civil Magistrate's Power* respecting RELIGION; I suppose it needful to look back to the *End,* and therefore to the *Original* of it: By which Means I suppose a just Notion may be formed of what is properly *their Business* or the *Object* of *their Power;* and so without any insuperable Difficulty we may thence learn what is out of that Compass.

That the SACRED SCRIPTURES are the *alone Rule* of *Faith* and *Practice* to a *Christian,* all *Protestants* are agreed in; and must therefore inviolably maintain, that every Christian has *a Right of judging for himself* what he is to believe and practice in Religion according to that Rule: Which I think on a full Examination you will find perfectly inconsistent with any Power in the civil Magistrate to make any penal Laws in Matters of Religion. Tho'

Protestants are agreed in the *Profession* of that Principle, yet too many in *Practice* have departed from it. The Evils that have been introduced thereby into the Christian Church are more than can be reckoned up. Because of the great Importance of it to the Christian and to his standing fast in that *Liberty* wherewith CHRIST has made him free, you will not fault me if I am the longer upon it. The more firmly this is established in our Minds; the more firm shall we be against all Attempts upon our *Christian Liberty*, and better practice that *Christian Charity* towards such as are of different Sentiments from us in Religion that is so much recommended and inculcated in those sacred Oracles, and which a just Understanding of our *Christian Rights* has a natural Tendency to influence us to. And tho' your Sentiments about some of those Points you demand my Thoughts upon may have been different from mine; yet I perswade my self, you will not think mine to be far from the Truth when you shall have thoroughly weighed what follows. But if I am mistaken in the Grounds I proceed upon or in any Conclusion drawn from true Premises, I shall be thankful to have the same pointed out: Truth being what I seek, to which all must bow first or last.

To proceed then as I have just hinted, I shall *First*, briefly consider *the Origin and End of Civil Government*.

First, As to *the Origin*—Reason teaches us that *all Men* are *naturally equal* in Respect of *Jurisdiction* or *Dominion* one over another. Altho' true it is that *Children* are not born *in* this full State of Equality, yet they are born *to* it. Their *Parents* have a Sort of Rule and Jurisdiction over them when they come into the World, and for some Time after: But it is but a temporary one; which arises from that Duty incumbent on them to take Care of their Offspring during the imperfect State of Childhood, to preserve, nourish and educate them (as the Workmanship of their own almighty MAKER, to whom they are to be accountable for them,) and govern the Actions of their yet ignorant Nonage, 'till *Reason* shall take its Place and ease them of that Trouble. For GOD having given *Man* an *Understanding* to direct his Actions, has given him therewith a *Freedom* of *Will* and *Liberty* of *Acting*, as properly belonging thereto, within the Bounds of *that Law* he is under: And whilst he is in a State wherein he has no Understanding of his own to direct his Will, he is not to have any Will of his own to follow: He that understands for him must will for him too.—But when he comes to such a State of *Reason* as made the *Father* free, the same must make the *Son* free too: For the *Freedom* of *Man* and *Liberty* of *acting* according to his own *Will* (without being subject to the Will of another) is grounded on his having *Reason*, which is able to instruct him in *that Law* he is to govern himself by, and make him know how far he is left to the Freedom of his own Will. So that we are *born Free* as we are *born Rational*. Not that we have the *Exercise* of either as soon as born; *Age* that brings one, brings the other too. *This natural Freedom* is not a Liberty for every one to do what he pleases without any Regard to any *Law;* for a *rational* Creature cannot but be made under a *Law* from its MAKER: But it consists in a *Freedom* from any *superiour Power on Earth*, and not being under the Will or legislative Authority of *Man*, and having only the *Law of Nature* (or in other Words, of its MAKER) for his Rule.

And as Reason tells us, all are born thus *naturally equal*, i.e. with an *equal Right* to their *Persons;* so also with an equal Right to their *Preservation;* and therefore to *such Things* as Nature affords for their *Subsistence*. For which Purpose GOD was pleased to make a Grant of *the Earth in common* to the *Children of Men*, first to *Adam* and afterwards to *Noah* and *his Sons:* as the Psalmist says, *Psal.* 115. 16. And altho' no one has originally a private Dominion exclusive of the rest of Mankind in the Earth or its Products, as they are consider'd in this their natural State; yet since GOD has given *these Things* for the Use of Men and given them *Reason* also to make Use thereof to the best Advantage of Life; there must of Necessity be a *Means* to *appropriate* them some Way or other, before they can be of any Use to any particular Person. And *every Man* having a *Property* in his own *Person,* the *Labour of his Body* and *the Work of his Hands* are properly his own, to which no one has Right but himself; it will therefore follow that when he removes any Thing out of the State that Nature has provided and left it in, he has *mixed his Labour* with it and joined something to it that is his own, and thereby makes it his Property. He having removed it out of the *common State* Nature placed it in, it hath by *this Labour* something annexed to it that excludes the common Right of others; because *this Labour* being the unquestionable Property of the Labourer, no Man but he can have a Right to what that is once joined to, at least where there is enough and as good left in common for others. Thus *every Man* having a *natural Right* to (or being the Proprietor of) his own *Person* and his own *Actions* and *Labour* and to what he can honestly acquire by his Labour, which we call *Property;* it certainly follows, that no Man can have a Right to the *Person* or *Property* of *another:* And if every Man has a Right to his *Person* and *Property;* he has also a Right to *defend* them, and a Right to all the *necessary Means of Defence,* and so has a Right of *punishing* all Insults upon his Person and Property.

But because in *such a State of Nature,* every Man must be *Judge* of the Breach of the Law of Nature and *Executioner* too (even in his own Case) and the greater Part being no strict Observers of Equity and Justice; the *Enjoyment* of Property in this State is *not very safe. Three Things* are wanting in this State (as the celebrated *Lock* observes) to render them safe; *viz.* an *established known Law* received and allowed by common Consent to be the Standard of Right and Wrong, the common Measure to decide all Controversies between them. For tho' the Law of Nature be intelligible to all rational Creatures; yet Men being biassed by their Interest as well as ignorant for Want of the Study of it, are not apt to allow of it as a Law binding to them in the Application of it to their particular Cases. There wants also a *known and indifferent Judge* with Authority to determine all Differences according to the established Law: for Men are too apt to be partial to themselves, and too much wanting in a just Concern for the Interest of others. There often wants also in a State of Nature, a *Power to back and support the Sentence* when right, and give it due Execution.—Now to remedy these Inconveniencies, *Reason* teaches Men to *join in Society*, to unite together into a Commonwealth under some Form or other, to make a Body of Laws agreable to the Law of Nature, and institute one common Power to see them observed.—It is they who thus unite together, *viz.* the People, who make and alone have Right to make the Laws that are to take Place among them; or which comes to the same Thing, appoint those who shall make them, and who shall see them executed.—For every Man has an equal Right to the Preservation of his Person and Property; and so an equal Right to establish a Law, or to nominate the Makers and Executors of the Laws which are the Guardians both of Person and Property.

Hence then the Fountain and Original of all civil Power is from the People, and is certainly instituted for their Sakes; or in other Words, which was the *second Thing* proposed, *The great End of civil Government*, is *the Preservation of their Persons, their Liberties and Estates, or their Property.* Most certain it is, that it must be for their own Sakes, the rendering their Condition better than it was in what is called a State of Nature (a State without such establish'd Laws as before mentioned, or without any common Power) that Men would willingly put themselves out of that State. It is nothing but *their own Good* can be any rational Inducement to it: and to suppose they either should or would do it on any other, is to suppose rational Creatures ought to change their State with a Design to make it worse. And *that Good* which in such a State they find a need of, is no other then a *greater Security of Enjoyment of what belonged to them.* That and that only can then be the true Reason of their uniting together in some Form or other they judge best for the obtaining that greater Security. *That greater Security* therefore of Life, Liberty, Money, Lands, Houses, Family, and the like, which may be all comprehended under that of *Person* and *Property,* is the *sole End* of all *civil Government.* I mean not that all civil Governments (as so called) are thus constituted: (tho' the *British* and some few other Nations are through a merciful Providence so happy as to have such.) There are too, too many arbitrary Governments in the World, where the People don't make their own Laws. These are not properly speaking *Governments* but *Tyrannies;* and are absolutely against the *Law* of GOD and *Nature.* But I am considering Things as they be in their own Nature, what Reason teaches concerning them: and herein have given *a short Sketch* of what the celebrated Mr. *Lock* in *his Treatise of Government* has largely demonstrated; and in which it is justly to be presumed all are agreed who understand the natural Rights of Mankind.

Thus having seen what the *End* of *civil Government* is; I suppose we see a fair Foundation laid for the Determination of the *next Thing* I proposed to consider: Which is, *What Liberty or Power belonging to Man as he is a reasonable Creature does every Man give up to the civil Government whereof he is a Member.*——Some Part of their natural Liberty they do certainly give up to the Government, for the Benefit of Society and mutual Defence, (for in a political Society *every one* even an *Infant* has the whole Force of the Community to protect him) and something therefore is certainly given up to the Whole for this Purpose.——Now the Way to know what Branches of natural Liberty are *given up*, and what *remain* to us after our Admission into civil Society, is to consider *the Ends* for which Men enter into a State of Government.—For so much Liberty and no more is departed from, as is necessary to secure those Ends; the rest is certainly our own still. And here I suppose with the before-mentioned noble Assertor of the Liberties of humane Nature; *all that is given up* may be reduced to *two Heads.*—1st. The *Power* that every one has in a State of Nature *to do whatever he judgeth fit*, for the *Preservation* of his *Person* and *Property* and that of others also, within the Permission of the Law of Nature, he gives up to be regulated by Laws made by the Society, so far forth as the *Preservation* of himself (his *Person* and *Property*) and the rest of that Society shall require. And, 2. The *Power* of *punishing* he wholly gives up, and engages his natural Force (which he might before employ in the Execution of the Law of Nature by his own single Authority as he thought fit) to assist the executive Power of the Society as the Law thereof shall require. For (he adds) being now in *a new State* wherein he is to enjoy many Conveniencies, from the Labour Assistance and Society of others in the same Community, as well as Protection from its whole Strength; he is to part also with as much of his natural Liberty and providing for himself, as the Good and Safety of the Society shall require; which is not only *necessary* but *just*, since the other Members of the Society do the like. Now if the giving up *these Powers* be *sufficient* to answer *those Ends* for which Men enter into a State of Government, *viz.* the better Security of their Persons and Properties; then no more is parted with; and therefore *all the rest* is ours still. This I rest on as certain, that *no more natural Liberty or Power is given up than is necessary for the Preservation of Person and Property.*

I design not to mention many Particulars which according to this Rule I suppose are not parted with by entering into a State of Government: what is reducible to *one* or *two general Heads* is sufficient to our present Purpose. —Tho' as I pass I cannot forbear taking notice of *one Point of Liberty* which all Members of a free State and particularly *Englishmen* think belonging to them, and are fond of; and that is the *Right* that *every one* has *to speak his Sentiments openly* concerning *such Matters as affect the good of the whole.* Every Member of a Community ought to be concerned for the *whole,* as well as for *his particular Part:* His Life and all, as to this World is as it were embarked in the same Bottom, and is perpetually interested in the good or ill Success thereof: Whenever therefore he sees a *Rock* on which there is a Probability the Vessel may split, or if he sees a *Sand* that may swallow it up, or if he foresees a *Storm* that is like to arise; his own Interest is too deeply concerned not to give Notice of the Danger: And the Right he has to his own Life and Property gives him a Right to speak his Sentiments. If the *Pilot* or *Captain* don't think fit to take any Notice of it, yet it seems to be certain they have no Right to stop the Mouth of him who thinks he espys Danger to the whole Ships Crew, or to punish the well-meaning Informer. A Man would scarce deserve the Character of a *good Member of Society* who should resolve to be silent on all Occasions, and never mind, speak or guard against the Follies or Ignorance or Mistakes of those at the Helm. And Government rather incourages than takes away a Liberty, the Use of which is so needful and often very beneficial to the Whole, as Experience has abundantly shown.

But not to detain you here,

I. The Members of a civil State or Society do *retain* their natural Liberty *in all such Cases* as have *no Relation* to the *Ends* of such a Society.—In a State of Nature Men had a Right to read *Milton* or *Lock* for their Instruction or Amusement: and why they do not retain this Liberty under a Government that is instituted for the *Preservation* of their *Persons* and *Properties*, is inconceivable. From whence can such a Society derive any Right to hinder them from doing that which does not affect the *Ends* of that Society? Should a Government therefore restrain the free Use of *the Scriptures*, prohibit Men the reading of them, and make it Penal to examine and search them; it would be a manifest Usurpation upon the common Rights of Mankind, as much a Violation of natural Liberty as the Attack of a Highwayman upon the Road can be upon our civil Rights. And indeed with respect to the *sacred Writings*, Men might not only read them if the Government did prohibit the same, but they would be bound by a higher Authority to read them, notwithstanding any humane Prohibition. The Pretence of any Authority to restrain Men from reading the same, is wicked as well as vain.—But whether in some Cases that have no Relation to the *Ends* of Government and wherein therefore Men retain their natural Liberty; if the civil Authority should attempt by a Law to restrain Men, People might not be oblig'd to submit therein, is not here at all the Question: tho' I suppose that in such Case wherein they ought to submit, the Obligation thereto would arise from some other Consideration, and not from the supposed Law; there being no binding Force in a Law where a rightful Authority to make the same is wanting.

II. The Members of a civil State do *retain their natural Liberty or Right* of *judging for themselves in Matters of Religion.* Every Man has an equal Right to follow the Dictates of his own *Conscience* in the Affairs of *Religion.* Every one is under an indispensable Obligation to *search the Scripture* for himself (which contains the whole of it) and to make the best Use of it he can for his own Information in the Will of GOD, the Nature and Duties of Christianity. And as every Christian is so bound; so he has an *unalienable Right* to *judge* of the *Sense and Meaning* of it, and to follow his Judgment wherever it leads him; even an equal Right with any Rulers be they Civil or Ecclesiastical. —This I say, I take to be an original Right of the humane Nature, and so far from being given up by the Individuals of a Community that it cannot be given up by them if they should be so weak as to offer it. Man by his Constitution as he is a *reasonable* Being capable of the Knowledge of his MAKER; is a *moral* and *accountable* Being: and therefore as every one is accountable for himself, he must reason, judge and determine for himself. That Faith and Practice which depends on the Judgment and Choice of any other Person, and not on the Person's own Understanding Judgment and Choice, may pass for Religion in the Synagogue of *Satan,* whose Tenet is that Ignorance is the Mother of Devotion; but with no understanding Protestant will it pass for any Religion at all. No Action is a religious Action without Understanding and Choice in the Agent. Whence it follows, the Rights of Conscience are sacred and equal in all, and strictly speaking unalienable. This *Right* of *judging every one for himself in Matters of Religion* results from the Nature of Man, and is so inseperably connected therewith, that a Man can no more part with it than he can with his *Power* of *Thinking:* and it is equally reasonable for him to attempt to strip himself of the *Power* of *Reasoning,* as to attempt the vesting of another with this Right. And whoever invades this Right of another, be he *Pope* or *Caesar,* may with equal Reason assume the other's Power of Thinking, and so level him with the Brutal Creation.—A Man may alienate some Branches of his Property and give up his Right in them to others; but he cannot transfer the *Rights* of *Conscience,* unless he could destroy his rational and moral Powers, or substitute some other to be judged for him at the Tribunal of GOD.

But what may further clear this Point and at the same Time shew the *Extent* of this *Right* of *private Judgment* in Matters of *Religion,* is this Truth, That the *sacred Scriptures* are the alone Rule of Faith and Practice to every individual Christian. Were it needful I might easily show, the sacred Scriptures have all the Characters necessary to constitute a just and proper Rule of Faith and Practice, and that they alone have them.—It is sufficient for all such as acknowledge the divine Authority of the Scriptures, briefly to observe, that GOD the Author has therein declared he has given and designed them to be our only Rule of Faith and Practice. Thus says the Apostle *Paul, 2 Tim.* 3. 15, 16; That they *are given by Inspiration from* GOD, *and are profitable for Doctrine, for Reproof, for Correction, for Instruction in Righteousness; that the Man of GOD may be perfect, thoroughly furnished unto every good* Work. So the Apostle *John* in his Gospel, Chap. 20. Ver. 31. says; *These Things are written that ye might believe that JESUS is the CHRIST, the SON of GOD, and that believing ye might have Life through his Name.* And in his *first Epistle,* Chap. 5. Ver. 13. *These Things have I written, that ye may know that ye have eternal Life, and that ye may believe on the Name of the* SON *of* GOD. These Passages show that what was written was to be the standing Rule of Faith and Practice, compleat and most sufficient for such an End, designed by infinite Wisdom in the giving them, containing every Thing needful to be known and done by Christians, or such as believe on the Name of the SON of GOD. Now inasmuch as the Scriptures are the only Rule of Faith and Practice to a Christian; then every one has an unalienable Right to read, enquire into, and impartially judge of the Sense and Meaning of it for himself. For if he is to be governed and determined therein by the Opinions and Determinations of any others, the Scriptures cease to be a Rule to him, and those Opinions or Determinations of others are substituted in the Room thereof. But you will say, *The Priest's Lips should keep Knowledge, and they should seek the Law at his Mouth,* Mal. 2. 7.—Yes; that is, it is their Duty to explain the Scriptures, and the People's Duty at the same Time to search the Scriptures to see whether those Things they say are so. *Acts* 17. 11. The Officers CHRIST has commissioned in his Church, as *Pastors* or *Bishops,* are to teach his Laws, to explain as they are able the Mind and Will of CHRIST laid down in the Scriptures; but they have no Warrant to make any Laws for them, nor are their Sentiments the Rule to any Christian, who are *all commanded* to *prove all Things,* to *try the Spirits whether they be of GOD.* I Thes. 5. 21. I Joh. 4. 1. *I speak as to wise Men,* says PAUL, *judge ye what I say,* I Cor. 10. 15. These and many other Texts I might have alledg'd, entirely answer the Objection, and establish the Point before us.

* * *

But say you once more; 'That the civil Authority must have Power to make such religious Establishment which I have been impleading, in order to have *Unity of Faith* and *Uniformity of Practice* in Religion. These you suppose necessary to Peace and good Order in the State; and that this *Unity* etc. is effected by such a religious *Establishment,* of which we are speaking; and consequently we must suppose them vested with Power to make such a one.'—Much Weight I know has been laid upon this Argument by the Lovers of *spiritual Tyranny,* and many ignorant unthinking People have been amused and deceived by it: But if we will look closely into it, it will appear lighter than Vanity. For

1. *Unity of Faith* and *Uniformity of Practice* in Religion, never was nor can be effected in a *Christian State* by any such legal Establishment of Religion pleaded for in the above-mentioned Argument. By a *Christian State,* I mean at least such a one, where the *sacred Scriptures* lie open to the People: and therefore I don't intend, to consider this Proposition relative to a *Popish State*, where People's Eyes being put out, they are more easily induced to follow their Leaders; tho' it be also true that *this Unity of Faith* is not found among them that are bound in the strongest Chains of human Establishments. This has been tried in *Protestant States*, to make all think and practice alike in Religion by legal Establishments and annexed Penalties: but it never produced this Effect. It were easy if needful to multiply Instances: but it is sufficient to our Purpose to Instance in *our own Nation*; where this Method has been tried ever since the Reformation, and as constantly found ineffectual for the accomplishing this Uniformity, for the Sake of which these legal Establishments have been pretended to be made. So far is this Method from bringing about an *Unity of Faith*, that this is not found even with them that submit to a legal Establishment. It is notoriously known, that the *Clergy* of the *Church of England* are bound to *subscribe* to the *thirty nine Articles,* i.e. to the Truth of *Calvinistick* Principles: But has this *Subscription* answer'd its End? Is it not known, that they subscribe those Articles in as widely distant and contradictory Senses as were ever put on the most dubious Passage in the Bible. And the Truth is, if we consider the almost *infinite Variety* with respect to the *Understandings*, *Tempers* and *Advantages* of Men for Improvement in Knowledge; it must be evident, that *this Uniformity* of Opinion and Practice in Religion, (as it has not) so it never can be

produced by the Art and Policy of Man. A Scheme for an artificial Conformity in Aspect, Shape and Stature of Body, is not a whit more ridiculous, than an Attempt to depress and contract the Understandings of some, to stretch the Capacities of others, to distort and torture all, 'till they are brought to *one Size*, and *one Way of Thinking and Practice.* So that if this Unity of Faith and Uniformity of Practice in Religion is *necessary* to the Peace of the State; —then it follow, that the civil Authority have a rightful Power to put to Death or banish all that cannot in Conscience conform to their religious Establishment. It will be to no Purpose for the avoiding this Consequence, to say; 'the civil Magistrate may not rise so high, or may affix some lower Penalties for Non-compliance with his Establishment:' For if this Conformity to his Establishment be *necessary* to the Peace of the State, then the civil Magistrate has a Right to prevent a Non-compliance with such Establishment; and if lesser Penalties will not do it, (as Experience has perpetually shown they will not) then they must rise so high as *Death*, or *Banishment:* For a Right to prevent such Non-compliance, that does not amount to a Right to prevent it effectually, is no Right to prevent it at all. So that on this Hypothesis, *all Non-conformists* to the religious Establishment of any State, are to be rooted out by *Death*, or *Banishment* as fast as they appear: Which both Experience and the Nature of Things evidence will be continual; the cutting off all that appear to Day will no ways hinder others from appearing so To-morrow. Whence it is but a *genuine Consequence*, that civil Government is one of the greatest Plagues that can be sent upon the World; since it must, in order to keep Peace in it, be perpetually destroying Men for no other Crime but *judging for themselves* and *acting* according to their *Consciences* in Matters of Religion; (and so perhaps very often the best Men in the State:) and all this in vain too, as to the proposed End, *viz.* Uniformity of Practice in Religion, that being for ever out of their reach.

2. Such Unity, or Uniformity in Religion is *not necessary* to the Peace of a civil State. Since God has formed the Understandings of Men so different, with respect to Clearness, Strength, and Compass, and placed them in such very different Circumstances; a Difference of Sentiments in some Things in Religion, seems natural and unavoidable: and to suppose this does in its own Nature tend to the public Mischief of the State, seems little less then arraigning infinite Wisdom. From thence will arise greater Reason and Scope for mutual Forbearance and Christian Charity. But it will certainly be found on Reflection, that it has no ill Aspect on the civil State. Have we not known Persons of different Sentiments and Practices in religious Matters, as *Presbyterians, Congregationalists, Church-Men* (as commonly called) *Baptists* and *Quakers*, all living in the same Community in Quiet and Peace with one another? I mention not *Papists*; because tho' the Principles of a *consistent Protestant*, naturally tend to make him a good Subject in any civil State, even in a *popish* one, and therefore ought to be allowed in every State; yet that is not the Case with the *Papist*: for by his very Principles he is an Enemy or Traytor to a *Protestant State:* and strictly speaking *Popery* is so far from deserving the name of *Religion*, that it is rather a Conspiracy against it, against the Reason, Liberties, and Peace of Mankind; the visible Head thereof the *Pope* being in Truth the Vice-gerent of the *Devil, Rev.* 13. 2. To pretend that such as own the sacred *Scriptures* to be the alone Rule of Faith and Practice in Religion, can't live in Peace and Love as good Neighbours and good Subjects, tho' their Opinions and Practices in religious Matters be different, is both false in Fact, and a vile Reproach cast upon the *Gospel*, which breaths nothing but *Benevolence* and *Love* among Men:

and while it plainly teaches the Right of private Judgment in every one, it most forcibly enjoins the Duties of mutual *Forbearance* and *Charity.* That golden Precept of our blessed LORD; *Whatsoever ye would that Men should do unto you, do ye even so to them,* Math. 7. 12, well taught and enforced by the Teachers of the Gospel, would (if I may use the Word) infinitely more tend to make Christians of the several Denominations in the State, good Neighbours and good Subjects, then this whimsical Notion of Uniformity. Which if it had always had its due Force on the Minds of Men, we should never have heard of the *Necessity* of Uniformity in Religion to the Peace of the State, nor any such legal Establishment of Religion I have been impleading. That Precept being a sacred Guard to the unalienable Rights of Conscience, which are always invaded by such Establishments.

But if you say, 'that *different Sects* in Religion aiming at Superiority, and endeavouring to suppress each other, form contrary Factions in the State; which tends to distress and thwart the civil Administration.'—I answer; The civil Authority's protecting all in their just Rights, and particularly this inestimable and unalienable one, *the Right of private Judgment* in Matters of *Religion,* is the best Guard against the Evil supposed in the Objection. Besides, this is no more a *natural Consequence* of Men's thinking differently in Religion, than of different Judgments about *Wit,* or *Poetry, Trade,* or *Husbandry.*

Or if you farther suppose, 'that *Religion* is a Matter of much greater Importance than these Things, and demands therefore a more warm and active Zeal.' Be it so; Nothing farther follows from thence, than that we should endeavour to support its Honour in a Way suited to its Excellency, to instruct one another in its grand Principles and Duties, and recommend it by calm and strong Perswasion.—It is by *Truth* CHRIST'S Kingdom is set up, as he himself has taught us, *Luk.* 18. 37. And it is a most unnatural Excess of Zeal, for the pretended Defence of Religion, to renounce *Humanity*, and that equitable Regard and kind Affection, which are unalterably due from one Man to another.

If it be again said, 'that tho' these above-mentioned Evils are directly contrary to the true Genius and Spirit of the Christian Religion; yet they are the *actual Consequence* of a Variety of Sects, exceeding fond of their particular Schemes.' I answer; they are only *accidental Abuses* to which the best Things are liable: The same Argument may be urged against *Reason*, and *every Branch* of natural and civil *Liberty*. It is equally conclusive as the *Papists* have used it against the *Laity's* having the *Bible; viz.* the Consequence of People's having the Bible in their Hands to read, has been the rising up of a *Variety* of *Sects* in the christian World, and therefore they ought not to be permitted the Use of it. As no such Conclusion can be drawn against every Body's having the *Bible* from such Premises; so in the Case before us, no Conclusion against the *Right of private Judgment* for our selves in Matters of *Religion*, can be drawn from these Inconveniencies; which do not spring directly from it, but arise entirely from different Causes; from *Pride*, or foolish *Bigotry*, that either does not understand, or pays no Regard to the unalienable Rights of Conscience.

3. Such legal Establishments have a direct *contrary* Tendency to the *Peace* of a Christian State. As the *Exercise of private Reason*, and free Enquiry in a strict and constant Adherence to the sacred *Scriptures* as the only Rule of Faith and Practice, is the most likely Means to produce Uniformity in the essential Principles of Christianity as well as Practice; so this is certainly the most sure Method of procuring Peace in the State. No Man having any Reason to repine at his Neighbour's Enjoyment of that Right, which he is not willing to be without himself; and on the

same Grounds he challenges it for himself, he must be forced to own, that it is as reasonable his Neighbour should enjoy it. But then on the other Hand, *every Claim of Power* inconsistent with this Right, (as the making such a human Establishment of Religion of which we are speaking) is an *Encroachment* on the Christian's Liberty; and so far therefore he is in a State of *Slavery:* And so far as a Man feels himself in a State of Slavery, so far he feels himself unhappy, and has Reason to complain of that Administration which puts the Chain upon him. So that if *Slavery* be for the *Peace* of the civil State; then such Establishments as we are speaking of, tend to promote the Peace of the State: *i.e.* what makes the Subjects *miserable,* really makes them *happy.* And as it necessarily tends to the Misery of some, so it also promotes *Bigotry, Pride,* and *Ambition* in such as are fond of such Establishments: which have from Time to Time broken out in Extravagancies and Severities (upon good Subjects) in Men of Authority and Influence, and into Rage and Fury, Hatred and Obloquy, and such like Wickednesses, in the impotent and commoner Sort. This has been the Case in all Places, more or less, as well as in our own Nation. Thus when K. *Henry* threw off the *Popish Tyranny,* he would not destroy and put an End to the Exercise of that unjust Power, but only transferred it to *himself,* and exercised it with great Severity. The same unjust Dominion over the Consciences of Men was again exercised in the Reign of *Elizabeth;* who (tho' otherwise a wise Princess) yet being of an high and arbitrary Temper, pressed *Uniformity* with Violence; and found Bishops enough, *Parker, Aylmer, Whitgift* and *others,* to cherish that Temper, and promote such Measures. *Silencings, Deprivations, Imprisonments, Fines* etc. upon the Account of Religion, were some of the powerful *Reasonings* of those Times. The Cries of innocent Prisoners, widowed Wives, and starving Children, made no Impression on their Hearts: Piety and Learning with them were void of Merit; Refusal of Subscriptions, and Non-conformity, were Crimes never to be forgiven. At the Instigation of that persecuting Prelate *Whitgift*, Archbishop of *Canterbury*, the *High Commission Court* was established; which had a near Resemblance to the *Court of Inquisition:* (A fine Invention to promote Uniformity) Which by the Cruelties practiced in it in the *two following Reigns*, was render'd the Abhorrence of the Nation; so that it was dissolved by *Parliament*, with a *Clause*, that *no such Court should be erected for the future.* A Creature framed to promote the wretched Designs of such Persecutors, was her weak Successor *James* the First, who gave the *Puritans* to understand—*That if they did not conform, he would either hurry them out of the Kingdom, or else do worse.* The Bishops supported by such an *inspired King*, according to *Whitgift's* impious and sordid Flattery, pursued the Maxim to accomplish Uniformity by Persecution. The grievous Severities and numerous Violences exercised on Non-conformists in *that* and the *next* Reign, under that tyrannical Prelate *Laud,* (said in Parliament by Sir *Harbottle Grimstone,* to be *the great and common Enemy of all Goodness and good Men*) are well known by all truly acquainted with the History of those Times: As well as the cruel Injustice exercised *after the Restoration* on great Numbers of as good Subjects as any in the Nation; meerly because they could not come up to this *Uniformity* pleaded for, and enquired according to their Measure of Knowledge after the Truth, and desired to worship GOD according to their Consciences: until the late great Deliverer (WILLIAM the IIId. of happy Memory) of the *British* Nation from *Popery* and *Slavery*, freed those miserable Sufferers (noble Confessors for the Truth) from a Yoke of Bondage laid upon them, and gave them *a Law* for the Security of their *Christian Liberty;* this *Right of private Judgment* I have been pleading for. And that this has promoted *Peace* in the State, Experience since has proved; as well as former Experience made it most evident, that the Incroachments upon this Right of private Judgment, by such legal Establishments, have been exceeding prejudicial to the Peace of the State: It being impossible but that such Methods should cause and perpetuate Schisms and Divisions of the Church, and disturb and disquiet the State; since *the Wrath of Man cannot work the Righteousness of GOD;* and since civil Punishments have no Tendency to convince the *Conscience*, but only to inflame the *Passions* against the Advisers and Inflicters of them. And as History gives us so dreadful an Account of the melancholy and tragical Effects of this Practice, one would think, that no People who have any Regard for the Peace of the Flock of CHRIST, who know the Worth of Liberty, would be fond of such legal Establishments, or any such Methods as encroach upon Christian Liberty, the most valuable of all our Rights.

Thus I think I have fully answered all your *Objections* against my *second Corollary.* I therefore proceed to a *third.*

III. That the *civil Authority* ought to *protect all their Subjects* in the Enjoyment of *this Right of private Judgment* in Matters of *Religion*, and the *Liberty* of *worshipping* GOD according to their *Consciences.* That being the *End* of civil Government (as we have seen) *viz.* the greater Security of Enjoyment of what belongs to every one, and *this Right of private Judgment,* and *worshipping* GOD according to their *Consciences,* being the *natural and unalienable Right* of *every Men,* what Men by entering into civil Society neither did, nor could give up into the Hands of the Community; it is but a just Consequence, that they are to be *protected* in the *Enjoyment* of *this Right* as well as any other. A worshipping Assembly of

Christians have surely as much Right to be *protected* from Molestation in their Worship, as the Inhabitants of a Town assembled to consult their civil Interests from Disturbance *etc.* This Right I am speaking of, is the most valuable Right, of which every one ought to be most tender, of universal and equal Concernment to all; and *Security* and *Protection* in the Enjoyment of it the just Expectation of every Individual. And the civil Magistrate in endeavouring and doing this, most truly comes up to the Character of *a nursing Father* to the Church of CHRIST. If this had been *protected* as it ought to have been, what infinite Mischief to the Christian Church had been prevented? From the Want of a due Care of this, the *Clergy* through Pride and Ambition assumed the Power of prescribing to, imposing on and domineering over the Consciences of Men; civil Rulers for their own private Ends helping it forward; which went on 'till it produced the most detestable *Monster* the Earth ever had upon it, the *Pope,* who has deluged the Earth with the Blood of Christians. This being the true Spirit of *Popery,* to impose their Determinations on all within their Power by any Methods which may appear most effectual: and those *civil Magistrates* that suffered and helped that *Beast* to invade this Right, did therein *commit Fornication with her; and give her their Strength and Power;* and so instead of proving *Fathers* to their People, proved the cursed *Butchers* of them. It has been by asserting and using this Right, that any of the *Nations* who *have been drunk with the Wine of her Fornication,* have *come out from her Abominations:* and would the civil Magistrates of those Nations, who at this Day worship the Beast, but protect their Subjects in *this natural Right* of *every one's judging for himself in Matters of Religion,* according to that alone Rule the *Bible;* that settled Darkness of Ignorance, Error and Idolatry, which now involves them, would vanish as the Darkness of the Night does by the rising of the Sun. How unspeakably would the Advantages be, arising from the Protection of this Right, did they reach no further than to the Estates, Bodies, and Lives of Men?

All *Reformations* are built on this single Principle I have been pleading for, from which we should never depart: yet it must be owned and deserves to be lamented, that the Reformed have too much departed from this Principle upon which they at first set up; whence it has come to pass that Reformations in one Place and another have not been more perfect. For the Prince of Darkness has always found Means this Way to make a Stand against the most vigorous Efforts; and if any Advantages have been gained in any Point, to secure a safe Retreat, by infatuating Men with that strange Sort of Pride, whereby they assume to themselves only, but allow to none else, a Power of domineering over the Consciences of others, Religion will certainly lie under Oppression if this unjust Authority be transferred, to *Decrees of Councils, Convocations, Injunctions of civil Magistrates*, or from one Man or any Order of Men to another; as it is if we have any other Rule of Faith and Practice in Religion, besides the *Bible.* It were easy to enlarge on the vast Advantages and Happiness of admitting no other Rule or Guide but the sacred *Scriptures* only: thence would flow the greatest Blessings to Mankind, Peace and Happiness to the World: so that if there be any Rights and Liberties of Men that challenge *Protection* and *Security* therein from the civil Magistrate, it is *this natural Right of private Judgment in Matters of Religion*, that the sacred *Scriptures only may become the Rule to all Men in all religious Matters*, as they ought to be. In a Word, this is the surest Way for the Ease and Quiet of Rulers, as well as Peace of the State, the surest Way to engage the Love and Obedience of all the Subjects. And if there be divers religious Sects in the State, and the one attempts to offend the other, and the Magistrate interposes only to keep the Peace; it is but a natural Consequence to suppose—that in such Case they all finding themselves equally *safe*, and *protected* in their Rights by the civil Power, they will all be equally obedient. It is the Power given to one, to oppress the other, that has occasioned all the Disturbances about Religion. And should the Clergy closely adhere to these Principles, instead of their being reproached for Pride and Ambition, as the Sowers of Strife and Contention and Disturbance of the Peace of the Church of God; they would be honoured for their Work's sake, esteemed for their Character, loved as Blessings to the World, heard with Pleasure, and become successful in their Endeavours to recommend the Knowledge and Practice of Christianity.

IV. It also follows from the preceeding Principles, that *every Christian* has *Right* to *determine* for himself *what Church to join himself to;* and *every Church* has *Right* to *judge* in *what Manner* GOD is to be *worshipped* by them, and *what Form of Discipline* ought to be observed by them, and the *Right* also of *electing their own Officers.* (For Brevity Sake I put them all together) From this *Right* of *private Judgment* in Matters of *Religion*, sufficiently demonstrated in the foregoing Pages, it follows, that no Christian is obliged to join himself to *this* or *the other Church*, because any Man or Order of Men command him to do so, or because they tell him the Worship and Discipline thereof is most consonant to the sacred Scriptures; For no Man has Right to judge for him, whether the Worship and Discipline of *this* or *the other* Church be most agreeable to the sacred Scriptures; and therefore no other can have Right to determine for him to which he ought to join himself: This Right therefore must lie with every Christian. As this is the Right of each *Individual;* so also of a *Number* of them agreeing in their Sentiments in these

Things, to agree to observe the Ordinances of Christ together, for their mutual Edification according to the Rules of the Gospel, which makes a particular Christian Church. And having voluntarily agreed together for such an End, no Man or Order of Men has any Authority to prescribe to them, *the Manner* of their *worshipping* GOD, or enjoining any *Form of Church Discipline* upon them. So a *Number of such Churches* (who are all endowed with Equality of Power) have Right to judge for themselves, whether it be most agreeable to the Mind of CHRIST, to *consociate* together in any *particular Form*; as for Instance, of *Presbyteries*, or *Synods*, or the like. And if they should do so, such Agreements of their's cannot be made a binding Rule to them, by any Law of Man; As has been demonstrated in the preceeding Pages. These Churches are all of them as free to think and judge for themselves, as they were before such Agreement; their Right of private Judgment not being given up, but reserved entire for themselves, when they entered into any such supposed Agreement. And if on Experience of such a Method of Regimen as they have agreed to, and farther Light, they judge any of them, there is good Reason for them to forbear practising farther in that Form; they are not held to continue therein, but have Right to act according to their present Light; they having no other Rule but the sacred *Scripture*, they have always a Right to act their Judgment according to that Rule. So also if a greater or lesser *Number* of Christians in any particular Church, shall judge another Way of Worship, or Method of Discipline, more agreeable to the *Mind* of CHRIST, than what is practised in that Church; they have *Right* to *withdraw*, and to be *embodied* by themselves. As they ought to signify this Desire to their *Brethren*, so *they* ought to *consent:* for they can have no Right to hold them to themselves: and this without any Breach of Charity on either Side; or of after Communion, so long as they hold to

CHRIST the Head, and are agreed in the great *Essentials* of Christianity. So also from the same Premisses it follows, that every Church or worshipping Assembly has the *Right* of *choosing its own Officers:*—Tho' it may ordinarily be a Point of Prudence for a Church destitute of a Pastor, to consult Pastors of other Churches where they may be supplied with a Person suitable for that Office; yet that no Way supposes, the full *Power of Election* does not lie with the Church. It is for the *better improving* their *Power of Election*, that such a Method is ever to be taken, and not because they have not the Power of Election in themselves. Nor can they be bound to this, if they see good Reason to act otherwise, (as the Case has sometimes hapned and often may.) *Nor can they be at all bound* to *elect* the *Person recommended:* They are to prove him themselves, and be fully satisfied in his Ministerial Gifts and Qualifications, and may herein be controuled by no Power whatever. It is their own good, their everlasting Interest that is concerned, and if they judge his Doctrine not agreeable to the sacred Scriptures, that he is not qualified as he ought to be for a Gospel Minister they have Right to reject him. As they have a Right of judging the Doctrines taught them by the sacred Scriptures; and of rejecting the same if not agreeable thereto, so it necessarily follows they have equal Right to refuse such a one for their Teacher, who does not teach according to the Scriptures.

But if it be demanded how this Power can be exercised, must every Individual be agreed in the Person, or no Election made?

I answer,

1. Such a universal Agreement is not necessary, the Election may be made by a Majority. Experience has shewn where the Candidate has had the Gospel Qualifications for the Office, the Concurrence in the

Choice has been universal, at least so general as to bring no Difficulty in the Exercise of this Right. So when there has been any considerable Number who judged they had any weighty Reason against the Election made by a Majority, Experience has also shewn the Majority's denying themselves of that Choice, and trying farther, has issued happily for the whole. In such Cases, 'tis certain, *Wisdom is profitable to direct.* And that Rule of our Saviour's, *Math.* 7. 12. will go a great Way in keeping Churches in the peaceable Exercise of this Right.

2. Where a minor Part cannot in Judgment acquiesce in the Choice made by the major Part of the worshipping Assembly, they have a Right to withdraw and choose a Minister for themselves, or if not able to support one may attend divine Worship in a neighbouring Church, where they find they may do it to greater Edification. They are all equally vested in the same Right, and hold it independent one of another, and each one independent of the whole, or of all the rest. So that the greater Number can have no Right to impose a Minister on the lesser. It is not here as in civil Societies where the Right of each Individual is subjected to the Body, or so transferred to the Society, as that the Act of theMajority is legally to be considered as the Act of the whole, and binding to each Individual. As to what concerns Men's civil Interests, there is nothing in the Nature of Things to hinder or prevent its being lawful or best, so to transfer their Power to the Community. But it is not so in religious Matters, where Conscience and Men's eternal Interests are concerned. If the Power of acting be transferred in this Case, as in that of civil Societies (now mentioned) Thus, if for Instance, the Majority should elect an *Arminian* Teacher, the minor Part must be so concluded by that Choice, as to submit to such a One as their Teacher, when at the same Time it may be directly against their Consciences to receive such Doctrines or such a

Teacher. But since the Rights of Conscience may not be touched, the Right of electing a Teacher is not transfer'd to the Body by the Individuals, as civil Rights may be in civil Societies. That Principle of Supposition, which any Ways infer, an Infringement upon the Rights of Conscience, cannot be true; as that does, which supposes a Majority may impose a Minister on a lesser Part.

If to avoid what I have asserted, that in such Case a minor Part may withdraw and choose a Minister for themselves, it be here said—That they may remove their Habitations——

I Answer, Since this Right of electing a Teacher for themselves does truly remain with them, after the Choice made by the Majority, that Right may be exercised by them, and why not in one Part of the civil State as well as another? They are guilty of no Crime for which they should be banished by the State, nor of any Thing whereby they have forfeited a Right of possessing their present Freeholds: their Right to their Freeholds remains, and consequently their Right to exercise their Christian Rights where they be, and have a Right to remain.—It is to no Purpose here to say, Perhaps the Legislature has fixed the Bounds of the Parish.—For the Legislature can make civil Societies, and may fix the Bounds of Towns and Parishes for civil Purposes; yet they can't make Churches, nor may they make any Laws that interfere with the Rights of Christians.—Nor is it to any Purpose to say, This would open a Door to a great Multiplication of Churches: For how many populous Places, as well as *Boston*, have tried it, and found Religion and Peace best promoted on these Principles; nor is there a probability that Churches will by this Means be increased beyond their Ability to support their Ministers.

By what I have said you will find some other of your Queries answer'd, without my making particular Application, and therefore I leave that for you to do at your own Leisure: And should here finish my Letter, but that you insist on my giving you my Sentiments on a Law made in your Colony *May* 1742, Intitled *An Act for regulating Abuses, and correcting Disorders in Ecclesiastical Affairs:* Which it seems, thro' the fond Opinion some Persons among you had of it, was thrust into one of our publick News Papers, soon after it was passed; under which every wise By-stander, that was a hearty Friend to your civil and religious Interests, was ready to write, *Tell it not in Gath* etc.

I shall not descend into every Particular that might be offered upon it—Some few Remarks may suffice.

1. The Law is founded on this false Principle, *viz.* That the civil Authority hath Power to establish a Form of Church-Government by penal Laws. The Act relates wholly to Matters of an ecclesiastical Nature: and as it supposes, the civil Magistrate has Authority by penal Laws to regulate ecclesiastical Matters, so consequently to establish an ecclesiastical Constitution by penal Laws. It appears from the Preamble to the Act, that the declared Design of it is to keep Persons from deviating from the ecclesiastical Discipline established by Law, in the Year 1708 and that under the Penalties by this Law enacted,—But that they have no such Authority, has been fully demonstrated in the foregoing Pages, which I need not repeat. Whence it must follow, that the Act is fundamentally wrong, being made without any Authority. Be pleas'd to reflect one Minute on this Power challenged by this Law, to correct, and that by penal Laws, such Disorders as are purely of an ecclesiastical Nature, and see the Consequence of it. One Disorder to be corrected is, A Minister's preaching out of his own Parish undesired by the Minister and major Part of the Church where he shall so preach. If the civil Magistrate has this Power the Act supposes, if he judges it to be a

Disorder for the Minister to preach in his own Parish on a Week Day, he may then restrain him: or if he thinks it a Disorder that there should be any public Prayers but by a set printed Form, he may then restrain all to such a Form. It is plain, if the civil Magistrate has Authority to correct ecclesiastical Disorders, he has a Right to judge what is a Disorder in the Church, and restrain the same. If he may execute this in one Instance, he may in another: and every Thing is on this Principle liable to be disallowed in the Worship of God, which does not suit with the civil Magistrate's Opinion. Whatever he judges to be a Disorder, is so by this Principle, and may be restrained accordingly. And so farewell all Christian Liberty.—It signifies nothing to say, your civil Magistrates are so sound in the Faith, there's no Danger they will go so far. I hope so indeed with you; tho' you can't tell what those or others in succeeding Times may do. It is no new Thing for civil Authority to make dreadful Havock of the Liberties and Religion of Christians; but the Argument, you see, proceeds upon the Nature of Things. The Principle, that Law stands upon, you may plainly see, is directly inconsistent in its own Nature, with the unalienable Rights of Christians. What sad Effects have been felt in our own Nation, in some former Reigns, from this very Principle's being put in Practice; who at all acquainted with History can be ignorant? While they were executing what they were pleased to call wholsome Severities on *Dissenters,* they were only in their Judgment correcting Disorders in ecclesiastical Affairs. If this Power belongs to the civil Authority, as such, it must belong to those in one State as well as another; and is as justly challenged by the civil Authority in *France,* as in *New-England.* Let it be but once supposed the civil Magistrate has this Authority, where can you stop? what is there in Religion not subject to his Judgment? All must be Disorder in Religion, which he is pleased to call so; you can have no more of the external Part of Religion than he is pleased to leave you, and may have so much of Superstition as he is pleased to enjoin under the Head of Order. So that this Law stands on no better a Foundation, than what infers the Destruction of Christian Liberty.

* * *

I come now to the last Paragraph, which runs thus:

That if any *Foreigner* or *Stranger* that is not an Inhabitant within this Colony, including as well such Persons, that have no ecclesiastical Character, or License to preach, as such as have received Ordination or License to preach by any Association or Presbytery, shall presume to preach, teach or publickly to exhort in any Town or Society within this Colony, without the Desire and License of the settled Minister and the major Part of the Church of such Town or Society; or at the Call and Desire of the Church and Inhabitants of such Town or Society, provided that it so happen that there is no settled Minister there; that every such Teacher or Exhorter shall be sent (as a *vagrant* Person) by Warrant from any one Assistant or Justice of the Peace from Constable to Constable, out of the Bounds of this Colony.

Since which, you tell me, there has been last *October* an Addition made, *viz.*

That whoso thus offends shall pay the Costs of his Transportation; and if he returns again and offends in such Sort, it is made the Duty of any Assistant or Justice of the Peace that shall be informed thereof, to cause such Person to be apprehended and brought before him, and if found guilty, to give Judgment that such Person shall become bound in the penal Sum of an *hundred Pounds* lawful Money, to his peaceable and good Behaviour until the next County Court, in the County where the Offence shall be committed, and that such Person will not offend again in like Manner; and the County Court may (if they see Cause) further bind *etc.* during their Pleasure.—

Occasioned, as I am informed, by that good Gentleman Mr. *Finley's* coming at the Direction of a *Presbytery* in the *New-Jersey* Government, who had been applied to for a Minister, and preaching to a Presbyterian Church at *Milford*, who had join'd themselves to that Presbytery, and put themselves under their Care; for which being transported out of the Government, he returned and preached to a congregational Church at *New-Haven*, who had been allowed, as well as the former at *Milford*, to be a Society for the worshipping of God, by the County Court at *New-Haven*, by Virtue of a Law formerly made for the Ease of such as soberly dissent from the Way of Worship and Ministry established by the Laws of *Connecticut;* and for this he was adjudged by the civil Authority to be transported again, which was but in Part effected thro' the Negligence of some Officer; and, I'm told, he returned and preached again.—This his Preaching and Exhorting, it seems, *greatly disquieted and disturbed the People;* as the Preamble to this Act expresses it.——Is it not strange, the preaching of that peaceable and humble Christian (as you confess his Behaviour bespoke him to be while in the Colony) unto a Number of People, who had Right to hear the Gospel preached from him, should *greatly disquiet and disturb* such as had their Choice in hearing others! Or could it *disquiet* and *disturb* any Minds except such as can't bear their Christian Neighbours should enjoy their unalienable Rights!—But to return to the before mentioned last Paragraph, I observe, that *any Stranger, not an Inhabitant in the Colony, who has received Ordination or License to preach from any* ASSOCIATION *or* PRESBYTERY, *that shall presume to preach undesired,* as expressed in the Paragraph, is liable to be treated as a *Vagrant,* unworthy to tread on that Spot of Earth: But if he should happen to be licensed by the Patriarch of *Greece*, a Super-intendant of *Denmark*, or any Bishop, he may escape the Lash of this Law. If the coming in of a Stranger and preaching in such a Manner be such a Breach of the Peace, as is punishable by the State, why should there be such *Partiality?* Why should Dr. *Watts's* preaching in such Manner in *Connecticut* be a greater Crime, because ordained by a *Presbytery*, than any other Stranger's doing so that was licensed by a Patriarch or Bishop, *etc.*—However, that is much less to be wondered at, than such Treatment as this Law subjects orthodox Ministers to, even the best Ministers of Christ upon Earth, for a mere Non-conformity to a certain Point of Order, that never took Place (I suppose) in any Church upon Earth.

But to be as brief as may be in the Consideration of this Paragraph; Let the Question be, if you please, exactly according to the Words, *viz.* Whether a civil State has rightful Authority to *banish* or thrust out a confessedly *orthodox Minister* of Jesus Christ, tho' a Foreigner or Stranger, for only *preaching the Gospel* to a Number, without the Desire of the Incumbent, and major Part of the Church in the Parish wherein he shall so preach; the said Minister being supposed to have a *Right* to Protection, and a *Right* to remain in that State, until he does something to *forfeit* it?—I have truly stated it, because I have mentioned the very supposed *Crime* for which such Foreigners or Strangers are to be thrust out of the Government; and I must necessarily suppose them *true* or *orthodox* Ministers of Christ, because *this Law* supposes them so, since it speaks of such as are *ordained* or *licensed by any Association or Presbytery* not within that Government; which includes all such as are on this Continent, as well as *Great-Britain* (at least) all of which are esteemed *orthodox*. I put in the last Words, because they really relate to the Subjects of the King of *Great Britain*, from whom the Government holds it *Charter*, and so to any Persons in the Plantations, as well as on the Isle of *Great Britain*, who have a Right therefore to be treated as *Englishmen,* or Fellow-Subjects under King GEORGE, and so may be truly said to have a Right to remain in the Colony, in such a Sense as you will not allow to any belonging to another Kingdom. I don't mention this because I would go into the Consideration of what particular Powers may be in your *Charter,* different from others; tho' I confess, I can't find any Words in your *Charter,* that express or imply a Power to do any Thing that is pretended to be done by this Law, to establish or regulate by Law any Matters of an ecclesiastical Nature, to impose any civil Pains or Penalties in Matters of Conscience, relating to the Worship of God. But neither your Colony, nor any other in the King's Dominions, have any rightful Authority to do as is here supposed, according to the Question, as I have truly stated it. Let me here take a plain Case to illustrate the Point. *Wickliff* arose a Light in *England,* while Popery prevailed: be it supposed, he instructed a few in the Truth, but neither Bishop nor Incumbent of the Parish would give Leave for his preaching. However, he goes on preaching the Gospel, and the People will hear him. In this Case, the King and Parliament had no rightful Authority to banish *Wickliff,* or turn him out from the Island, for his so preaching. For, as has been already shewn in the preceeding Pages, *the End of civil Government being the Preservation of Person and Property, it would be a plain departing from the End of civil Government, to inflict any Punishment on* Wickliff *for his so preaching.* What the civil Authority is obliged to defend and secure, is not hurt at all by the supposed Action of *Wickliff;* and it is really acting against the Design of the civil Magistrate's Trust, to hurt an innocent Subject.—Besides, the Right of private Judgment in Matters of Religion being unalienable, and what the civil Magistrate is rather oblig'd to protect his Subjects equally in, both *Wickliff,* and they who desired to hear him, had a just Right to remain where they were, in the Enjoyment of that Right, free from all Molestation from any Persons whatsoever; agreeable to what has been sufficiently evidenced in the foregoing Pages.—On the other Hand, see the *Absurdity* of supposing that the civil Magistrate had rightful Authority to have sent away *Wickliff.* If the Magistrate had Right to send him away because the *standing Clergy* were unwilling he should preach (that being one of the Cases supposed in this Law) then the civil Authority must have had equal Right to send any *other* such Person away, as fast as they appeared; and consequently they must be supposed to have had rightful Authority to hold their Subjects in the worst *Slavery,* i. e. to keep them from the Exercise of their *private Judgment* in Matters of *Religion;* a Power to do which never was nor could be vested in the civil Magistrate, by the People, by any original Compact, which is truly supposed the Foundation of all civil Government. It alters not the Nature of civil Government, whether the Magistrate be Protestant or Papist, Christian or Pagan. What of Right appertains to the civil Magistrate by Virtue of his *Office,* must also necessarily belong to him, tho' Popish, or Heathen. The Supposal therefore that the civil Magistrate in *England* at that Day had rightful Authority to have sent away *Wickliff,* for preaching the Gospel without Leave of the Clergy, is big with too great an Absurdity, for a consistent Protestant to swallow. Suppose then these *Colonies* to have existed at that Time, or *Great Britain* and these Colonies *Popish* now, as *Great-Britain* was then, and *Wickliff* to come into any of them and preach in some Parish without the Consent of the Incumbent, at the Desire of a Number of People, it is certain, in this Case none of these Colonies could have any rightful Authority to thrust him out of their Borders, or do any Thing like it.—The *same Reasons* must conclude against these Colonies Authority to transport him, for coming and preaching *now* without an Incumbent's Leave at the Desire of a Number, as in the former Case; the same Principles and Reasoning will hold equally true, applied to any such Instance as now before us, any Time since the Reformation from Popery. The civil *Peace* is no Ways broken by this Action of *preaching*, of which we are speaking: But indeed if any should take Occasion from it, to contend and quarrel with their Neighbours, as Papists and Heathens have sometimes done, the Apostle (*James* 4. 1.) has shown us the true Spring thereof, the *Lusts* in Men's Hearts; the Outbreakings of which in *Injuries* to their Neighbours, fall under the civil Magistrate's Cognizance.—And the Rights of *Conscience and private Judgment* in Matters of *Religion* are unalterably the same: And 'tis a Scandal to Christians, to contend and quarrel with their Neighbours for enjoying them, and inexcusable in a Protestant State to make any Infringement upon them. And it was on these very Principles, which I here Advance (and by which this Law must fall) that our first *Reformers* acted, and on which all Reformations must be built. And tho' our Nation in Times past under the Influence of a biggotted Clergy, and arbitrary weak or popish Princes, have made Laws founded on Principles contrary to these I have been pleading for; yet they seem in a great Measure rooted out of the Nation: and these Principles of Truth have taken Root, and been growing ever since the happy *Revolution*, and Act of *Toleration;* and 'tis to be hoped, will prevail and spread more and more, until all spiritual Tyranny, and lording it over the Consciences of Men, be banished out of the World.

But I shall finish with observing, That by Virtue of the *Act of Toleration*, all his Majesty's Subjects are so freed from the Force of all *Coercive Laws* in Matters of *Religion*, relating to Worship and Discipline, that they act their own *private Judgment*, without Restraint:—That *any Number* of

Christians, greater or less, hear *any Protestant Minister* they desire, without Controul from the Will of others, or Authority of the civil State:—Since this is the Case, and withal as plain as the Sun in the Meridian, that where such a *Law* as this I have been considering, takes Place, *There* People are abridged of that *Christian Liberty*, which the same Persons would enjoy under the present Constitution, if they were in *England*. And how far therefore it falls short of denying and secluding them from the Benefit of the *Act of Toleration*, I leave you to say, who well know, that it is expresly provided by the Terms of your *Charter*, that *the Laws to be made in Virtue of it, shall not be contrary to the Laws of* England. This Right of private Judgment and Liberty now mentioned, is confessed and secured to you by that Law which was the Glory of the Reign of WILLIAM and MARY; but by your Law now before me, it is denied to you. How you will clear it from a *Contrariety* to the former, I know not. Nor is this about a trivial Matter, or what is dependent upon the Will of your Legislature. The Rights of *Magna Charta* depend not on the Will of the Prince, or the Will of the Legislature; but they are the inherent natural Rights of *Englishmen*: secured and confirmed they may be by the Legislature, but not derived from nor dependent on their *Will*. And if there be any Rights, any Priviledges, that we may call natural and unalienable, this is one, *viz.* the Right of *private Judgment*, and Liberty of worshipping God according to our Consciences, without controul from human Laws. A Priviledge more valuable than the civil Rights of *Magna Charta*.—This we hold, not from *Man*, but from GOD: which therefore no Man can touch and be innocent. And all the Invaders of it will certainly find, when they shall stand at his Bar, from whom we hold this, *that* CHRIST *will be King in his own Kingdom*.—In the mean Time, it stands Christians in Hand to hold fast this Priviledge, and to be on their

Guard against all Attempts made upon it. And I doubt not, those Ministers who were apprehensive of this, and freely addressed the Legislative Body of *Connecticut* (as I hear was done *October* 1742.) for a Repeal of this Law, did therein what was pleasing to their great Lord and Master which is in Heaven. They acted becoming such as durst not themselves, and were willing to do what lay in their Power that others might not, *Lord it over God's Heritage.* Not that I would insinuate, that there were no others *like-minded* with them—but that therein they set an excellent Example for others to copy after, and what was proper to awaken the Attention of Christians. It has commonly been the Case, that Christian *Liberty,* as well as Civil, has been lost by little and little; and Experience has taught, that it is not easy to recover it, when once lost. So precious a *Jewel* is always to be watched with a careful Eye: for no People are likely to enjoy Liberty long, that are not zealous to preserve it. . . .

---

19. JONATHAN MAYHEW ON THE RIGHT OF REVOLUTION

Jonathan Mayhew (1720–1766) graduated from Harvard College in 1744 and three years later became minister of the West Church in Boston. There he lived up to the reputation he had acquired in college for radical religious views, tending toward unitarianism and deism. Deeply suspicious of the Anglican church and of its proselyting

---

From Jonathan Mayhew, *A Discourse concerning Unlimited Submission and Non-Resistance to the Higher Powers: With some Reflections on the Resistance made to King Charles I* (Boston: D. Fowle and D. Gookin, 1750), pp. 25–55.

efforts in New England, he chose the anniversary of the execution of Charles I to challenge the Anglicans by reaffirming the right of rebellion against tyrants in a sermon on Romans XIII. Though he himself had arrived at theological views that his ancestors would not have approved, his interpretation of their politics struck a chord that would become familiar throughout New England in the next decades.

Let us now trace the apostle's reasoning in favor of submission to the *higher powers,* a little more particularly and exactly. For by this it will appear, on one hand, how good and conclusive it is, for submission to those rulers who exercise their power in a proper manner: And, on the other, how weak and trifling and inconnected it is, if it be supposed to be meant by the apostle to show the obligation and duty of obedience to tyrannical, oppressive rulers in common with others of a different character.

The apostle enters upon his subject thus—*Let every soul be subject unto the higher powers; for there is no power but of God: the powers that be, are ordained of God.* Here he urges the duty of obedience from this topic of argument, that civil rulers, as they are supposed to fulfil the pleasure of God, are the ordinance of God. But how is this an argument for obedience to such rulers as do not perform the pleasure of God, by doing good; but the pleasure of the devil, by doing evil; and such as are not, therefore, *God's ministers*, but the devil's! *Whosoever, therefore, resisteth the power, resisteth the ordinance of God; and they that resist, shall receive to themselves damnation.* Here the apostle argues, that those who resist a reasonable and just authority, which is agreeable to the will of God, do really resist the will of God himself; and will, therefore, be punished by him. But how does this prove, that those who resist a lawless, unreasonable power, which is contrary to the will of God, do therein resist the will and ordinance of God? Is resisting those who resist God's will, the same thing with resisting God? Or shall those who do so, *receive to themselves damnation! For rulers are not a terror to good works, but to the evil. Wilt thou then not be afraid of the power? Do that which is good; and thou shalt have praise of the same. For he is the minister of God to thee for good.* Here the apostle argues more explicitly than he had before done, for revereing, and submitting to, magistracy, from this consideration, that such as really performed the duty of magistrates, would be enemies only to the evil actions of men, and would befriend and encourage the good; and so be a common blessing to society. But how is this an argument, that we must honor, and submit to, such magistrates as are not enemies to the evil actions of men; but to the good; and such as are not a common blessing, but a common curse, to society! *But if thou do that which is evil, be afraid: For he is the minister of God, a revenger, to execute wrath upon him that doth evil.* Here the apostle argues from the nature and end of magistracy, that such as did evil, (and such only) had reason to be afraid of the *higher powers;* it being part of their office to punish evil doers, no less than to defend and encourage such as do well. But if magistrates are unrighteous; if they are *respecters of persons;* if they are partial in their administration of justice; then those who do well have as much reason to *be afraid,* as those that do evil: there can be no safety for the good, nor any peculiar ground of terror to the unruly and injurious. So that, in this case, the main end of civil government will be frustrated. And what reason is there for submitting to that government, which does by no means answer the design of government? *Wherefore ye must needs be subject not only for wrath, but also for conscience sake.* Here the apostle argues the duty of a chearful and conscientious submission to civil government, from the nature and end of magistracy as he had before laid it down, i. e.

as the design of it was to punish evil doers, and to support and encourage such as do well; and as it must, if so exercised, be agreeable to the will of God. But how does what he here says, prove the duty of a chearful and conscientious subjection to those who forfeit the character of rulers? to those who encourage the bad, and discourage the good? The argument here used no more proves it to be a sin to resist such rulers, than it does, to *resist the devil*, that he may *flee from us*. For one is as truly the *minister of God* as the other. *For, for this cause pay you tribute also; for they are God's ministers, attending continually upon this very thing*. Here the apostle argues the duty of paying taxes, from this consideration, that those who perform the duty of rulers, are continually attending upon the public welfare. But how does this argument conclude for paying taxes to such princes as are continually endeavouring to ruin the public? And especially when such payment would facilitate and promote this wicked design! *Render therefore to all their dues; tribute, to whom tribute is due; custom, to whom custom; fear, to whom fear; honor, to whom honor.* Here the apostle sums up what he had been saying concerning the duty of subjects to rulers. And his argument stands thus—"Since magistrates who execute their office well, "are common benefactors to society; and may, in that re-"spect, be properly stiled *the ministers and ordinance* "*of God;* and since they are constantly employed in the "service of the public; it becomes you to pay them tribute "and custom; and to reverence, honor, and submit to, them "in the execution of their respective offices." This is apparently good reasoning. But does this argument conclude for the duty of paying tribute, custom, reverence, honor and obedience, to such persons as (although they bear the title of rulers) use all their power to hurt and injure the public? such as are not *God's ministers*, but *satan's?* such as do not take care of, and attend upon, the public interest, but their own, to the ruin of the public? that is, in short, to such as have no natural and just claim at all to tribute, custom, reverence, honor and obedience? It is to be hoped that those who have any regard to the apostle's character as an inspired writer, or even as a man of common understanding, will not represent him as reasoning in such a loose incoherent manner; and drawing conclusions which have not the least relation to his premises. For what can be more absurd than an argument thus framed? "Rulers are, "by their office, bound to consult the public welfare and the "good of society: therefore you are bound to pay them trib- "ute, to honor, and to submit to them, even when they "destroy the public welfare, and are a common pest to "society, by acting in direct contradiction to the nature "and end of their office."

Thus, upon a careful review of the apostle's reasoning in this passage, it appears that his arguments to enforce submission, are of such a nature, as to conclude only in favour of submission *to such rulers as he himself describes;* i.e. such as rule for the good of society, which is the only end of their institution. Common tyrants, and public oppressors, are not intitled to obedience from their subjects, by virtue of any thing here laid down by the inspired apostle.

I now add, farther, that the apostle's argument is so far from proving it to be the duty of people to obey, and submit to, such rulers as act in contradiction to the public good, † and so to the design of their office, that it proves *the direct contrary.* For, please to observe, that if the end of all civil government, be the good of society; if this be the thing that is aimed at in constituting civil rulers; and if the motive and argument for submission to government, be

†This does not intend, their acting so in *a few particular instances,* which the best of rulers may do through mistake, &c. but their acting so *habitually;* and in a manner which plainly shows, that they aim at making themselves great, by the ruin of their subjects.

taken from the apparent usefulness of civil authority; it follows, that when no such good end can be answered by submission, there remains no argument or motive to enforce it; if instead of this good end's being brought about by submission, a *contrary end* is brought about, and the ruin and misery of society effected by it, here is a plain and positive reason against submission in all such cases, should they ever happen. And therefore, in such cases, a regard to the public welfare, ought to make us with-hold from our rulers, that obedience and subjection which it would, otherwise, be our duty to render to them. If it be our duty, for example, to obey our king, merely for this reason, that he rules for the public welfare, (which is the only argument the apostle makes use of) it follows, by a parity of reason, that when he turns tyrant, and makes his subjects his prey to devour and to destroy, instead of his charge to defend and cherish, we are bound to throw off our allegiance to him, and to resist; and that according to the tenor of the apostle's argument in this passage. Not to discontinue our allegiance, in this case, would be to join with the sovereign in promoting the slavery and misery of that society, the welfare of which, we ourselves, as well as our sovereign, are indispensably obliged to secure and promote, as far as in us lies. It is true the apostle puts no case of such a tyrannical prince; but by his grounding his argument for submission wholly upon the good of civil society; it is plain he implicitly authorises, and even requires us to make resistance, whenever this shall be necessary to the public safety and happiness. Let me make use of this easy and familiar *similitude* to illustrate the point in hand—Suppose God requires a family of children, to obey their father and not to resist him; and inforces his command with this argument; that the superintendence and care and authority of a just and kind parent, will contribute to the happiness of the whole family; so that they ought to obey him for their own sakes more than for his:

Suppose this parent at length runs distracted, and attempts, in his mad fit, to cut all his children's throats: Now, in this case, is not the reason before assigned, why these children should obey their parent while he continued of a sound mind, namely, *their common good*, a reason equally conclusive for disobeying and resisting him, since he is become delirious, and attempts their ruin? It makes no alteration in the argument, whether this parent, properly speaking, loses his reason; or does, while he retains his understanding, that which is as fatal in its consequences, as any thing he could do, were he really deprived of it. This similitude needs no formal application—

But it ought to be remembred, that if the duty of universal obedience and non-resistance to our king or prince, can be argued from this passage, the same unlimited submission under a republican, or any other form of government; and even to all the subordinate powers in any particular state, can be proved by it as well: which is more than those who alledge it for the mentioned purpose, would be willing should be inferred from it. So that this passage does not answer their purpose; but really overthrows and confutes it. This matter deserves to be more particularly considered.—The advocates for unlimited submission and passive obedience, do, if I mistake not, always speak with reference to kingly or monarchical government, as distinguished from all other forms; and, with reference to submitting to the will of the king, in distinction from all subordinate officers, acting beyond their commission, and the authority which they have received from the crown. It is not pretended that any person besides kings, have a divine right to do what they please, so that no one may resist them, without incurring the guilt of factiousness and rebellion. If any other supreme powers oppress the people, it is generally allowed, that the people may get redress, by resistance, if other methods prove ineffectual. And if any officers in a kingly government, go beyond the limits of that power which they have derived from the crown, (the supposed original source of all power and authority in the state) and attempt, illegally, to take away the properties and lives of their fellow subjects, they may be *forcibly* resisted, at least till application can be made to the crown. But as to the sovereign himself, he may not be resisted in any case; nor any of his officers, while they confine themselves within the bounds which he has prescribed to them. This is, I think, a true sketch of the principles of those who defend the doctrine of passive obedience and non-resistance. Now there is nothing in scripture which supports this scheme of political principles. As to the passage under consideration, the apostle here speaks of civil rulers in *general;* of all persons in *common,* vested with authority for the good of society, without any particular reference to one form of government, more than to another; or to the supreme power in any particular state, more than to subordinate powers. The apostle does not concern himself with the different forms of government.* This he supposes

*The essence of government (I mean *good* government; and this is the *only* government which the apostle treats of in this passage) consists in the *making* and *executing of good laws*—laws attempered to the common felicity of the *governed.* And if this be, *in fact,* done, it is evidently, in it self, a thing of no consequence at all, what the *particular* form of government is;—whether the legislative and executive power be lodged in *one and the same* person, or in *different* persons;—whether in *one* person, whom we call an *absolute monarch;*—whether in a *few,* so as to constitute an *aristocrasy;*—whether in *many,* so as to constitute a *republic;* or whether in *three co-ordinate branches,* in such manner as to make the government *partake* something of *each* of these forms; and to be, at the same time, *essentially different* from them *all.* If the *end* be attained, it is enough. But no form of government seems to be so unlikely to accomplish this *end,* as *absolute monarchy*——Nor is there any one that has so little pretence to a *divine original,* unless it be in this sense, that God *first* introduced it into, and thereby overturned, the common wealth of *Israel,* as a *curse* upon that people for their *folly* and *wickedness,* particularly in *desiring* such a government. (See I *Sam.* viii. chap.) Just so God, before, sent *Quails* amongst them, as a *plague,* and a *curse,* and not as a *blessing. Numb.* chap. xi.

left intirely to human prudence and discretion. Now the consequence of this is, that unlimited and passive obedience, is no more enjoined in this passage, under monarchical government; or to the supreme power in any state, than under all other species of government, which answer the end of government; or, to all the subordinate degrees of civil authority, from the highest to the lowest. Those, therefore, who would from this passage infer the guilt of resisting kings, in all cases whatever, though acting ever so contrary to the design of their office, must, if they will be consistent, go much farther, and infer from it the guilt of resistance under all other forms of government; and of resisting *any petty officer* in the state, tho' acting beyond his commission, in the most arbitrary, illegal manner possible. The argument holds equally strong in both cases. All civil rulers, as such, are the *ordinance* and *ministers of God;* and they are all, by the nature of their office, and in their respective spheres and stations, bound to consult the public welfare. With the same reason therefore, that any deny unlimited and passive obedience to be here injoined under a republic or aristocrasy, or any other established form of civil government; or to subordinate powers, acting in an illegal and oppressive manner; (with the same reason) others may deny, that such obedience is enjoined to a king or monarch, or any civil power whatever. For the apostle says nothing that is *peculiar to kings;* what he says, extends equally to *all* other persons whatever, vested with any civil office. They are all, in exactly the same sense, the *ordinance of God;* and the *ministers of God;* and obedience is equally enjoined to be paid to them all. For, as the apostle expresses it, *there is* NO POWER *but of God:* And we are required to *render to* ALL *their* DUES; and not MORE than their DUES. And what these *dues* are, and to *whom* they are to be *rendered,* the apostle *sayeth not;* but leaves to the reason and consciences of men to determine.

Thus it appears, that the common argument, grounded upon this passage, in favor of universal, and passive obedience, really overthrows itself, by proving too much, if it proves any thing at all; namely, that no civil officer is, in any case whatever, to be resisted, though acting in express contradiction to the design of his office; which no man, in his senses, ever did, or can assert.

If we calmly consider the nature of the thing itself, nothing can well be imagined more directly contrary to common sense, than to suppose that *millions* of people should be subjected to the arbitrary, precarious pleasure of *one single man;* (who has *naturally* no superiority over them in point of authority) so that their estates, and every thing that is valuable in life, and even their lives also, shall be absolutely at his disposal, if he happens to be wanton and capricious enough to demand them. What unprejudiced man can think, that God made ALL to be thus subservient to the lawless pleasure and phrenzy of ONE, so that it shall always be a sin to resist him! Nothing but the most plain and express revelation from heaven could make a sober impartial man believe such a monstrous, unaccountable doctrine, and, indeed, the thing itself, appears so shocking—so out of all *proportion,* that it may be questioned, whether all the *miracles* that ever were wrought, could make it credible, that this doctrine *really* came from God. At present, there is not the least syllable in scripture which gives any countenance to it. The hereditary, indefeasible, divine right of kings, and the doctrine of non-resistance which is built upon the supposition of such a right, are altogether as fabulous and chimerical, as transubstantiation; or any of the most absurd reveries of ancient or modern visionaries. These notions are fetched neither from divine revelation, nor human reason; and if they are derived from neither of those sources, it is not much matter from *whence they come, or whither they go.* Only it is a pity that such doctrines should be propagated in society, to raise factions and rebellions, as we see they have, in fact, been both in the *last,* and in the *present,* REIGN.

But then, if unlimited submission and passive obedience to the *higher powers,* in all possible cases, be not a duty, it will be asked, "How far are we obliged to submit? If "we may innocently disobey and resist in some cases, why "not in all? Where shall we stop? What is the measure of "our duty? This doctrine tends to the total dissolution of "civil government; and to introduce such scenes of wild "anarchy and confusion, as are more fatal to society than "the worst of tyranny."

After this manner, some men object; and, indeed, this is the most plausible thing that can be said in favor of such an absolute submission as they plead for. But the worst (or rather the best) of it, is, that there is very little strength or solidity in it. For similar difficulties may be raised with respect to almost every duty of natural and revealed religion.—To instance only in two, both of which are near akin, and indeed exactly parallel, to the case before us. It is unquestionably the duty of children to submit to their parents; and of servants, to their masters. But no one asserts, that it is their duty to obey, and submit to them, in all supposeable cases; or universally a sin to resist them. Now does this tend to subvert the just authority of parents and masters? Or to introduce confusion and anarchy into private families? No. How then does the same principle tend to unhinge the government of that larger family, the body politic? We know, in general, that children and servants are obliged to obey their parents and masters respectively. We know also, with equal certainty, that they are not obliged to submit to them in all things, without exception; but may, in some cases, reasonably, and therefore innocently, resist them. These principles are acknowledged upon all hands, whatever difficulty there may be in fixing the exact limits of submission. Now there is at least as much difficulty in stating the measure of duty in these two cases, as in the case of rulers and subjects. So that this is really no objection, at least no reasonable one, against resistance to the *higher powers:* Or, if it is one, it will hold equally against resistance in the other cases mentioned. —It is indeed true, that turbulent, vicious-minded men, may take occasion from this principle, that their rulers may, in some cases, be lawfully resisted, to raise factions and disturbances in the state; and to make resistance where resistance is needless, and therefore, sinful. But is it not equally true, that children and servants of turbulent, vicious minds, may take occasion from this principle, that parents and masters may, in some cases be lawfully resisted, to resist when resistance is unnecessary, and therefore, criminal? Is the principle in either case false in itself, merely because it may be abused; and applied to legitimate disobedience and resistance in those instances, to which it ought not to be applied? According to this way of arguing, there will be no true principles in the world; for there are none but what may be wrested and perverted to serve bad purposes, either through the weakness or wickedness of men.*

*We may very safely assert these two things in general, without undermining government: One is, That no civil rulers are to be obeyed when they enjoin things that are inconsistent with the commands of God: All such disobedience is lawful and glorious; particularly, if persons refuse to comply with any *legal establishment of religion*, because it is a gross perversion and corruption (as to doctrine, worship and discipline) of a pure and divine religion, brought from heaven to earth by the *Son of God,* (the only King and Head of the *christian* church) and propagated

A people, really oppressed to a great degree by their sovereign, cannot well be insensible when they are so oppressed. And such a people (if I may allude to an ancient *fable*) have, like the *hesperian* fruit, a DRAGON for their *protector* and *guardian:* Nor would they have any reason to mourn, if some HERCULES should appear to dispatch him—For a nation thus abused to arise unanimously,

through the world by his inspired apostles. All commands running counter to the declared will of the supreme legislator of heaven and earth, are null and void: And therefore disobedience to them is a duty, not a crime.—Another thing that may be asserted with equal truth and safety, is, That no government is to be submitted to, at the *expence* of that which is the *sole end* of all government,—the common good and safety of society. Because, to submit in this case, if it should ever happen, would evidently be to set up the *means* as more valuable, and above, the *end:* than which there cannot be a greater solecism and contradiction. The only reason of the institution of civil government; and the only rational ground of submission to it, is the common safety and utility. If therefore, in any case, the common safety and utility would not be promoted by submission to government, but the contrary, there is no ground or motive for obedience and submission, but, for the contrary.

Whoever considers the nature of civil government must, indeed, be sensible that a great degree of *implicit confidence*, must unavoidably be placed in those that bear rule: this is implied in the very notion of authority's being originally a *trust,* committed by the people, to those who are vested with it, as all just and righteous authority is; all besides, is mere lawless force and usurpation; neither God nor nature, having given any man a right of dominion over any society, independently of that society's approbation, and consent to be governed by him—Now as all men are fallible, it cannot be supposed that the public affairs of any state, should be always administred in the best manner possible, even by persons of the greatest wisdom and integrity. Nor is it sufficient to legitimate disobedience to the *higher powers* that they are not so administred; or that they are, in some instances, very ill-managed; for upon this principle, it is scarcely supposeable that any government at all could be supported, or subsist. Such a principle manifestly tends to the dissolution of government; and to throw all things into confusion and anarchy.—But it is equally evident, upon the other hand, that those in authority may abuse their *trust* and power *to such a degree,* that neither the law of reason, nor of religion, requires, that any obedience or submission should be paid to them; but, on the contrary, that they should be totally *discarded;* and the authority which they were before vested with, transferred to others, who may exercise it more to those good purposes for which it is given.—Nor is and to resist their prince, even to the dethroning him, is not criminal; but a reasonable way of indicating their liberties and just rights; it is making use of the means, and the only means, which God has put into their power, for mutual and self-defence. And it would be highly criminal in them, not to make use of this means. It would be stupid tameness, and unaccountable folly, for whole nations to suffer *one* unreasonable, ambitious and cruel man, to wan-

this principle, that resistance to the *higher powers*, is, in some extraordinary cases, justifiable, so liable to abuse, as many persons seem to apprehend it. For although there will be always some petulant, querulous men, in every state—men of factious, turbulent and carping dispositions,—glad to lay hold of any trifle to justify and legitimate their caballing against their rulers, and other seditious practices; yet there are, comparatively speaking, but few men of this *contemptible character*. It does not appear but that mankind, in general, have a disposition to be as submissive and passive and tame under government as they ought to be.—Witness a great, if not the greatest, part of the known world, who are now groaning, but not murmuring, under the heavy yoke of tyranny! While those who govern, do it with any tolerable degree of moderation and justice, and, in any good measure act up to their office and character, by being public benefactors; the people will generally be easy and peaceable; and be rather inclined to flatter and adore, than to insult and resist, them. Nor was there ever any *general* complaint against any administration, *which lasted long*, but what there was good reason for. Till people find themselves greatly abused and oppressed by their governors, they are not apt to complain; and whenever they do, in fact, find themselves thus abused and oppressed, they must be stupid not to complain. To say that subjects in general are not proper judges when their governors oppress them, and play the tyrant; and when they defend their rights, administer justice impartially, and promote the public welfare, is as great *treason* as ever man uttered;—'tis treason,—not against one *single* man, but the state—against the whole body politic;—'tis treason against mankind;—'tis treason against common sense;—'tis treason against God. And this impious principle lays the foundation for justifying all the tyranny and oppression that ever any prince was guilty of. The people know for what end they set up, and maintain, their governors; and they are the proper judges when they execute their *trust* as they ought to do it;—when their prince exercises an equitable and paternal authority over them;—when from a prince and common father, he exalts himself into a tyrant—when from subjects and children, he degrades them into the class of slaves;—plunders them, makes them his prey, and unnaturally sports himself with their lives and fortunes—

ton and riot in their misery. And in such a case it would, of the two, be more rational to suppose, that they that did NOT *resist,* than that they who did, would *receive to themselves damnation.* And

This naturally brings us to make some reflections upon the resistance which was made about a century since, to that unhappy prince, KING CHARLES I; and upon the ANNIVERSARY of his death. This is a point which I should not have concerned myself about, were it not that *some men* continue to speak of it, even to this day, with a great deal of warmth and zeal; and in such a manner as to undermine all the principles of LIBERTY, whether civil or religious, and to introduce the most abject slavery both in church and state: so that it is become a matter of universal concern.—What I have to offer upon this subject, will be comprised in a short answer to the following *queries; viz.*

For what reason the resistance to king *Charles* the *First* was made?

By whom it was made?

Whether this resistance was REBELLION,* or not?

How the *Anniversary* of king *Charles's* death came *at first* to be solemnized as a day of fasting and humiliation?

And lastly,

Why those of the episcopal clergy who are very high in the principles of *ecclesiastical authority,* continue to speak of this unhappy man, as a great SAINT and a MARTYR?

For what reason, then, was the resistance to king *Charles,* made? The general answer to this inquiry is, that it was on account of the *tyranny* and *oppression* of his reign. Not a great while after his accession to the throne,

*N. B. I speak of rebellion, treason, saintship, martyrdom, &c. throughout this discourse, only in the *scriptural* and *theological sense.* I know not how the *law* defines them; the study of *that* not being my employment—

he married a *french catholic;* and with her seemed to have *wedded* the politics, if not the religion of *France,* also. For afterwards, during a reign, or rather a tyranny of many years, he governed in a perfectly wild and arbitrary manner, paying no regard to the constitution and the laws of the kingdom, by which the power of the crown was limited; or to the solemn oath which he had taken at his coronation. It would be endless, as well as needless, to give a particular account of all the illegal and despotic measures which he took in his administration;—partly from his own natural lust of power, and partly from the influence of wicked councellors and ministers.—He committed many illustrious members of both houses of parliament to the *tower,* for opposing his arbitrary schemes.—He levied many taxes upon the people without consent of parliament;—and then imprisoned great numbers of the principal merchants and gentry for not paying them.—He erected, or at least revived, several new and arbitrary courts, in which the most unheard-of barbarities were committed with his knowledge and approbation—He supported that more than fiend, arch-bishop *Laud* and the clergy of his stamp, in all their church-tyranny and hellish cruelties—He authorised a book in favor of *sports* upon the *Lord's day;* and several clergymen were persecuted by him and the mentioned *pious* bishop, for not reading it to the people after *divine service*—When the parliament complained to him of the arbitrary proceedings of his corrupt ministers, he told that *august body,* in a rough, domineering, unprincely manner, that he wondred any one should be so foolish and insolent as to think that he would part with the meanest of his servants *upon their account*—He refused to call any parliament at all for the space of twelve years together, during all which time, he governed in an absolute lawless and despotic manner—He took all opportunities to encourage the *papists,* and to promote them to the highest offices of honor and trust—He (probably) abetted the horrid massacre in *Ireland*, in which two hundred thousand protestants were butchered by the roman catholics.—He sent a large sum of money, which he has raised by his arbitrary taxes, into *Germany*, to raise foreign troops, in order to force more arbitrary taxes upon his subjects.—He not only by a long series of actions, but also in *plain terms*, asserted an absolute uncontroulable power; saying even in one of his speeches to parliament, that as it was blasphemy to dispute what God might do; so it was sedition in subjects to dispute what the king might do.—Towards the end of his tyranny, he came to the house of commons with an armed force,* and demanded five of its principal members to be delivered up to him—And this was a prelude to that unnatural war which he soon after levied against his own dutiful subjects; whom he was bound by all the laws of honor, humanity, piety, and I might add, of *interest* also, to defend and cherish with a paternal affection—I have only time to hint at these facts in a general way, all which, and many more of the same tenor, may be proved by good authorities: So that the *figurative* language which St. *John* uses concerning the just and beneficent deeds of our blessed Saviour, may be applied to the unrighteous and execrable deeds of this prince, *viz. And there are also many other things which* king Charles *did, the which, if they should be written every one, I suppose that even the world itself, could not contain the books that should be written.* Now it was on account of king *Charles*'s thus assuming a power above the laws, in direct contradiction to his coronation oath, and governing the greatest part of his time, in the most arbitrary op-

*Historians are not agreed, what number of soldiers attended him in this monstrous invasion of the priviledges of parliament—Some say 300, some 400: And the author of *The history of the kings of Scotland*, says 500.

pressive manner; it was upon this account, that that resistance was made to him, which, at length, issued in the loss of his crown, and of *that head* which was unworthy to wear it.

But by whom was this resistance made? Not by a private *junto;*—not by a small seditious *party;*—not by a *few desparadoes,* who, to mend their fortunes, would embroil the state;—but by the LORDS and COMMONS of *England.* It was they that almost unanimously opposed the king's measures for overturning the constitution, and changing that free and happy government into a wretched, absolute monarchy. It was they that when the king was about levying forces against his subjects, in order to make himself absolute, commissioned officers, and raised an army to defend themselves and the public: And it was they that maintained the war against him all along, till he was made a prisoner. This is indisputable. Though it was not properly speaking the parliament, but the army, which put him to death afterwards. And it ought to be freely acknowledged, that most of their proceeding, in order to get this matter effected; and particularly the court by which the king was at last tried and condemned, was little better than a mere mockery of justice.—

The next question which naturally arises, is, whether this resistance which was made to the king *by the parliament,* was properly *rebellion,* or not? The answer to which is plain, that it was not; but a most righteous and glorious stand, made in defence of the natural and legal rights of the people, against the unnatural and illegal encroachments of arbitrary power. Nor was this a rash and too sudden opposition. The nation had been patient under the oppressions of the crown, even to *long suffering;*—for a course of many years; and there was no rational hope of redress in any other way—Resistance was absolutely necessary in order to preserve the nation from slavery, misery and ruin. And who so proper to make this resistance as the lords and commons;—the whole representative body of the people;—guardians of the public welfare; and each of which was, in point of legislation, vested with an equal, co-ordinate power, with that of the crown?* Here were

*The *english* constitution is originally and essentially *free*. The character which *J. Caesar* and *Tacitus* both give of the ancient *Britains* so long ago, is, That they were extremely *jealous of their liberties,* as well as a people of a *martial* spirit. Nor have there been wanting frequent instances and proofs of the same glorious spirit (in both respects) remaining in their posterity ever since,—in the struggles they have made for liberty, both against foreign and domestic tyrants.—Their kings hold their title to the throne, solely by grant of parliament; i. e. in other words, by the voluntary consent of the people. And, agreably hereto, the prerogative and rights of the crown are stated, defined and limited by law; and that as truly and strictly as the rights of any inferior officer in the state; or indeed, of any private subject. And it is only in this respect that it can be said, that "the king can do no wrong." Being restrained by the law, he cannot, while he confines himself within those just limits which the law prescribes to him as the measure of his authority, injure and oppress the subject.—The king, in his coronation oath, swears to exercise only such a power as the constitution gives him: And the subject, in the oath of allegiance, swears only to obey him in the exercise of such a power. The king is as much bound by his oath, not to infringe the legal rights of the people, as the people are bound to yield subjection to him. From whence it follows, that as soon as the prince sets himself up above law, he loses the king in the tyrant: he does to all intents and purposes, unking himself, by acting out of, and beyond, that sphere which the constitution allows him to move in. And in such cases, he has no more right to be obeyed, than any inferior officer who acts beyond his commission. The subjects obligation to allegiance *then* ceases of course: and to resist him, is no more *rebellion,* than to resist any foreign invader. There is an essential difference betwixt *government and tyranny;* at least under such a constitution as the *english.* The former consists in ruling according to law and equity; the latter, in ruling contrary to law and equity. So also, there is an essential difference betwixt resisting a tyrant, and rebellion; The former is a just and reasonable self-defence; the latter consists in resisting a prince whose administration is just and legal; and this is what denominates it a crime.—Now it is evident, that king *Charles's* government was illegal, and very oppressive, through the greatest part of his reign: And, therefore, to resist him, was no more rebellion, than to oppose any foreign invader, or any other domestic oppressor.

two branches of the legislature against *one*;—two, which had law and equity and the constitution on their side, against one which was impiously attempting to overturn law and equity and the constitution; and to exercise a wanton licentious *sovereignty* over the properties, consciences and lives of all the people:—Such a *sovereignty* as some inconsiderately ascribe to the supreme Governor of the world.—I say, inconsiderately; because God himself does not govern in an absolutely arbitrary and despotic manner. The power of this Almighty King (I speak it not without caution and reverence; the power of this Almighty King) is *limited by law;* not, indeed, by *acts of parliament,* but by the eternal *laws* of truth, wisdom and equity; and the everlasting *tables* of right reason;—tables that cannot be *repealed*, or *thrown down* and *broken* like those of *Moses.*—But king *Charles* sat himself up above all these, as much as he did above the written laws of the realm; and made mere humor and caprice, which are no rule at all, the only rule and measure of his administration. And now, is it not perfectly ridiculous to call resistance to such a tyrant, by the name of *rebellion?—the grand rebellion?* Even that—parliament, which brought king *Charles* II. to the throne, and which run *loyally mad*, severely reproved one of their own members for condemning the proceedings of that parliament which first took up arms against the former king. And upon the same principles that the proceedings of this parliament may be censured as wicked and rebellious, the proceedings of those who, since, opposed king *James* II, and brought the prince of *Orange* to the throne, may be censured as wicked and rebellious also. The cases are parallel.—But whatever *some* men may *think*, it is to be hoped that, for their own sakes, they will not dare to *speak* against the REVOLUTION, upon the justice and legality of which depends (in part) his present MAJESTY'S right to the throne.

If it be said, that although the parliament which first opposed king *Charles*'s measures, and at length took up arms against him, were not guilty of rebellion; yet certainly those persons were, who condemned, and put him to death; even this perhaps is not true. For he had, in fact, *unkinged* himself long before, and had forfeited his title to the allegiance of the people. So that those who put him to death, were, at most only guilty of *murder;* which, indeed, is bad enough, if they were really guilty of *that;* (which is at least disputable.) *Cromwell,* and those who were principally concerned in the (*nominal*) king's death, might possibly have been very wicked and designing men. Nor shall I say any thing in vindication of the reigning *hypocrisy* of those times; or of *Cromwell's* male-administration during the *interregnum*: (for it is *truth,* and not a *party,* that I am speaking for.) But still it may be said, that *Cromwell* and his adherents were not, properly speaking, guilty of *rebellion;* because he, whom they beheaded was not, properly speaking, *their king;* but a *lawless tyrant.*—much less, are the whole body of the nation at that time to be charged with rebellion on that account; for it was no *national act;* it was not done by a *free* parliament. And much less still, is the nation at present, to be charged with the great sin of rebellion, for what their *ancestors* did, (or rather did NOT) a century ago.

But how came the *anniversary* of king *Charles*'s death, to be solemnized as a day of fasting and humiliation? The true answer in brief, to which inquiry, is, that this fast was instituted by way of *court* and *complement* to king *Charles* II, upon the *restoration.* All were desirous of making their court to him; of ingratiating themselves; and of making him forget what had been done in opposition to his *father,* so as not to revenge it. To effect this, they ran into the most extravagant professions of affection and loyalty to him, insomuch that he himself said, that it was a *mad* and *hair brain'd* loyalty which they professed. And amongst other strange things, which his first parliament did, they ordered the *Thirtieth* of *January* (the day on which his father was beheaded) to be kept as a day of solemn humiliation, to deprecate the judgments of heaven for the rebellion which the nation had been guilty of, in that which was no national thing; and which was not rebellion in them that did it —Thus they soothed and flattered their new king, at the expence of their liberties:—And were ready to yield up freely to *Charles* II, all that enormous power, which they had justly resisted *Charles* I, for usurping to himself.

The last query mentioned, was, Why those of the *episcopal clergy* who are very high in the principles of *ecclesiastical authority,* continue to speak of this unhappy prince as a *great Saint* and a *Martyr?* This, we know, is what they constantly do, especially upon the 30th of *January;*—a day sacred to the *extolling* of *him,* and to the *reproaching* of those who are not of the *established church. Out of the same mouth* on this day, *proceedeth blessing and cursing; there with bless they their God, even* Charles, *and therewith curse they* the dissenters: And their *tongue can no man tame; it is an unruly evil, full of deadly poison.* King *Charles* is, upon this solemnity, frequently compared to our Lord Jesus Christ, both in respect of the *holiness* of his life, and the greatness and injustice of his *sufferings;* and it is a wonder they do not add something concerning the *merits* of his death also—But *blessed Saint* and *royal martyr,* are as humble titles as any that are thought worthy of him.

Now this may, at first view, well appear to be a very strange *phenomenon.* For king *Charles* was really a man black with guilt and *laden with iniquity,* as appears by his crimes before mentioned. He liv'd a tyrant; and it was the oppression and violence of his reign, that brought him to his untimely and violent end at last. Now what of saintship or martyrdom is there in all this! What of saintship is there in encouraging people to *profane* the *Lord's Day?* What of saintship in falshood and perjury? What of saintship in repeated robberies and depredations? What of saintship in throwing real saints, and glorious patriots, into gaols? What of saintship in overturning an excellent civil constitution;—and proudly grasping at an illegal and monstrous power? What of saintship in the murder of thousands of innocent people; and involving a nation in all the calamities of a civil war? And what of martyrdom is there, in a man's bringing an immature and violent death upon himself, by *being wicked overmuch?* Is there any such thing as grace, without goodness! As being a follower of Christ, without following him? As being his disciple, without learning of him to be just and beneficent? Or, as saintship without sanctity?* If not, I fear it will be hard to prove this man a saint. And verily one would be apt to suspect that *that church* must be but *poorly stocked* with saints and

*Is it any wonder that even persons who do not *walk after their own lusts,* should *scoff* at *such saints* as this, both in the *first* and in the *last days,* even *from everlasting to everlasting?* 2 Pet. iii. 3, 4.—But perhaps it will be said, that these things are MYSTERIES, which (although very true in themselves) *lay-understandings* cannot comprehend: Or, indeed, any other persons amongst us, besides those who being INWARDLY MOVED BY THE HOLY GHOST, have taken a trip across the *Atlantic* to obtain *episcopal ordination* and *the indelible character.*—However, if these *consecrated gentlemen* do not quite despair of us, it is hoped that, in the abundance of their charity, they will endeavour to *illucidate* these *dark* points; and, at the same time, explain the creed of *another of their eminent saints,* which we are told, that unless we *believe faithfully,* (i. e. *believingly*) *we cannot be saved:* which creed, (or rather *riddle*) notwithstanding all the labours of the *pious*—and *metaphysical* Dr. *Waterland,* remains somewhat *enigmatical* still.

martyrs, which is forced to adopt such enormous sinners into her *kalendar*, in order to swell the number.

But to unravel this *mystery of* (*nonsense* as well as of) *iniquity*, which has *already worked* for a *long time* amongst us; or, at least, to give the most probable solution of it; it is to be remembered, that king *Charles*, this *burlesque* upon saintship and martyrdom, though so great an oppressor, was a true friend to the *Church;*—so true a friend to her, that he was very well affected towards the *roman catholics;* and would, probably, have been very willing to unite *Lambeth* and *Rome*. This appears by his marrying a true *daughter* of that true *mother of harlots;* which he did with a dispensation from the *Pope*, that supreme BISHOP; to whom when he wrote he gave the title of MOST HOLY FATHER. His queen was extremely bigotted to all the follies and superstitions, and to the *hierarchy*, of *Rome;* and had a prodigious ascendency over him all his life. It was, in part, owing to this, that he (probably) abetted the massacre of the protestants in *Ireland;* that he assisted in extirpating the *french* protestants at *Rochelle;* that he all along encouraged *papist*, and popishly effected *clergymen*, in preference to all other persons, and that he upheld that monster of wickedness, ARCH-BISHOP LAUD, and the bishops of his stamp; in all their church-tyranny and diabolical cruelties. In return to his kindness and indulgence in which respects, they caused many of the pulpits throughout the nation, to ring with the divine absolute, indefeasible right of kings; with the praises of *Charles* and his reign; and with the damnable sin of resisting the *Lord's anointed*, let him do what he would. So that not *Christ*, but *Charles*, was commonly preached to the people.—In *plain english*, there seems to have been an impious bargain struck up betwixt the *scepter* and the *surplice,* for enslaving both the *bodies* and *souls* of men. The king appeared to be willing that the clergy should do what they would,—set up a monstrous hierarchy like that of *Rome,*—a monstrous inquisition like that of *Spain* or *Portugal,*—or any thing else which their own pride, and the devil's malice, could prompt them to: *Provided always,* that the clergy would be *tools* to the crown; that they would make the people believe, that kings had God's authority for breaking God's law; that they had a commission from heaven to seize the estates and lives of their subjects at pleasure; and that it was a damnable sin to resist them, even when they did such things as deserved more than damnation.—This appears to be the true key for explaining the *mysterious* doctrine of king *Charles's* saintship and martyrdom. He was a saint, not because he was in his life, a good *man,* but a good *churchman;* not because he was a lover of *holiness,* but the *hierarchy;* not because he was a friend to *Christ,* but the *Craft.* And he was a martyr in his death, not because he bravely suffered death in the cause of truth and righteousness, but because he died an enemy to liberty and the rights of conscience; i.e. not because he died an enemy to *sin,* but *dissenters.* For these reasons it is that all bigotted clergymen, and friends to church-power, paint this man as a saint in his life, though he was such a mighty, such a *royal sinner;* and as a martyr in his death, though he fell a sacrifice only to his own ambition, avarice, and unbounded lust of power. And from prostituting their praise upon king *Charles,* and offering him that incense which is not his due, it is natural for them to make a transition to the dissenters, (as they commonly do) and to load them with that reproach which they do not deserve; they being generally professed enemies both to civil and ecclesiastical tyranny. WE are commonly charged (upon the *Thirtieth of January*) with the guilt of putting the king to death, under a notion that it was our ancestors that did it; and so we are represented in the blackest colours, not only as scismaticks, but also as traitors and rebels and all that is bad. And these *lofty* gentlemen usually rail upon this head, in such a manner as plainly shows, that they are either grosly ignorant of the history of those times which they speak of; or, which is worse, that they are guilty of the most shameful prevarication, slander and falshood.—But every *petty priest*, with a *roll* and a *gown*, thinks he must do something in imitation of his *betters*, in *lawn*, and show himself a *true son* of the church: And thus, through a foolish ambition to appear *considerable*, they only render themselves *contemptible*.

But suppose *our* fore-fathers did kill their *mock* saint and martyr a century ago, what is that to *us* now? If I mistake not, these gentlemen generally preach down the doctrine of the *imputation of Adam's sin to his posterity*, as absurd and unreasonable, notwithstanding they have solemnly subscribed what is equivalent to it in *their own articles of religion*. And therefore one would hardly expect that they would lay the guilt of the king's death upon *us*, altho' *our fore-fathers* had been the only authors of it. But this conduct is much more surprising, when it does not appear that *our* ancestors had any more hand in it than *their own*.—However, bigotry is sufficient to account for this, and many other *phenomena*, which cannot be accounted for in any other way.

Although the observation of this *anniversary* seems to have been (at least) superstitious in its *original*; and although it is often abused to very bad purposes by the established clergy, as they serve themselves of it, to perpetuate strife, a party spirit, and divisions in the christian church; yet it is to be hoped that one good end will be answered by it, quite contrary to their intention: It is to be hoped, that it will prove a standing *memento*, that *Britons* will not be *slaves;* and a warning to all corrupt *councellors* and *ministers*, not to go too far in advising to arbitrary, despotic measures—

To conclude: Let us all learn to be *free*, and to be *loyal.* Let us not profess ourselves vassals to the lawless pleasure of any man on earth. But let us remember, at the same time, government is *sacred*, and not to be *trifled* with. It is our happiness to live under the government of a PRINCE who is satisfied with ruling according to law; as every other *good prince* will—We enjoy under his administration all the liberty that is proper and expedient for us. It becomes us, therefore, to be contented, and dutiful subjects. Let us prize our freedom; but not *use our liberty for a cloke of maliciousness.* There are men who strike at *liberty* under the term *licentiousness.* There are others who aim at *popularity* under the disguise of *patriotism.* Be aware of both. *Extremes* are dangerous. There is at present amongst *us*, perhaps, more danger of the *latter*, than of the *former.* For which reason I would exhort you to pay all due Regard to the government over us; to the KING and all in authority; and to *lead a quiet and peaceable life.*—And while I am speaking of loyalty to our *earthly Prince*, suffer me just to put you in mind to be loyal also to the supreme RULER of the universe, *by whom kings reign, and princes decree justice.* To which king eternal immortal, invisible, even to the ONLY WISE GOD, be all honor and praise, DOMINION and thanksgiving, through JESUS CHRIST our LORD. AMEN.

20. FROM THE SOCIAL LADDER TO THE SEPARATION OF POWERS

Abraham Williams (1727–1784), pastor of the church at Sandwich, Massachusetts, was not an outstanding thinker. His election sermon of 1762 is memorable, not because of any originality or forceful expression, but simply because it illustrates the transformation that had taken place in Puritan ideas. Williams's immediate purpose was conservative, to discourage a political dispute that had broken out against the royal governor; but by this time, even in the hands of a conservative, the old ideas sound radical. Williams affirms that the voice of the people is the voice of God; and while he urges every man to keep in his place, he applies his admonition much more directly to the officers of government than he does to the people at large.

AN ELECTION SERMON.

I COR. XII. 25.

That there should be no Schism in the Body, but that the Members should have the same Care one for another.

As the natural Body consists of various Members, connected and subservient one to the other, each serving some valuable Purpose, and the most perfect and happy

---

Abraham Williams, A *Sermon Preach'd at Boston, Before the Great and General Court or Assembly Of the Province of the Massachusetts-Bay in New England, May 26, 1762* (Boston: S. Kneeland, 1762). The sermon is printed here in its entirety.

State of the Body results from all the Members regularly performing their natural Offices; so collective Bodies, or Societies, are composed of various Individuals, connected together, related & subservient to each other. Every Person has his proper Sphere, and is of Importance to the *whole;* and the public Peace and Welfare is best secured and promoted, by every Member attending to the proper Business of his particular Station. This Resemblance between the natural Body and Societies, being so obvious, affords a striking Argument from *Analogy* from one to the other, and was improved, with good Effect, by the ancient *Sages*, to appease Commotions, perswade to Contentment, and a faithful Discharge of all relative Duties.

The Apostle *Paul* has applied this Argument to Christian Societies, and from hence strongly inforced *Unity, Peace* and *Harmony, Justice* and *Truth, Fidelity* and *Kindness:* By a beautiful Allusion to the natural Body, he reproves the improper Behaviour of the Corinthians, in their Use of the spiritual Gifts, bestowed for the Edification of the Church, as well as their own Benefit; and directs them to such an Improvement, as would render them all harmonious, and highly advantageous to themselves, to the Church, and to the World.

As the natural Body is *one,*—though it have many Members, yet they are all so adjusted and fitted one to the other, as never to interfere,—none is superfluous,—each contributes it's Part to the Perfection and Happiness of the Body:—So the Body of Christ is *one,*—all it's Members are related to one another—tho' their Gifts and Stations are different, yet they are all consistent, and ought to be so used, as to promote the Peace and Edification of the Church; that there be no *Schism,* Discord or Division in the Body; but that all the Members consider their mutual

Relations and Dependencies, and duly perform the Duties of their respective Stations, and thus express their *Care one for another.*—The Christian Church would be happy, if a due Regard was paid to the Apostle's Argument.

The same Reasoning is evidently applicable to civil Societies; and were their Members of all Ranks influenced thereby, it would greatly promote their Peace and Happiness.

In this View, I shall take the Liberty to improve my Text as an Introduction to some Observations, concerning the—Origin—Nature—and End of civil Societies and Government;—the various Orders and Ranks necessary to answer the Purposes of Society;—and the Obligations the different Orders are under faithfully to discharge the Duties of their Stations, to answer the general Ends of Government, *that the Members have the same Care one for another, and there be no Schism in the Body.*

As to the origin of civil Societies or Governments; the Author of our Being, has given Man a Nature fitted for, and disposed to Society. It was not good for Man at first to be *alone*; his Nature is social, having various Affections, Propensities and Passions, which respect Society, and cannot be indulged without a social Intercourse: The natural Principles of Benévolence, Compassion, Justice, and indeed most of our natural Affections, powerfully incite to, and plainly indicate, that Man was formed for Society. To a Man detached from all Society, many essential Parts of his Frame are useless—are troublesome: He is unable to supply himself with many Materials of Happiness, which require the Assistance and Concurrence of others: Most of the *Conveniencies* of Life require the *Concurrence* of *several.* If we suppose a Man without exterior Assistance, able to procure what is barely *necessary* to his *Being,*—at best it would be with Difficulty,—but in Sickness and the Decline of Life, would be impossible: yet allowing it possible, all the Elegancies and Comforts of Life would be wanting. If we examine the Materials of our temporal Happiness, we shall find they chiefly result from Society: from hence proceed the Pleasures,—of Books,—Conversation,—Friends,—Relations, and all the social and relative Virtues. So that the social Nature of Man, and his natural Desire of Happiness, strongly urge him to Society as eligible;—to which, if we add, the natural Principle of Self-Preservation, the Dangers Mens Lives and Properties are exposed to, when considered as unconnected with others, Society will appear necessary.

All Men being naturally equal, as descended from a common Parent, endued with like Faculties and Propensities, having originally equal Rights and Properties, *the Earth being given to the Children of Men* in general, without any *difference, distinction, natural Preheminence,* or *Dominion* of one over another, yet Men not being equally industrious and frugal, their Properties and Enjoyments would be unequal. This would tempt the idle and imprudent, to seize what they had not laboured for; which must put the industrious and honest upon Methods of Self-defence, and dispose them to unite in Societies for mutual Security, against the Assaults of rapacious Men, as well as voracious Animals. The social Affections of human Nature, and the Desire of the many Conveniencies, not to be obtain'd or enjoyed, without the concurrence of others, probably, first induced Men to associate together: and *Envy, Ambition, Covetousness,* and *Sensuality,* so much prevailing in the *depraved* Nature of Man, since the *Apostacy,* obliged them to enter into closer Connections, Combinations and Compacts, for mutual Protection and Assistance. Thus civil Societies and Governments would be formed;

which in this View appear to be natural. Small Societies being formed, interfering Interests, and Men's unruly *Lusts*, would cause *Wars:*—The same Principle of Self-Preservation, upon which they at first associated, would induce several of these small Societies to unite & form greater Bodies; from which Coalition, with the natural Increase of Mankind, all civil Societies and Governments, probably arose. In this Way, *Government comes from God,* and is his *Ordinance. The Kingdom is the Lords, and he is Governor among the Nations*; (Psal. 22. 28.) *By him Kings reign, and Princes decree Justice, even all the Judges of the Earth,* (Prov. 8. 15, 16.) *He has made the Earth, and given it to whom it seemeth meet to him;* (Dan. 2. 20.) *He changes Times and Seasons, and ruleth in the Kingdoms of Men,* (Dan. 4. 17.) *There is no Power but of God—The Powers that be, are ordained of God &c.* (Rom. 13. ch.) The Meaning is, That God is the *supreme Governor* and *Disposer* of all Things.—His *alwise Providence* super-intends all Events, particularly those relating to Mankind: And Government is a divine Constitution, founded in the Nature and Relations of Things,—agreable to the Will of God,—what the Circumstances of his Creatures require:—And when Men enter into civil Societies, and agree upon rational Forms of Government, they act right, conformable to the Will of God, by the Concurrence of whose Providence, Rulers are appointed. Thus the origin of Government is from God, tho' it be an *human Ordinance* or *Creature,* (I Pet. 2. 13.) and immediately proceeds from Men; as all other Blessings and Things advantageous to Mankind, proceed from him, tho' visibly effected by second Causes.

The End and Design of civil Society and Government, from this View of it's Origin, must be to secure the Rights and Properties of it's Members, and promote their Welfare; or in the Apostle's Words, *that Men may lead quiet and peaceable Lives in Godliness and Honesty,* (1 Tim. 2.1.) i.e. that they may be secure in the Enjoyment of all their Rights and Properties righteously acquired, and their honest Industry quietly possess it's proper Rewards, and they enjoy all the Conveniencies of a social Life, to which Uprightness entitles them; and that Men may peaceably practice *Godliness,*—may worship & serve the supreme Being, in the Way they believe most acceptable to him, provided they behave peaceably, and transgress not the Rules of Righteousness in their Behaviour towards others.

In all Governments, *Magistrates* are *God's Ministers,* designed *for Good to the People.* The End of their Institution, is to be Instruments of Divine Providence, to secure and promote the Happiness of Society; to *be Terrors to the doers of Evil,*—to prevent and punish Unrighteousness, and remedy the Evils occasioned thereby; and *to be a Praise,* a Security and Reward *to them that do well,* (Rom. 13. ch.) The End and Design of Government, is to secure Men from all Injustice, Violence and Rapine, that they may enjoy their Rights and Properties; all the Advantages of Society, and peaceably practice Godliness:—that the Unjust and Rapacious may be restrained, the ill Effects of their Wickedness be prevented, the secular Welfare of all be secured and promoted.

The Nature of civil Society or Government, is a temporal worldly Constitution, formed upon worldly Motives, to answer valuable worldly Purposes. The Constitution, Laws and Sanctions of civil Society respect this World, and are therefore essentially distinct and different from the *Kingdom of Christ,* which is *not of this World,* (Joh. 18. 36.) The Notion of a civil Society, includes a Number of Persons combined together for civil Purposes.

As in a *State of Nature prior to Government,* every Man has a Right to the Fruits of his own Labour, to defend it from others, to recover it when unjustly taken away, or an Equivalent; and to a Recompence for the Damage and Trouble caused by this unrighteous Seizure; and to take reasonable Precautions for Security against future Rapine; So when civil Societies are formed, *the Community is naturally possessed of all the civil Rights of it's Members.* Men reasonably surrender to the Society the Right they before had of judging in their own Case, and of executing those righteous Judgments: It is therefore the Right, and is the Business of the Society, to defend it's Members; to secure their Properties, from foreign Invasions; and to preserve Order and Peace, and execute Justice between it's own Members. The Law of Nature (or those Rules of Behaviour, which the Nature God has given Men, the Relations they bear to one another, and the Circumstances they are placed in, render fit and necessary to the Welfare of Mankind) is the *Law* and *Will* of the *God of Nature,* which all Men are obliged to obey. Almighty God, as Head of the System, and Supreme Governor of the Universe, will suitably animadvert upon every Violation. And every Man, prior to Government, is authorized, by the universal King, so far as his Happiness is interrupted, his Property disturbed or injured, by any Violation of these immutable Laws of Equity, to vindicate his own Right, and inflict adequate Punishment on the Invader; not from a Spirit of Revenge,—or to cause Misery for it's own Sake;—but to inflict such Penalties, as will probably prevent future Injuries, and render Mens Right and Properties, as secure as they were before this dangerous Example of Injustice. In civil Society this Right, is in general, transfer'd to the Body, or Government, who *have* a Right, and it is their Duty, to punish those Violations of the Laws of

Nature, whereby the People's Properties are injured. Every Society has a Right to publish, and execute equitable Laws and Rules, for the civil Order, Peace and Welfare of the People;—for ascertaining and securing their Rights and Properties, with suitable Penalties to the Transgressors: Which Laws are, or ever ought to be, only the Laws of Nature explained and applied, both Laws and Sanctions being founded in Reason and Equity. Things unreasonable, or absolutely indifferent (if such there be) ought not to be imposed by Law. A Law without a Penalty is of no Force; and to subject a Man to suffer, for *doing* or *forbearing* what in the Nature of things is *indifferent*, is wrong and unreasonable. Men's outward Behaviour only affects, or may injure the Properties and Enjoyments of others; this therefore is all the Society ought, 'tis indeed all it can command. Human Laws can't controul the Mind.—The Rights of Conscience, are unalienable; inseperable from our Nature;—they ought not—they cannot possibly be gven up to Society. Therefore *Religion,* as it *consists* in *right Sentiments, Affections* and *Behaviour* towards God,—as it is chiefly *internal* and *private,* can be regulated only by God himself:—Yet civil Societies have a Right, it is their Duty, to encourage and maintain social public Worship of the Deity, and Instructions in Righteousness; for without *social Vertues, Societies can't subsist*; and *these Vertues can't be expected, or depended on,* without a belief in, and regard to, the supreme Being, and a future World: Consequently, a religious *Fear* and Regard to God, ought to be encouraged in every Society, and with this View, publick social Worship and Instructions in social Virtues, maintained. This is consistent with an entire *Liberty of Conscience* as to *Forms* and *additional Principles, and Duties,* which however important with Respect to *another* World; it is possible Men may think and act *differently* about, and yet practice that Piety and Virtue, which the Nature and Ends of civil Society require.

Upon the whole, the general Idea of a civil Society or Government, is a Number of Persons united by Agreement, for mutual Defence and Convenience in this World, with a Power of making and executing Laws, or of publishing those Laws of Nature, which respect Mens civil Rights and Properties, and inflicting reasonable Punishment upon Transgressors.

As to the various Orders and Ranks necessary to answer the Purposes of civil Society,—A Society without different Orders and Offices, like a Body without Eyes, Hands and other Members, would be uncapable of acting, either to secure its internal Order and Well-being, or defend itself from external Injuries. Whatever Power is in the Society, unless it be united, under one Direction, will be useless, or hurt instead of serving the Community. The natural Laws of Reason and Equity, Carelessness may over-look, or Prejudice and Vice misunderstand, or pervert: In many Cases more Attention and Care is requisite to discover them, than most will allow: And the general Security and Happiness of Mankind depending on the Knowledge and Observation of these Rules of Equity,—Persons of Penetration, Attention and Uprightness, ought to be employed for this Purpose; and when thus discover'd, the Reasonableness and Obligation of them, may immediately appear to Persons that of themselves would never have investigated them. The Transgression of these natural Laws of Equity must be punished, to compensate the Injured, and prevent future Offences: Unless proper Persons are appointed for this Purpose in Societies, it will probably be omitted, or unduly multiplied, and *Schism* and Confusion be in the Body. Therefore as a Society has a Right to defend itself, and regulate its own Members; to secure their Rights and Properties from the Violence of one another, as well as from foreign Enemies,—it is expedient, and even necessary, to have established Forms of civil Government; —Some to guide and direct their publick Affairs, and secure their Rights with Relation to other Societies;—some to search into and publish the natural Laws of Equity, with proper Sanctions, which relate to Society in general, and to that Society in particular under it's peculiar Circumstances;—And some to execute these Laws, punish Evildoers, adjust Differences, and determine Men's Rights and Properties according to them. These Considerations shew the Necessity of different Orders, with various Subordinations, to answer the Ends of Society.—The Forms of Government are various, every Society having a Right to chuse that which appears best; and if upon Trial it prove inconvenient, to alter it for a better. Persons that manage the Affairs of Government, may be considered as distinct from the *Governed,* but in Reality, they are closely united in one Body,—have a common Interest,—and are appointed for their *Benefit.*—All these *Orders* and *Ranks*, in the *Body politic,* however *distinct* one from the other, having *different Provinces* and *Duties*, designed for *different Purposes*, and immediately answering *different Ends,* are in themselves *Harmonious,* and when *properly conducted, coincide and center in one grand End,*—the Security and Happiness of the whole, *and of every Member.*

This leads me to consider,

The Obligations of the different Orders and Ranks in civil Society, to attend to their respective Duties, that they may answer the important Ends of Society; *that the Mem-*

bers have the same Care one for another, and there be no Schism in the Body.

As in the natural Body, the several Members have their distinct Offices, for which they are adapted, and when in their proper Order, they perform their natural Functions, the Body is in it's most perfect State; so in the politic Body, when it's several Orders attend to their respective Duties, proper to their Rank; the Welfare of the whole Community, and of every Individual, is secured and promoted. In the natural Body, if the Eye would do the Office of the Ear, or the Ear of the Eye; Discord and Confusion would ensue, and the usurped Office not be performed: the same holds proportionably in the civil Body. 'Tis the Concern of every Person, in every Station, to attend to his proper Duty, and mind his own Business, if he would be a good Member of Society and promote the public Weal. Schisms will rend the Body, if the Members forsake their proper Sphere, and act out of Character.

The great Ends of Society,—the secure Enjoyment of our Rights and Properties, can't ordinarily be obtained, unless the various Ranks and Offices, carefully perform their respective Duties—Whatever Precedency, some may claim above others, and whatever Subordinations in Rank, there may be, yet the *Dignity* and *Authority,* of *each,*—of *all,* is *derived* from the *whole Society,* for whose Good they are ordained by HIM, from whom originally all Power proceeds. As in a natural, so in the civil Body, all the Parts are harmonious; there is no superfluous Order, none whose real Interest is detached from, or inconsistent with, the public Good. The Peace and Prosperity of the Community depends upon the regular Discharge of the relative Duties incumbent on the various Members: To a faithful and honest Performance of which Duties, the Nature and Relations of Things indispensably oblige them.

If we consider some of the principal Orders in civil Society, it will be very evident that the public Security and Happiness greatly depends on their Fidelity to their Trusts, which proves their Obligation.

The Business of *Legislation* is very important, and the Capacity, Fidelity, and public Spirit, of those concerned in it, are closely connected with the public Welfare. They are to investigate and publish the Rules of Equity, as the Circumstances of Things require, and to annex such Sanctions as Reason directs, to secure the Rights & Properties of the Society, and of every Individual: The due Performance whereof requires a penetrating and calm Mind, an upright and benevolent Heart: Whereas Carelessness, selfish Passions, and private Interest, acting in this Sphere, will produce the greatest Disorders and Injuries.—Rules by which the Lives and Properties of Men are to be determined, ought to be demonstrably good and righteous.

As it is of the greatest Importance to Society, therefore those to whom this great Trust is committed, of making Laws, are from the Ends of Society, and the Nature of their Office, under the strongest Obligations, rationally and faithfully to discharge the Duties of their exalted Station. A *Fault here* will produce the greatest *Schism,* and may *ruin* the Body; but *Wisdom* and *Uprightness,* will most effectually secure and promote the public Good, the Order, Harmony, Peace and Prosperity of the whole, and engage the Members to a due *Care one for another.*

The *Application* and *Execution* of *Laws* made for the *public Good,* is another *great Trust* in civil Society. The

Peace and Welfare of the Community, the Security and Enjoyment of every Individual, much depend upon the *Skill* and *Uprightness* of those to whom it is committed. The End of their Institution, is to be a Terror to evil Doers, and a Praise to those that do well. Laws are published to be observed: The Fitness of them is the Reason and Ground of their Obligation:—The Security & Happiness of Society depend upon their Observation. As it is fit that Persons be appointed to execute these Laws, the Society must greatly suffer, and the Ends of it be frustrated, if they neglect their Business:—Communities may be ruined, if they pervert those Laws, design'd for general Security, to the Prejudice of it's Members—. But a faithful Execution of these Rules of Equity, and a due Punishment of Transgressors, will secure the innocent and honest; and answer the great Purposes of civil Society. They that execute equitable Laws, establish Peace & Righteousness, make others, and are themselves good Members of the Body, and express a proper Care for the other Members.

The Persons whose Business it is to secure the Society against foreign Enemies, are obliged to exert themselves with Courage, Prudence and Fidelity, to defend the Public, because the Security and Continuance of civil Societies, under God, greatly depends on their Wisdom, Virtue and Fortitude.

The public Good is promoted, and therefore the People in general who constitute the Body, are obliged in their private Stations and Occupations, to mind their own Business, with Industry, Frugality and Uprightness,—treating others, as they would reasonably desire to be treated by them,—observing the equitable Laws of the Community, rendering Obedience, Honour and Tribute to those that are employed in the important Affairs of the Public, and are *God's Ministers to them for Good.*

I might proceed to other Orders of the Common Wealth, and shew their Obligation to a proper Discharge of their relative Duties, from the Nature and Ends of civil Society, as well as from the plain Precepts of our holy Religion; but the Point seems to require no further Illustration. I shall therefore endeavour to offer some pertinent Reflections.

And,

1. Let us gratefully acknowledge the Goodness of divine Providence, in favouring us with so wise and good a civil Government: A Constitution the best proportioned and adapted to answer the Ends of civil Society, to secure the Enjoyment of our private Properties, and every Satisfaction and Advantage of social Life. By a happy Mixture and Union of the several Forms of Government; most of the Inconveniencies of each are avoided, and the peculiar Advantages of each secured.—A Government, so prudently and righteously administred, that most of our Laws are just and reasonable; and in general, equitably executed. If we take a Survey of other Nations—their Forms of Government,—the Menaces of their Rulers—the Poverty and Slavery of the common People,—we shall find abundant Reason for Gratitude to God, *who maketh* us *to differ: He hath not dealt so with* other *Nations—Praise ye the Lord.* The great Governor of the World, imperceptibly, yet effectually influences the Minds of Men, in Ways adapted to their rational Nature, to execute his own divine Schemes, with Relation to this World & the next, to our temporal and everlasting Interest. His wise and good Providence is to be acknowledged in all Revolutions of Government; and we ought sincerely to praise him, for placing us under a Government, so wise and good in its Constitution and Administration.

2. Let us humbly adore and praise the supreme Lord of the Universe, that he has so remarkably interposed, for the Preservation of our civil Constitution, and that he gives us so reasonable Hopes of it's Continuance to the latest Generations. We still enjoy our Liberties and Properties, and the same free and good Government, notwithstanding the Attempts of domestic Traitors, arbitrary bigotted Tyrants, and foreign unrighteous Enemies, in former and later Times: *He that sitteth on High, to whom Victory belongs, has confounded the Devices of the Crafty,* and *scatered* those that *delight in,* and prompted by the *Lusts* of Ambition and Covetousness, injuriously began *War.* Whatever new Enemies join the unrighteous Cause, yet from the Justice of our Cause, the Deliverances and Successes already afforded us by the Lord of Host, the almighty Judge, that will do Right, we have Reason to hope and trust, he will still favour us, and bring to nought the Combinations of unreasonable Men, and that the Cause of Truth and Right shall finally prevail.

3. Let all concerned in the Administration of Government, be excited to Unanimity & Fidelity in their respective Trusts; to prevent as much as possible any *Schism* in the *Body,* and by expressing their Care for the Members, promote public Harmony and Prosperity. However different their Ranks, Offices and Duties, they are all connected, and tend when properly conducted, to one End. There is no Discord or interfering in the *Constitution;* and if there be among those that administer public Affairs, it indicates a *Defect* in *Capacity* or *Integrity*—it arises from unruly Lusts or turbulent Passions, and not from the Nature of their Offices. As in the Body, every Member ought to perform it's proper Office, and not that of others; so in Government, since there must be various Orders and Subordinations, every Person's Concern is to *act his own Part well;* not envying or usurping what belongs to others. As the

natural Body is more frequently destroyed by internal Disorders, than external Violence; so Factions, Divisions, and Parties in the State, (fomented by those whose Business it is to preserve Order & Peace,) are more dangerous, and have more frequently proved fatal than foreign Enemies. It is a great,—a scandalous Immorality,—a crying Sin against God,—an insufferable Injury to Men—to accept a Trust—an important Trust,—and *even* to *neglect* it,—much *more* to *abuse* it,—to improve it to different Purposes from what was intended, to Purposes inconsistent with, or subversive of the good Ends proposed by their Employers:—This is an Iniquity deserving the Indignation of Mankind, and may expect the Wrath and Curse of God in this and the future World.

In a wise civil Constitution, all the Orders and Offices, tend by different Ways to the same Point, the public Good; the Way to this, in general, is *plain* and *easy*, to those that will *attend*, and are *disposed* to walk in it. Private Views, selfish Lusts, and haughty Passions, lead another Way; and when these are cloaked over with specious Pretences to public Good, we may naturally expect, Tergiversations, Intrigues, and all the artful Labyrinths of Machiavillian Politicks.

The Nature and End of Government is not so mysterious, but a Person of *common Sense*, with *tolerable Application*, may attain a competent Knowledge thereof, and with an *upright Heart, honourably perform any Part* Providence may assign him. Therefore, since the Happiness of Society, so much depends upon the faithful Discharge of the Duties of the various Offices, and all who are well disposed, can so easily perform them; this shews the Obligation, and should be a powerful Motive to Fidelity, as they will answer it at the Tribunal of the great Judge, when he calls them to account for their Talents.

4. This Subject may suggest suitable Reflections, to those at the Head of our political Body, by reminding them, of what I ought to suppose they already know,—the Nature and Importance of their Trust, and the Obligations they are under to Uprightness, Fidelity and Unanimity.

We may esteem it a Happiness, that the Gentleman, who fills the most exalted Station in our Government, whose Consent is necessary to our Laws, is so well acquainted with the Laws of our Nation (in general so agreeable to the Law of Nature)—born and educated in a Land of Liberty, under the best civil Government;—whose *Interest* it is—to whom it must be natural to *defend* and *secure* the *Rights and Liberties of British Subjects:*—who is particularly acquainted with the Importance of Understanding and Knowledge, Uprightness and Fidelity, in the executive Part of Government—Under whose Administration, therefore we may reasonably expect, no arbitrary, illegal Measures, no unreasonable, trifling, or unrighteous Laws—that all Officers of his Nomination and Appointment, will be Persons of known Capacity and Integrity, and in all Respects the fittest for their respective Posts;—that so far as his Influence extends, Piety and Virtue, Peace and Union, Order and Fidelity in every Trust, will generally prevail among all Ranks;—that his Administration, will be wise and equitable, and happy to himself and to us;—that when all secular Honours shall cease, He may receive a Crown of Glory, that fadeth not away.

In the political Body, by the *Voice of the People*, which in this Case is the *Voice of God*, the honourable his Majesty's Council, and House of Representatives, are raised to the most important Trust.—They are as Eyes to the Body, to direct the Way: *If the Eye be single*, be sincere, *the Body is full of Light*, will be properly directed; but if the Eye be depraved, the Body is exposed to numberless Inconveniencies and Disasters. 'Tis their Business to discover and publish the Rules of Equity, and inforce them with proper Sanctions. The *Law of Nature*, which is the *Constitution of the God of Nature*, is universally obliging, —it varies not with Men's Humours or Interest, but is immutable as the Relations of Things: Human Laws bind the Conscience only by their Conformity hereto—Laws ought to be plain and intelligible, consistent with themselves, —with Reason,—with Religion.—Government ought to be supported by it's Members, in exact Proportion to the Benefits they enjoy, and the Protection they receive from it. Those therefore who conduct these Affairs, we have Reason to expect will pay a due Regard to them.—As a public Spirit, a rational Desire and Endeavour to promote the publick Welfare, ought to animate all the Members of the Community; so it should be more conspicuously the Character of those intrusted with public Affairs. 'Tis their proper Business, to which they should continually attend, to preserve the public from Damage,—to promote social Virtue, Peace and Happiness: To this End they ought to encourage social Worship,—Instructions in Righteousness,—well regulated Schools and Means of Education.—The civil and religious Liberties of the Community ought to be held inviolable, by all the Members, especially by those at the Head of Government.

As the Community has originally the Right to chuse it's Magistrates, so it seems prudent to retain so much of this Right, as is consistent with Order and Peace; which may require other Methods for continuing some Officers than was expedient, or practicable for their first Appointment.—There appears a peculiar Propriety in, many Advantages result from, a considerable Part of the Legislature being frequently chosen, from all Parts of the Society: Hereby it's true State is better known; and those arbitrary Principles and Practices too apt to prevail where Power is hereditary or long continued, are check'd, and their fatal Influence prevented—As the apparent Danger of natural Death often restrains many Extravagances, and causes Men to practice many Duties, which are not regarded when this Danger is removed; so probably there may be something analogous to this in elective Offices. Therefore the annual Choice of two Branches of our Legislature, is *generally tho't* a valuable Priviledge, that properly improved greatly conduces to the publick Safety and Welfare.—By Virtue of this Priviledge one Branch of the Legislature is this Day to be chosen, for the ensuing Year. —The honourable *Gentlemen*, intrusted with this important Affair, as the *public Good* was the *End*, they ought, and professed to have in View, in *seeking* and *accepting* this Trust; with *Reason we expect,—and have good Right to expect*, that in the Choice of Councellors, the public Welfare will be their sole Aim:—that sinister Views will not be allowed in the *least Degree* to biass their Minds;—that partial Affections, natural Relations, private Piques, or Passions, will not be permitted in *any Measure* to influence their Choice.—The Supreme Legislator of Mankind, has graciously condescended to describe the Character suited to this Trust.—(Exod. 18. 21.) *Provide out of all the People, able Men.* Persons of Wisdom and Capacity to *discern between Good and Evil; that fear God,* have a Sense of his Perfections, that reverence his Authority, fear his Displeasure, believe themselves accountable to him, and pay a due Regard to his Approbation: *Men of Truth,* Sincerity, Uprightness and Faithfulness in every Trust; *hating Covetousness*, not govern'd by private Interests, but truly regarding the public Good.—The Ruler in Israel, was obliged to *write a Copy of the Law, and read therein all the Days of his Life*, (Deut. 17. 18.) Proportionably, in other Governments, the Care of the Public should be committed only to such Persons as pay a suitable Regard to the Laws established by the great Governor of the World.—Societies of Christians act an imprudent Part, to trust their public Affairs to those who pay no Regard to their holy Religion, —who disbelieve it,—whose Tempers and Lives are manifestly inconsistent with it. Christianity fairly proposed, has sufficient Evidence, to engage the assent of upright, impartial Minds; and there is reason to distrust the Capacity or Integrity of the Person that rejects it:—While he behaves well, and lives honestly, he ought peaceably to enjoy the Protection of Government; yet it is a Reflection upon Christians, if they are obliged to chuse Persons of this Character into Places of great Trust. Once more, Rulers should be *Men known among their Tribes;* (Deut. 1. 13.) Persons whose good Characters are known & established; who will probably behave well in whatever Station they are placed. These Qualifications must be regarded by the Electors, as they will answer it to God, to the Community, or to their own Consciences.

Those who are called *Gods,*—who by divine Providence, are raised to important Stations; particularly, who conduct the weighty Affairs of this Day; ought to remember, that there is *One higher than They;—who judgeth among the Gods;* (and tho' they may not in legal Form be accountable to their Constituents, yet) to Him they are accountable for all their Talents. *He sitteth upon the Circle of the Earth, and views all the Children of Men; and with Him is no respect of Persons:* He has said, that *the Gods,* those raised to the highest Authority over their Fellows, *shall die like other Men*; and *after Death, is the Judgment*; when they that have been *faithful in little,* and rightly improved their temporal Trust, shall be crowned with everlasting Honours; but the unfaithful, however great and dignified—shall in vain try to hide themselves in Caves of the Earth *from the Face of him that sitteth on the Throne, and from the Wrath of the Lamb.—He that is wise will consider these Things.*

Finally, let us all of every Rank and Order, consider our selves as Members of the civil Body, who have our proper Sphere of Action; and whatever Part Providence has assign'd us, let us perform it well. It is not our Concern, who fills this or that Station, provided the Duties of it are faithfully performed, and *there be no Schism in the Body.* If the public Good be promoted, we ought to be content, tho' we may imagine *our selves*, or some of our Friends, better qualified for some Posts, than the present Possessors. *Our* proper *Concern* is to be *faithful* to *our own Trust*, not making a Schism in the Body, but expressing a real Care and good Will for the other Members: Thus we shall preserve Harmony, and promote general Happiness.

Government is a natural and a divine Ordinance, and when tolerably answering the good Ends of it, ought quietly to be submitted to, for Conscience sake. Did we more cultivate Love to God, and to Mankind, this mutual Care for one another, would more prevail, and fewer Schisms be in the Body: Public Vertue would diffuse public Peace, Tranquility and Happiness. Did we consider and improve the Text in the view the Apostle used it, as a Motive and Reason for Peace and Faithfulness, as Members of the Body of Christ, it would render us *good Members of civil Society.* Let this then be our Endeavour, to be true and living Members of Christ's Body; in the Ways of his Appointment, let us seek an Union to and Interest in him, and pray that his Spirit, as a vital Principle may animate us, that we may be sincerely pious toward God, universally righteous toward Men, strictly sober with Regard to ourselves; then we shall be at Peace with God, and with one another. We shall be true Members of his Church here, peaceable and useful Members of the Body politic; and when all civil Societies shall be disbanded,—all secular Honours laid in the Dust,—and civil Distinctions be no more,—we shall be Members of the General Assembly and

Church of the First-born in Heaven, where universal Love, Order and Virtue, shall reign with uninterupted and everlasting Peace, Harmony and Felicity. *Amen.*

---

21. GOVERNMENT CORRUPTED BY VICE, AND RECOVERED BY RIGHTEOUSNESS

BY SAMUEL LANGDON

Samuel Langdon (1723–1797) took office as president of Harvard College in 1774. In the following year came the battles of Lexington and Concord. Though the official government of Massachusetts was at a standstill and the royal governor confined within the city of Boston by a patriot army, the General Court assembled as an extra legal Congress at Watertown and proceeded with business as usual. That meant an election in May, with an election sermon from one of the colony's leading ministers. Langdon was designated for the task and delivered the following address, in which the reader of the previous documents will recognize many old ideas applied to the purpose of encouraging American resistance to British rule.

Samuel Langdon, *Government Corrupted by Vice, and recovered by Righteousness. A Sermon Preached Before the Honorable Congress of the Colony Of the Massachusetts-Bay in New England, Assembled at Watertown, On Wednesday the 31st Day of May, 1775* (Watertown, 1775). The sermon is printed here in its entirety.

A SERMON.

ISAIAH I. 26.

And I will restore thy Judges as at the first, and thy Counsellors as at the beginning: afterward thou shalt be called, the City of Righteousness, the faithful City.

SHALL we rejoice, my Fathers and Brethren, or shall we weep together, on the return of this Anniversary, which from the first settlement of this Colony has been sacred to Liberty, to perpetuate that invaluable privilege of chusing, from among ourselves, wise men, fearing God, and hating covetousness, to be honorable Counsellors, to constitute one essential branch of that happy government which was established on the faith of royal Charters?

On this day, the people have from year to year assembled, from all our towns, in a vast congregation, with gladness and festivity, with every ensign of joy displayed in our Metropolis, which now, alas! is made a garrison of mercenary troops, the strong hold of despotism. But how shall I now address you from this Desk, remote from the Capital, and remind you of the important business which distinguished this day in our Kalendar, without spreading a gloom over this assembly, by exhibiting the melancholy change made in the face of our public affairs?

We have lived to see the time when British Liberty is just ready to expire;—when that constitution of government which has so long been the glory and strength of the English nation, is deeply undermined and ready to tumble into ruins;—when America is threatned with cruel oppression, and the arm of power is stretched out against New-England, and especially against this Colony, to compel us to submit to the arbitrary acts of legislators who are not our representatives, and who will not themselves bear the least part of the burdens which, without mercy, they are laying upon us. The most formal and solemn grants of Kings to our ancestors are deemed by our oppressors as of little value; and they have mutilated the Charter of this Colony in the most essential parts, upon false representations, and new invented maxims of policy, without the least regard to any legal process. We are no longer permited to fix our eyes on the faithful of the land, and trust in the wisdom of their counsels, and the equity of their judgment; but men in whom we can have no confidence,—whose principles are subversive of our liberties,—whose aim is to exercise lordship over us, and share among themselves the public wealth:—men who are ready to serve any master, and execute the most unrighteous decrees for high wages, —whose faces we never saw before, and whose interests and connexions may be far divided from us by the wide atlantick,—are to be set over us as counsellors and judges, at the pleasure of those who have the riches and power of the nation in their hands, and whose noblest plan is to subjugate the Colonies first, and then the whole nation to their will.

That we might not have it in our power to refuse the most absolute submission to their unlimited claims of authority, they have not only endeavored to terrify us with fleets and armies sent to our Capital, and distressed and put an end to our trade, particularly that important branch of it, the fishery; but at length attempted, by a sudden march of a body of troops in the night, to seize and destroy one of our magazines, formed by the people merely for their own security; if, after such formidable military preparations on the other side, matters should be pushed to an extremity. By this, as might well be expected, a skirmish was brought on; and it is most evident, from a variety of concurring circumstances, as well as numerous depositions both of the prisoners taken by us at that time, and our own men then on the spot only as spectators, that the fire began first on the side of the King's troops. At least five or six of our inhabitants were murderously kill'd by the Regulars at Lexington, before any man attempted to return the fire, and when they were actually complying with the command to disperse: and two more of our brethren were likewise kill'd at Concord-Bridge by a fire from the King's soldiers, before the engagement began on our side. But whatever credit falshoods transmited to Great-Britain, from the other side, may gain, the matter may be rested intirely on this,—that he that arms himself to commit a robbery, and demands the traveller's purse, by the terror of instant death, is the first aggressor, though the other should take the advantage of discharging his pistol first and killing the robber.

The alarm was sudden; but in a very short time spread far and wide: the nearest neighbours in haste ran together, to assist their brethren, and save their country. Not more than three or four hundred met in season and bravely attacked and repulsed the enemies of liberty, who retreated with great precipitation. But by the help of a strong reinforcement, notwithstanding a close pursuit, and continual loss on their side, they acted the part of Robbers and Savages, by burning, plundering, and damaging almost every house in their way, to the utmost of their power, murdering the unarmed and helpless, and not regarding the weaknesses of the tender sex, until they had secured themselves beyond the reach of our terrifying arms.*

*Near the Meeting-house in Menotomy two aged helpless men who had not been out in the action, and were found unarmed in a house where the Regulars enter'd, were murdered without mercy. In another house in that neighbourhood a woman in bed with a new born infant, about a week old, was forced by the threats of the soldiery, to escape, almost naked, to an open outhouse; her house was then set on fire, but soon extinguished by one of the children which had laid concealed till the enemy was gone. In Cambridge a man of weak mental powers, who went out to gaze at the regular army as they pass'd, without arms, or thought of danger, was wantonly shot at and kill'd by those inhuman butchers, as he sat on a fence.

That ever memorable day, the nineteenth of April, is the date of an unhappy war openly begun, by the Ministers of the King of Great-Britain, against his good subjects in this Colony, and implicitly against all the colonies.——But for what?——Because they have made a noble stand for their natural and constitutional rights, in opposition to the machinations of wicked men, who are betraying their Royal Master, establishing popery in the British dominions, and aiming to enslave and ruin the whole nation, that they may enrich themselves and their vile dependents with the public treasures, and the spoils of America.

We have used our utmost endeavors, by repeated humble petitions and remonstrances,——by a series of unanswerable reasonings published from the Press, in which the dispute has been fairly stated, and the justice of our opposition clearly demonstrated,——and by the mediation of some of the noblest and most faithful friends of the British constitution, who have powerfully plead our cause in Parliament,——to prevent such measures as may soon reduce the body politic to a miserable, dismembered, dying trunk, though lately the terror of all Europe. But our King, as if impelled by some strange fatality, is resolved to reason with us only by the roar of his Cannon, and the pointed arguments of musquets and bayonets. Because we refuse submission to the despotic power of a ministerial Parliament, our own Sovereign, to whom we have been always ready to swear true allegiance,——whose authority we never meant to cast off,——who might have continued happy in the cheerful obedience of as faithful subjects as any in his dominions,——has given us up to the rage of his Ministers, to be seized at sea by the rapacious commanders of every little sloop of war and piratical cutter, and to be plundered and massacred by land by mercenary troops, who know no distinction betwixt an enemy and a brother, between right and wrong; but only, like brutal pursuers, to hunt and seize the prey pointed out by their masters.

We must keep our eyes fixed on the supreme government of the ETERNAL KING, as directing all events, setting up or pulling down the Kings of the earth at his pleasure, suffering the best forms of human government to degenerate and go to ruin by corruption; or restoring the decayed constitutions of kingdoms and states, by reviving public virtue and religion, and granting the favorable interpositions of his providence. To this our text leads us; and though I hope to be excused on this occasion from a formal discourse on the words in a doctrinal way, yet I must not wholly pass over the religious instruction contained in them.

Let us consider——That for the sins of a people God may suffer the best government to be corrupted, or entirely dissolved; and that nothing but a general reformation can give good ground to hope that the public happiness will be restored, by the recovery of the strength and perfection of the state, and that divine providence will interpose to fill every department with wise and good men.

Isaiah prophesied about the time of the captivity of the ten tribes of Israel, and about a century before the captivity of Judah. The kingdom of Israel was brought to destruction, because its iniquities were full; its counsellors and judges were wholly taken away, because there remained no hope of reformation. But the sceptre did not entirely depart from Judah, nor a lawgiver from between his feet, till the Messiah came: yet greater and greater changes took place in their political affairs; their government degenerated in proportion as their vices increased, till few faithful men were left in any public offices; and at length, when they were delivered up for seventy years into the hands of the king of Babylon, scarce any remains of their original excellent civil polity appeared among them.

The Jewish government, according to the original constitution which was divinely established, if considered merely in a civil view, was a perfect Republic. The heads of their tribes, and elders of their cities, were their counsellors and judges. They called the people together in more general or particular assemblies, took their opinions, gave advice, and managed the public affairs according to the general voice. Counsellors and judges comprehend all the powers of that government; for there was no such thing as legislative authority belonging to it, their complete code of laws being given immediately from God by the hand of Moses. And let them who cry up *the divine right of Kings* consider, that the only form of government which had a proper claim to a divine establishment was so far from including the idea of a King, that it was a high crime for Israel to ask to be in this respect like other nations; and when they were gratified, it was rather as a just punishment of their folly, that they might feel the burdens of court pageantry, of which they were warned by a very striking description, than as a divine recommendation of kingly authority.

Every nation, when able and agreed, has a right to set up over themselves any form of government which to them may appear most conducive to their common welfare. The civil Polity of Israel is doubtless an excellent general model, allowing for some peculiarities; at least some principal laws and orders of it may be copied, to great advantage, in more modern establishments.

When a government is in it's prime, the public good engages the attention of the whole; the strictest regard is paid to the qualifications of those who hold the offices of the state; virtue prevails; every thing is managed with justice, prudence, and frugality; the laws are founded on principles of equity rather than mere policy; and all the people are happy. But vice will increase with the riches and glory of an empire; and this gradually tends to corrupt the constitution, and in time bring on it's dissolution. This may be considered not only as the natural effect of vice, but a righteous judgment of heaven, especially upon a nation which has been favor'd with the blessings of religion and liberty, and is guilty of undervaluing them, and eagerly going into the gratification of every lust.

In this chapter the prophet describes the very corrupt state of Judah in his day, both as to religion and common morality; and looks forward to that increase of wickedness which would bring on their desolation and captivity. They were *a sinful nation, a people laden with iniquity, a seed of evil doers, children that were corrupters, who had forsaken the Lord, and provoked the holy One of Israel to anger.* The whole body of the nation, from head to foot, was full of moral and political disorders, without any remaining soundness. Their religion was all mere ceremony and hypocrisy; and even the laws of common justice and humanity were disregarded in their public courts. They had Counsellors and Judges, but very different from those at the beginning of the common-wealth. Their Princes were rebellious against God, and the constitution of their country, and companions of thieves, giving countenance to every artifice for seizing the property of the subjects into their own hands, and robbing the public treasury. Every one loved gifts and followed after rewards; they regarded the perquisites more than the duties of their office; the general aim was at profitable places and pensions; they were influenced in every thing by bribery; and their avarice and luxury were never satisfied, but hurried them on to all kinds of oppression and violence, so that they even justified and encouraged the murder of innocent persons to support their lawless power, and increase their wealth. And God in righteous judgment left them to run into all this excess of vice to their own destruction, because they had forsaken him, and were guilty of wilful inattention to the most essential parts of that religion which had been given them by a well attested Revelation from heaven.

The Jewish nation could not but see and feel the unhappy consequences of so great corruption of the state. Doubtless they complained much of men in power, and very heartily and liberally reproached them for their notorious misconduct. The public greatly suffered and the people groaned, and wished for better rulers and better management. But in vain they hoped for a change of men and measures and better times, when the spirit of religion was gone, and the infection of vice was become universal. The whole body being so corrupted, there could be no rational prospect of any great reformation in the state, but rather of its ruin; which accordingly came on in Jeremiah's time. Yet if a general reformation of religion and morals had taken place, and they had turned to God from all their sins; if they had again recovered the true spirit of their religion; God, by the gracious interpositions of his providence, would soon have found out methods to restore the former virtue of the state, and again have given them men of wisdom and integrity, according to their utmost wish, to be Counsellors and Judges. This was verified in fact, after the nation had been purged by a long captivity, and returned to their own land humbled, and filled with zeal for God and his law.

By all this we may be led to consider the true cause of the present remarkable troubles which are come upon Great-Britain and these Colonies; and the only effectual remedy.

We have rebelled against God. We have lost the true spirit of christianity, tho' we retain the outward profession and form of it. We have neglected and set light by the glorious gospel of our Lord Jesus Christ, and his holy commands and institutions. The worship of many is but meer compliment to the Deity, while their hearts are far from him. By many the gospel is corrupted into a superficial system of moral philosophy, little better than ancient Platonism. And after all the pretended refinements of Moderns in the theory of christianity, very little of the pure practice of it is to be found among those who once stood foremost in the profession of the Gospel. In a general view of the present moral state of Great Britain it may be said—*There is no truth, nor mercy, nor knowledge of God in the land. By swearing, and lying, and killing, and stealing, and commiting adultery,* their wickedness breaks out; and one murder after another is committed, under the connivance and encouragement even of that authority by which such crimes ought to be punished, that the purposes of oppression and despotism may be answered. As they have increased, so have they sinned; therefore God is changing their glory into shame. The general prevalence of vice has changed the whole face of things in the British government.

The excellency of the constitution has been the boast of Great-Britain, and the envy of neighbouring nations. In former times the great departments of the state, and the various places of trust and authority, were filled with men of wisdom, honesty, and religion, who employed all their powers, and were ready to risque their fortunes, and their lives for the public good. They were faithful counsellors to Kings; directed their authority and majesty to the happiness of the nation; and opposed every step by which despotism endeavoured to advance. They were Fathers of the people, and sought the welfare and prosperity of the whole body. They did not exhaust the national wealth by luxury and bribery, or convert it to their own private benefit, or the maintenance of idle useless officers and dependents; but improved it faithfully for the proper purposes, for the necessary support of government, and defence of the kingdom. Their laws was dictated by wisdom and equity; and justice was administred with impartiality. Religion discover'd it's general influence among all ranks, and kept out great corruptions from places of power.

But in what does the British nation now glory?—In a meer shadow of it's ancient political system?—In titles of dignity without virtue?—In vast public treasures continually lavished in corruption, till every fund is exhausted, notwithstanding the mighty streams perpetually flowing in?——In the many artifices to stretch the prerogatives of the crown beyond all constitutional bounds, and make the king an absolute monarch, while the people are deluded with a meer phantom of liberty? What idea must we entertain of that government, if such an one can be found, which pretends to have made an exact counterbalance of power between the sovereign, the nobles and the commons, so that the three branches shall be an effectual check upon each other, and the united wisdom of the whole shall conspire to promote the national felicity; but which, in reality, is reduced to such a situation that it may be managed at the sole will of one court favorite? What difference is there betwixt one man's *choosing*, at his own pleasure, by his single vote, the majority of those who are to represent the people; and his *purchasing in* such a majority, according to his own nomination, with money out of the public treasury, or other effectual methods of influencing elections?—And what shall we say, if in the same manner, by places, pensions, and other bribes, a minister of state can at any time gain over a *nobler majority* likewise, to be intirely subservient to his purposes; and moreover persuade his *royal master* to resign himself up wholly to the direction of his counsels? If this should be the case of any nation from one seven years end to another, the bargain and sale being made sure for such a period, would they still have reason to boast of their excellent constitution?—Ought they not rather to think it high time to restore the corrupted dying state to its original perfection?—I will apply this to the Roman senate under Julius Caesar, which retained all its ancient formalities, but voted always only as Caesar dictated. If the decrees of such a senate were urged on the Romans as fraught with all the blessings of Roman liberty, we must suppose them strangely deluded, if they were persuaded to believe it.

The pretence for taxing America has been, that the nation contracted an immense debt for the defence of the American Colonies; and that as they are now able to contribute some proportion towards the discharge of this debt, and must be considered as part of the nation, it is reasonable they should be taxed, and the Parliament has a right to tax and govern them, in all cases whatever, by it's own supreme authority. Enough has been already published on this grand controversy, which now threatens a final separation of the Colonies from Great-Britain.——But can the amazing national debt, be paid by a little trifling sum, squeezed from year to year out of America, which is continually drained of all its cash by a restricted trade with the parent country, and which in this way is taxed to the government of Britain in a very large proportion? Would it not be much superior wisdom, and sounder policy, for a distressed kingdom to retrench the vast unnecessary expences continually incurred by its enormous vices?—To stop the prodigious sums paid in pensions, and to numberless officers, without the least advantage to the public?—to reduce the number of devouring servants in the Great Family?—to turn their minds from the pursuit of pleasure, and the boundless luxuries of life, to the important interests of their country, and the salvation of the common wealth?—Would not a reverend regard to the authority of divine revelation, an hearty belief of the gospel of the grace of God, and a general reformation of all those vices which bring misery and ruin upon individuals, families and kingdoms, and which have provoked heaven to bring the nation into such perplexed and dangerous circumstances, be the surest way to recover the sinking state, and make it again rich and flourishing? Millions might annually be saved, if the kingdom were generally and thoroughly reformed; and the public debt, great as it is, might in a few years be cancelled by a growing revenue, which now amounts to full ten millions per annum, without laying additional burdens on any of the subjects. But the demands of corruption are constantly increasing, and will forever exceed all the resources of wealth which the wit of man can invent, or tyranny impose.

Into what fatal policy has the nation been impelled by its public vices! To wage a cruel war with its own children in these colonies, only to gratify the lust of power, and the demands of extravagance! May God, in his great mercy recover Great Britain from this fatal infatuation; shew them their errors; and give them a spirit of reformation, before it is too late to avert impending destruction. May the eyes of the King be opened to see the ruinous tendency of the measures into which he has been led, and his heart inclined to treat his American Subjects with justice and clemency, instead of forcing them still farther to the last extremities! God grant some method may be found out to effect a happy reconciliation, so that the colonies may again enjoy the protection of their Sovereign, with perfect security of all their natural rights, and civil and religious liberties.

But, alas! have not the sins of America, and of New-England in particular, had a hand in bringing down upon us the righteous judgments of heaven? Wherefore is all this evil come upon us? Is it not because we have forsaken the Lord? Can we say we are innocent of crimes against God? No surely; it becomes us to humble ourselves under his mighty hand, that he may exalt us in due time. However unjustly and cruelly we have been treated by man, we certainly deserve, at the hand of God, all the calamities in which we are now involved. Have we not lost much of that spirit of genuine christianity, which so remarkably appeared in our ancestors, for which God distinguished them with the signal favors of providence when they fled from tyranny and persecution into this western desert? Have we not departed from their virtues? Tho' I hope and am confident, that as much true religion, agreeable to the purity and simplicity of the gospel, remains among us, as among any people in the world; yet in the midst of the present great apostacy of the nation's professing christianity, have not we likewise been guilty of departing from the living God? Have we not made light of the gospel of salvation, and too much affected the cold, formal, fashionable religion of countries grown old in vice, and overspread with infidelity? Do not our follies and iniquities testify against us? Have we not, especially in our Seaports, gone much too far into the pride and luxuries of life? Is it not a fact open to common observation, that profaness, intemperance, unchastity, the love of pleasure, fraud, avarice, and other vices, are increasing among us from year to year? And have not even these young governments been in some measure infected with the corruptions of European Courts?—Has there been no flattery; no bribery; no artifices practised, to get into places of honor and profit, or carry a vote to serve a particular interest, without regard to right or wrong? Have our Statesmen always acted with integrity? And every Judge with impartiality, in the fear of God? In short, have all ranks of men shewed regard to the divine commands, and joined to promote the Redeemer's kingdom, and the public welfare? I wish we could more fully justify ourselves in all these respects. If such sins have not been so notorious among us as in older countries, we must nevertheless remember, that the sins of a people who have been remarkable for the profession of godliness, are more aggravated by all the advantages and favors they have enjoyed, and will receive more speedy and signal punishment; as God says of Israel——*You only have I known of all the families of the earth, therefore will I punish you for all your iniquities.**

The judgments now come upon us are very heavy and distressing, and have fallen with peculiar weight on our Capital; where, notwithstanding the plighted honor of the chief Commander of the hostile troops, many of our brethren are still detained as if they were captives; and those that have been released have left the principal part of their subsistance, which is withheld by arbitrary orders, contrary to an express treaty, to be plunder'd by the army.**

Let me address you in the words of the prophet—O Israel, *return unto the Lord thy God for thou hast fallen by thine iniquity*—My brethren, let us repent and implore

---

*Amos 3.2.

**Soon after the battle at Concord, General Gage stipulated with the Select Men of Boston, that if the Inhabitants would deliver up their arms, to be deposited in Fanueil Hall, and return'd when circumstances would permit, they should have liberty to quit the town, and take with them all their effects. They readily complied; but soon found themselves abused, With great difficulty, and very slowly, they obtain passes; but are forbidden to carry out any thing besides houshold furniture and wearing apparel. Merchants and Shopkeepers are obliged to leave behind all their merchandise, and even their Cash is detained. Mechanics are not allowed to bring out the most necessary tools for their work. Not only their family stores of provisions are stopt; but it has been repeatedly and credibly affirmed, that poor women and children have had the very smallest articles of this kind taken from them, which were necessary for their refreshment while they travelled a few miles to their friends; and that even from young children, in their mothers arms, the cruel Soldiery have taken the morsel of bread given to prevent their crying, and thrown it away. How much better for the Inhabitants to have resolved, at all hazards, to defend themselves by their arms against such an enemy, than suffer such shameful abuse!

the divine mercy. Let us amend our ways, and our doings; reform every thing which has been provoking to the most high, and thus endeavor to obtain the gracious interpositions of providence for our deliverance.

If true religion is revived by means of these public calamities, and again prevails among us; if it appears in our religious assemblies,—in the conduct of our civil affairs,—in our armies,—in our families,—in all our business and conversation,—we may hope for the direction and blessing of the Most High, while we are using our best endeavors to preserve and restore the civil government of this Colony, and defend America from slavery.

Our late happy government is changed into the terrors of military execution. Our firm opposition to the establishment of an arbitrary system is called *Rebellion*, and we are to expect no mercy but by yielding property and life at discretion. This we are resolved at all events not to do; and therefore, we have taken arms in our own defence, and all the Colonies are united in the great cause of liberty.

But how shall we live while civil government is dissolved? What shall we do without *Counsellors* and *Judges?* A state of absolute anarchy is dreadful. Submission to the tyrany of hundreds of imperious masters, firmly embodied against us, and united in the same cruel design of disposing of our substance and lives at their pleasure, and making their own will our law in all cases whatever, is the vilest slavery, and worse than death.

Thanks be to God, that he has given us, as men, natural rights independent on all human laws whatever; and that these rights are recognized by the grand Charter of British Liberties. By the *law of nature* any body of people, destitute of order and government, may form themselves into a civil society according to their best prudence, and so provide for their common safety and advantage. When one form is found, by the majority, not to answer the grand purpose in any tolerable degree, they may by common consent put an end to it, and set up another: only as all such great changes are attended with difficulty, and danger of confusion, they ought not to be attempted without urgent necessity, which will be determined always by the general voice of the wisest and best members of the community.

If the great servants of the public forget their duty, betray their trust and sell their country, or make war against the most valuable rights and privileges of the people; reason and justice require that they should be discarded, and others appointed in their room, without any regard to formal resignations of their forfeited power.

It must be ascribed to some supernatural influence on the minds of the main body of the people through this extensive continent, that they have so universally adopted the method of managing the important matters necessary to preserve among them a free government, by corresponding committees and congresses, consisting of the wisest and most disinterested patriots in America, chosen by the unbiased suffrages of the people assembled for that purpose, in their several towns, counties and provinces. So general agreement, thro' so many provinces of so large a country, in one mode of self preservation, is unexampled in any history: and the effect has exceeded our most sanguine expectations. Universal tumults, and all the irregularities and violence of mobish factions, naturally arise when legal authority ceases. But how little of this has appeared in the midst of the late obstructions of civil government! Nothing more than what has often happened in Great-Britain and Ireland, in the face of the civil powers in all their strength: nothing more than what is frequently seen in the midst of the perfect regulations of the great city of London: And, may I not add, nothing more than has been absolutely necessary to carry into execution the spirited resolutions of a people too sensible to deliver themselves up to oppression and slavery. The judgment and advice of the Continental Assembly of Delegates have been as readily obeyed, as if they were authentic acts of a long established parliament. And in every colony, the votes of a congress have had equal effect with the laws of great and general courts.

It is now ten months since this Colony has been deprived of the benefit of that government which was so long enjoyed by charter. They have had no general assembly for matters of legislation, and the public revenue. The courts of justice have been shut up; and almost the whole executive power has ceased to act. Yet order among the people has been remarkably preserved; few crimes have been committed punishable by the judge; even former contentions betwixt one neighbour and another have ceased; nor have fraud and rapine taken advantage of the imbecility of the civil powers.

The necessary preparations for the defence of our liberties required not only the collected wisdom and strength of the colony, but an immediate chearful application of the wealth of individuals to the public service, in due proportion; or a taxation which depended on general consent. Where was the authority to vote, collect, or receive the large sums required, and make provision for the utmost extremities?—A *Congress* succeeded to the honors of a *General Assembly*, as soon as the latter was crush'd by the hand of power. It gained all the confidence of the people. Wisdom and prudence secur'd all that the laws of the former constitution could have given. And we now observe, with astonishment, an army of many thousands of well disciplined troops suddenly assembled, and abundantly furnished with all necessary supplies in defence of the liberties of America.

But is it proper or safe for the colony to continue much

longer in such imperfect order? Must it not appear rational and necessary, to every man that understands the various movements requisite to good government, that the many parts should be properly settled, and every branch of the legislative and executive authority restored to that order and vigour on which the life and health of the body politic depend? To the honorable Gentlemen, now met in this new Congress as the Fathers of the People, this weighty matter must be referred. Who knows but in the midst of all the distresses of the present war to defeat the attempts of arbitrary power, God may in mercy restore to us our Judges as at the first, and our Counsellors as at the beginning.

On your wisdom, religion, and public spirit, Honored Gentlemen, we depend, to determine what may be done as to the important matter of reviving the form of government, and settling all necessary affairs relating to it in the present critical state of things, that we may again have law and justice, and avoid the danger of anarchy and confusion. May GOD be with you, and by the influences of his spirit direct all your counsels and resolutions for the glory of his name, and the safety and happiness of this colony. We have great reason to acknowledge with thankfulness the evident tokens of the divine presence with the former congress; that they were led to foresee present exigencies, and make such effectual provision for them. It is our earnest prayer to the Father of Lights, that he would irradiate your minds, make all your way plain, and grant you may be happy instruments of many and great blessings to the people by whom you are constituted, to New-England, and all the united Colonies.

Let us praise our God for the advantages already given us over the enemies of Liberty; particularly, that they have been so dispirited by repeated experience of the efficacy of our arms; and that in the late action at Chelsea, when several hundreds of our soldiery, the greater part open to the fire of so many cannon, swivels, and musquets from a battery advantageously situated, from two armed cutters, and many barges full of marines, and from ships of the line in the harbour, not one man on our side was killed, and but two or three wounded; when, by the best intelligence, a great number were killed and wounded on the other side, and one of their cutters was taken and burnt, the other narrowly escaping with great damage.*

If God be for us, who can be against us? The enemy has reproached us for calling on his name, and professing our trust in him. They have made a mock of our solemn Fasts, and every appearance of serious christianity in the land. On this account, by way of contempt, they call us *saints;* and that they themselves may keep at the greatest distance from this character, their mouths are full of horrid blasphemies, cursing and bitterness, and vent all the rage of malice, and barbarity. And may we not be confident that the Most High, who regards these things, will vindicate his own honor, and plead our righteous cause against such enemies to his government, as well as our liberties. O, may our Camp be free from every accursed thing! May our Land be purged from all it's sins! May we be truly a holy people, and all our towns cities of righteousness! Then the Lord will be our refuge and strength, a very present help in trouble; and we shall have no reason to be afraid though thousands of enemies set themselves against us round about,—tho' all nature should be thrown into tumults and convulsions. He can command the stars in their courses to fight his battles, and all the elements to wage war with his

---

*This action was in the night following the 27th current, after our soldiery had been taking off the cattle from some islands in Boston harbour. By the last information we have been able to procure, about 105 of the King's troops were killed, and 160 wounded in the engagement.

enemies. He can destroy them with innumerable plagues, or send faintness into their hearts, so that the men of might shall not find their hands. In a variety of methods he can work salvation for us, as he did for his people in ancient days, and according to the many remarkable deliverances granted in former times to Great-Britain and New England, when Popish machinations threatned both countries with civil and ecclesiastical tyranny.*

May the Lord hear us in this day of trouble, and the name of the God of Jacob defend us; send us help from his sanctuary; and strengthen us out of Zion. We will rejoice in his salvation, and in the name of our God we will set up our banners; let us look to him to fulfil all our petitions.

---

*When we consider the late Canada Bill; which implies, not merely a *toleration* of the Roman-catholic religion, (which would be just and liberal) but a *firm establishment* of it through that extensive province, now greatly enlarged to serve political purposes; by which means multitudes of people, subjects of Great Britain, which may hereafter settle that vast country, will be tempted, by all the attachments arising from an establishment, to profess that religion, or be discouraged from any endeavors to propagate reformed principles; have we not great reason to suspect, that all the late measures respecting the Colonies have originated from popish schemes of men who would gladly restore the race of Stewart and who look on popery as a religion most favorable to arbitrary power? It is plain fact, that *Despotism has an establishment* in that province equally with the Roman-catholic Church. The Governor, with a Council very much under his power, has by his commission almost unlimited authority, free from the clog of Representatives of the people. However agreable this may be to the genius of the French, English Subjects there will be discouraged from continuing in a country, where both they and their posterity will be deprived of the greatest privileges of the British constitution, and in many respects feel the effects of absolute monarchy. Lord Littleton in his defence of this detestable Statute, frankly concedes, that it is an *establishment* of the Roman-catholic religion, and that part of the policy of it was to provide a check upon the New England Colonies. And the writer of an Address of the people of Great-Britain to the inhabitants of America, just published, expresses himself with great precision when he says, that Statute "*gave toleration to ENGLISH Subjects.*"

22. EZRA STILES ON THE RIGHTS OF THE PEOPLE

Ezra Stiles (1727–1795), who was president of Yale from 1778 to 1795, emulated both the theology and the politics of his ancestors. In his old age he composed a history of the three judges of Charles I who sought refuge in Connecticut after the Restoration of Charles II. While thus engaged he heard of the execution of Louis XVI and was shocked to discover that his friends disapproved it. Stiles believed that Louis had earned his fate as surely as Charles I had; and he turned from his researches to write a polemical defense of tyrannicide and of the Jacobin societies that had overthrown the French monarchy. A hurried, disordered, yet eloquent performance, it marks the final adjustment of Puritan political thought to the needs of a democratic republic.

So again monarchs contemplate Jacobin Societies with horror and dread, and this with great reason.—They need not be so viewed by republics. The Jacobin Societies have proved the salvation of France. They have been the bulwark of liberty. Their excesses are to be coerced by government; but their suppression and extinction is unnecessary and impossible. "The popular societies are the columns of the revolution.—They shall not be shaken," said president Cambeceres. Violent and unjust in many things they may be, and so sometimes are congresses, assemblies, parliaments, not therefore to be dissolved, for

---

From Ezra Stiles, *A History of Three of the Judges of King Charles I* (Hartford: Elisha Babcock, 1794), pp. 272–290.

they may be generally right. Would it be wise to wish the extinction of the winds, which are salutary and beneficial for navigation and for clarifying the atmosphere, because sometimes attended with hurricanes? They may be set up against a good government indeed, but their efforts against it must ultimately be inefficacious and harmless. Because they sometimes succeed in overturning a tyranny, will it follow that there is even a possibility of their succeeding against a good policy? The experiment is yet to be made. Hitherto there has existed no good polity to try them upon. In the nature of things they will become self-correctors of their own irregularities and excesses; and harmonization of the public sentiment must result from their diffusive deliberations. Nay, the strength of a general and uniform support to the administration of a good policy must arise. Their discussions, circulation of intelligence, and communication of light, must eventually form, digest and unify the national judgment. None but tyrants need fear them. The national convention has not feared them, but rejoiced in their support. Congress in 1775 did not fear the body of the people in America, though sometimes wild and anarchical. A policy which shall have sustained their ventilation and discussion, will be firm. The end being answered, and the care of the public consigned into the hands of constitutional government, these societies will spontaneously disappear; nor rise again unless called forth on great occasions worthy their attention.

I said that men would judge of historical events according as they are principled in politics. Monarchies of all modes are contemplated with a suspicious eye, by communities at large; which in their turn contemplate republics, of any and almost every form, with attention and pleasure. There once was a time, and it is not yet past, when the sovereigns of Europe could not contemplate but with horror and disgust, the Prince of Orange, and Holland, dissolving their feudal submission to their lord paramount, the revolt of the house of Braganza from Spain, the more recent erection of the self-created kingdom of Prussia, or the self-created republics of Switzerland, and the United States. But all these examples come up into operative and efficacious view in the present age; and are contemplated with sympathetic consolation by states struggling with the tyranny of kings.

Self-erected sovereignties, whether monarchical or republican bid fair for considerable duration; while popular societies, are either defeated, or go to rest of course, when their end is accomplished. Their coerced extinction would prove as fatal to liberty and the rights of man, as the forceable suppression or extinction of letters or the liberty of the press. Both ever have done, and ever will do much mischief; both do infinitely more good: both are the combined conservators of the public liberty, in philosophy, religion, politics. They are excellently adapted to frame the public mind to wisdom, and to an acquiescence founded in diffusive conviction and information of that wherein consists the public interest, the general welfare of society. There is no alternative between their right to assemble, and the abolition of liberty. Extinguish this right in England and in every sovereignty, and the people are slaves. If at any time extravagant, a prudent insertion of counsel, and circulation of it through the popular societies may generally correct and rectify these extravagances, excesses into which they, are usually betrayed by false brethren or enemies masqued. It is their unalienable right to meet and deliberate, even for the purpose of systematically altering the policy, provided they peaceably submit to obey the policy and laws in being, until regularly altered by public consent. If assembling even for this open and direct purpose is to be adjudged treason, the change and rectification of the most tyrannous polity can never be effected, but by spontaneous recourse to the tremendous alternative of arms. If the popular societies sometimes err, it is not always, it is not usually from malicious and inimical views, but from defective and partial information among those the best disposed for the public good, or, as I said, from tories, which covertly, insidiously and unawares insert themselves as marplots. If well informed, it is impossible the community at large can be inimical to the public good. Enough of this general disposition for the public good may be found in every community at large, to counteract and nullify the injuries of factions. And the common people will generally judge right, when duly informed. The general liberty is safe and secure in their hands. It is not from deficiency of abilities to judge, but from want of information, if they at any time as a body go wrong. Upon information from an abundance of enlightened characters always intermixt among them, they will ultimately always judge right, and be in the end the faithful guardians and support and security of government. Nothing will kill a faction, like the body of a people if consulted. A faction may beat a faction, at a pretty fair and even conflict; but in a fair and full contest, it can never beat the people. The great art of factions is to keep the decision from the body of the people. But let a matter be fairly brought before the people, and they will not only determine it, but will judge and determine right. It is the insidious art of parties and politicians to keep things concealed from the people, or if they are alarmed and assemble, to excite parties, sow dissentions, and prevent as much as possible the question from coming up fairly before them, instead of harmoniously endeavoring in a fair, open and candid manner, to lay things clearly before them, and thus honestly endeavoring to form and obtain the public mind. And thus they ever attempt, and are too successful in deceiving, instead of a frank and open appeal to the people. But shall this cunning prevail forever? Politicians, with too much reason, say it will. I, who am no politician, but a prophet, say it will not. Almost all the civil polities on earth are become so corrupt and oppressive, as that they cannot stand before a well formed system of revolutionary societies. Those of the United States and France will sustain them without injury or eversion. The reformation of all others, must commence in associations, which by government will be considered and treated as factionary and treasonable, but will enlarge and spread into a system of revolutionary societies. In all states these will be frowned upon, and suppressed as treasonable. Their suppression and persecution will pour oil on the flame. They will burst out again and again, till they will carry all before them, till real treason shall be accurately defined not to the sense of aristocrats or the present usurped reigning powers, but to the general sense of the community. And such a law of treason will be infallibly supported by the community. This done every association will know what it may, and what it may not do, with impunity. Till this is done, the spirit of enlightened liberty is become so great, and ready to burst forth under oppressive and intolerable irritations, that it will risque all consequences, until all the present policies shall be fairly brought to the tribunal of the public sense. Then no one can doubt the result. Factionary societies begun even with the primary and direct design of overturning government, if the government or polity be supported by the general sense, will fall: otherwise they will bring on and adduce at length extensive discussions which enlighten the public, defeat insidious and partial cunning, and bring forward an open and firm support of good and acceptable government. Should they at any time surrender, or duped and outwitted by counter factions, be prevailed upon to betray the public liberty, the community will deserve slavery a little longer, until again aroused to energy, unity, wisdom. Thus England has now for a century been suffering a national punishment or chastisement, brought upon them by their own folly, for being duped by the insidious cavalier faction, which overturned the happy constitution of Oliver's republican polity. When at length brought to their senses, and a conviction of their national folly, they will break out and burst forth with united and irresistable vigour, and recover and rectify themselves. The French have for ages been duped by court factions, but have at length recovered their national rights and liberties, by a voluntary, united, bold and daring exertion, by an effort which makes all Europe to tremble. So it will be in England. The forcible suppression of societies there will only accelerate their revolution and political regeneration. More must be done for the satisfaction of the national sense and spirit of liberty, than parliament ever can, or ever will do, unless they shall call a national convention, which they never will do. The national spirit impressed with despair of redress, will become desparate. All confidence in parliament lost: then to your tents, O Israel! The national interest and welfare will take care of itself; and this with an unconquerable violence and impetuosity!

The English nation flattered themselves at the Restoration—revolution—accession of the House of Hanover:—Have been deceived and disappointed at each epoch, and find themselves as before, or rather more closely enchained and bastiled. The same conviction seizes the patriots of the present as of the last century. Never has the nation really despaired of all possibility of redress till now. Now at length *nationally despairing* of the present polity, they will be filled with very energetic feelings. They feel anew what was felt of old. New wine put into old bottles, may possibly burst the bottles.

In every state, good or bad, there will always be a number of restless, subtil, crafty, turbulent and ungovernable spirits; who by writings and intrigues, will be exciting discontent and stirring up mischief: and will molest and embarrass the best as well as the worst administration. Society will always have to encounter such characters. But calm discussion, and giving time for insidious projections to take their course and run their race, they may be wisely managed, contravened and defeated, especially after the public have felt and tasted some of the ill consequences into which they are plunged by such artifices and delusory stratagems. And perhaps voluntary associations, without noticing them as seditious, are as proper theatres for them to display and spend themselves upon as any other. Faction may be turbulent and successful, applied to monarchy and aristocracy—self-defeated, when applied to the community at large. Experiments in the old governments, in the Grecian and Roman, in antient and modern history, will be no precedent to count upon, in judging their effect on the new republican polities.—The public will not be ultimately duped by factions or factionary societies, though assembling with the greatest freedom. They will be harmless, till they arm, and then they become amenable to the laws, which if made by the public, the public will effectually support, even finally by military coercion.

Absolute monarchs have in all ages permitted individuals, subjects and slaves, to petition their King.—Even the Dey of Algiers, the Sultan of Constantinople, the Sophi of Persia, will receive the petition of slaves. The same thing is permitted in England; where it has hitherto been also permitted, especially since the suppression of villainage, for subjects assembled in popular, and even systematical societies, to petition the King or Parliament for redress of grievances, for or against bills depending in parliament, for or against the repeal of laws already enacted. So far they may go with impunity, and without liability to criminal processes for sedition or treason. This is a conceded right in England. But to assemble for the direct purpose of altering the constitution of King, Lords and Commons, is by statute, sedition, and arming in consequence, treason.—Thus it follows that reformation by the people is impossible. Let the constitution become corrupt into the most absolute and conjunct tyranny, it is however inviolable. There then exists a case, in which tyranny ought not, cannot be *justly* and legally corrected and abolished by the people. Will not the same reasoning apply for the perpetuity and irreformableness of any the most despotic governments? Will not these principles terminate in the universal eversion of liberty, in the universal establishment of universal tyranny? And is there no justifiable expedient, no public measure of redress, whose assumption and adoption may be justified upon the high, transcendant and paramount principles of public justice, right, liberty? If there is, it will lead to and terminate in the justification of voluntary societies, assembled to consult the public good, augmenting, multiplying and diffusing themselves into a system of popular assemblies, for enlightening, forming, digesting, and collecting the general sense of the community, whose polity needs amendment. It should seem therefore, that however iniquitous and pernicious some may be, yet *all* assemblies for the express purpose of altering and changing the polity, are *not* to be reprobated, as unjustifiable, seditious and traitorous. It remains to settle this point for all nations, that it is as justifiable to assemble for altering the polity, as for petitioning a national council, whose polity and constitution the whole nation approve, without the least desire of subverting or altering it. When this shall have become the universal conviction, national assemblies will become universal: and such polities as will not sustain their revision and discussion must fall. Thus it may be seen all the present corrupt polities are gone. But it is said, by parity, popular assemblies may be instituted against the new conceived polities, in endless progress, *ad infinitum.* Very true: and let them be so. If upon revision, they find the polity sound and good, one to satisfaction, as sooner or later, after a few revisions, they will find, they will of course leave it untouched, return home, report and diffuse and generate universal acquiescence, satisfaction and submission; and thus strengthen the whole community into one firm and united bulwark for its support and defence. Afterwards they will feel no occasion for popular assemblies, unless upon agitated bills, and very seldom for this end, all readily acquiescing in the determination and enactment of the national council, if frequently elected, which can have no other interest but that of the people. The very notion of petitioning parliaments, national councils, or kings, for rights and liberties, is a badge of slavery, founded on the supposition that they have both the power and disposition to counteract the interest of the governed. This abolished, petitioning dies of course; and will be securely confined to the wisdom and fidelity of the council. They are empowered, entrusted and confided in for this very purpose. A good policy will generally enact wise and good laws, to which obedience ought to be exacted, if necessary among turbulent spirits, by the united military force of the citizens, not foreign force. Yet former good legislators have erred, and those of a best polity may err again, and enact laws which ought to be disobeyed and resisted. What must be done in this case? Agreeable to the custom of all kings and nobility throughout Europe in the middle ages, Evenus, a King of Scotland, caused a law to pass, by which all the wives and daughters of noblemen were subjected to his lust, and those of the plebians to the lust of his nobility. "*Tulit legem Evanus ut cuivis liceret, pro opibus quot alere posset, uxores ducere; ut rex nuptias sponsarum nobilium, nobiles plebeiarum praelibarent pudicitiam, ut plebeiorum uxores cum nobilitate communes essent.*" Could it be supposed possible that Congress should re-enact such a licentious law in favor of privileged orders, of any description of men, it would exasperate and unite so many plebeian husbands, and in the United States even wives too, in resistance, and even arming for defence, as that it would be wise to reverse it. Here resistance would be justifiable, even to arming and civil war. In this case, whether successful or unsuccessful, the resistance would be just. But from a few such supposed cases and extraordinary instances of error, we are not to infer that we are justifiable in resisting any and every law which we think and feel to be oppressive. In elective republics there is another way always open, which will always be effectual for the redress of even real grievances. Defer and endure till the next election, and then send up men that shall abolish the law. They will either do it, or bring back reasons which will convince their constituents. Numerous have been the instances of this in the New-England republics the last and present century—and the public have been satisfied. There is no need to alter the polity for this end. In an elective republic factionary resistance and insurrection ought to be repressed by military coercion, not by foreign troops, but by citizens, who will cheerfully lend their aid, in the support of an act agreeable to the general sense of the community. If not agreeable to the general sense, it ought to be repealed, till by becoming convinced of its expediency they shall re-enact it. But it is next to impossible that such a thing can be enacted by a national council standing on biennial, or triennial, or short elections. Dissatisfactions may and will arise, will be manifested; and if general, yet there is no need of arming for resistance, which would be and must necessarily be treated as sedition and treason. If general among the constituents, and they cannot be enlightened to see the reason and justice of the law, the obnoxious act will be reversed, even by the existing senate. If not, the next election will return members who will cancel and rectify the error, if there is one. It is therefore next to impossible to suppose a case in an elective republic, wherein resistance can be justifiable. Because redress may be at all times effected in another and more peacable and satisfactory way, without endangering the public tranquility, or disturbing the public order of the general government, and especially without eversion of the constitution.

But although insurrection and resistance may perhaps never be just in an elective government; it will not follow but that they may be sometimes justifiable in a despotic government, and especially when the polities and constitutions are so radically corrupt, as that the very polity itself ought to be changed and rectified. And here resistance is justifiable, whether successful or not. Whether the attempt and enterprize shall be prudent and wise, may be a question, when we confer with flesh and blood, but whether just in the view of right reason, need not be questioned. The polities of all the European nations are become so radically corrupt and oppressive, that the welfare of mankind requires that they should be renovated. This would be best for human society. Why should despotism and oppression be entailed to subsequent generations? Why is it not just that the ages of tyranny should be succeeded by the ages of liberty? Under the obstinate and persevering opposition of the reigning powers this emancipation cannot be made but by the people. This must commence, as I have said, in popular societies, connected, spreading and growing up into a general popular exertion. If oppression occasions their rise, they must take their fate. The enterprize is arduous, but combined national enthusiasm in the cause of liberty is of great and awful force. All Europe is ripening with celerity for a great revolution; the area is commencing of a *general revolution.* The amelioration of human society must and will take place. It will be a conflict between Kings and their subjects. This war of Kings, like that of Gog and Magog, will be terrible. It will, for there is no other way, it will commence and originate in voluntary associations among subjects in all kingdoms. Eluded supplications and petitions for liberty, will be followed by armaments for the vindication of the rights of human nature. The public ardor will be kindled, and a national spirit and exertion roused, which undiscouraged, unsubdued by many defeats, will ultimately carry away all before it. So that popular societies will be attended with very different effects, when directed against an unjust and tyrannous polity, from those which will attend them when directed against a sound and well constructed one. In the one case they will prove obnoxious and harmless; in the other alarming and terrible. In popular governments they may sometimes proceed to operate on elections, reverse wise and excellent laws for a time, and lay aside excellent characters, some of their best and most useful friends, and reward their merits with public ingratitude; but they will substitute others in their room, who collectively will do well, and the polity will go on, and the government proceed regularly, though in new hands. But they will generally preserve a succession of worthy characters. In the other case they will demolish polities, overturn thrones, eject aristocrats, and institute new elective governments —differently policied perhaps, but uniformly elective.

When popular societies are set on foot, if the polity be so well settled to the general sense, as that they shall turn out but a minority, and yet this minority should be so considerable and daring as to arm against the constitution, civil war or a war of citizens ensues, and there remains no umpire, until victory declares it. In that exigency it becomes of necessity that the law of the state should declare such associations seditious, traiterous and rebellious. And the same must take place, be the polity just or unjust, provided the majority of the community concur in it. But it remains to be experimented by future ages, whether there will often if ever exist such a minority combination against a polity once, and especially repeatedly settled with satisfactory revisions, by the collective body of the people, especially where frequent revisions are appointed and provided in the constitution; and whether an insurrection generally discountenanced, will not give way and be easily suppressed with or without force, and perhaps only by light and the fraternal persuasions of fellow-citizens.—Against a generally acceptable polity, every popular effort of minority associations will die away and come to nothing, terminating in the confirmation and strengthening the polity to an impregnable inviolability. Against such a bulwark of the united people, the efforts of a cluster of popular societies will prove but *bruta fulmina,* harmless, and self-defeated as well as self-created. But if the polity be a bad one, such a cluster may be subdued, may possibly increase, acquire irresistible strength and carry all before it. The little quarrel of the Marli brought on the *bellum sociale.* Not all the Bastiles nor Botany Bays, no enforcement of the existing laws against sedition, can prevent the spread and progress of this conviction of the possible right, utility and necessity of popular assemblies at least to contemplate the public state, and in given cases even to regenerate the policy. And when this shall have become a little more the general conviction of nations, they will burst forth, and originate and devise modes of public exertion, adequate to the accomplishment of a complete revolution in any polity. Nor will the present age of light and liberty rest in any thing short of this. The nations will never sit down content with this, that a defective constitution is irremediable. They will not despair; they will find a remedy somewhere, an efficacious remedy not to be defeated by aulic manoeuvres and circumventions either of policy or force. No measures of any actual existing government can ultimately defeat this. Every Botany Bay decision in England will contribute to the acceleration and insurance of such an event. And perhaps England will be the next to try the political experiment, after France; even in the sure foreseen road to liberty, being marked with horror and blood. Exasperated despair will be fruitful in expedients, and bold, adventurous, and successful in enterprize. The public sense on the present state of the English constitution must sooner or later be tried. It can be tried only in these assemblies in the nature of things. These might for this end be called by the existing ruling powers. But the ruling powers certainly never will do it. It can then never be done but by spontaneous origination. This is the only alternative. This closed, liberty is gone, tyranny is inviolable. Will the world sit down quiet and submissive under this last gloomy, solitary, swinish conclusion? In the spirit of prophecy, I say, nay!

Should the express, real, true and only object of the voluntary societies in England, or the recovery of *annual parliaments* and *universal suffrage*, they would be guilty of no crime against the laws or the state. But should they arm, that moment it becomes sedition—and punishable as such—if the existing powers shall prove able to subdue an armed minority, which may at length become an armed people. In this event all is reduced to hostility and civil war: a conflict ensues till victory declares itself. "Universal suffrage and annual parliaments are legitimate and constitutional objects of pursuit."

A reform in parliament is necessary in the public conviction, even of the parliament itself as well as the nation at large. How far it should proceed is a doubt, whether by an equitable appointment of the representation to the one hundred and fifty thousand electors of shires, cities, and boroughs; or by universal suffrage? Mr. Pitt, as well as Burke, Fox, and others were once for a reform in the commons; and Pitt publicly avowed in parliament, annual parliaments, and universal suffrage, the very principles avowed in the British convention at Edinburgh. But the French revolution changed their minds, or rather, affected that *now* was not the proper time, or that it ought to be procrastinated to a time, which he now foresees can never be found, which is in effect convincing him, that what he once advocated ought never to be done, because he now foresees it never can be done, without the sure danger of the demolition of royalty and nobility. The haughtiness of high dominion can never give up, until it is too late. It is intended by court politicians that the dissonance of opinion as to the mode of reform shall nullify the whole. They are content to have the question most liberally agitated, but never to be settled and determined: that the partizans should discuss themselves out of breath, as in a chancery suit, and in despair to leave all to an *uti possidetis*. Circulating this *ultimatum* among all the partizans of the ministry, it is purposed and assuredly expected to worry out the public spirit, and go on with the present system, until all shall feel it incurable, and tamely acquiesce.

The national debt is considered as combining and holding all together. It is supposed to be fatally endangered by a revolution, and especially by the change of a monarchy into a republic. But it is as easy to secure a national credit in the one as the other. Holland, Venice, America, and I believe France will shew that national credit, stocks and funds may be as secure in a republic as in a monarchy. If in a revolution it shall be provided that the public debt shall be taken upon the new polity, all would be secure, unless the debt, as it may be, should be so heavy as to be impossible to be supported. But how powerful soever a public debt may be towards consolidating and holding the polity together, there are great exigencies, in which it will lose this force. A debt of three hundred millions sterling did not withhold the Roman empire from dissolution, when its fate was expired. There are certain political tempests which carry away all before them. The national debt of England will not repel a revolution, when the body of the people are brought to exert their force; which they certainly will do, when thoroughly sick of their polity: a crisis very fast approaching.

But if a reform, contrary to all court intention and expectation, must come on; the question will arise, shall the parliament do this, or the people? The parliament may seem to attempt, think to amuse the nation, but dare not to adventure a reform even of one house, and much less of both. And therefore from a concurrence of various motives, both houses feeling themselves to stand or fall together, will unite in the most firm and decided opposition to it, and risque the most sanguinary measures to defeat every attempt, and prevent, obstruct, and suppress every movement efficaciously tending to a real reform; unless it may be they may propose so trifling and so ineffectual a reform, as will rather mock and irritate, than give national satisfaction. Add to this, that though they allow the people to fancy and conceive that they have rights and liberties, and suffer them to boast of them, declaim upon them and glory in them, as long as the politicians see them chained and fettered; yet really in their hearts and secret counsels, they at bottom most cordially hold, that the herd cannot govern themselves; and as to participation in government the swinish multitude have no rights and liberties, or which is the same thing, none originally and independently, none but what are held at the concession of the King and parliament. And the few ascending from the plebeians into parliament, soon lose their plebeian principles and become assimilated to the aristocracy. The two hundred and fifty nobles therefore and five hundred and fifty commons, or their venal majorities, become a combined Phalanx against the people, set and firmly united against any ultimate and real alteration or reform of the polity. There remains therefore that the struggle must be given up. It will not be given up. The feelings of aristocracy are totally different from the feelings of the people. The preposterous conduct of the ministry and parliament for now almost half a century have so involved and oppressed the nation, as to precipitate a revolution. A national enquiry is unavoidable. It has taken place in France; it will take place in every sovereignty in Europe; it will take place in England sooner or later.—The mode cannot be predicted, saving only that it will be a popular one. A real Saxon meycle-gemot must be resumed.

The English parliament is such a mockery on representation, that the nation will never rest in its present state. And it must sooner or later be altered. The agitations for effecting this inevitable alteration will bring on and advance other political discussions, terminating in a republican renovation. So absurd and disproportionate is the representation in parliament, that it strikes all with disgust, as an insult on the majesty of the people. Of the five hundred and fifty members, it appears that in England, two thousand six hundred and eleven persons elect and return three hundred and twenty seven members; and in Scotland, of the forty-five members to represent two millions of people, ninety-eight persons elect one third, and the other thirty are elected by about one thousand four hundred.

When the present national storm is a little over, parliament will attempt to appease the public spirit by apportioning the representation. So far it will be well.—But they will see that this will not satisfy. They will enlarge the election, but will not proceed to universal or general suffrage. This may rest the national spirit for the present, and respite further popular exertions, perhaps for another generation, perhaps not. However they will by both these measures give the precedent of a principle, on which the public will prescribe for further enlargements and amendments. Liberty must be disputed and gained by inches. The cure of the national disorder is not yet effected. The designation of all public offices is to be regulated. If left in the hands of the monarch, sole appointment will ever give him power to command and subject both houses to his will. The possibility of this autocratical controul in the crown remains to be extinguished. The nobility will be with the King. All this will ultimately sooner or later bring on a struggle with aristocracy, which must be fought out with blood, and then the nation will become a republic. Half a century will complete this. Or at least it will be accomplished in some given time.

Politicians should look upon irritated human nature, and consider the extent of passive national endurance. They may view it in the Roman empire, in the history of the reformation from the pontificate, in the English history from king John to this time, in the Baron's wars, in the endurance of the Duke of Alva; in short in a thousand similar instances in the histories of nations. Look at the French revolution, look at the American revolution; instead of looking to Caesar, to the vanquishments of tyranny, to the invasion of the Gauls by the Franks, the Saxon, Danish, and Norman conquests, the English illegitimate conquest of Ireland, and the other successful conflicts of tyranny: and in numerous other examples, they may find that tyranny, however adventurous, is not always successful. But they will be taught by none of these. They will find, however, that the temerity of incensed Englishmen will, as in the last century, risque blood and every consequence. The conflict once begun, though none can foresee the means, yet it requires no spirit of prophecy to foresee the event. The end will be accomplished, as sure as the downfall of the Roman empire. The road however to this end must be strewed with blood. But will any madly adventure this? They will. And there must and will arise more Cromwells, Kosciuskos, Whalleys, Fairfaxes; more Warrens, Muirs, Palmers, and Geralds, must suffer martyrdom. Three or four more hereditary monarchies and aristocracies must be fought and hunted down, before the rest will submit to the empire of liberty, law and reason. Oh Parliament! O English Nation! you have before you to fight out, not whether a Stuart, Nassau, or Brunswick, this or that family, shall reign; no longer a war among Kings, a conflict between interfering and claiming sovereigns—but a more interesting, real and solemn conflict awaits you—a conflict between the people and sovereigns and hereditary aristocrats, and in connexion with them in England, a plebeian assembly, or delusory shadow of fictitious, popular, unreal representation, tacked on fallaciously to support them. But let us be assured the conflict will be severe and bloody—it will however assuredly take place—and its end will be glorious! During the fiery trial, we of the United States, shall contemplate this struggle with heart-feeling solicitude, and share with the parent state, from which we still glory to have descended, in the joys and exultations of the final triumphs of liberty. We sprang from England, and still read and study her histories with as much attention and sympathetic feeling, as our brethren, from whom we have been cruelly dismembered. And our reflexions are made and uttered here, with the most liberal, unembarrassed and unbounded freedom, a freedom unknown even in England, that land, of all the transatlantic regions, the land of free discussion and liberty.

It is not alien or foreign from our purpose, but directly in point to adduce these strictures and observations, or to attend to the present state of things in England and Europe; because they have issued from 1641, and are but the progress of the conflict of ages; and because in their struggles with tyranny, the nation find themselves obliged to recur to the principles of the last century, and resume the work, which Oliver and the Judges once achieved before them, and put into the hands of the nation, and which they were foolishly duped to give back and surrender to the flattering and ever delusory promises of tyranny. If the existing polities will not reform themselves, as they certainly will not, all must come to the conclusion of the enlightened patriots of past ages, and especially of the last century, who were more deeply studied in the principles of polity and dominion, than the civilians that any other age ever produced. After every the most profound discussion of the subject, every one must finally come to a conclusion, which their progenitors clearly discerned and boldly announced, that in such an exigence, there remains the only alternative of submission or rebellion. And though every other rebellion is unjustifiable, yet such an exigence may be adjudged to necessitate and justify rebellion—for it is said, "rebellion to tyrants is obedience to God."

INDEX